The Politics of Neglect

UNDER THE EDITORSHIP OF
RICHARD P. LONGAKER

The Politics of Neglect:
The Environmental Crisis

Edited by
Roy L. Meek
John A. Straayer
Colorado State University

HOUGHTON MIFFLIN COMPANY • BOSTON

New York • Atlanta • Geneva, Illinois • Dallas • Palo Alto

Preface

Environmental destruction has emerged as one of the most salient political issues of the 1970s. There is growing recognition that reckless exploitation of the natural environment is a threat not only to the good life but to all life. There is further recognition that collective decisions of public agencies must be substituted for the private, uncoordinated decisions which have led to the current state of affairs. Today the political system is charged with the responsibility of devising programs to ameliorate the environmental crisis; and pollution abatement, population control, natural resource preservation, and land-use planning for the urban environment have become priority items on the agenda of government. The readings in this book survey some of the major dimensions of the environmental crisis as well as the political constraints upon action intended to reduce the resulting stress.

The editors of this volume share a number of convictions about the nature of this crisis and the political response to it. First, we believe that before any significant progress can be made toward solving the problems which collectively constitute the current concern, an informed and aroused public must be created. Second, we believe that the design of effective programs demands a great deal of costly and time-consuming research into the nature of the problem and alternative ways to solve it. Third, we believe that, even with an ideal mix of public support and systematic research, remedial efforts will be slow and incremental at best. Fourth, we believe that even incremental advance is possible only if environmental considerations are made a significant part of private and public decision-making. A broader set of perspectives, or a systems approach, must be utilized if remedial action is to be effective and not create further environmental problems. Lastly, we believe that whereas environment alarmists can help in the early stages of developing public concern, their activities alone can not go very far toward solving concrete environmental problems. A long-term, broadly based commitment to correction and protection is required, both to sustain the costs in time and money of dealing with the ecological problems we face and to compensate for the necessary changes in preferences and life styles. The selections in this book reflect, in one way or another, these shared beliefs.

A number of people contributed substantially to the production of this book. Of greatest help, of course, were those who wrote and permitted publication of the articles which are included. Additionally, Frank Shelton of Houghton Mifflin and Richard Longaker of UCLA were of significant assistance. Finally, the work of Miss Becky Burdette of Colorado State University was indispensable.

Roy L. Meek
John A. Straayer

Colorado State University
Fort Collins, Colorado

Contents

Chapter 5 • Contamination of the Water

Chapter 6 • The Future and the Environmental Crisis

The Politics of Neglect

Environmental Quality: The New War

*The great question of the seventies is, shall we surrender to our surround-
ings, or shall we make peace with nature and begin to make reparations
for the damage we have done to our air, to our land and to our water?*[1]

With the coming of the 1970s the United States finds itself engaged in yet another
war. This war is being waged on college campuses; in local, state, and national
legislative assemblies; through the press and the electronic media; and in countless meetings of citizens, special interest groups, and industrial leaders. It is a
war to end environmental pollution and to bring on environmental quality. Unlike
wars which seek to destroy life, this war seeks to preserve life. At stake is the
continued existence of open spaces, clean air and water, fish and wildlife, and even
man himself.

This new war on environmental pollution is actually a continuation and an in-
tensification of an old struggle. Groups like the Sierra Club and the Audubon
Society have for decades championed the cause of the wild river, the unmolested
forest, and the preservation of nature in general.[2] Many articulate voices from
Thoreau to Rachel Carson have cried out for the conservation, preservation, and
protection of nature and natural beauty and against their destruction by the great
predator, Man.[3] In the past, most activities against the spoilers were carried on by
small, well-organized groups, or by individuals. Although such individual and
group activity was sometimes successful, its scope was generally limited to narrow
issues and to problems involving a specific threat to a part of the natural environment. Such activity, for example, has arisen in the past in reaction to plans of
army engineers to drain swamps for development purposes or channel streams for
flood control, to plans of Southwestern interests to flood a portion of the Grand

---

[1] *Richard M. Nixon,* 1970 Presidential State of the Union Message.

[2] *Perhaps a classic example of such group activity involved the Sierra Club's rather successful efforts in 1965 to torpedo congressional passage of the Central Arizona Project
legislation.*

[3] *See Henry David Thoreau,* Walden: A Writer's Edition *(New York: Holt, Rinehart & Winston,
1966) and Rachel Carson,* Silent Spring *(Boston: Houghton Mifflin, 1962).*

Canyon to bring more water to central and southern Arizona, and to plans to use scenic beaches or wilderness areas for industrial development.

The new elements in the current war are the significant enlargement and increased visibility of the participating public, the scope of the issues at stake, and the prevailing atmosphere of crisis. To be exact, then, we have not entered into a new war, but into a new phase of an old one. This phase promises to transform the issue of environmental quality into one of the major political concerns of the 1970s. No longer are small cadres of bird watchers and wilderness purists doing battle alone on limited fronts with developers and governmental agencies. No longer is the struggle carried on in a few poorly attended monthly meetings, or through the use of occasional mailouts and Washington lobbyists. The war has now caught the attention of increasing numbers of housewives, students, governmental officials, and community leaders, and drawn their energies into it. Perhaps most importantly, the new war stems not simply from a romantic longing to protect the birds and communicate with nature, but rather from a deeply rooted concern for human survival. There is concern that in our efforts to solve problems and provide life's amenities (e.g., using D.D.T. to kill bugs), we may have upset the balance of nature. In short, there is some fear that our scientific and technological society, with its tremendous capacity for production and consumption, and its uncontrolled population growth, may have turned out to be a doomsday machine.

This new war is cutting into the ranks of those who have done service in the struggles of the sixties — the war on inflation, the war on poverty, the war for racial justice, and the war against war itself. Many housewives who in the past protested against rising beef prices are now engaged on the side of those attempting to achieve and maintain environmental quality. Many self-proclaimed radicals have left other issues to fight against proposed variances in air pollution ordinances, and they have been joined by large numbers of their less radical colleagues.[4]

The interest in environmental problems has not been limited to the "ivory towered campuses." Conservation — even survival — have become major political issues. President Nixon made pollution abatement and general environmental quality a major theme in his 1970 State of the Union Message. In late 1969, the governors of Hawaii and Colorado were sharply criticized for speeches in which they promoted the growth of their states. Their critics argued that growth could only mean more despoiling of the environment. High-pollution industries are increasingly unwelcome in local communities. Look magazine has recently carried articles entitled "Mankind's Last Chance"; "Assault on the Everglades"; "America the Beautiful?"; "Danger"; "Land Lovers"; "Epic of Garbage"; and "Hawaii: Paradise in Peril?" Intense criticism of both private activity and public policy in the area of environmental quality has been similarly displayed as a major theme in many other organs of the press.[5]

Whereas earlier campaigns for environmental quality were carried on primarily

[4] Not only has the decrease in anti-Vietnam activity on college campuses paralleled the increase in concern with environmental quality, but many of those involved in the "new war" were leaders in the anti-Vietnam movements.

[5] See, for example, Look, January 13, 1970; September 19, 1969; November 4, 1969; April 29, 1969; and Life, September 5, 1969 and November 14, 1969.

by preservationist groups and tended to concentrate on problems and issues that were limited in time and space, the new attack goes forward on many fronts at once. The object in danger is no longer perceived as a single dam, an isolated river, or a section of a public park or state forest. Rather, it is the entire human environment, namely, the nation and the world. There is growing concern not only with dirty air and water, but also with problems of population, ecological balance, and man's capacity to survive. Those engaged in this new war wonder not only about oil slicks, the Everglades, land use planning, and urban smog and noise, but also about the very nature of the environmental crisis, its root causes, and their consequences.

Implicit in this burst of new activity is the realization that the problems are too large, too complex, too interrelated, and too immediate to be attacked by individual effort alone. They are problems for the entire society and demand society's full, organized power. Among the leadership of the nation there is an awareness that the preconditions for victory in this struggle are a "systems" approach to environmental problem solving and the development of overarching efforts at the public policy level.

The battle for environmental quality has been translated into demands for new public policy. Supporters of environmental quality have made it a political problem by placing it on the agenda of government, making governmental officials responsible for viable solutions.

The political system is thus faced with the need to develop solutions to problems such as air pollution, water pollution, and insufficiently effective land use planning, which are rooted in the very development of an urban, industrial society. These problems inhere in the rapid population growth accompanying such societies and, in the United States, in the ideological structures associated with such development.

Many of the most serious problems of environmental quality go back to the industrial revolution. Scientific knowledge, a money economy, new forms of power, new modes of production, and new methods of transportation and communication appeared during the eighteenth and nineteenth centuries and stamped their imprint upon American society. These essentially technological advances, wedded to public policies, contributed to the development of an urban, industrial society. The birth and growth of new forms of power, production, and transportation led to a productive system based on the factory, which drew to a centralized location large numbers of workers in search of work. Increased mechanization and economies in agricultural production drove many from the farm to the factory and city for jobs. Industrialization and the factory thus precipitated the development of an urbanized society with its accompanying problems of pollution.[6]

In the twentieth century, continued technological advance, population growth, and public policy have joined to extend the development of an urban society to a suburban one and have spread already existing pollution. The continued growth of cities and the creation of suburban offshoots were made possible by additional "gifts" of technology — the automobile, bus, train, expressway, and mass com-

<hr>

[6] A good discussion of this is contained in Robert Presthus, The Organizational Society (New York: Alfred A. Knopf, 1962).

munication. Public sponsorship of roadway systems has permitted people to work in one location and live in another; and public support of widespread consumer credit has allowed millions of Americans to purchase automobiles and single-family housing outside the core city. These developments have generated mazes of expressways, millions of automobiles, polluted air, garish strip commercial development, and rather haphazard residential land use planning and development. In short, technology, mass production, the highway, the automobile, mass communication, low-cost housing, government-insured loans, and other forms of technological development and public policy have combined to produce many of the problems which we consider to be serious threats today to the quality of the environment, if not to life itself.

These environmental problems are seldom isolated sets of conditions that can be resolved by an independent public policy effort for each problem. Air and water pollution, for example, relate not only to offending foundries and paper mills, but also to regional economic systems, to use of the automobile, and to the expressway systems and life styles of millions of urban and suburban Americans. Thus, air and water pollution are tied not only to certain industries and certain methods of production, but also to public transportation policy, economic systems, and a host of social and psychological factors.

Attacks upon environmental problems, therefore, must be balanced and made on all fronts. The failure to account for certain social-psychological factors in attempting to counter air pollution, for example, may reduce public support for a proposed remedial policy and its acceptance if adopted. Likewise, the failure to account for economic factors could easily damage certain industries, and in turn cause unemployment.

It is apparent that several difficult problems are inherent in the search for environmental quality. The first involves the identification of undesirable conditions and the definition of the preferred environmental state. Consideration must be given to such questions as "What is environmental quality?" and "Environmental quality for whom?" No one would deny that certain conditions are almost universally abhorrent; hardly anyone "likes" badly polluted air or oil slicks. But human values vary widely, and what is "quality of environment" to a father of five who supports his family by working in a stream-polluting paper mill or air-polluting foundry is not likely to be the same to a professor of wildlife biology who lives in a plush suburb. The professor and his neighbors may want very badly to clean up the air or the stream; and the worker may agree as long as the action does not affect industry in a way that forces a job layoff. The difficult policy problem here is to find workable alternatives between dirty water and unemployment.

The first and perhaps most difficult step in seeking "environmental quality" is to decide whose notion of quality is to dominate. Contrary to the image projected by the mass media of beautiful streams and meadows, multiple publics hold a variety of views of the good life. Environmental planning thus must take account of the views of large numbers of human beings.

A second and related problem involves the many interlocking ties among the components of human and physical systems. Strategies for altering one part of the environment or a specific set of behavior patterns nearly always affect other elements in both systems. For example, the abatement of stream pollution through the imposition of discharge restrictions on a paper or steel mill will have economic implications for the company and, depending upon the time allowed for compliance, may influence regional employment. Likewise, attacks upon air pollution or uncontrolled land use may affect patterns of transportation, employment, and recreation, as well as living costs.

A third problem in environmental planning concerns the accommodation of new policies and programs with those of the past. The difficulties and costs — human, physical, and financial — of adopting and implementing new programs are greatly increased by the need to modify existing programs, behavior patterns, skills, or physical plant. Decision-makers are, therefore, understandably reluctant to adopt radical changes in policy. Costs already "sunk" into the production and distribution of automobiles, for example, generate stiff resistance to the adoption of new types of propulsion. Likewise, the costs of existing expressway systems greatly restrict the options for new urban transportation schemes.

A fourth difficulty grows out of the incongruous relationship between physical and political systems. The United States is heavily fragmented politically, especially in its urban areas. A metropolitan area which may constitute a readily identifiable social and economic system may contain hundreds of governmental units. Similarly, a single watershed (or "airshed") may cover a wide, politically atomized region. The frequent result of this phenomenon is the difficulty encountered in attempting to package public problems.[7] Air pollution, water pollution, mass transit, land use planning, and so forth thus become hard to deal with because they affect large, irregularly shaped areas where public responsibility for problem solving is greatly diffused.

Finally, perhaps the most critical of all problems in environmental planning are those relating to public acceptability and support. In theory, no plans in a democracy should be made and implemented unless they fully and accurately reflect public desire. In practice, two major obstacles arise: (1) the impossibility of identifying any single public interest, and (2) the infrequency with which the public articulates its interest, except when coaxed to do so by leadership. But realistically as well as theoretically, it is important that public acceptability be carefully considered in planning; as the record of acceptance of metropolitan reform and reorganization so clearly documents, the most expensive and "rational" plans will generally come to naught unless real or potential political resistance is identified and overcome. Resistance is best defeated by strong and lasting bases of political and financial support. All too often narrow vision, selfishness, and the tradition of free enterprise, profit, and immediate individual gain are pressures which even the most well-meaning politicians or political system must fight. Only in this way can they develop standards that will benefit not only the next generation but succeeding ones, too.

Like many wars, the war for environmental quality results from intense emotional commitment and demands quick, complete, low-cost victory. It requires us to

---

[7] The concept of "problem packaging" is developed by Vincent Ostrom et al., "The Organization of Government in Metropolitan Areas: A Theoretical Inquiry," American Political Science Review, Vol. 60 (December 1961), pp. 831-842.

attempt to order our lives and institutions in a manner that will achieve an illusory "perfect" balance between man and his natural environment, a balance that some say was present some time in the golden past. For them this is a campaign for a return to a balance of nature; it is a war to end all wars. Although romanticism and emotional commitment may be necessary and sufficient stimuli to launch such a war and sustain those engaged in the pursuit of victory, they cannot assure success against an evasive, powerful, diffuse enemy which can be subdued only through a long, costly struggle. It is probably meaningless to speak of victory in this context, since victory, to many, demands a permanent struggle for human survival. If man is to survive and if the world is not to become a worse place in which to live, serious attention must be given to the complexity of the survival problem and the costs and consequences of proposed solutions. The present crisis itself, at least in part, is the result of the application of technological solutions to narrow problems without considering the effects on the total environment.

In the struggle for environmental quality, emotion and symbols can be both functional and dysfunctional. On the positive side, they can be used to rally an effective public around the environmental problem. If skillfully developed, and employed, and related to concrete environmental problems by a dedicated leadership, emotion and symbols can markedly help to recruit and mobilize an articulate and effective public for the pursuit of a better environment.

On the other hand, emotional symbols do not do much to help spot the problems or develop the strategies and tactics necessary to meet the crisis of our times. The despoilers of the environment are not always clearly identifiable, nor are their activities always blatant or dramatic. To be sure, there are purposeful polluters who pour great quantities of noxious materials into the air and water in order to reap quick and enormous profits. But much of the threat to the environment results from the activities of a different type of polluter. It is produced by the poor man who, lacking alternative means of transportation, drives a defective automobile to work to maintain a livelihood for himself and his family; by the suburban masses who commute from bedroom suburbs to industrial and business locations; by the small industrialist who is economically unable to modernize his plant but whose furnishing of employment thins the ranks of the unemployed; by the farmer who uses pesticides and insecticides in order to maintain necessary levels of productivity to meet the needs of an ever more crowded nation and world; by the airline which relies on noisy jet aircraft; and by individuals who carelessly litter the nation's highways and byways.

These, then, are a few examples of the sources of threat to environmental quality. They should suffice to illustrate the point that pollution is not a great conspiracy which can be resolved by "more power to the people." Rather, the problem of pollution, like the quest for "quality of life," is extremely costly and complicated. Its solution demands patience, resolve, and a longterm commitment at all levels of government and the private sector to use scientific knowledge wisely to create a better environment. It requires the use, not abuse, of technology. It necessitates careful and complete identification of the physical, social, economic, and political dimensions of environmental problems, and of the interrelatedness of the many factors forming the environmental crisis. It calls for careful and accurate assessment of probable costs and the consequences of each approach to the problem. Finally, progress toward a better environment will come only from a firm, constant political leadership that is capable of identifying problems, building bases of political support, and securing the resources needed to put across both remedial and preventive environmental improvement programs.

Many of the problems which comprise the threat to the human environment cannot be resolved through our present level of technology. And many others, which technically can be resolved, would exact a price for such resolution which we would be unwilling to pay. Technological advance is clearly needed, therefore, to carry on the battle — unless, of course, we are willing to put up with unemployment, a declining standard of living, and a lopsided distribution of the costs and benefits to society.

Even assuming the development of sufficient technological information to resolve the most persistent and obvious pollution problems at cost levels acceptable to the society as a whole, we are still left with difficult problems. Who will bear the costs for scientific inquiry? Who will pay for changes demanded by new technology? How questions like these must be answered is a matter of public policy, and they are sure to provoke controversy. The easy answer is always to let someone else pay. The industrialist may see pollution abatement as a public good for which the public should pay. Local government may see it as a matter of national concern. The national government may insist on local involvement, and citizens may turn down bond issues to support the necessary programs.

At the root of the search for a quality environment, therefore, are the problems of definition and cost allocation. Somebody's version of the good life will dominate; someone else's will not. Some people will pay; others will not. Open spaces and beautiful structures may mean long hours of travel to work for some, and the inability to acquire decent housing for others. Parks and wilderness areas may seem necessary to some, and a waste of precious resources to others. For some, attempts at population control will seem an invasion of privacy. For others, it will appear essential to avoid the destruction of a quality environment. The war for survival and a quality environment involves science, technology, dollars, and public support. But first and foremost it involves politics — the resolution of conflict.

The readings that follow have a dual purpose. They are designed both to explore certain physical dimensions of environmental problems, and to dramatize the political and economic complexities lodged in the efforts to solve them. They emphasize the social, political, economic, and technological context within which these physical problems exist and solutions must be developed. They indicate some of the considerations that must be taken into account in calculating the costs and consequences of these efforts. They point to feasible and possible activities as well as to utopian dreams.

1

The Ecological Crisis

What we call the "ecological crisis" is caused by the combination of a broad array of physical conditions and social problems. On the one hand, this crisis grows out of the scarcity of natural resources, their conservation, and responsible allocation to human needs. It also involves the more elusive concept of "quality of life" and its preservation against threats of pollution, solid waste, pesticides, urban decay, population explosion, and noise.

Although most of the physical conditions at the base of modern environmental problems are not new, the growth and concentration of population and rapid industrial and technological change have brought them to the surface in increasingly intense forms. The resulting state of affairs has made attempts to solve environmental problems all the more urgent, and has transformed them into priority items on the public agenda. The problem of environmental policy, in short, has been converted dramatically into a vital matter of public policy formation. Having become a major competitor for the attention and resources of public agencies, the ecological crisis is rapidly becoming one of the most significant political issues in the American polity.

In formulating public policy designed to remove the barriers to environmental quality, policy makers face a variety of social, economic, political, and technological factors. The interdependence of these factors and the relationships among natural environment, social structure, and technological development demand a comprehensive approach to public policy formation rarely found in the American political system. Traditionally, American public policy has developed in a disjointed and piecemeal manner focussing upon rather narrow social and technological problems. Regarding environmental quality, most of the relevant decisions reached have been made by private individuals and groups whose unrelated and uncoordinated decision-making has imposed intense pressures upon the natural and social environments and has threatened the ecological balance. Examples abound. Pesticides and herbicides have been widely used to reduce crop losses from insect infestations and noxious plants, with little regard to the effect upon fish and wildlife. The ecology of the city has been determined by private judgments concerning the location of housing, industrial sites, and office complexes, with little regard to the impact upon population concentration. Pollution abatement has frequently progressed, with little effort to assess its economic and social costs. And freeways have been constructed, with little attention to the effect on social patterns, the development of ghettos, and pollution.

In the past, public policy formation and private decision-making have tended to occur in response to short-run needs and obvious, narrowly defined problems. This has often led to unanticipated, dysfunctional consequences for both the ecology and core values of our society. Efforts to correct the imbalance and improve remedial policies must now be made, and greater attention must be paid henceforth to the consequences of those policies for our ecology and basic values.

The development of such policies may require a substantial reordering of political processes, governmental structures, and individual values. These changes will have to be guided by a new social knowledge capable of creating alternative policies and of evaluating their consequences for ecological control and the values of both the individual and society.

The thesis of this chapter is that the ecological crisis is imposing a new set of responsibilities on the American polity. The political system, as currently organized, is ill suited for the comprehensive ecological approach required for effective action. Policy tends to emerge from political compromises made by a number of individuals, groups, and agencies, each seeking to maximize its special version of the public good.

Substantial changes in methods of policy formation and implementation may be required. These changes may strike at many values deeply held by society. Drastic changes will therefore be slow in coming — if they come at all. At least one basic requisite of change will be the development of tools that appropriately conceptualize the problems and evaluate alternatives in terms of their effect on the distribution of values.

The four selections in this chapter, which sketch the major dimensions of the environmental crisis, present some of the barriers to attaining environmental quality. Their authors illustrate some of the causes of the present crisis, and they describe the fragmented nature of the policy process, pointing to the need for a broader frame of reference and a more comprehensive and integrated approach to remedial policy. Further, they indicate the deficiencies in such criteria for decision-making as the analysis of costs and benefits, and they call for the development of new resources, new institutional arrangements, new knowledge, and new criteria to aid the decision-makers of tomorrow.

In the opening selection, Professor Paul Ehrlich introduces us to the "environmental crisis" with a clearly alarmist view of the future. In a dramatic scenario he describes the "end of the oceans" which is to occur in 1979, as well as a series of events which foreshadow this climax in the preceding decade. These events include the decline of the world fishing industry, the failure of the "green revolution," massive urban decay, widespread sickness and disease, increasingly serious air pollution, and the breakdown of water systems. Ehrlich places much of the blame for these catastrophic developments on an alliance of crassly selfish American business interests and their lackeys in the United States government bureaucracy. He also suggests that the Russians, in the misuse of technology and science, have done little better. Professor Ehrlich comes perilously close to implying that the curtain is about to be rung down for keeps.

In the second article, Harvey Wheeler argues that a new politics of ecology is emerging which will increasingly shape the activities and very nature of the American political system. The primary goals of the new politics are to find means to achieve ecological balance and ways to calculate the hidden social costs of public policy and social choice. Substantial political and social changes are needed to achieve the goals of the new politics. The shifting of concentrations of population in a manner that reduces the stress on the ecological system must occur. And if comprehensive policy making is to emerge, the American party system and the legislative process which depend on traditional pressure group politics and state and local autonomy must be reordered.

Following Mr. Wheeler, Professor Lieber suggests that despite evidence of increased governmental recognition and concern, performance in attacking problems of the environment leaves something to be desired. Professor Lieber points up some of the shortcomings of past activities and some of the difficulties in the creation and application of remedial policy.

In the final selection, Aaron Wildavsky rejects the idea that environmental problems are primarily either technological or economic. The major problem is basically political and is rooted in both the organization of the American political system and the distribution of values among individuals and groups within the system. He argues that any changes in the making and administering of public policies will have a sharp impact on the allocation of costs and benefits. Yet at present, Professor Wildavsky suggests, we are unable to make choices based upon solid information as to the implications of various courses of action.

Eco-Catastrophe!

PAUL EHRLICH*

The end of the ocean came late in the summer of 1979, and it came even more rapidly than the biologists had expected. There had been signs for more than a decade, commencing with the discovery in 1968 that DDT slows down photosynthesis in marine plant life. It was announced in a short paper in the technical journal, *Science*, but to ecologists it smacked of doomsday. They knew that all life in the sea depends on photosynthesis, the chemical process by which green plants bind the sun's energy and make it available to living things. And they knew that DDT and similar chlorinated hydrocarbons had polluted the entire surface of the earth, including the sea.

But that was only the first of many signs. There had been the final gasp of the whaling industry in 1973, and the end of the Peruvian anchovy fishery in 1975. Indeed, a score of other fisheries had disappeared quietly from over-exploitation

*Reprinted with the permission of Paul R. Ehrlich and the Editors of Ramparts. From *Ramparts* (September 1969), pp. 24-28.

and various eco-catastrophes by 1977. The term "eco-catastrophe" was coined by a California ecologist in 1969 to describe the most spectacular of man's attacks on the systems which sustain his life. He drew his inspiration from the Santa Barbara offshore oil disaster of that year, and from the news which spread among naturalists that virtually all of the Golden State's seashore bird life was doomed because of chlorinated hydrocarbon interference with its reproduction. Eco-catastrophes in the sea became increasingly common in the early 1970's. Mysterious "blooms" of previously rare microorganisms began to appear in offshore waters. Red tides — killer outbreaks of a minute single-celled plant — returned to the Florida Gulf coast and were sometimes accompanied by tides of other exotic hues.

It was clear by 1975 that the entire ecology of the ocean was changing. A few types of phytoplankton were becoming resistant to chlorinated hydrocarbons and were gaining the upper hand. Changes in the phytoplankton community led inevitably to changes in the community of zooplankton, the tiny animals which eat the phytoplankton. These changes were passed on up the chains of life in the ocean to the herring, plaice, cod, and tuna. As the diversity of life in the ocean diminished, its stability also decreased.

Other changes had taken place by 1975. Most ocean fishes that returned to fresh water to breed, like the salmon, had become extinct, their breeding streams so dammed up and polluted that their powerful homing instinct only resulted in suicide. Many fishes and shellfishes that bred in restricted areas along the coasts followed them as onshore pollution escalated.

By 1977 the annual yield of fish from the sea was down to 30 million metric tons, less than one-half the per capita catch of a decade earlier. This helped malnutrition to escalate sharply in a world where an estimated 50 million people per year were already dying of starvation. The United Nations attempted to get all chlorinated hydrocarbon insecticides banned on a worldwide basis, but the move was defeated by the United States. This opposition was generated primarily by the American petrochemical industry, operating hand in glove with its subsidiary, the United States Department of Agriculture. Together they persuaded the government to oppose the U.N. move — which was not difficult since most Americans believed that Russia and China were more in need of fish products than was the United States. The United Nations also attempted to get fishing nations to adopt strict and enforced catch limits to preserve dwindling stocks. This move was blocked by Russia, who, with the most modern electronic equipment, was in the best position to glean what was left in the sea. It was, curiously, on the very day in 1977 when the Soviet Union announced its refusal that another ominous article appeared in *Science*. It announced that incident solar radiation had been so reduced by worldwide air pollution that serious effects on the world's vegetation could be expected.

II

Apparently it was a combination of ecosystem destabilization, sunlight reduction, and a rapid escalation in chlorinated hydrocarbon pollution from massive Thanodrin applications which triggered the ultimate catastrophe. Seventeen huge Soviet-financed Thanodrin plants were operating in underdeveloped countries by 1978.

They had been part of a massive Russian "aid offensive" designed to fill the gap caused by the collapse of America's ballyhooed "Green Revolution."

It became apparent in the early '70s that the "Green Revolution" was more talk than substance. Distribution of high yield "miracle" grain seeds had caused temporary local spurts in agricultural production. Simultaneously, excellent weather had produced record harvests. The combination permitted bureaucrats, especially in the United States Department of Agriculture and the Agency for International Development (AID), to reverse their previous pessimism and indulge in an outburst of optimistic propaganda about staving off famine. They raved about the approaching transformation of agriculture in the underdeveloped countries (UDCs). The reason for the propaganda reversal was never made clear. Most historians agree that a combination of utter ignorance of ecology, a desire to justify past errors, and pressure from agro-industry (which was eager to sell pesticides, fertilizers, and farm machinery to the UDCs and agencies helping the UDCs) was behind the campaign. Whatever the motivation, the results were clear. Many concerned people, lacking the expertise to see through the Green Revolution drivel, relaxed. The population-food crisis was "solved."

But reality was not long in showing itself. Local famine persisted in northern India even after good weather brought an end to the ghastly Bihar famine of the mid-'60s. East Pakistan was next, followed by a resurgence of general famine in northern India. Other foci of famine rapidly developed in Indonesia, the Philippines, Malawi, the Congo, Egypt, Colombia, Ecuador, Honduras, the Dominican Republic, and Mexico.

Everywhere hard realities destroyed the illusion of the Green Revolution. Yields dropped as the progressive farmers who had first accepted the new seeds found that their higher yields brought lower prices — effective demand (hunger plus cash) was not sufficient in poor countries to keep prices up. Less progressive farmers, observing this, refused to make the extra effort required to cultivate the "miracle" grains. Transport systems proved inadequate to bring the necessary fertilizer to the fields where the new and extremely fertilizer-sensitive grains were being grown. The same systems were also inadequate to move produce to markets. Fertilizer plants were not built fast enough, and most of the underdeveloped countries could not scrape together funds to purchase supplies, even on concessional terms. Finally, the inevitable happened, and pests began to reduce yields in even the most carefully cultivated fields. Among the first were the famous "miracle rats" which invaded Philippine "miracle rice" fields early in 1969. They were quickly followed by many insects and viruses, thriving on the relatively pest-susceptible new grains, encouraged by the vast and dense plantings, and rapidly acquiring resistance to the chemicals used against them. As chaos spread until even the most obtuse agriculturists and economists realized that the Green Revolution had turned brown, the Russians stepped in.

In retrospect it seems incredible that the Russians, with the American mistakes known to them, could launch an even more incompetent program of aid to the underdeveloped world. Indeed, in the early 1970's there were cynics in the United States who claimed that outdoing the stupidity of American foreign aid would be physically impossible. Those critics were, however, obviously unaware that the Russians had been busily destroying their own environment for many years. The virtual disappearance of sturgeon from Russian rivers caused a great shortage of caviar by 1970. A standard joke among Russian scientists at that time was that they had created an artificial caviar which was indistinguishable from the real thing — except by taste. At any rate the Soviet Union, observing with interest the progressive deterioration of relations between the UDCs and the United States, came up with a solution. It had recently developed what it claimed was the ideal insecticide, a highly lethal chlorinated hydrocarbon complexed with a special agent for penetrating the external skeletal armor of insects. Announcing that the new pesticide, called Thanodrin, would truly produce a Green Revolution, the Soviets entered into negotiations with various UDCs for the construction of massive Thanodrin factories. The USSR would bear all the costs; all it wanted in return were certain trade and military concessions.

It is interesting now, with the perspective of years, to examine in some detail the reasons why the UDCs welcomed the Thanodrin plan with such open arms. Government officials in these countries ignored the protests of their own scientists that Thanodrin would not solve the problems which plagued them. The governments now knew that the basic cause of their problems was overpopulation, and that these problems had been exacerbated by the dullness, daydreaming, and cupidity endemic to all governments. They knew that only population control and limited development aimed primarily at agriculture could have spared them the horrors they now faced. They knew it, but they were not about to admit it. How much easier it was simply to accuse the Americans of failing to give them proper aid; how much simpler to accept the Russian panacea.

And then there was the general worsening of relations between the United States and the UDCs. Many things had contributed to this. The situation in America in the first half of the 1970's deserves our close scrutiny. Being more dependent on imports for raw materials than the Soviet Union, the United States had, in the early 1970s, adopted more and more heavy-handed policies in order to insure continuing supplies. Military adventures in Asia and Latin America had further lessened the international credibility of the United States as a great defender of freedom — an image which had begun to deteriorate rapidly during the pointless and fruitless Viet-Nam conflict. At home, acceptance of the carefully manufactured image lessened dramatically, as even the more romantic and chauvinistic citizens began to understand the role of the military and the industrial system in what John Kenneth Galbraith had aptly named "The New Industrial State."

At home in the USA the early '70s were traumatic times. Racial violence grew and the habitability of the cities diminished, as nothing substantial was done to ameliorate either racial inequities or urban blight. Welfare rolls grew as automation and general technological progress forced more and more people into the category of "unemployable." Simultaneously a taxpayers' revolt occurred. Although there was not enough money to build the schools, roads, water systems, sewage systems, jails, hospitals, urban transit lines, and all the other amenities needed to support a burgeoning population, Americans refused to tax themselves more heavily. Starting in Youngstown, Ohio in 1969 and followed closely by Richmond, California, community after community was forced to close its schools or curtail educational operations for lack of funds. Water supplies, already marginal in quality and quantity in many places by 1970, deteriorated quickly. Water rationing occurred in 1723 municipalities in the summer of 1974, and hepatitis and epidemic dysentery rates climbed about 500 per cent between 1970-1974.

III

Air pollution continued to be the most obvious manifestation of environmental deterioration. It was, by 1972, quite literally in the eyes of all Americans. The year 1973 saw not only the New York and Los Angeles smog disasters, but also the publication of the Surgeon General's massive report on air pollution and health. The public had been partially prepared for the worst by the publicity given to the U.N. pollution conference held in 1972. Deaths in the late '60s caused by smog were well known to scientists, but the public had ignored them because they mostly involved the early demise of the old and sick rather than people dropping dead on the freeways. But suddenly our citizens were faced with nearly 200,000 corpses and massive documentation that they could be the next to die from respiratory disease. They were not ready for that scale of disaster. After all, the U.N. conference had not predicted that accumulated air pollution would make the planet uninhabitable until almost 1990. The population was terrorized as TV screens became filled with scenes of horror from the disaster areas. Especially vivid was NBC's coverage of hundreds of unattended people choking out their lives outside of New York's hospitals. Terms like nitrogen oxide, acute bronchitis, and cardiac arrest began to have real meaning for most Americans.

The ultimate horror was the announcement that chlorinated hydrocarbons were now a major constituent of air pollution in all American cities. Autopsies of smog disaster victims revealed an average chlorinated hydrocarbon load in fatty tissue equivalent to 26 parts per million of DDT. In October, 1973, the Department of Health, Education and Welfare announced studies which showed unequivocally that increasing death rates from hypertension, cirrhosis of the liver, liver cancer and a series of other diseases had resulted from the chlorinated hydrocarbon load. They estimated that Americans born since 1946 (when DDT usage began) now had a life expectancy of only 49 years, and predicted that if current patterns continued, this expectancy would reach 42 years by 1980, when it might level out. Plunging insurance stocks triggered a stock market panic. The president of Velsicol, Inc., a major pesticide producer, went on television to "publicly eat a teaspoonful of DDT" (it was really powdered milk) and announce that HEW had been infiltrated by Communists. Other giants of the petrochemical industry, attempting to dispute the indisputable evidence, launched a massive pressure campaign on Congress to force HEW to "get out of agriculture's business." They were aided by the agrochemical journals, which had decades of experience in misleading the public about the benefits and dangers of pesticides. But by now the public realized that it had been duped. The Nobel Prize for medicine and physiology was given to Drs. J. L. Radomski and W. B. Deichmann, who in the late 1960s had pioneered in the documentation of the long-term lethal effects of chlorinated hydrocarbons. A Presidential Commission with unimpeachable credentials directly accused the agrochemical complex of "condemning many millions of Americans to an early death." The year 1973 was the year in which Americans finally came to understand the direct threat to their existence posed by environmental deterioration.

And 1973 was also the year in which most people finally comprehended the indirect threat. Even the president of Union Oil Company and several other industrialists publicly stated their concern over the reduction of bird populations which had resulted from pollution by DDT and other chlorinated hydrocarbons. Insect populations boomed because they were resistant to most pesticides and had been freed, by the incompetent use of those pesticides, from most of their natural enemies. Rodents swarmed over crops, multiplying rapidly in the absence of predatory birds. The effect of pests on the wheat crop was especially disastrous in the summer of 1973, since that was also the year of the great drought. Most of us can remember the shock which greeted the announcement by atmospheric physicists that the shift of the jet stream which had caused the drought was probably permanent. It signalled the birth of the Midwestern desert. Man's air-polluting activities had by then caused gross changes in climatic patterns. The news, of course, played hell with commodity and stock markets. Food prices skyrocketed, as savings were poured into hoarded canned goods. Official assurances that food supplies would remain ample fell on deaf ears, and even the government showed signs of nervousness when California migrant field workers went out on strike again in protest against the continued use of pesticides by growers. The strike burgeoned into farm burning and riots. The workers, calling themselves "The Walking Dead," demanded immediate compensation for their shortened lives, and crash research programs to attempt to lengthen them.

It was in the same speech in which President Edward Kennedy, after much delay, finally declared a national emergency and called out the National Guard to harvest California's crops, that the first mention of population control was made. Kennedy pointed out that the United States would no longer be able to offer any food aid to other nations and was likely to suffer food shortages herself. He suggested that, in view of the manifest failure of the Green Revolution, the only hope of the UDCs lay in population control. His statement, you will recall, created an uproar in the underdeveloped countries. Newspaper editorials accused the United States of wishing to prevent small countries from becoming large nations and thus threatening American hegemony. Politicians asserted that President Kennedy was a "creature of the giant drug combine" that wished to shove its pills down every woman's throat.

Among Americans, religious opposition to population control was very slight. Industry in general also backed the idea. Increasing poverty in the UDCs was both destroying markets and threatening supplies of raw materials. The seriousness of the raw material situation had been brought home during the Congressional Hard Resources hearings in 1971. The exposure of the ignorance of the cornucopian economists had been quite a spectacle — a spectacle brought into virtually every American's home in living color. Few would forget the distinguished geologist from the University of California who suggested that economists be legally required to learn at least the most elementary facts of geology. Fewer still would forget that an equally distinguished Harvard economist added that they might be required to learn some economics, too. The overall message was clear: America's resource situation was bad and bound to get worse. The hearings had led to a bill requiring the Departments of State, Interior, and Commerce to set up a joint resource procurement council with the express purpose of "insuring that proper consideration of American resource needs be an integral part of American foreign policy."

Suddenly the United States discovered that it had a national consensus: population control was the only possible salvation of the underdeveloped world. But that same consensus led to heated debate. How could the UDCs be persuaded to limit their populations, and should not the United States lead the way by limiting its own? Members of the intellectual community wanted America to set an example. They pointed out that the United States was in the midst of a new baby boom: her birth rate, well over 20 per thousand per year, and her growth rate of over one per cent per annum were among the very highest of the developed countries. They detailed the deterioration of the American physical and psychic environments, the growing health threats, the impending food shortages, and the insufficiency of funds for desperately needed public works. They contended that the nation was clearly unable or unwilling to properly care for the people it already had. What possible reason could there be, they queried, for adding any more? Besides, who would listen to requests by the United States for population control when that nation did not control her own profligate reproduction?

Those who opposed population controls for the U.S. were equally vociferous. The military-industrial complex, with its all-too-human mixture of ignorance and avarice, still saw strength and prosperity in numbers. Baby food magnates, already worried by the growing nitrate pollution of their products, saw their market disappearing. Steel manufacturers saw a decrease in aggregate demand and slippage for that holy of holies, the Gross National Product. And military men saw, in the growing population-food-environment crisis, a serious threat to their carefully nurtured Cold War. In the end, of course, economic arguments held sway, and the "inalienable right of every American couple to determine the size of its family," a freedom invented for the occasion in the early '70s, was not compromised.

The population control bill, which was passed by Congress early in 1974, was quite a document, nevertheless. On the domestic front, it authorized an increase from 100 to 150 million dollars in funds for "family planning" activities. This was made possible by a general feeling in the country that the growing army on welfare needed family planning. But the gist of the bill was a series of measures designed to impress the need for population control on the UDCs. All American aid to countries with overpopulation problems was required by law to consist in part of population control assistance. In order to receive any assistance each nation was required not only to accept the population control aid, but also to match it according to a complex formula. "Overpopulation" itself was defined by a formula based on U.N. statistics, and the UDCs were required not only to accept aid, but also to show progress in reducing birth rates. Every five years the status of the aid program for each nation was to be re-evaluated.

The reaction to the announcement of this program dwarfed the response to President Kennedy's speech. A coalition of UDCs attempted to get the U.N. General Assembly to condemn the United States as a "genetic aggressor." Most damaging of all to the American cause was the famous "25 Indians and a dog" speech by Mr. Shankarnarayan, Indian Ambassador to the U.N. Shankarnarayan pointed out that for several decades the United States, with less than six per cent of the people of the world had consumed roughly 50 per cent of the raw materials used every year. He described vividly America's contribution to worldwide environmental deterioration, and he scathingly denounced the miserly record of United States foreign aid as "unworthy of a fourth-rate power, let alone the most powerful nation on earth."

It was the climax of his speech, however, which most historians claim once and for all destroyed the image of the United States. Shankarnarayan informed the assembly that the average American family dog was fed more animal protein per week than the average Indian got in a month. "How do you justify taking fish from protein-starved Peruvians and feeding them to your animals?" he asked. "I contend," he concluded, "that the birth of an American baby is a greater disaster for the world than that of 25 Indian babies." When the applause had died away, Mr. Sorensen, the American representative, made a speech which said essentially that "other countries look after their own self-interest, too." When the vote came, the United States was condemned.

IV

This condemnation set the tone of U.S.-UDC relations at the time the Russian Thanodrin proposal was made. The proposal seemed to offer the masses in the UDCs an opportunity to save themselves and humiliate the United States at the same time; and in human affairs, as we all know, biological realities could never interfere with such an opportunity. The scientists were silenced, the politicians said yes, the Thanodrin plants were built, and the results were what any beginning ecology student could have predicted. At first Thanodrin seemed to offer excellent control of many pests. True, there was a rash of human fatalities from improper use of the lethal chemical, but, as Russian technical advisors were prone to note, these were more than compensated for by increased yields. Thanodrin use skyrocketed throughout the underdeveloped world. The Mikoyan design group developed a dependable, cheap agricultural aircraft which the Soviets donated to the effort in large numbers. MIG sprayers became even more common in UDCs than MIG interceptors.

Then the troubles began. Insect strains with cuticles resistant to Thanodrin penetration began to appear. And as streams, rivers, fish culture ponds and onshore waters became rich in Thanodrin, more fisheries began to disappear. Bird populations were decimated. The sequence of events was standard for broadcast use of a synthetic pesticide: great success at first, followed by removal of natural enemies and development of resistance by the pest. Populations of crop-eating insects in areas treated with Thanodrin made steady comebacks and soon became more abundant than ever. Yields plunged, while farmers in their desperation increased the Thanodrin dose and shortened the time between treatments. Death from Thanodrin poisoning became common. The first violent incident occurred in the Canete Valley of Peru, where farmers had suffered a similar chlorinated hydrocarbon disaster in the mid-'50s. A Russian advisor serving as an agricultural pilot was assaulted and killed by a mob of enraged farmers in January, 1978. Trouble spread rapidly during 1978, especially after the word got out that two years earlier Russia herself had banned the use of Thanodrin at home because of its serious effects on ecological systems. Suddenly Russia, and not the United States, was the *bête noir* in the UDCs. "Thanodrin parties" became epidemic, with farmers, in their ignorance, dumping carloads of Thanodrin concentrate into the sea. Russian advisors fled, and four of the Thanodrin plants were leveled to the ground. Destruction of the plants in Rio and Calcutta led to hundreds of thousands of gallons of Thanodrin concentrate being dumped directly into the sea.

Mr. Shankarnarayan again rose to address the U.N., but this time it was Mr. Potemkin, representative of the Soviet Union, who was on the hot seat. Mr. Potemkin heard his nation described as the greatest mass killer of all time as Shankarnarayan predicted at least 30 million deaths from crop failures due to overdependence on Thanodrin. Russia was accused of "chemical aggression," and the General Assembly, after a weak reply by Potemkin, passed a vote of censure.

It was in January, 1979, that huge blooms of a previously unknown variety of diatom were reported off the coast of Peru. The blooms were accompanied by a massive die-off of sea life and of the pathetic remainder of the birds which had once feasted on the anchovies of the area. Almost immediately another huge bloom was reported in the Indian Ocean, centering around the Seychelles, and then a third in the South Atlantic off the African coast. Both of these were accompanied by spectacular die-offs of marine animals. Even more ominous were growing reports of fish and bird kills at oceanic points where there were no spectacular blooms. Biologists were soon able to explain the phenomena: the diatom had evolved an enzyme which broke down Thanodrin; that enzyme also produced a breakdown product which interfered with the transmission of nerve impulses, and was therefore lethal to animals. Unfortunately, the biologists could suggest no way of repressing the poisonous diatom bloom in time. By September, 1979, all important animal life in the sea was extinct. Large areas of coastline had to be evacuated, as windrows of dead fish created a monumental stench.

But stench was the least of man's problems. Japan and China were faced with almost instant starvation from a total loss of the seafood on which they were so dependent. Both blamed Russia for their situation and demanded immediate mass shipments of food. Russia had none to send. On October 13, Chinese armies attacked Russia on a broad front. . . .

V

A pretty grim scenario. Unfortunately, we're a long way into it already. Everything mentioned as happening before 1970 has actually occurred; much of the rest is based on projections of trends already appearing. Evidence that pesticides have long-term lethal effects on human beings has started to accumulate, and recently Robert Finch, Secretary of the Department of Health, Education and Welfare expressed his extreme apprehension about the pesticide situation. Simultaneously the petrochemical industry continues its unconscionable poison-peddling. For instance, Shell Chemical has been carrying on a high-pressure campaign to sell the insecticide Azodrin to farmers as a killer of cotton pests. They continue their program even though they know that Azodrin is not only ineffective, but often *increases* the pest density. They've covered themselves nicely in an advertisement which states, "Even if an overpowering migration [sic] develops, the flexibility of Azodrin lets you regain control fast. Just increase the dosage according to label recommendations." It's a great game—get people to apply the poison and kill the natural enemies of the pests. Then blame the increased pests on "migration" and sell even more pesticide!

Right now fisheries are being wiped out by over-exploitation, made easy by modern electronic equipment. The companies producing the equipment know this. They even boast in advertising that only their equipment will keep fishermen in business until the final kill. Profits must obviously be maximized in the short run. Indeed, Western society is in the process of completing the rape and murder of the planet for economic gain. And, sadly, most of the rest of the world is eager for the opportunity to emulate our behavior. But the underdeveloped peoples will be denied that opportunity—the days of plunder are drawing inexorably to a close.

Most of the people who are going to die in the greatest cataclysm in the history of man have already been born. More than three and a half billion people already populate our moribund globe, and about half of them are hungry. Some 10 to 20 million will starve to death *this year*. In spite of this, the population of the earth will increase by 70 million souls in 1969. For mankind has artificially lowered the death rate of the human population, while in general birth rates have remained high. With the input side of the population system in high gear and the output side slowed down, our fragile planet has filled with people at an incredible rate. It took several million years for the population to reach a total of two billion people in 1930, while a *second two billion will have been added by 1975!* By that time some experts feel that food shortages will have escalated the present level of world hunger and starvation into famines of unbelievable proportions. Other experts, more optimistic, think the ultimate food-population collision will not occur until the decade of the 1980's. Of course more massive famine may be avoided if other events cause a prior rise in the human death rate.

Both worldwide plague and thermonuclear war are made more probable as population growth continues. These, along with famine, make up the trio of potential "death rate solutions" to the population problem—solutions in which the birth rate-death rate imbalance is redressed by a rise in the death rate rather than by a lowering of the birth rate. Make no mistake about it, *the imbalance will be redressed*. The shape of the population growth curve is one familiar to the biologist. It is the outbreak part of an outbreak-crash sequence. A population grows rapidly in the presence of abundant resources, finally runs out of food or some other necessity, and crashes to a low level or extinction. Man is not only running out of food, he is also destroying the life support systems of the Spaceship Earth. The situation was recently summarized very succinctly: "It is the top of the ninth inning. Man, always a threat at the plate, has been hitting Nature hard. It is important to remember, however, that NATURE BATS LAST."

The Politics of Ecology

HARVEY WHEELER*

Until little more than six months ago, "new politics" referred to either the protest movement or late-model mass-media campaigning. Today, however, a third new politics is springing up. It is being given urgency by a growing public alarm over all varieties of pollution. War protest has yielded to demonstrations against the rape of the environment. Youth is turning away from Marxists like Herbert Marcuse and flocking to ecologists like Paul Ehrlich. The message is ecocide, the environment being murdered by mankind. Each day brings to light a new ecological crisis. Our dense, amber air is a noxious emphysema agent; farming — anti-husbandry — turns fertile soil into a poisoned wasteland; rivers are sewers, lakes cesspools, and our oceans are dying.

The early warning signals seemed unrelated and were easily ignored. Five hundred Londoners died of a summer smog attack. New York, blacked out and turned off, became dysfunctional. Union Oil's Platform A sprang a leak and converted Santa Barbara's postcard beaches into a sludge swamp. Traffic congestion made driving slower than walking. Airways threatened to become as dangerous as freeways. Cities, unable to function, closed schools and reduced public services. As power blackouts became seasonal, power demands rose and pushed pollution levels — thermal and hydrocarbon — to higher readings. Mathematical ecologists, such as Kenneth Watt, estimate that the United States is approaching the point where the interstitial energy required to keep the system going is greater than the energy it employs productively: Overhead costs overwhelm output. Our entire social order faces an ecosystem "depression" that will make 1929 look like a shower at a garden party.

It is imperative to correct one common fallacy — one especially popular among the young. Technology is not the culprit. Admittedly, the misuse of technology is part of the problem, but the essence of the real problem is what Watt calls the ecocidal asymptote. It is to the new politics of ecology what $E = mc^2$ was to the thermonuclear era.

The ecocidal asymptote runs as follows: Statistical studies of the pattern of exploitation of every natural resource can be plotted as two curves. One represents the rate of depletion of a resource, the other represents the technological capacity for its exploitation. Both curves are exponential; that is, in the beginning they rise very gradually. But their rate of increase is always rising, pushing their curves up ever more steeply until they reach a vertical explosion. Both follow the same pattern at the same rate, exploding, asymptotically, at the same time.

As an illustration, consider the ocean's fisheries — the blue whale, the salmon, the tuna. In the beginning, the supply is virtually unlimited, and harvesting techniques make little or no dent in the available supply. Soon fishing techniques im-

*Reprinted with permission from the author and the editors of *Saturday Review*. Copyright 1970 Saturday Review, Inc. From *Saturday Review* (March 7, 1970), pp. 51-52, 62-64. Abridged. The author is Senior Fellow at the Center for the Study of Democratic Institutions.

prove, and, as they do, they gradually overtake reproduction rates; supplies decline as techniques improve. As this situation becomes apparent, it spurs on competition to get more and more while the getting is good. Ever more efficient fishing techniques are invented, and their rate of efficiency rises in direct ratio to the depletion of the resource until the point arrives when the ultimate in fishing technology coincides with the extinction of the species. This "falling together" of the technology and resource depletion curves is the ecocidal asymptote. It is the inimical process that characterizes our age, the enemy of the new politics of ecology. The death of one resource leads to the depletion of another; one technological fix begets another. Each of our ecocidal crises is interconnected with all the others, and none can be solved in isolation. The politics of ecology is architectonic.

The new politics of ecology, however, is not merely an outgrowth of the old politics of conservation. Conservation has a long and revered history, tracing back to such men as John Muir and Clifford Pinchot. This conservationist tradition, somewhat ineffectual in the past, is acquiring a new vitality today. In fact, entire states, largely in the American Northwest, are known for their being officially conservation-minded. Washington, Oregon, and Montana are prominent examples. Conservationist slogans gain in popularity each day: "Keep Arizona Clean"; "Preserve Washington's Water" (and keep it out of California); "Stamp Out Billboards"; "Save Lake Tahoe." Rotarians and Yippies unite in "GOO"—"Get Oil Out of Santa Barbara"; and the cry of that great conservationist Howard Hughes is voiced: "Don't let the AEC shake down Caesar's Palace." These are laudable examples of conservationist politics, but all share the basic characteristics of the conservationism of the past; all are local, piecemeal efforts, and all rely upon traditional pressure-group tactics.

Today, we can count approximately 126 Congressmen who have publicly identified themselves as a conservationist bloc. A new bill introduced by Congressman Richard L. Ottinger and others proposes to guarantee all citizens the right to enjoy a healthful environment. Yet, such efforts are still in the mode of the old politics. They have a new twist, a new power base, and a new constituency. This new lease on life for the old mode of conservationist politics is not difficult to understand. It is an outgrowth of the leisure industries spawned by our affluent society. It is, to oversimplify, the politics of tourism. Conservationism is a gut issue in the West. It means preserve our state as an enclave of natural beauty and tourist attractions.

But the new politics of ecology means something quite different. A few examples will sharpen these differences. The essential political problem of the future is, first, to figure out how to preserve general ecological balances, and, second, how to calculate hidden social costs so as to determine how much is really being spent on side effects such as a new freeway, the three-car family, and the SST. Complete ecological harmony is impossible to achieve, but the "trade-offs" necessary to approach it as closely as possible must become known.

There is no such thing as an atmosphere without any pollution. However, it is obvious that certain kinds of air pollution deriving from fossil fuels already have reached perilous levels. This is not merely a question of unsightliness nor even of the threat of a rise in lung cancer and emphysema. Even more serious hazards may develop if pollution particles are carried by superjets from the lower atmosphere into its upper, turbulence-free layers. Scientists warn that these jet contrails may not be dispersed and could act as an insulation layer between earth and sun, cooling the earth and leading to a new Ice Age. Of course, no one is certain what will really happen. We are in much the same position as when DDT was introduced; nobody knew for certain what its cumulative effects would be. Today, it does not seem inconceivable that pollution particles could quickly clog the upper atmosphere, and before we knew it utter havoc would be upon us.

Obviously, pollution must be reduced, but again we are not dealing in absolutes. We must know what levels are tolerable, and we must know the conveniences or desires that must be sacrificed to maintain these levels. New mass transit systems may be required. Individual desires to own several automobiles will have to be curtailed. And this is but the beginning. Ecologists tell us we shall have to mount a revolution of declining expectations. Gadgets will have to go. Creature comforts will have to give way to culture comforts. Americans today are at 1788. Never again will they or their children enjoy as many material conveniences. This is the real revolution implicit in the new politics of ecology.

What level of public education should we and can we maintain? How much are we willing to pay for it? How can we finance that level? Can we continue to support schools from state land taxes? Is it just to do so? Must we institute a national educational system? To answer these questions we must know the optimum size of an urban community, and how population should be distributed in our clustered communities. In short, we shall have to find out exactly what life in a megalopolis really costs, and whether or not we are getting our money's worth.

What degree of smog is created by population density? Perhaps the same number of people could live in roughly the same area, and even own the same number of cars if they displayed different density patterns with lower ratios of travel between residence and work. Simple freeway tariff schedules could alter traffic patterns immediately by penalizing over-powered and under-occupied vehicles. But we don't know. We don't know how much interstitial overhead energy we waste in a city like New York, merely trying to hold its parts together and keep it operating. We shall have to learn how to calculate the interstitial requirements of cities of different types and sizes to determine the optimum balance between urban amenities and overhead costs. We have no real measures of the price we pay for slums in all sorts of ways—poor health, substandard living conditions, crime, and so on. We do know that slums are high statistics areas; in them are concentrated most of everything bad, and at the end of each statistic lies a dead body.

Automation reduces the number of people required for factory and office operations, making huge cities unnecessary as well as uneconomic. Industrialists have known this for a long time. But what about the city as a cultural center? If we reduced cities to the size of fifty thousand or even a hundred thousand people, wouldn't we have to sacrifice our great cultural centers, our theaters, our museums, our libraries? The answer is no, we would expand them, improve them, and make them more widely available to all. We speak already of the museum without walls, meaning that the treasures of the entire world can now be exhibited everywhere.

Microfilm libraries plus computer terminals make it possible for everybody everywhere to use the Library of Congress as well as the British Museum and the Bibliothèque Nationale.

What of the theater, the symphony, the ballet? Of course, recordings and television spread them to all, in one sense. Even great "living" theaters and symphonies are possible in very small cities. Vienna was relatively small when it reached its musical apex. Our greatest cultural traditions have been produced in very small cities. Seventeenth-century London abounded with genius; by modern standards it was but a mini-town. Ancient Athens was even smaller, and Plato and Aristotle thought it far too large at that. There is no reason why the same thing cannot be done again. At least, failure would not be due to smallness. All we really need is to decide to produce the cultural conditions necessary to elicit similarly high achievements. Gross size, far from a prerequisite, is an insuperable hindrance.

To answer such questions and to implement the answers will be one of the chief tasks of the politics of the future. We've never asked these questions of politics in the past. But, today, we can have everything that is really valuable about our large cities, and at the same time avoid the disagreeable and expensive side effects due to size. These are ecological questions, and, even though we may be able to answer them soon, there will still be no way to transmit this ecological wisdom to the average citizen for rational and deliberate application at the polls. Yet, this is exactly what we must be able to do in the near future. We shall require a new kind of party system with a new kind of participational democracy seeking solutions to ecological problems. Finally, we shall require a new kind of deliberation or legislative process to grow out of the new politics of ecology, and we shall have to relate to it in something like the way the existing legislative process related to our traditional party system.

Let us take the second problem first, for although it is generally understood that our party system is inadequate, the deficiencies of our legislative system have received scant attention. Reflect for a moment on the fact that our legislatures and our party system are well-tailored to each other. Our parties are, as the textbooks say, loose confederations of state and local boss systems. The key element is "state and local." This means that the representatives selected through our present electoral system arrive at our legislative chambers representing the interests of their local districts. An implicit assumption is that all our primary problems and conflicts will arise from the clash of local interests—conflicts relating to the interests people acquire because they live in one place rather than another. Since before James Madison—the man who provided the underlying rationale for this system of politics —we have trusted that this pluralistic, territorially based expression of interests would produce the general interest, almost as if guided by an unseen hand.

But the issues described earlier are not related to any specific territory as such. Nor are they capable of solution through the expression of local interests. On the contrary, the critical problem—the source of our indictment of the old politics—is that its foundation is too restricted and particularistic to cope with the characteristic problems of our times. Technology-related problems know no territorial bounds, and they defy locally based efforts to deal with them. The same is true for science-related issues. Our present political system is unable to bring all such problems together for resolution within an ecological framework. Yet, this is what we must do.

The characteristic political problems of the present arise from disorders of the entire ecological order. Their solutions are to be found, not through the traditional interaction of local interests and pressure-group politics, but through a new politics of the whole—politics considered architectonically, as the ancients called it. This requires a politics that is more speculative and less mechanistic; it requires us to do our lobbying in the realm of thought as well as in the corridors of power. Our most pressing political problems now have their origins in science and technology. Their solutions will require a new politics especially designed to cope with science and technology, a politics based on what Teilhard de Chardin called the "noösphere," instead of our accustomed politics based on real estate. It follows that entirely new policy-forming institutions will be needed to deal with the ecological politics of the noösphere. Legislatures must be redesigned accordingly. But, of course, before all this can happen, the popular base from which representatives are chosen must be given a new foundation. The scientific-biological-technological revolution that awaits us around the corner of post-industrial time demands entirely new ecological parties. Their outlines are not hard to foresee.

One portent of the new politics occurred in California in 1969. Over the decades, the Sierra Club—a tradition-oriented pressure group of the Pinchot type—had grown into a potent political force. An internal crisis resulted in the defeat of its activist wing. Shortly thereafter, the deposed leadership, forming around the John Muir Society, announced the establishment of a new political movement to be devoted to ecological concerns. Of course, this was not thought of as a new political party, but, nonetheless, it used language that looked ahead to something like the new politics called for above. Whether or not this particular movement prospers, ecological parties promise to be the wave of the future, providing the underpinning required to produce the novel legislative institutions the future will require.

How would such a party system actually operate? How would it differ in essential structure and mode of operation from the electoral and precinct organizations of the past? Again, in California, a technological breakthrough occurred in 1969 that may provide the informational and educational components required to enable voters to make intelligent ecological choices as they function politically in the future.

A team of multidisciplinary experts headed by Kenneth Watt designed a model that would ultimately contain mathematical expressions for almost every conceivable problem concerning the state of California. All these expressions will be programed into a complex computerized analytical system whose formulas alone will run to 5,000 pages. When finished some five years hence, it will be capable of revealing the multifarious interrelationships of each part of the model. The result will be an architectonic mathematical model of California considered as a complete ecological system. Watt calls this the "Model of a Society." Such computer programs will help us to find out how any given problem relates to all others. Suppose we must decide whether to vote for or against a bond issue to raise funds for a new school system. At the present, our choice is determined largely by whether or not we favor public education. But countless other considerations are involved. How would residential patterns be affected? How would traffic on streets and freeways be changed? What new public utilities would be required? How about other services such as fire and police? Would these changes lead to a relocation of shopping centers? What would all these changes add up to? Would they produce the kind of future we want? Computers are not foolproof, and computer models are even less so. We don't expect perfection from either people or machines. All we expect is a device to help us make our decisions on a somewhat more systematic basis. Not only politics would be affected, planning would also change. Those who make new proposals would have to calculate their full ecological consequences well in advance of offering them to the public. The result would be a profound shift in the terms on which political deliberation occurs. The voter would be able to visit computer terminals with multimedia display consoles where the foreseeable implications of alternative policies would be portrayed in pictures, figures, and graphs.

Mathematicians, ecologists, and social scientists working together can lay the beginnings of a new participatory democracy that will be as well-suited to the conditions of the post-industrial era as was the old, grassroots democracy to the simpler conditions of the nineteenth century, and it can all be realized within a decade. But this is only the beginning. In the more distant future, we shall require even more ingenious innovations to bring our underprivileged and our undereducated back into politics.

The first component will be what systems engineers call the multimedia home: not the home we already know with radio, television, and tape recorders. Rather, what is envisioned is an entirely new assortment of media installations with a revolutionary new domestic architecture to accompany it. All communications media can be integrated into a complete acculturational system. Each family can then "program" the entire "informational" input coming into its home. All the pictorial, the graphic, the sound, and print media can be considered as a whole. All sources of knowledge would become accessible to each home. Every data bank would be a potential reservoir to be drawn upon when needed. Obviously, protection of each person's right of privacy must be insured; appropriate personal safeguards must be perfected before these new systems can be made available. Beyond this, other data access criteria might include need to know, and ability to assimilate, qualifications.

Subscription to separate newspapers, magazines, book clubs, and encyclopedias would continue, but for general acculturational purposes it would no longer be necessary. Indeed, save for amusement and leisure occupations, the "mix" of one's own overall multimedia diet need not be left to impulse or passing whim. On the contrary, each person would have the ability—the possibility—of preprograming his overall cultural environment for a period reaching far into the future, just as we do now when we embark on a high school or a college degree program. Adjustments in the programing mix would require revision on a regular basis—semiannually, for example—to comport with family and social changes, and in accord with changing individual interests and varying rates of development. Conceivably, we can design individualized programs to realize cultural, educational, and professional goals whose consummation may lie twenty years or more in the future. Variability and change can be imagined as a branching pattern that reaches into the future, just as trees branch upward in ways that can never be predicted at the start.

Certified professional counselors will be required to assist each family select the integrated cultural development programs of its choice, with appropriate variations to account for the special needs of each member. These professional programers will be comparable to the investment brokers who help wealthy clients play their long-range investment portfolios. But once programs are under way, self-motivation can be counted on to take over. This is what happens today with the best of our new programed instruction systems. Students learn at their own pace, but whatever that pace, they do learn. And they so love what they learn that it often becomes necessary to pry them away from their lessons.

In principle, this new system is similar to the original eighteenth-century concept of the encyclopedia, which was designed to "encircle" everything then known, so each man, on his own, could take "all knowledge for his province." At the time of the first encyclopedia, it was very nearly possible to realize both goals, at least if the reader already had a fairly large working vocabulary. By the mid-nineteenth century, however, knowledge in general and science in particular had grown so complex that no encyclopedia could fully encompass everything that was known. And even if it could have, the departments of learning had become too complex to be understood by any but experts. Ph.D.s in botany, for example, were no better off than illiterates, if they tried to read an encyclopedia article on plasma physics or molecular biology. However, multimedia programing systems can now restore the original aim of the encyclopedia. Moreover, neither prior learning, nor even literacy itself, is any longer a precondition to the assimilation of high cultural status. A well-programed system can provide even functional illiterates with the essentials of higher learning. Of course, education and culture are only the civic essentials. Multimedia homes can embrace the entire range of human activities, with leisure, amusement, and frivolity provided according to individual desire. Each part of each program can be tailored to each person's wants, needs, and talents.

All this is technologically possible today. It is only necessary for us to devote our scientific resources to bringing it about. If that is done, we can move toward the realization of one of man's oldest dreams. All our citizens, the most lowly as well as the most favored, can enjoy the highest fruits of civilization. The optimistic conclusion is that we no longer need despair of democracy's future prospects because of the increased complexity of the problems of the post-industrial world. The very technological advances that are bringing about this new world will also make it possible to produce a citizenry able to comprehend and cope with them, ushering in a new era in the history of democracy.

Public Administration and Environmental Quality

HARVEY LIEBER*

Environment, ecology, and quality of life are currently fashionable words. A recent Gallup poll found that more than 85 per cent of the population is concerned about environmental pollution and that three out of four people said they would be willing to pay some additional taxes to improve our natural surroundings. Auto stickers urge us to ban DDT. Walter Hickel wins confirmation from a concerned Senate only after pledging to have the Department of Interior zealously fight for environmental enhancement. The United Nations calls a conference on the worldwide problems of the human environment.

Yet despite the rising national and international concern over the deterioration of the environment there has been an institutional and political lag. Public administration theory and practice has hardly faced up to the problem of environmental management, except for repeating the traditional dogmas. Few middle-level theories or administrative models which would be of aid in the control and abatement of pollution, for example, have been proposed . . . .

In the year since the *Public Administration Review* devoted an entire issue to environmental policy we have experienced (to use only water pollution cases) an oil spill in Santa Barbara, a Rhine River fish kill, a fire on the oily Cuyahoga River, and seizure by the Food and Drug Administration of 22,000 pounds of Lake Michigan salmon with dangerous levels of DDT. In addition, controversy is growing over ocean disposal of nerve gas, deep well storage of toxic wastes, the construction of a giant jetport bordering Everglades National Park, and thermal pollution from nuclear power plants. At the same time Congress has taken more than two years to reach agreement on a bill controlling oil, vessel, thermal, lake, and acid mine pollution while a proposal for long-term financing of sewage treatment works is stalled. Also, articles have recently appeared exposing the severe administrative and political difficulties the Federal Water Pollution Control Administration is experiencing in trying to carry out its water quality mission. Thus it appears that in this "transitional stage of complexity and uncertainty" public administration has so far failed to act "with the intelligence, vigor, and self-consciousness that the situation demands."

Environmental Problems

A wide and diffuse range of concerns is subsumed under the subject heading of environmental problems. Besides air, water, noise, and solid waste pollution, this term often is expanded to include other amenities of life such as beautification, recreation, and at times urban structure and stress, transportation, food and drugs, even population problems.

*Reprinted with permission of the author and the editors of *Public Administration Review*. From *Public Administration Review* (May/June, 1970), pp. 277-286. Abridged and footnotes deleted.

Environmental disasters such as acute air pollution "episodes," hepatitis outbreaks from eating polluted clams, or the accidental death of 6,000 sheep by nerve gas attract headlines. Less prominent but no less threatening are the quiet crises: the gradual disappearance of San Francisco Bay, the death of Lake Erie from eutrophication, or the water supply courses that are declining in quality and purity.

Consider the following possible harmful environmental effects, chosen at random from this year's scientific and popular literature:

—A slow heating up of the earth's atmosphere and climate through a steady increase of carbon dioxide, released by burning oil and coal. Or, conversely:

—A gradually colder climate, through the cooling effects of accelerating quantities of smoke and dust.

—Increased incidence of lung cancer caused by asbestos in mining, building, and construction materials.

—Teenage deafness as a result of the sonic boom of loud rock music.

—A proposed sea-level canal to join the Atlantic and Pacific Oceans near Panama, to be created by nuclear detonation which may have disastrous effects on the climate, currents, food industries, species, and general bioecology of 10,000 miles of coastline.

—Earthquakes and ground water contamination caused by the deep well storage of toxic chemical wastes.

—Migrant workers poisoned by continual contact with parathion, a chemical pesticide.

—Acid wastes, surface subsidence, and fires in the accumulation of solid wastes and debris of underground mining.

—The Mediterranean as a fished-out, typhoid laden, dying body of water from overloading by untreated sewage and industrial wastes.

—Irrigated crops adversely affected by boron contained in the new presoak detergents.

—Nitrate poisoning of babies from children's food containing traces of artificial nitrogen fertilizers.

—Mutagenesis, or chromosome changes in body and germinal cells caused by ingesting hallucinogenic drugs, pesticides, food ingredients (caffeine) and additives (cyclamates), industrial chemicals, and solvents.

Most of these asserted threats are still open to verification and are the subject of intense scientific controversy. Nevertheless they offer us some idea of the "unanticipated environmental hazards resulting from technological intrusions." And they also raise the possibility that we may have to plan and manage our environment in such a manner as to prevent or at least minimize some of these irreversible effects.

Aside from these more exotic cases, few can today doubt that "normal" air, water, and land pollution is increasing or that our general biophysical environment is deteriorating. Our mounting waste disposal problems can be quickly described and documented:

> As long as our population size, density, and industrialization were low, our environment—our air, land and water—could absorb these wastes and no great problems arose.
>
> We now face a new situation: Rapid population growth, predicted to double

in 50 to 60 years; demand for water tripling while population doubles; increasing output of wastes and increasing pollution of our air, land, and water from all sources, municipal, industrial, agricultural, recreational; new types of wastes from industry, new chemicals which are more difficult to manage and control; increasing urbanization, industrialization, and use of technology, rising levels of income and increased outdoor recreation, all of which help to increase demand for clean water, pure air, and unlittered land.

... the pollution problems will probably increase as the economy grows. If, for example, industrial production tends to grow 4½ percent per year, it will have increased fourfold by the year 2000 and almost tenfold by 2020. Unless there are changes in technology or the composition of output, the total weight of the materials going through the economy, and the wastes generated, will have increased by a like amount. ...

If all municipal wastes were treated and if the effectiveness of treatment were raised to 85 percent, on average, actual municipal discharges into rivers would still be greater in 1980 than they were in 1962, and would have doubled by 2020. If on the other hand, we raised the effectiveness of all treatment to 95 percent, municipal waste discharges into rivers would probably decline over the next 60 years. But 95 percent goes to the outer limits of present technology, and would perhaps triple or quadruple treatment costs.

One estimate puts the costs of building and operating treatment plants that would remove at least 85 percent of the organic wastes from both municipal and industrial effluents by 1973 at over $20 billion, or $4 or $6 billion a year.

Within twenty years life on our planet will be showing the first signs of succumbing to pollution. The atmosphere will later become unbreathable for men and animals; life will cease in rivers and lakes and plants will wither from poisoning.

This last "alarmist" prediction comes from Unesco! Adding it all up, there is reason to believe that the recent American Museum of Natural History exhibition, "Can Man Survive?" was not entirely mistitled.

Technology under Fire

When New York City mayoral candidate Norman Mailer was asked what he would do about the smoke blowing over from New Jersey, he replied, perhaps only partly in jest, that he would blow up the factories which were causing the air pollution.

This perceptive writer's remark expressed some of the current second thoughts about the blessings of modern technology, which many now view as an uncontrolled 20th century Frankenstein monster which threatens to poison nature and contaminate our planet. Rather than a revolt against technology, it would be more accurate to speak of a backlash, against the unforeseen and harmful byproducts of our machine age. Factories, power plants, automobiles, and jets, once considered signs of progress, now also symbolize major environmental threats. This is a recent but nevertheless, widespread, even worldwide, phenomenon.

The Taylorites and other scientific managers applauded the introduction of time-saving devices and attempted to devise more efficient means of utilizing such machines. Later students of administration recognized that successful production rates and outputs made it necessary that attention be given to worker morale and interpersonal behavior. However, until recently few questioned the goals and products of the organization, its ends or its priorities; efficiency and growth were accepted as the highest good.

We are now living in what has variously been called a post-industrial, a new industrial, or a technetronic society. A generation which has been shaped by the impact of technology and is aware of its perils can question the purpose and priority of even such a fabulous technological feat as Apollo 11. It wryly notes that man's first act on the moon was to pollute it with chemicals from his engine exhaust while later jettisoning behind him a sizeable accumulation of solid wastes.

Similarly other probably technological successes such as our chemical and bacteriological warfare program and the supersonic transport plane are being increasingly attacked for their unplanned but extremely harmful environmental byproducts. You cannot stop progress—yet an expressway that would impair the historic quality of the New Orleans French Quarter has just been vetoed and a moratorium is in effect on building or annexation proceedings in New Jersey communities that have inadequate sewage treatment facilities. We have not yet reached the point where we are ready to seriously consider W. H. Ferry's proposal of a two-year ban on technological innovation to give us time to catch up on its side effects. However, we are beginning to pause before embarking on projects that are advanced in the name of progress and modernization and justified solely on the basis of immediate economic benefits.

The Scientific Response to the Challenge

The realization that "we have become victims of our own technological genius" has spurred initial scientific and governmental responses. The scientific community, especially biologists, has been among the most concerned and active in environmental controversies. This involvement may be due to immediate research interests or perhaps it arises from guilt feelings. In any case, three basic ideas which have been advanced by scientists—pollution as a system, spaceship earth, and recycling—are becoming part of the basic theoretical framework of environmental management policy, and so will be discussed before turning to public administration theory in a strict sense.

Under the concept of environmental systems, pollution is viewed as one total system, whose outward manifestations may differ in form. Thus air, water, and solid waste pollution are all interdependent. For example, straw was found to be the most effective beach cleanup material at Santa Barbara. Useful for oil pollution removal, its disposal by burning could have posed a serious air pollution problem. The final solution, however, was to bury the straw, which brings us to the third part of our interrelated pollution system—solid waste disposal or land pollution.

Awareness of the finite resources and the very limited assimilative capacity of our planet has given rise to the simile of "spaceship earth," a closed production system whose wastes must be repurified for the sake of survival. Thus the concept of recycling rather than disposal is gaining widespread acceptance. If one views pollution as "a resource out of place," then reuse rather than throw away becomes a guiding commandment and conservation rather than exploitation acquires a newer and more sophisticated meaning.

Technology, the application of science to practical tasks, is a two-edged sword. It concentrates on immediate economic benefits and often ignores long-range environmental impact. Yet at the same time its inventions promise to reverse the trend towards environmental degradation. Besides those scientists and engineers manning the barricades, such as Barry Commoner, there are others at work developing technological alternatives. A breakthrough in pest control, new energy sources, or alternatives to the internal combustion engine would be of obvious benefit in eliminating some of the present technologically caused problems. Less spectacular ideas, such as easily degradable beer cans, would also help. Other scientists are beginning to concentrate on utilizing waste for beneficial purposes, such as warm water irrigation from thermal pollution to stimulate plant growth and to protect fruit trees from killing frost; converting dairy whey into saleable food products; using domestic sewage as compost; and deriving protein from petroleum wastes, yeast from industrial wastes, and sugars from pulp wastes.

The accelerating pace of technological innovation has also spurred scientific interest in futurism, which looks toward the year 2000 and beyond. Alarmed by the hazards, conflicts, and crises which may be caused by uncontrolled social and technological change, physical and social scientists are joining forces in systematic long-range forecasting. The President has recently formed a National Goals Research Staff in the White House which will assess the long-range consequences of present social trends and evaluate alternative courses of action. This too is an indication of the rapid acceptance of the need for planning and preparing for the hidden environmental costs of such changes through environmental early warning systems.

Congressional Initiative

Congress, rather than the Executive Branch, has historically been the most responsive to demands for stepped-up air and water pollution control. Similarly recent congressional initiatives for a recognition of the seriousness of present ecological trends and the need for a reassessment of general environmental policies have been followed by the Nixon Administration's present emphasis on this problem.

In particular, Senators Jackson, Muskie, and Nelson, and Congressman Daddario have performed a valuable educational function by alerting the public to environmental threats. The 91st Congress has been blessed with an abundance of legislative proposals on the environment, to the point where individual competition for legislative honors and intercommittee jurisdictional rivalries at one time threatened the passage of any bill.

The most significant recent legislative accomplishment has been passage of S 1075, Senator Jackson's National Environmental Policy Act of 1969. It contains a declaration of national environmental policy and goals, establishes a Council on Environmental Quality, and provides for review of federal programs for their impact on environmental quality.

S 1075 recognizes "that each person should enjoy a healthful environment" along with "a responsibility to contribute to the preservation and enhancement of the environment." It declares a national policy to prevent and eliminate damage to the environment and "to create and maintain conditions under which man and nature can exist in productive harmony." PL 91-190 also seeks to:

assure for all Americans safe, healthful, productive, and esthetically and culturally pleasing surroundings;

attain the widest range of beneficial uses of the environment without degradation, risk to health or safety, or other undesirable and unintended consequences;

preserve important historic, cultural, and natural aspects of our national heritages, and maintain, wherever possible, an environment which supports diversity and variety of individual choice;

achieve a balance between population and resource use which will permit high standards of living and a wide sharing of life's amenities; and

enhance the quality of renewable resources and approach the maximum attainable recycling of depletable resources.

S 1075 established a three-member independent advisory group in the Executive Office of the President which is modeled after the Council of Economic Advisers. This is the Council on Environmental Quality which is to study environmental trends and federally related programs and submit an annual report to the President on the state and condition of the environment.

Under Title II of S 7, sponsored by Senator Muskie, a White House Office of Environmental Quality is to be established to give the Council an operating staff and professional expertise. The chairman of the Council would be the director of this high-level office which would have an annual authorization of more than one million dollars and which would be directed to send its annual report to all standing congressional committees with jurisdictional involvement in environmental matters.

The most controversial part of the National Environmental Policy Act directs every government agency to adjust its policies and carry out its functions in conformance with the stated congressional policy on the environment. A finding on environmental impact and effects would be required by the responsible agency official in every recommendation or report on proposals for legislation and other major federal actions which significantly affect the quality of the environment.

In addition to this Act, other more far-reaching legislative proposals in the 91st Congress would create a Department of Conservation and Environment (S 2312), a Department of Natural Resources (S 1446) or a Department of Resources, Environment, and Population (HR 12000). This reorganized department would generally be made up of most of the established Interior Department bureaus and other related agencies (e.g., National Air Pollution Control Administration, Consumer Protection and Environmental Health Service, Forest Service, Environmental Science Services Administration). In any case, the Congress clearly intends to upgrade and stress the need to take environmental considerations into federal programs and actions.

Executive Action

During its first year in office the Nixon Administration was as unable as its predecessors to make its performance match its environmental quality promises. The sole innovation was the creation by Executive Order of an advisory Cabinet-level body, paralleling the National Security and Urban Affairs Councils, to review environmental policies and programs and suggest improvements. This interdepartmental coordinating body rarely met and failed to live up to its stated function to serve as "the focal point for this Administration's efforts to protect all of our natural resources."

However, a series of presidential statements and messages indicate that environmental problems now have top priority, to the point where the Administration has almost preempted pollution as a political issue. Although initially unenthusiastic about the National Environmental Policy Bill, President Nixon upon signing it on January 1, 1970, strongly praised the new legislation, saying that it was a "particularly fitting" first act of the new decade. He then followed up his statement that "it is literally now or never" by selecting three distinguished conservationists for the Council and by proposing in his first State of the Union Message a national growth policy which would stress qualitative improvements rather than quantitative growth.

An ambitious presidential message of February 10 proposed a 51-point program of legislative and executive actions concerning water and air pollution, solid waste management, parklands and recreation, and organizing for action. Succeeding presidential statements and a study of possible consolidation and reorganization of environmental agencies also show a continuing awareness of the immensity of these problems and a willingness to tackle them.

Nevertheless, the effectiveness of the government's environmental policy will in the final analysis be judged not by the organizational mechanisms it establishes but on the basis of the specific actions and priorities it imposes. Also, as Sundquist has pointed out, environmental quality is not a single issue to be resolved like medicare or social security; rather it is a series of continuing fights and use conflicts, with entrenched interests, such as oil companies, waging a series of strong rearguard actions.

At present expectations are high but the possibility of delivery is debatable. For example, the technology is generally well in hand (although not without some very troublesome exceptions) for the control of pollution. The cost of control, however, is quite high—for water pollution alone, 20 to 30 billion dollars over the next five years and perhaps 100 billion dollars over the next 20 years. And the gap between promise and performance is most striking when one compares the difference between money authorized and funds actually appropriated for air and water pollution control and for water and sewer grants.

The government is lagging administratively as well. Air pollution standards are several years from completion and the water pollution control program is also faltering from lack of sewage treatment plant construction funds. Less than half of the states have water quality standards that are fully acceptable to the Secretary of the Interior.

The phenomenon of commitment far outstripping resources is of course not unique to this area. Despite Vietnam, inflation, and hard-core city problems, the Administration now pledges to fully devote itself to upgrading the quality of our life. However even when money is available it will be difficult to change direction—

the classic example of distorted priorities being the billions of government sub-sidies for the construction of the SST with its unresolved sonic boom problems and the meagre amount spent by the government for research on alternatives to the smoggy internal combustion engine.

Environmental Quality and Administration

Until the 1960's, environmental quality was an issue of little public or academic interest, despite the rising levels of contamination. In this decade it has emerged as a major concern and political problem. With the advent of prosperity and economic security for most Americans, quantitative "bread and butter" issues have declined in importance. However, certain intangible aspects of living — beautifica-tion, air, water, noise, the quality of life — have become increasingly significant.

We are now in the middle stage of tentative actions and gropings toward solu-tions. Environmental quality activities have not broken fresh ground in terms of innovative policies and new institutional arrangements. Programs have generally been undertaken on an ad hoc basis without the benefit of much elucidation from public administration theory. Confronted with a wide range of emerging environ-mental problems, administrative theory's answer to the litany of doom has been an antiquated catechism whose key phrases — regional and coordination — fail to reflect political reality.

Consider the following syllogism:

1. Air pollution does not respect political boundary lines.
2. Existing local and state agencies deal with air pollution on a limited, piece-meal, and uncoordinated basis.
Therefore — 3. An areawide agency covering the entire problem-shed would be the most effective unit to deal with the problem.

But whether through interstate compact, council of government, or special district, there is hardly a single effective regional air pollution agency functioning today. With the possible exception of the Delaware River Basin Commission, the same could be said for water pollution control. As in the case of metro governments, the immense political difficulties in organizing areawide control operations vitiate the apparent administrative advantages attributed to such regional agencies.

• • •

"Coordination" instead of "fragmentation" is often advocated for environmental policy disputes in the hope that an optimal solution can be reached. Such over-optimistic attitudes only succeed in masking genuine clashes of interests which are not easily reconciled, such as the preservation vs. development fights that occur in many of our estuarine zones. In this search for harmony some are reluctant to recog-nize the basic economic and interagency conflicts that are present in most environ-mental policy issues.

It remains to be seen how well a Cabinet body or a White House staff will be able to "coordinate" conflicting uses and interests such as the differing attitudes of the Departments of Agriculture and Health, Education, and Welfare over the use of pesticides, or the dissimilar views of the Atomic Energy Commission and the Department of the Interior over the efforts of nuclear detonations.

Similarly, the stress on finding alternatives that are feasible often overlooks the catalytic role that "unrealistic" threats of outright banning play in eliminating environmental threats. We already know that bills banning over-sudsy detergents spurred the industry into developing biodegradable detergents; one may wonder what effect recent legislation passed by the California Senate banning the use of DDT or the sale of internal combustion engines by 1975 will have on manufacturers.

Finally, "reorganization" is often used in conjunction with coordination by advocates of superenvironment departments. If the lessons of the Federal Water Pollution Control Administration are in any way instructive, they show that transfer from the Department of Health, Education, and Welfare to the Interior Department has had a traumatic effect in terms of personnel turnover without any appreciable benefits; further although FWPCA, and Fish and Wildlife Service, and the U.S. Geological Survey were all under one departmental umbrella, there was still insufficient consideration of environmental impact by the Department of the Interior in awarding Santa Barbara oil drilling and production leases.

• • •

Concern over the biophysical environment may merely be a broadening of previous conservation interests. However, the new conservation has also been transformed to stress not just preserving nature, but managing the entire environment, man-made as well as natural. Pinchot and Muir led us to the realization that our natural resources were limited; today we recognize that our ability to absorb our wastes is equally restricted. Not only are our traditional physical resources diminishing, but our air, open space, and natural beauty is equally threatened. As a result of increasing, possibly catastrophic, levels of pollution, man himself is an endangered species.

The early conservationists stressed multiple use; the ecologists now urge reuse. From an earlier interest in U.S. forests, soil, and water, our concerns have expanded to include the global effects of the complex interaction of society, environment, and technology.

One observer has attributed the generation gap to the horrendous threats of the future—nuclear war, overpopulation, and pollution—being built into the flesh and blood of the young. Indeed, college students are now seizing upon quality of life issues and channelling their idealism into crusades for cleaner air and water. Concern over threats to coastal zones, rivers, and mountains has resulted in "ecological activism," a union of old-line conservationists and youthful militants employing political pressure and communications techniques, staging confrontations and demonstrations. This environmental mobilization is symbolized by the April 22 "Earth Day" or the national teach-in and day of protest on high school and college campuses. On the more academic side, there has been a dramatic rise in the number of environmental law and conservation courses being taught on the campuses as well as the mushrooming number of environmental studies centers and pollution symposia. These events sparked by those who will inherit our polluted planet have served to highlight the environmental crisis to a growing conservation constituency.

As a result we are beginning to develop an ecological conscience or "the emergence of a concept of public responsibility for the environmental welfare of the American people" and for the long-range consequences of our technological actions. This ethic values a livable environment over economic expansion and recognizes an individual's right to live in a pleasant environment "free from improvident destruction or pollution."

With our higher standard of living we have broadened our concerns to include qualitative social and moral questions as well as economic issues. From preventing diseases and death we are now equally interested in reaching an optimal state of well being and in enjoying the amenities of life. These enlarged areas of interest may be indicated by the gradual shift of terminology from "sewage" to "water pollution" to "water resources" to "water quality." Yet the gap between private consumption and public needs is still one of the basic characteristics of the Effluent Society.

We have reached an awareness of the seriousness of these problems, but our political structures are still not keeping up with changes in the biophysical environment. The challenge of the 1970's will be to confront the difficult policy problems of institutional arrangements and establish effective systems for environmental management and enhancement.

Aesthetic Power or the Triumph of the Sensitive Minority over the Vulgar Mass: A Political Analysis of the New Economics

AARON WILDAVSKY*

How does the "old economics" of natural resources differ from the "new economics"? The old economics was mostly economics. The new economics is mostly politics. The agonizing question confronting the new economics has troubled political theorists from the time of the Hebrew prophets to this very day: How shall society be organized so that the preferences of the morally or aesthetically sensitive minority will triumph? Where majorities are rarely mobilized, the question may be rephrased to ask how our *good* minority may prevail over their *bad* minority. If only a superior few truly love the remote and virgin wilderness, for instance, how may this opportunity for solitary communion with nature be preserved against hostile masses or rival elites? The new economics of natural resources appears to be designed to answer this question indirectly without quite raising it to a conscious level.

The terms new economists use to describe the deterioration of the natural en-

*Reprinted with permission from *Daedalus* (Fall, 1967), pp. 1115-1127. Footnotes deleted.

vironment are sufficiently expressive to convey the feeling behind them. The landscape has been assaulted and degraded, if not raped; genocide has been practiced against certain animal species; the air threatens to become a poisonous gas; the odor of dead fish testifies to the pollution of our water; human marauders invade and despoil isolated areas. The tone is strident; the mood, a mixture of rage and disgust. The metaphors belong more to the battlefield than the market place. It is not surprising, then, that Athelstan Spilhaus urges us to take risks in enhancing the environment comparable to those we would take in war; nor that Nathaniel Wollman suggests a political structure with administrative environmental boards possessing "the power and authority that is now accorded the military establishment . . . because the penalty of inexpert decisions may be just as disastrous for the human race as the effect of military weapons." Unfortunately, the old economics does not provide the necessary weapons for what many evidently see as the war for environmental quality.

In the beginning, the rationale for the Conservation Movement was one of preserving basic resources that were becoming increasingly scarce. Wood, coal, and iron were essentially fixed in given lumps; use was a kind of desecration. As demand increased and supply decreased in an industrial society, these resources would become more and more valuable. The larger the part played by natural resources in the economy and the higher their price in comparison with other goods, the easier it was to make an economic case for protecting them. To the extent that the votes of a misguided or ignorant people would not protect these precious resources through the political arena, the symbolic casting of ballots in the more rational economic market place would restrict use by raising prices. If politics were involved at all, it would be not for economic reasons, but merely to undo the evil restrictions upon the free market that special interests had worked out with conniving politicians.

Even when economic theorists arrived at a justification for governmental intervention to overcome certain imperfections in the market place, the political arena proved vexing. When a large dam would impose costs on those who did not benefit from it, for example, it was deemed appropriate for the government to intervene to rectify the situation. But, as it turned out, the politicians marched to music of their own and were only remotely interested in following the lead of economic science. The interest rate, that old puritan arbiter between present consumption and future desires, was kept artificially low so that many projects were justified on economic grounds without valid reason. Cost-benefit analysis, designed to increase national income by assuring that the benefits to whoever received them would exceed the costs to whoever paid them, was twisted out of shape in notorious fashion. Things were arranged so that general taxpayers received less and the direct beneficiaries far more than their economically justifiable shares. A project with a low benefit-cost ratio might be joined with another having a much higher ratio so that the "new" combined project could qualify. So-called intangibles like recreation values were credited with increasingly large shares of the benefits, thus representing a "finagle" factor that could be enlarged almost at will to provide justification. A decentralized party system and a highly fragmented national political system with strong regional interests proved resistant to making decisions on economic grounds. Comments about narrow local interests, selfish minorities, and violations of the public interest filled the economic literature. While politics was proving so disappointing, the former economic rationale for protecting resources suffered severe blows.

The market mechanism, together with man's remarkable technical ingenuity, drastically changed the supply-and-demand relationships for many natural resources. New sources of supply were continuously discovered, and new products substituted for old. Industrial and farm production grew exceedingly large and immensely more efficient. Consequently, the prices of resource commodities continually decreased in comparison with those of other goods and services. The contribution of natural resources to Gross National Product showed a corresponding, proportionate drop. The decline in the price of resource commodities made it more difficult to justify special treatment on the grounds of economic efficiency. The contribution that these resources made to production was too small, and it is getting smaller. This change in the economic importance of resources lies behind the plaintive cry that it is not possible to justify on economic grounds most large programs designed to improve the quality of the natural environment.

Re-evaluations of the abundance of natural resources illustrate another aspect of their new position. We now know that we have more forest resources than we had thought and that new growth may exceed demand. Although water may be in short supply in some areas, technological advance and the shift of existing supplies to more productive uses should provide amounts more than adequate for the future. Despite the hue and cry about the advancing tentacles of the monster called urbanization, only 2 or 3 per cent of the nation's land is or will be devoted to urban uses in the next few decades. The immediate conclusion is all too evident. Resource problems will, by and large, not be critical for economic purposes. A technological advance here or a local adjustment there will take care of the worst difficulties. From a strictly economic viewpoint, nothing much need be done.

The terrible difficulty for economists is that problems of environmental quality do not look so bad as they ought. If present modes of economic justification are used, there is no way of preserving the basic values these men hold as users of the natural environment. To have personal values done in by professional values is no fun at all. Hence, a "new economics" has emerged to get around the old. If the old economics will not let you have what you know is right, it follows that a new economics is evidently needed. The term *new economics of natural resources* is used to designate an emerging trend, . . . and permits economists to avoid direct confrontation with political problems by bringing in aesthetic factors to make economic analysis come out "right."

Since the new economists of today are the old economists of yesterday, a certain ambivalence about their enterprise might be expected. It is tempting to retain an economic vocabulary for essentially non-economic processes. The deep woods with clear lakes, white-water streams, and rare animal species may be called unique and irreplaceable, like the White House or the Liberty Bell or a man's children or his sweetheart. One could say that no price is too high for these treasures except that the concept "price" is really inapplicable. These treasures are not to be bought and sold at all. They are literally "priceless"—that is, outside any market.

The usual system for determining what is allowable in the market place is political or in some sense deeply traditional or social, but in no case may it be called economic. The old economist considers it ridiculous for a society to spend $20 billion to rid itself entirely of water pollution when marginal benefits of spending the largest fraction of that sum elsewhere would be much higher. The new economist says "why not" and invents rationales. After all, at current rates of economic growth, $20 billion a year represents only a few months delay in reaching a GNP that much higher. This marginalist fallacy, a variant of the old argument that for want of a nail a war was lost, suffers from a fatal defect. We can all think of huge expenditures to accomplish highly cherished ends that could be justified if only people would wait a little while longer to become richer. All the wilderness areas and fine old buildings might be preserved for even less, and many experimental cities might be built. The wealth is here. Presumably, all that is required is the will. We undoubtedly can have some of the things some of us want, but not all the things all of us want. Otherwise, there would be no problem of scarcity, no need for allocation. This is not a new economics but a "non-economics."

The old economists cried out against the use of "finagle factors" that might in some sense be important, but that could not be measured in the market place. In preference to having such factors expanded or contracted at will, they preferred that these be brought to the attention of decision-makers who could take them into account. To do otherwise would be to compromise fatally the economic part of the analysis. The new economists are tempted to abandon this position. Maintaining the wilds may be justified, without being able to specify size or cost or conditions, on the grounds that people like to leave a legacy to their children. Outdoor recreation may be alleged to have great psychic benefits, though demonstrating its dimensions or comparing it with television or people-watching on crowded streets is another matter. Yet alternative expenditures may also serve some values people hold, and the economic problem is to justify one expenditure rather than another on something more than personal grounds. Surely economics is not to become a parody of a parody, the social-science version of Saul Bellow's *Henderson the Rain King* who plunges throughout time and continents shouting ever more loudly, "I want, I want."

No one will argue that the values of economic man in the market place are the only ones that count. Who is so vulgar and insensitive as to claim that only what is objectively demonstrable is important? Will progress be made, however, by undermining the rationale for economic analysis or by concealing intransigent political problems under an economic guise? The new economics poses for itself essentially political problems. Which decisions shall be made through the market and which not? What decision structures will best assure environmental quality? How can aesthetic feelings be translated into public policy? What happens if strong aesthetic impulses are shared by only a small minority? Consideration of the problems surrounding public preferences will help throw the many political dilemmas into sharper focus.

Let us assume, for the moment, that all problems of directly measuring public preferences in regard to the quality of the environment were solved through opinion surveys or other devices. Would our problems of allocating resources then be solved? In one sense, they would be solved all too well. The problem of the interpersonal comparison of utilities, the relative preferences among different people for shares in things like housing, transportation, space exploration, or ballet, must be solved before environmental quality may be given its place. If the results of the survey are accepted, then all allocation problems in society have been solved. Such a state of affairs is usually called utopia.

Suppose, however, that some people prefer a different mix of goods than was provided in the grand allocation mechanism. Perhaps they are among the relatively small groups that intensely desire long canoe trips through completely wild areas and have been outvoted (or "outpreferenced") by others who want skin diving near where they live or who prefer large indemnities to black people to repay them for decades of service in slavery. These minorities would certainly challenge the existing state of preferences. They might argue, as democratic theorists have through the ages, that strict majority rule should not prevail. Minorities like themselves should be given some proportionate share of good things (though it is doubtful whether they would agree that every minority, including ones opposed to their desires, should get similar consideration regardless of what they wanted). The wilderness minority might say that people should not get what they want, but what they ought to have, according to the principles of the sensitive few. Perhaps many people decide in ignorance and ought to be educated before their preferences are counted or weighed equally with those of the more knowledgeable. Things might be different if people were encouraged through subsidies to experience elementary contact with nature which would in turn alter their previous preferences. What turns out to be crucial is not merely knowledge of preferences but a set of rules for putting them together so that policy decisions emerge. Yet we have not even mentioned the knotty problems of accounting for intensity of preferences. Should the intense minority triumph over the apathetic majority? Should we satisfy the widespread norm of equality by treating all citizens equally or only equals equally? Extraordinary difficulties arise when public preferences must be translated into public policy.

Should their sensitivities be sufficiently outraged, the wilderness minority might question the procedures through which public preferences for governmental expenditures are determined. The use of opinion polls to derive a rank order of public preferences is suspect in many ways. The process of seeking preferences may create preferences where none existed before. People may feel they have to respond to a questionnaire without ever having thought of the matter before or having any real preference. Many citizens may discover that they have preferences only after an act to which they can respond has taken place. It is difficult to get people of low education to understand the wording of questions and the complex choices involved. Highly educated people will also have trouble sorting out their feelings if they are required to make a series of comparisons leading to a ranking of some fifteen or twenty major areas of public policy. If the ranking is performed by a survey analyst, the rules for determining the hierarchy of preferences may be challenged as inadequate or controversial. Political leaders like the President are known to influence the determination of public preferences from time to time. What a President may get from a survey, therefore, is an echo of his own voice.

Since opinion is mutable, the opposition can say that if they will just work harder, public preferences will come closer to their values in the future. Although the temptation is understandably great, the hard problems of making interpersonal comparisons of utility cannot be avoided by fobbing off the task on other people through an opinion survey.

For the old economics, the political system unfortunately did not produce decisions that met the strict criteria of economic rationality. It was desirable economically, for example, to take into account as many measurable consequences for others as possible. The larger the area covered, the greater is the number of externalities that can be internalized within the analysis. If economic criteria were to be followed, bargaining, horse-trading, log-rolling, or other practices that might introduce inconsistencies had to be kept to a minimum. Thus, a unitary government with highly centralized parties and powerful hierarchical leadership would appear to be preferable to a federal system with extremely decentralized parties and fragmented leadership continuously engaged in bargaining to accommodate the most diverse range of interests. But the desirability and feasibility of abolishing the federal system, the separation of powers, and decentralized parties are not usually considered because such matters go beyond economic analysis.

The new economics need not face the same problems. It is concerned, after all, with getting away from rigid economic analysis and the strict application of efficiency criteria. Its practitioners are committed to values favoring the enhancement of environmental quality. The new economists are advocates as well as scholars. For them, policy outcomes cannot simply be the result of a set of analytic procedures. They want some results and not others. They want to develop the best arguments they can for securing the results they favor. In cases of doubt and indeterminacy, the new economists want the values they favor included rather than excluded. But they are inhibited by a nostalgia for the credibility accorded to the old economists they once were. Caught between the desire to insure certain outcomes and the pull of their economist's conscience, they risk being neither economists nor effective advocates.

The new economics is in danger of misconstruing its mission. Its goals are laudatory (that is, I share them), but they cannot be achieved by self-deception. Little is to be gained and much lost by compromising the old economics. It should be perfected according to its own lights, so that at least part of the spectrum of values will be properly illuminated. What is first required is an accurate statement of the political problems involved in realizing environmental values.

There is no evidence to suggest widespread and intense support for drastically improving the quality of the environment. Most people are probably indifferent. Some care a little, but are unwilling to sacrifice much. Only a relatively small minority cares deeply enough to make significant sacrifices. The best available evidence comes from a survey of attitudes toward government programs conducted in 1961 by Eva Mueller through the Michigan Survey Research Center. The survey is especially valuable because people were asked whether they would give up income in the form of higher taxes in order to pay for expenditures they believed desirable. Of fourteen types of public policy mentioned, the item called "Parks, recreation facilities" provides a fair test of public support for improving the environment. No doubt more people care about parks than about the remote back-woods, but 10 per cent of the people interviewed have no opinion on these resource programs, and 48 per cent think that existing governmental expenditure is about right. Thus, 58 per cent of the population is essentially indifferent to a change in public policy. It is true that a larger minority favors more rather than less expenditure (27 to 15 per cent), but the favorable minority declines by almost 400 per cent (27 to 7 per cent) when asked if they would pay higher taxes to support this resource

Attitudes Toward Government Programs

Program	More	Less	Same	No opinion	Total	More even if taxes had to be raised[2]
	%	%	%	%	%	%
Help for older people	70	3	23	4	100	34
Help for needy people	60	7	28	5	100	26
Education	60	7	25	8	100	41
Slum clearance, city improvement[1]	55	9	24	12	100	3
Hospital and medical care	54	9	28	9	100	25
Public works[1]	48	11	31	10	100	3
Defense, rearmament[2]	47	6	34	13	100	30
Support for small business[1]	37	11	31	21	100	3
Highway construction	36	10	45	9	100	13
Unemployment benefits	29	14	45	12	100	10
Parks, recreation facilities	27	15	48	10	100	7
Space exploration[2]	26	32	28	14	100	14
Support for agriculture	20	26	34	20	100	6
Help to other countries[2]	7	53	28	12	100	2

[1]Question asked only in June, 1961.
[2]Question asked only in November, 1961.
[3]Unavailable.

policy. Larger proportions of the population are willing to pay through higher taxes for help for the old and needy, education, defense, and highways. Indeed, the number of people willing to pay to explore outer space is twice that willing to pay to improve the earthly environment (14 per cent as compared to 7 per cent).

Public sentiment may have changed since 1961. Perhaps people would now be willing to pay more to deal with water pollution. When a candidate for governor of California suggests selling part of the state's wilderness areas, however, and still receives overwhelming endorsement by the electorate, it is difficult to believe that the wilderness minority is very large. Though small, the wilderness minority is not always impotent. Yet the victories recorded here and there all appear to stem from an intense campaign run by a few dedicated individuals. When this middle- and upper-class effort fails to materialize, nothing happens, except the loss of another site of scenic splendor.

The provision of subsidies on behalf of the aesthetic minority — subsidies like the British Broadcasting Company's Third Programme — might suggest that a unitary and centralized political system would be more receptive to demands of this nature. But this result depends on the existence of a privileged minority to which great deference is accorded. The cultural conditions for this phenomenon do not exist in the United States, nor, on other grounds, would many of us prefer such a situation. In America, a centralized political system that registered immediate majority demands could well wreak havoc with the policies preferred by the aesthetic minority. Bigger and better highways might always be preferred to clean air, or parks, or refuges for wildlife.

A system like the American one that provides special opportunities for skillful and well-organized minorities would appear well suited to the characteristics of the aesthetic few. How should they go about realizing their preferences? How can they mobilize their forces? What organizational structures and strategies are best suited to translating their preferences into public policy? What kinds of administrative arrangements will help obtain favorable results in the future? Although satisfactory answers are not likely to be immediately forthcoming, these questions are foremost among the right ones to ask.

There is no reason to suppose that the most aesthetically interested members of society are politically disadvantaged. They probably do not suffer from being denied the right to vote or from low educational attainments or poor family backgrounds that would deny them the skills necessary to compete in political life. Like those with special interests in theater or ballet or sailing, the aesthetic minority is likely to be composed of middle- or upper-class people who do not have to struggle for the necessities of life and can afford to be sensitive. Their problems of political mobilization are likely to be quite different from those of the poor and downtrodden. Given a choice between political activity in behalf of their preferences for environmental quality or individual economic action, they may well choose the latter. They can move to the suburbs to get away from air pollution or travel to where the remote wilderness still exists. Things may have to get worse before they find it less costly to spend time in political activity than in raising income to satisfy their aesthetic preferences. Yet they are also capable of reasonably long-run perspectives. The leaders of this minority must first convince people who share their preferences that political action is necessary now if they want their children to be able to enjoy a natural environment of higher quality in the future.

Political elites are far more likely to share the preferences of the aesthetic minority than are the mass of people. While long-term efforts of mass education may be desirable, short-term results depend on the men in power. Since various interests oppose certain specific measures, and alternative objects of expenditures compete for existing resources, ways must be found to enable public officials to support the policies most of them would like to see implemented. The questions of who will pay and how are crucial. In the best of all possible worlds, a new process is discovered that produces a good like wood pulp more cheaply and with far less noxious waste than before. Everyone gains, and no one loses; or those who win in one transaction compensate the losers in another. In most cases, however, the questions of who will pay and how much loom large. Costs can be transferred to large industries or to those who consume their products, to general taxpayers or to specific industries, to citizens or to foreigners, from one region or class of citizens to another. Citizens with low incomes are notorious for their willingness to seek greater public benefits, and their unwillingness to pay more taxes. The wealthy are famous for the ingenuity with which they escape the full burden of the income tax. The acknowledged principles of the public-finance literature — ability to pay and benefits received — are inadequate when there are severe disagreements over the justice and applicability of each principle. The difficulties are compounded when a desired objective, say reduction of air pollution, can be accomplished if and only if an objectionable mode of assigning costs is accepted. If it turns out to be much easier to pass the burden on in the form of hidden consumer taxes than to assess the polluters or desecraters of the wilderness, difficult choices must be made.

In the past, there has been considerable public support for conservation in some western states. Mass support may now be generated in various areas in regard to water and air pollution, but the possibilities of support may be slim for a subtle policy specifying so much reduction of pollution here, a little less there, and none someplace else (the kind of policy favored by the old economics). The price of mass support may be massive programs to wipe out pollution entirely. Again, a difficult choice may have to be made between too little effort to reduce pollution and too much.

Presently we do not have the knowledge that would enable us to choose the kinds of organizational structure that would lead to decisions in favor of improving environmental quality. We can, however, identify critical choices. The number of governmental organizations concerned with natural resources is already large and growing. These agencies traditionally perform specialized functions for a particular clientele and are closely tied to local interests and their congressional advocates. To these divisive forces are then joined narrow organizational loyalties. The legitimization of new functions by society, such as desalinization, pollution abatement, and highway beautification, has been accompanied by the creation of separate organizations to devise and implement programs. For people concerned with rationalizing policy in the resource field, the rapid proliferation of autonomous organizations is alarming. It points to the need for larger units or co-ordinating structures that will presumably produce decisions which take into account a wider range of values. Leaving aside questions of the feasibility and cost of such a change, it is not clear whether it would further the cause of the aesthetic minority. New and "narrow" agencies supporting environmental quality with ever greater determination might be preferable. Sub-units within larger multipurpose agencies dealing with extensive geographical areas might be used to great advantage in the cause of the aesthetic minority. We do not know and are hardly in a position to guess.

Another critical issue involves the choice between setting-up or strengthening a regulatory agency or trying to enact legislation that contains automatic incentives making it advantageous for the affected parties to do the right thing. When outrage over pollution or destruction of forests bursts out, it is tempting to pillory the offenders and to control their future conduct by establishing a regulatory commission of some sort. But the history of regulation has not been an entirely happy one. With the best of motives, the original regulatory passion begins to wane. The people whose interests are most directly affected maintain constant vigilance, while the rest of us turn to other pursuits. The regulatory agency is surrounded by the interests it is supposed to regulate. The inevitable accommodations may leave little regulation intact. Moreover, the existence of friendly regulatory bodies is used as a rationale for avoiding the necessity of other and possibly more stringent measures. We have little evaluated experience in developing incentives in the form of tax measures, bonuses for keeping land or water in certain conditions, support for competitive products, or other devices that might accomplish the task.

If action is to be based on some knowledge, the consequences of varying institutional arrangements for major values must be specified. In different times and places, there has been considerable variety in organizational arrangements and legal patterns. Knowledge of what results ensued under different conditions might give direction to future judgments. New techniques of organizational analysis also provide splendid opportunities for current research. The development of computer simulation models is especially promising. These models view organizations as problem-solving mechanisms that use certain rules for arriving at decisions in a complex environment. These rules can be derived from interviews and observations, and programmed on computers. By recapitulating the processes of decisions on computers, it should be possible to explain how the organization works. One can then experiment with alterations in the assumptions guiding the organization, its specific rules for decisions, and its environment, and determine how these changes affect its policy outputs. Organizational changes can be experimentally produced as a better guide to action than mere guesswork.

There is, in general, an appalling lack of information on the causes and consequences of environmental deterioration. If environmental quality is broadened to include the design of urban living (and hence poverty and race relations), the absence of knowledge is even more startling. The availability of better information might reveal a wider range of choice and thus result in different political decisions. There is overwhelming need for experimentation. We could use more than one experimental city. Thus, there is an important role for the man who does not find it becoming to devote his talent to direct political questions of mobilizing support to preserve the wilderness or the cultures of the city. He may feel that his desires are not more worthy than those of other men. Such a man may be prepared to have his minority preferences overridden. But by working to improve the information base for decision-making, he may hope to make everyone wiser about the scope of their interests and the possibilities of reconciliation with others.

We do not wish to restrict ourselves to the values appropriate to economic man in the market place. (Failure to preserve superb redwoods because the economic worth of the income produced by cutting them down exceeds their presently known aesthetic value would be tragic.) Nor do we wish to become mere schemers who, so long as they can muster the political power necessary to achieve their personal objectives, do not care about other people's feelings. (Failure to alleviate the psychic deprivation suffered by people who will lose their jobs if the redwoods are protected, and whose identity is bound up with the lumber trade rather than selling souvenirs to tourists, would be cruel.) Yet, like Dostoevski's underground man, whose appreciation of the endless depths of every question rendered him unfit for any action, the cost of taking everyone's preferences into account may be paralysis. Worse, it may result in grand opportunities foregone or in irreversible damage to the environment. Weak and frail as we are, beset by doubts and anxieties, undoubtedly partial in our views, we must act. If those who love the wilderness will not save it, who will?

2

Population:
The Basic Problem

Very likely the most basic problem facing those concerned with improving the quality of the environment in the United States is the tremendous growth of population. And the laissez faire attitude which surrounds the development of public policy to deal with population growth is certainly no help. As a consequence, there hovers over us the spectre of what we call "the population problem." This problem results from the many private and public decisions based on narrow, individual goals and made with little thought for their impact on the growth and distribution of the nation's population. Attempts to reverse the situation and control population growth are often met by stiff emotional resistance which places roadblocks in the way of attaining a more desirous public goal.

One of the major dimensions of the population problem is size. Owing to relatively recent medical and health advances, death rates among the very young and the very old have fallen sharply, resulting in substantially increased population size and increased pressure upon resources. Such population growth raises questions about the possibility of maintaining a reasonable quality of life, with such amenities as education, employment, material well-being, and recreational opportunities.

A second significant dimension of the population problem is age distribution. There are growing numbers of the very young and the very old — the two groups that demand the greatest amount of social services while contributing least to the resources that make these services available. Age distribution also helps to project patterns of future population growth. Thus, in efforts to frame effective population policy, age distribution and the consumptive needs and productive contributions of each age group must be taken into account.

The spatial distribution of the population presents additional problems. Although a high concentration of population may increase consumer choice of goods and services and economies of scale, it may also bring about major problems in transportation and distribution of commodities, traffic congestion, concentration of water and air pollution, and psychic tension.

Because control of population is considered one of the most significant environmental problems, there are increasing demands that solutions be developed through public policy. Yet there are those — some Catholics and blacks, for example — who say this is not an appropriate concern of government. They see in the issue such dramatic losses of private liberties that they believe the situation is worsened rather than improved by attempts to control population. In short, there is little consensus, and the alternatives proposed directly impinge upon the values of many individuals and groups.

Attempts to control population systematically conflict with many deeply valued moral precepts. These include the impropriety of impeding natural processes, as in contraception, and the taking of life, as in abortion. Some persons have even charged that proposed policies are thinly veiled attempts to practice genocide against minority groups. Thus, any suggestions to develop population policy are immediately met by efforts to block even relatively minor incentive programs, educational programs, and programs permitting freedom of choice. Such reactions are not hopeful omens of dramatic public programs to reduce population size significantly or even to change substantially the pattern of population distribution. As in many other areas, population policy is almost sure to come slowly, incrementally, and as the result of compromise.

The selections which follow in this chapter point up several dimensions of the "population problem" and call attention to the complexities and difficulties inherent in any attempt to formulate population policy. In the opening selection, Mr. Wolfers shows that in the past, the balance between the size of the population and the supportive environmental systems was maintained by nature through adjustments in birth and death rates. Mankind now has the technical and social means to avoid a return to this mechanism, but if no direct action is taken to maintain the balance through alternative means, nature will surely reassert its control. Mr. Wolfers traces the historical developments in agriculture, health, and other areas which, beginning about 1650, led to disruption of the natural balance. He insists that population control is needed and that central population planning may lie ahead.

In the second selection, Claire and W.M.S. Russell articulate the extreme view which holds that population growth constitutes a major threat to civilization. Generalizing from studies of animal behavior, they argue that population density is the prime cause of human aggression and that a proper population balance will lead to a sane and peaceful society.

Professor Blake's article challenges the notions that the poor should constitute a major target for population control programs and that they do not practice birth control at present because of a lack of information and the means to do so. She finds from available poll data that, contrary to much current opinion, they do want large families. Professor Blake suggests that the key to increased population control may lie less in family planning programs than in altering the social system to make marriage and parenthood less popular conventions.

In the final selection, Ralph Hallow touches on one of the more sensitive areas of population control—the opinion of many blacks that family planning is a governmental ploy to weaken black power by reducing the number of black people. Whether or not well founded, to the extent that this concern impedes the success of family planning programs, the ultimate losers are the poor—both black and white—who would like the same "freedom to choose sex without conception that [their] middle class counterpart[s] enjoy."

Problems of Expanding Populations

D. WOLFERS*

The current human ecological crisis derives from the great technical advances by which man has placed himself in the position of a (self)-protected species for whom natural ecological regulation is suspended. Inevitably his numbers have increased to the point where all the resources of the Earth cannot supply his wants.

There have been four distinct forms of organization of human life—arboreal, pastoral, agricultural and technological—and each change from a more primitive to a more advanced organization has been accompanied by the disturbance of an established population balance, followed by a phase of rapid growth, and then the re-establishment of demographic stability. We are at present involved in the latest of these transformations and, with the limited perspective of the human life-span, have difficulty in seeing how it will end.

In each of the three past states of demographic balance, corresponding to arboreal, pastoral and agricultural society, that balance was determined by natural principles so that, growth being inhibited by the unchanging abundance of resources, death rates automatically adjusted to the prevailing birth rate. This adjustment did not mean that birth and death rates were the same every year, but there were periodic peaks of deaths, brought about by famine, epidemic or war, which irregularly restored a supportable population density. The current imbalance is likely to be resolved on similar terms if direct action is not taken to avoid it. But we now have the technical and social means of restoring a balance on terms more acceptable to human aspirations than the natural balancing mechanism.

Population trends in the 10,000 years of the agricultural phase show that throughout this period minor improvements in the availability of resources made possible slow but distinct growth of world population at a rate somewhat less than one per thousand per year. Meanwhile, high birth and death rates (about forty per thousand) prevailed constantly, and populations were everywhere and at all times "young."

Early Disturbances of Balance

The first stirrings of disturbance of this balance are now seen to have begun in about 1650 when, in response to quite small improvements in agricultural practice, and perhaps also political organization, the rate of growth of world population more than trebled to about three per thousand per year. This change occurred simultaneously in Europe and Asia. In 1750, with the agricultural revolution in full swing and the effects of the industrial revolution beginning to be felt, it is clear that a major discontinuity had occurred in those countries that were affected; growth rates started increasing to levels like ten to fifteen per thousand per year. By now, production was leaping ahead of consumption and the determining factors of rates of growth ceased for the time being to be economic and became biological; the link between birth and death rates was broken and they were able to act as independent variables.

*Reprinted with permission from *Nature* (February 14, 1970), pp. 593-597. Figures deleted.

The first effect of this change was the disappearance of mortality peaks. Food production and distribution had so improved that adverse seasons no longer produced famine, and nutritional standards had so changed that even though conditions of crowding and sanitation may have been worse than ever, epidemic disease was no longer able to decimate populations. Political organization had become so macroscopic that the toll of warfare became too selective to have important demographic consequences. Next came a steady decline of annual death rates in response to innovations in environmental sanitation and curative medicine and rising standards of nutrition — a process still continuing although with diminishing returns. The third effect, delayed for more than a century after the initiation of the first, was the long steady decline in birth rate, stretching in the United Kingdom over the whole period 1880-1930. No contemporary analysis of the causes of this decline exists, but it is safe to say that it reflected the adjustments made by individuals to radical changes in conditions of economic and social competition. An important secondary effect of this decline in birth rates was the transformation of the population to an older age-distribution with a consequent braking effect on the decline in death rate and a temporary alleviation of the dependency burden.

From 1930 onwards little change has been registered in the demographic indices of developed countries, growth rates fluctuating between three and ten per thousand per year, with manifest full independence of death rates from birth rates.

The Developing World

Although such high growth rates cannot continue for ever, they can be sustained for some generations without bringing inevitable disaster. The current crisis arises from a recognition of the potential consequences of continuation of the quite different trends in the developing world.

By the beginning of the twentieth century, moderate growth rates of about ten per thousand prevailed in most agricultural lands. This situation reflected the pacification, aggregation and administration imposed by the colonial powers and tutelary agents. Public health advances, particularly in tropical medicine, began to reduce the force of epidemic scourges, and the concept of famine relief made some progress. It is, however, only since the Second World War that a manifestly insupportable imbalance has been recognized. Countries which in 1939 were economically and socially stagnating in subsistence agriculture emerged in 1945 with political groups determined to speed them into the maelstrom of the modern world. Not only was production set for continuous expansion and mechanization, but a new spirit of interdependence led to the limited redistribution of foodstuffs under the aegis of United Nations agencies and with the help of food surpluses in advanced countries. Although violence was involved in the achievement of political independence by many developing nations, the previous pattern of recurrent tribal raiding was prohibited by the consolidation of what were in pre-colonial days dozens or hundreds of autonomous groups into large nation states. With neither famine nor war to restrain numbers, the importance of the spectacular application of preventive medical techniques (often, as with DDT and penicillin, developed during the Second World War) was enhanced, and death rates declined throughout the world at an unprecedented rate.

Rate of Growth Today

... Growth rates in developing countries at present vary between twenty and forty per thousand per year, representing, on exponential projection, periods of doubling of between 18 and 35 years. The most generally accepted estimate of the current growth of world population is twenty-one per thousand (doubling every 33 years) with a strong accelerating trend. Estimates of the probable future of development of world population prepared by the UN Demographic Division suggest a total of 7,000 million by the year 2000 compared with the present 3,500 million.

The expansion of a species ten-fold in a mere fourteen generations is, of course, a remarkable success story—in view of the complexity of human requirements it is almost a miracle of adaptation. Furthermore, there can be no doubt that when the limits of sustenance are reached the increase will be arrested by the customary balancing mechanisms of ecological logic.

Although some people believe that the problem can therefore be safely left to solve itself, the likely resolution without deliberate action is not the introduction of low birth rates but the restoration of high death rates. The spontaneous orderly unfolding of a demographic–economic transition is most improbable in the circumstances of the developing world, for the cause and effect sequences which led to the slowing of European growth are all running in reverse. Population growth, death control and the expansion of the labour force are proceeding rapidly while those whose job it is to increase economic growth, birth control and employment opportunities strive to keep pace. The problems of capital formation are particularly acute, for not only are the demands for capital inputs to support the expanding population crippling, but the ruthless reservation of resources for capital at the expense of consumption, which darkened the lives of town dwellers in nineteenth century Europe and starved the peasants of Russia in the 1930s, is no longer morally acceptable. By increasing the denominator of every fraction, be it literacy rate, doctor-patient ratio, proportion of labour force gainfully employed, or income per head, a rapid rate of population growth leaves government and people producing frantically in order to maintain their situation. Although economies of scale may accrue as the population increases in some countries, in most the scale is already so great that no real effect of this kind can be demonstrated. While in some countries with vast hinterlands no perceptible change is taking place in the ratio of population to natural resources, in others this ratio is becoming critically high, and in yet others, principally small islands, actual space is running out. Because the flow of international migration is blocked in almost every channel and will surely remain so, these islands are experiencing the crisis in its most acute form. Because of these considerations, if no action is taken to limit population growth it is likely to continue with no substantial change in standard of living or national economy until the problem becomes too great to cope with and the system itself collapses under the administrative burden of numbers and the disappointment of perpetual deferment of hopes. If this should happen, large tracts of the Earth will return to jungle law, de-population will take place and an entirely new set of problems will arise.

This catastrophe is not an immediate prospect, nor likely to occur on a worldwide scale. Some favoured developing countries, such as Singapore, Venezuela and Israel, have rates of economic growth large enough to sustain the chain reaction of development long enough to produce the social changes which we assume to be sufficient to stimulate spontaneous fertility limitation; others are sufficiently sparsely populated in relation to their resources to be able to grow rapidly for a very long time before there is a qualitative change from rural poverty to chaotic destitution. But these countries will, if they do not act soon to limit growth rates, have missed the only foreseeable opportunity to build graciously advanced societies free of the tragic squalor which has accompanied industrialization and demographic transition in the western world.

World Situation

While each country faces its own population dilemma, the world as a whole is not exempt. The "green revolution" has given a temporary advantage in the race to keep world food supplies from becoming yet more inadequate to meet growing needs; modern public health makes it difficult to visualize uncontrollable pandemics sweeping the world; nuclear weapons appear at present to be held under firm restraint. The crucial areas of world concern are now atmospheric pollution, shortage of water and the potential exhaustion of minable minerals. In these respects we live in a fool's paradise where each has faith in the ability of the others to solve problems too difficult for himself. Aesthetically too, and in relation to the intangible "quality of life," more and more people, unable to visualize institutions which can preserve what man has held valuable in the past into a teeming future, view that future with perhaps unwarranted despair.

Action is, however, being taken. In almost all cases this takes the form of family planning programmes, fully organized by government, supported by government or permitted by government. The pattern of introduction of these programmes was, only 10 years ago, a rather unedifying spectacle in which enthusiastic voluntary agencies seemed to drag suspicious governments into a series of tentative steps. Only after feeling their way for some years did governments come to embrace programmes enthusiastically. This situation is now changing, and genuine government leadership is appearing in an encouragingly large number of countries.

Government reluctance, and in places opposition, stems from several considerations, of which the fear of provoking opposition and courting unpopularity is the least realistic and the most important. It is in dispelling the myth that most peasant populations would be outraged by exposure to birth control services and propaganda that the social survey has made its outstanding contribution to the solution of the problem. Sample surveys, referred to as KAP surveys (knowledge, attitude and practice), conducted in dozens of different settings, seem to have uncovered a very strong demand—commonly 70 to 80 per cent of female respondents—for the facilities for controlling fertility, and to have demonstrated that, almost regardless of the situation prevailing, most couples want relatively small families (three or four children). There have been some exceptions to these generalizations, particularly in tropical Africa.

Difficulty also arises in countries where political power is shared between two or more ethnic or tribal groups of approximately equal numbers. In these circumstances each group fears that their own members, by adopting family planning, will encompass their ultimate political extinction. The view is quite widely and influentially held in Africa and Latin America that "population control for the developing countries" is a manifestation of similar tribal thinking on a global scale by the developed countries, and this naturally is responsible for bitter opposition.

The unreal basis of official Roman Catholic thought on the subject hinders developments in predominantly Catholic countries, but family planning programmes with declared health and welfare objectives substituted for demographic aims are making headway.

Outcome of Programmes

It is too early to make more than the most tentative predictions of success or failure for family planning programmes, and it is likely that some will be successful and others fail. The population control objective requires that two stages be accomplished. First, the adoption of birth control by most of the population efficiently enough to ensure that births correspond closely with numbers desired, and, second, the reduction of numbers desired to the level where development success is assured.

The first is certainly an easier objective to attain than the second, but, except in a few cases, which as they appear come to be described as special, there is little encouraging to report yet. For reasons related to the austerity of Christian morality, contraceptive technology has received far too little attention from scientists in the past. The crisis has arrived when we have no satisfactory techniques of contraception to offer the clients recruited in these programmes. Methods which have proved successful for highly motivated western populations are either too difficult or unpleasant for the mildly motivated to use regularly (diaphragm, condom); have too many unwelcome side-effects (IUD, pill, injection); require an unrealistic degree of cooperation (pill) or are too ineffective (coitus interruptus, spermicidal preparations). Although many millions in the developing world are struggling to use these methods, follow-up studies show that no more than half are able to preserve with any one method for a prolonged period. The techniques of sterilization, particularly of males, are much more satisfactory, but their adoption requires a finality of decision which few can muster until their family sizes are already excessive. The uncertainty of survival in areas where rates of infant mortality are high is, of course, a further deterrent.

The demographic history of Japan in the 1950s and contemporary East Europe shows that the practice of abortion alone is capable of producing dramatic effects on the birth rate, but the applicability of this to less developed countries is dubious. Neither the level of motivation nor the availability of medical services is of the same order in most of these. Additionally, stubborn adherence to rigid interpretations of the sanctity of life, particularly in Moslem and Catholic countries, rules out this method at present.

It is not known whether the availability of more acceptable forms of contraception (and much current research is being devoted to their development) would have a favourable effect on the numbers of couples adopting contraception, but it is certain that it would enhance the effectiveness of practice of those who do.

The discrepancy between the proportions of any population studied who assert their willingness to practise contraception and those who actually do so when it is offered is very large, and offers a great challenge to the social scientist and psychologist to unravel the complexities of decision taking involved. One of the least understood factors is the part played by males in this process.

Family planning programmes with demographic objectives are recent innovations. The earliest was in 1952 (India) but remained in very low gear till 1964. The real history of such programmes dates back only to 1962. So far very few participating countries have recorded substantial gains, and there is no lack of critics who attribute these to factors other than deliberate programmes. Although no change has been recorded in the birth rates of countries such as India and Pakistan, it should be remembered that in these countries vital registration is grossly defective, that changes in the age structure of the population are producing conditions favourable to increasing birth rates and that millions of couples have attempted birth control for the first time during the past few years.

High Fertility Favoured

The complementary task of introducing the "small family norm" has, in spite of considerable effort, met even less demonstrable success. While families of three children or fewer "fit" urban, industrialized societies which put premiums on higher education and provide comprehensive welfare services, it is the large family which until recently has enjoyed advantages in the rural environment which still prevails for 80 per cent of people living in developing countries. Free labour for the farm and the security of numbers and continuity in ill health or old age were the principal economic gains, while the extended family system spread the very light burdens of child-rearing in such a way that each additional child was almost no extra burden. Because very high levels of child mortality prevailed until recently, it is not surprising that a mutually supporting structure of social, moral and religious doctrine has developed to protect and advance the ideal of high fertility. It matters little that, after a generation of rapid increase, fragmentation of farms has become more important than labour supply, and after a generation of independence the burden of education is growing to rival the benefits of mutual support; the time scale of change in social and economic institutions is now far more contracted than that of change in cultural outlook. Automatic re-acculturization cannot be relied on, and the task of changing attitudes falls to the propagandist, the educator, and perhaps soon the tax gatherer.

The "small family norm" will not, of course, make any headway where extreme levels of child mortality prevail, so that a precondition of lowering birth rates is the necessity for lowering death rates. The most urgent preparatory task is to improve the coverage and standards of maternal and child health services in rural areas of the developing world; this is, of course, enormously costly. It is only, however, in the context of a secure and comprehensive health service that family planning can cease to be a foreign gimmick and become a settled part of life.

Campaign Media

Posters, films, radio talks and earnest face to face encounters multiply throughout the developing world to bring the message that two or three children are enough, but, in the hectic urgency of this campaign, time has not been found to evaluate the efficacy of the media used. The possibility of attempting to indoctrinate school children is at last being canvassed, but there is resistance because of the sexual component involved. School activity, to be effective, must take place in primary schools, because too few children attend higher grades for a campaign to have worthwhile results. Numerous suggestions for giving financial incentives to parents to have small families or imposing penalties on those who have large ones have been made. Almost without exception these prove relatively easy to implement in the highly organized money economy of an industrial state, which does not need them, but quite impossible in areas of subsistence agriculture where taxpayers form a small elite of the population. Meanwhile, the world is not ready to surrender another of its primitive freedoms by accepting the introduction of licences for child-birth.

If no way has been found to manipulate family size norms, the same may be said for the determination of optimum levels to aim for. Although in a technologically stagnant world, with abundant space and goods, a case might be made for aiming at a zero rate of growth, this magic figure has no applicability to any actual situation in the world today.

Although many programmes express their objectives in terms of the attainment of specific rates of growth by a certain date, few if any of these objectives have a more rational basis than the hope that the objective can be attained. So many ecological studies have been made too late that there is clearly a great urgency for the revival of studies of optimal population growth so that, when conditions are achieved which permit the induction of massive changes in fertility, a rational policy will be possible.

The situation at present is undeniably confused, with hope and despair about even balanced. This is inevitable in the first decade of serious attempts to deal with a problem of this size. Clear outlines of the tasks to be performed are, however, beginning to emerge. Of these, surely the most difficult and most important is to reduce child mortality as far as possible and provide a comprehensive network of health services throughout the developing world. This is the carrier wave for broadcasting family planning. A process of re-acculturization must be accomplished, and this implies indoctrination of populations at impressionable ages — in early school years, and as a corollary it implies bringing the whole child population to school. To these extents, medical and educational, population control depends on progress in development. There are, however, activities which may bring results in relatively unpromising situations. It is agreed that too frequent child-bearing is physically harmful to women, and this may form the basis for the adoption of a more authoritarian attitude to the prescription of contraception by members of the medical profession and their agents. Were the provision of contraceptive techniques as routine a part of the after-care of childbirth as iron for the treatment of anaemia, or insulin for diabetes, great results might be achieved even in areas now hopelessly unprepared for radical social change.

Impact of Abortion

The liberalization of abortion laws will likewise have an impact, although necessarily one which is dependent on the availability of competent services to perform operations. Meanwhile the search for reliable and safe medical abortifacients must be pursued, as must the search for better contraceptives. For all its moral dubiety, abortion enjoys the enormous psychological advantages of the nine late over the timely one stitch.

It is not easy to assess the ultimate impact of the torrent of "educational" material now inundating adult populations in the developing world. There are good reasons to believe that this insistent reiteration may, after a relatively long time, quite suddenly bring about a change in popular attitudes. Familiarity and legitimation are powerful agents for the dissolution of resistance. Patience is therefore important.

If we look more than a generation or two ahead, we are forced to come to terms with the ecological basis of the problem. At present the human race is appalled by the recognition of its dramatic rise to maturity with the accompanying achievement of the potential for self-destruction, for irretrievable pollution of the environment, and for exhaustion of key materials as well as for overcrowding itself. An age of centralized planning is on us as part of the unavoidable logic of development and progress. That planning already involves production and agriculture, education and welfare, research and development, distribution and transportation, the siting and distribution of population and countless other aspects of our lives. It is inevitable that it will soon come to embrace the numbers and then the quality of population, for all else will come to depend on these.

The Sardine Syndrome:
Overcrowding and Social Tension

CLAIRE AND W.M.S. RUSSELL*

"In 1900, a visitor from another sphere might reasonably have decided that man, as one met him in Europe or America, was a kindly, merciful and generous creature. In 1940 he might have decided, with an equal show of justice, that this creature was diabolically malignant. *And yet it was the same creature under different conditions of stress.*" These words occur in *The Shape of Things to Come,* published (in 1933!) by H. G. Wells. For thousands of years, there have been two schools of thought about human aggression and its expression in violent crime, riot and war. Some people have said that human aggressiveness is human nature, an innate disposition in man. Other people, like Wells, have taken the view that human aggression is a response to intolerable frustrations, and that violence is a symptom of stresses in human societies and in their relations with their natural surroundings. The records of past history, right up to the middle of the present century, appear to favour this second view, that violence is a reaction to stress, notably the

* Reprinted by permission of Harold Ober Associates Incorporated. Copyright © Claire and W. M. S. Russell 1968. Adaptation as it appeared in the Ecologist Magazine, August 1970. Figures deleted.

stress of shortage of food. Clear evidence for this connection can be found by studying the incidence and severity of public violence in many times and places, such as Imperial China, Japan in the 17th and 19th centuries, Tudor England, 18th century France, and medieval Europe from Britanny to Bohemia. By 1932, evidence of this kind had convinced most civilized people that human aggression is a response to stress, and not an innate and ineradicable taint. This was the verdict of the members of the *American Psychological Association*, replying in that year to a questionnaire, by a majority of 346 to 10.

Affluent Aggression

But in the 1950's voices began to be heard again in favour of man's inherent aggressiveness. This change of opinion results from events in modern highly industrialized societies of W. Europe and N. America. These "affluent" societies have much higher national incomes than other nations, or than they themselves had in earlier periods. True, it has been estimated that nearly one-seventh of the British people, and more than one-quarter of the American people are living in serious poverty. Nevertheless, the affluent societies are genuinely affluent in one important sense. By comparison with Tudor England or Imperial China or *modern* India, most people in the affluent societies are free from really serious shortage of food. If violence is a response to stress, should not this real improvement have the effect of substantially reducing violence in these societies? What has actually happened is precisely the reverse. In England and Wales, between 1950 and 1960, the annual number of violent crimes per 100,000 people more than doubled. In the United States, between 1960 and 1967, violent crime increased nearly six times as fast as population. Does this mean that people are indeed inherently aggressive whatever their conditions?

At this point we can get new insight into the problem from studies of the simpler societies of monkeys (including apes), and especially from comparing their behaviour in the wild and in the zoo. By now we have accounts of some 15 species in the wild, at least eight of these same species in zoos or other close forms of confinement, and some species in a variety of different intermediate conditions. We find that differences between wild and zoo behaviour are common to all species studied, and amount to a total change or reversal of all aspects of social behaviour and social life. In monkeys living under completely relaxed conditions in the wild, quarrelling is always rare and violence is practically non-existent. In monkeys living under the stresses of an enclosure, quarrelling is frequent and violence appreciable, sometimes leading to serious wounds and death. This contrast applies to all the species studied: any monkey species in the zoo is more quarrelsome and violent than the same or other species in the wild. Hans Kummer made a direct comparison of hamadryas baboons living in the wild in Ethiopia with hamadryas baboons at the Zurich Zoo. He found that aggressive acts by males were 17.5 times as frequent in the zoo as in the wild, and that serious bite-wounds were commonplace in the zoo, though *never* occurring in the wild. This contrast seems to be typical for all monkey species studied.

Affluent Monkeys

The zoo monkeys are clearly getting an ample food supply, and can be regarded, so to speak, as materially "affluent" societies. What they lack is *space*, since a band of monkeys in the wild normally roams an area of several square miles, whereas a zoo community must make do with an area of several hundred square yards. Hans Kummer found in the wild hamadryas baboons that such quarrelling as did occur was commonest in areas where cliff-ledges (and hence *space* for resting in safety from predators) were in short supply. *Crowding* is the crucial stress. Further confirmation of this comes from observations on rhesus monkeys by C. H. Southwick at the Calcutta Zoo and by Hilary and Martin Waterhouse at the Bristol Zoo. At Calcutta, halving the cage area for the same number of monkeys roughly doubled the amount of aggressive behaviour. At Bristol, halving the number of monkeys in the same enclosed area reduced the frequency of fights by 75 per cent.

The uniform peacefulness of wild monkey bands reflects the nature of their social organization. The forms of social structure and political control vary between monkey species. In the patriarchal democracy of the hamadryas baboons, leadership is dispersed among all experienced males; in cynocephalus baboons and rhesus monkeys, a small establishment of leading males controls the society; in Japanese monkeys, though male leaders generally control the movements of the band, a male can only become a leader if he is acceptable to the leading females who live at the core of the band. The one form *never* found in relaxed wild conditions is arbitrary dictatorship by a single individual. In the more oligarchic societies there is a sort of constitutional president but he does not differ sharply in rank from his aides, and owes his position entirely to the support of his male colleagues and, in Japanese monkeys, to the approval of the females. In a group of cynocephalus baboons observed in Nairobi Park, for instance, the leader could be driven away from a piece of food by a stronger baboon if both were some distance from the rest of the band. But normally, whenever an argument arose, the leader's authority was supreme, for he was always loyally supported by two colleagues, and a group of three can outrank any trouble-making individual. At Takahashi, a Japanese monkey male, individually capable of dominating any other male in the band, could never enter the leader class, for every time he approached the centre of the band, where the leaders live, he was driven out by the leading females. From these and other instances it appears that a highly aggressive male cannot expect to rise high in a band of monkeys under relaxed conditions. Since his position is owed to support by others and not brute strength, the leader does not appear much higher in rank than his supporters; on the other hand, he need not fear displacement as his physical powers decline. In chimpanzees and hamadryas baboons, elderly males are known to be respected; and in two Japanese monkey bands the top leader has been seen to retain his position to the end of his life, thanks to the active support of his leading colleagues.

Benevolence and Rank

The basis of social rank among chimpanzees has recently been studied by Vernon Reynolds and Gillian Luscombe. The observations were made at a USAF base in New Mexico, and concerned a community of redundant chimponauts. These chimps had all been trained to work in space vehicles. As everyone knows, human astronauts have taken over their jobs. The apes were therefore gathered together in honourable retirement in a spacious enclosure of 30 acres at Holloman Base. They rapidly resynthesized a community similar in many ways to those Vernon Reynolds had observed in the wild in Uganda. In these relatively relaxed conditions, Reynolds and Luscombe made observations for six days on 34 individuals. Each individual was scored for the amount and kind of food he obtained. A clear-cut rank order emerged with marked differences between high ranking individuals, who ate plenty of their favourite fruits, and low-ranking chimps, who had to make do with monkey pellets.

Records were also made, for each individual, of all his social interactions with other individuals, that is everytime he did something in relation to another individual. These interactions were classified into two groups: aggressive and friendly. Aggressive interactions included slaps, bites and a stand-up threat display which made the threatened individual take to flight. Friendly interactions included grooming, greeting, play and the like. When all the scores were compared it was found that the chimps of high rank, evidently the most self-assertive ones, were *not* the ones with the most aggressive behaviour, but those with most friendly contacts, the best-liked individuals. The most successful chimp of all had nine times as many friendly contacts as the average score. The chief way to win friends and influence people was apparently to perform a noisy but unaggressive display, quite different from the threat display; this cheerful hooting and banging about seemed to attract friendly attention and interest, and led to numerous friendly contacts and high rank and privileges as a result. When two or more bands of chimps meet in the wild at a fruit tree, which has just come into season, they engage in a regular beat session which may go on for 55 minutes, drumming on tree-roots and rushing about the trees. This may help to arrange ranks and priorities among chimps who do not know each other well. Clearly, under relaxed conditions, self-assertion and aggression are totally different things, expressed in posturally different displays. In a wild monkey band, aggression is not the way to social advancement.

Dictatorship in Zoos

In the zoo, under sufficient crowding stress, dictatorship by a physically powerful individual is a commonplace observation. In rhesus colonies observed by Michael Chance at Regent's Park and by Vernon Reynolds at Whipsnade the top male was in each case an absolute dictator, of whom all other monkeys were terrified. In a group of chimpanzees in a small enclosure at Regent's Park, observed by Caroline Medawar, we can see the extreme contrast to the civilized community at Holloman Base. In this crowded group, the boss was a strong male with a positive dislike for personal friendly contacts: he would attack and viciously wound any of his subjects who made friendly approaches even to each other. In these conditions there has been a total reversal: high rank is now attained by brutal aggression and nothing else.

Between the two extremes, there are two intermediate situations. At Whipsnade, Reynolds drew up diagrams of the aggressive and friendly interrelations between each of the individuals in the colony. The chief male was found to be at the top of the aggressive hierarchy, liable to attack anyone below him, but also at the top of the friendly hierarchy, receiving grooming and friendly contact from many subordinates. In a community of rhesus monkeys at the Bristol Zoo, Hilary and Martin Waterhouse found *two* individuals at the top of the rank order in terms of food access and freedom of movement: one of these was at the top of an aggressive hierarchy, the other at the top of a friendly hierarchy. These two intermediate situations throw some light on the transition from a relaxed to a stressful society. Evidently, when a society is under sufficient stress, brute strength and ferocity take the place of friendly mutual support and responsible leadership.

It is no wonder the result is frequent quarrelling and not infrequent violence. A dictator monkey in a zoo colony, touchy about intrusion or disturbance in the confined space, is constantly liable to attack subordinates. He may suddenly rush upon a group of neighbours and scatter them — just as the police suddenly scattered a group of peaceful demonstrators in Lincoln Park, during the "police riot" in Chicago in the summer of 1968. In a study of 118 quarrels described by Reynolds among the rhesus colony at Whipsnade, we were able to identify a number of processes which in the wild make for peace, but which under the protracted stress of crowding actually spread, amplify, prolong and intensify quarrels. A wild leader will repress a quarrel between two others by means of a mild threat; the zoo dictator will simply attack one of them as a *punishment*. In the wild, a monkey suffering momentary frustration from a superior may work off his feelings by redirecting resentment into a threat against some monkey of still lower rank, who can simply move away. In the crowded community, a monkey punished by the dictator will go off and attack somebody else by way of *redirection*, illustrating the observation of the great law reformer Sir Samuel Romilly, that "cruel punishment will have an inevitable tendency to produce cruelty in the people." When one monkey threatens, a neighbouring monkey will often threaten in the same direction, even if he cannot see the object of the first one's threat. In the wild, this automatic reaction ensures prompt support for the leader from his colleagues, who are always close to him, in suppressing, by threat and without violence, aggression by subordinates. In the zoo, this same reaction causes other monkeys to join in the quarrel on the side of the aggressor. By all these means, quarrels reverberate round the crowded society. Monkeys of low rank are liable to become the butts of redirection by all the others. This mass redirection can reduce an individual to the status of an outcast. This happened to a male at Whipsnade, who finally had to be removed when the others broke his arm in their unprovoked persecution of him.

Stress-Induced Aggression

We have now seen that rank criteria, social structure and a variety of social interactions all change completely under stress. When brute strength becomes the basis of social order, females and young, as the weakest members of the society, are the principal victims. In relaxed conditions in the wild, male leaders show the utmost chivalry towards females and young, and protect them instantly from even mild attacks by others. Under stress, the dictators of the zoo colonies are capable of savagely biting and even killing females and young. In a colony of hamadryas baboons at Regent's Park, observed in the 1920's by Sir Solly Zuckerman, eight out of 61 males died by violence, but 30 out of 33 females and five out of five babies were killed in this way.

Monkeys, in short, have two totally different kinds of social behaviour, "kindly and merciful" on the one hand, "diabolically malignant" on the other. Some social mechanisms, as we have seen, are actually designed to promote peace under relaxed conditions and violence under stressful conditions. Other mammals present a similar picture of reversal of social behaviour under stress, notably under crowding. The fundamental change is in parental behaviour, from a protective to a competitive attitude. For, as the Dutch zoologist Adriaan Kortlandt has shown, parental behaviour is the starting point of all other mammalian social behaviour. In its relaxed and positive and its stressful and negative forms, it is the origin of love and hate. The advantages of positive social behaviour are obvious: what could be the significance of the diabolically malignant behaviour under stress? Studies with rapidly breeding mammals, such as rats and voles, have shown that a population bred in a confined space, though supplied with unlimited food, will not exceed a certain density. As soon as the population density reaches a certain level, the reversal of behaviour begins, and the tension and violence and attacks on females and young have the effect of halting population growth and even reducing the population for some time. V. C. Wynne-Edwards has pointed out that if a population of animals only began to fight when its food supply was running short, that supply could be irretrievably depleted. By reacting to crowding, a population can be reduced in time to allow the food supply to recover. The effects of crowding and violence are not restricted to death by wounds. There are physiological effects on the females which impair reproduction for a couple of generations, and a disturbance of the machinery of immunity which renders the animals vulnerable to infectious disease, so that epidemics complete the crash of the population. The whole system of reversal of social behaviour can thus be seen as a means of response to a crisis in which population is in danger of outrunning resources. It may, indeed, get out of hand and go too far; this may have happened to the red squirrel in Britain.

Civilized Mammals

Under relaxed conditions, then, mammals are incredibly peaceful and, so to speak, civilized. Under population pressure, their societies are brutally unequal, cruel, tense and violent. Where man is concerned, we can make no such easy comparison. For man has probably never, or hardly ever, enjoyed completely relaxed conditions. Technological advance is the outcome of human intelligence, but it has always hit human societies as if it were an external force, since they have never recognized the need to regulate and allow for its effects. Every such advance, changing the relation between human societies and their natural surroundings and resources, has made possible an increase in population: every time, the increase has gone on without regulation, so that sooner or later population outstripped resources. As a result, man has been under virtually continuous population stress, and hence virtually continuous social inequality, tension and violence. Hence some people have supposed that these evils are the normal inherent lot or nature of man. But while all mammals are capable of fiendish cruelty under stress, man differs from them all in having an even more highly developed positive parental urge. This is clear from the long and increasing period of parental care in man, and from the unique social achievements of our species, with refinements of social welfare even for adults, all stemming from our parental behaviour. Even under frightful stresses, where almost all mammals would kill their young, many human beings continue to love and protect them at great sacrifice to themselves. It is not the violence in man's desperately stressful career that should astonish us, but the quality of human intelligence and human feeling in the most awful circumstances.

Nevertheless, under sufficient stress, a proportion of human beings do wound, kill, even eat their own children, and thoroughly mammalian atrocities do occur in man. We do not have human societies in totally relaxed conditions for comparison, as we do with monkeys; but we can compare human societies under greater or lesser degrees of stress, in different places and times. When we do so, we find striking differences, enough to suggest that, if we could eliminate population stresses altogether and forever, our societies could eventually be as free, friendly and peaceful as those of wild monkeys, and of course infinitely more creative. F. H. McClintock and others studied the incidence of violent crime in London in 1950, 1957 and 1960. They found violent crime at first concentrated in areas of dense, bad housing. As the British population crisis continued, other districts also became densely populated, and violent crime spread to these, though it showed no sign of appearing in suburbs where housing was still good and population relatively sparse. At Newcastle, the city planning department recently studied various social and medical symptoms in different districts. The sharpest contrast was between the most crowded and least crowded third of the city. The most crowded third produced more than five times as many offences against the person, more than four times as many larcenies, seven times as many people on probation, three times as much juvenile delinquency, more than five times as many cases of neglect of children, five times as much venereal disease, and 43 per cent more prenatal deaths. In his *Autobiography* H. G. Wells thus described his life in a slum at Westbourne Park. "I looked, so to speak, through a hole in my life of some weeks more or less, into a sort of humanity coarser, beastlier and baser than anything I had ever known before. . . . I think the peculiar unpleasantness of that episode lies in the fact that we were all too close together. We were as congested . . . as zoo monkeys."

Population Crisis

The settled civilized populations of mankind have generally had high normal death rates, of 3–4 per cent annually, but even higher birth rates of 3.5–5 per cent, resulting in a natural annual increase of up to 1 per cent. If this had been the whole story, it has been calculated that by now the world population would form "a sphere of living flesh, many thousand light years in diameter, expanding with a radial velocity many times faster than the speed of light." In real life, as opposed to the wonderland of mathematics, nothing of the kind can happen: indefinite natural increase is absurdly impossible, and either birth rates come down or death rates go up. In fact, every time the human civilized populations seriously outran their resources, they entered a population crisis, marked by very acute social tensions, leading to extensive, unrestrained violence and stress, the collapse of the population under epidemics, and the decline and fall of many a civilization. These population cycles were out of phase in different regions; thus India succumbed to population crisis in the 18th century, China in the 19th, and hence the Europeans gained control in India a century earlier than they did in China. Europe was for long the least densely populated region of the civilized world, and most recent creative advances in technology and social organization were achieved in Europe during the precious respites between crises, when population was for a while in balance with resources. The current population crisis differs in two ways from previous ones: it is world-wide and it is marked by very low normal death rates, making for explosive population growth.

Our Violent Century

Our century is therefore exceptionally cruel and violent, and getting more so. Civilians, including women and children, made up five per cent of the dead in World War I, between 50 and 75 per cent of the dead in World War II and 84 per cent in Korea. According to Senator Edward Kennedy, quoted by *The Times* on December 3rd, 1969, more than 300,000 civilians had by then been killed in Vietnam since 1965. Even if we could tolerate the suffering and waste entailed by the population crisis response of social tension and violence, we can no longer afford it even for its old evolutionary function, since a world war with modern weapons, far from sparing our natural resources, would irretrievably damage them by its ecological effects. But we can avert all this. We can do what no animal can do. We can substitute voluntary birth control for involuntary death control, for what Paul Leyhausen has called "the old, cruel, methods by which Nature balanced our numbers." With our modern technological resources, and a reduced world population, we can find out how to create, for the first time, truly relaxed conditions for human societies. Everything we know of mammals and man suggests that, if we can do this, we can build a lasting, peaceful and creative civilization. We can choose whether our species is to be kindly, merciful and generous or diabolically malignant: for it is the same creature under different conditions of stress.

Population Policy for Americans:
Is the Government Being Misled?

JUDITH BLAKE*

Pressure on the federal government for "action" to limit population growth in the United States has intensified greatly during the past 10 years, and at present such action is virtually unchallenged as an official national goal. Given the goal, the question of means becomes crucial. Here I first evaluate the particular means being advocated and pursued in public policy, then I present alternative ways of possibly achieving the goal.

*Reprinted with permission from the author and the editors of *Science*. Copyright 1969 by the American Association for the Advancement of Science. From *Science*, Vol. 164 (May 2, 1969), pp. 522-529. Footnotes and tables deleted.

The prevailing view as to the best means is remarkably unanimous and abundantly documented. It is set forth in the 17 volumes of congressional hearings so far published on the "population crisis" (1); in "The Growth of U.S. Population," a report by the Committee on Population of the National Academy of Sciences (2); in a statement made by an officer of the Ford Foundation who was asked by the Department of Health, Education, and Welfare to make suggestions (3); and, finally, in the "Report of the President's Committee on Population and Family Planning," which was officially released this past January (4). The essential recommendation throughout is that the government should give highest priority to ghetto-oriented family-planning programs designed to "deliver" birth-control services to the poor and uneducated, among whom, it is claimed, there are at least 5 million women who are "in need" of such federally sponsored birth-control assistance.

By what logic have the proponents of control moved from a concern with population growth to a recommendation favoring highest priority for poverty-oriented birth-control programs? First, they have assumed that fertility is the only component of population growth worthy of government attention. Second, they have taken it for granted that, to reduce fertility, one sponsors birth-control programs ("family planning"). Just why they have made this assumption is not clear, but its logical implication is that population growth is due to births that couples would have preferred to avoid. Furthermore, the reasoning confuses couple control over births with societal control over them. Third, the proponents of the new policy have seized on the poor and uneducated as the "target" group for birth-control action because they see this group as the only remaining target for a program of voluntary family planning. The rest of the population is handling its family planning pretty well on its own: over 95 percent of fecund U.S. couples already either use birth-control methods or intend to do so. The poor, on the other hand — at least those who are fecund — have larger families than the advantaged; they not only use birth-control methods less but they use them less effectively. The family-planning movement's notion of "responsible parenthood" carries the implication that family size should be directly, not inversely, related to social and economic advantage, and the poor are seen as constituting the residual slack to be taken up by the movement's efforts. Why are the poor not conforming to the dictates of responsible parenthood? Given the movement's basic assumptions, there are only two answers: the poor are irresponsible, or they have not had the opportunity. Since present-day leaders would abhor labeling the poor irresponsible, they have chosen to blame lack of opportunity as the cause. Opportunity has been lacking, in their eyes, either because the poor have not been "educated" in family planning or because they have not been "reached" by family-planning services. In either case, as they see it, the poor have been deprived of their "rights." This deprivation has allegedly been due to the prudery and hypocrisy of the affluent, who have overtly tabooed discussion of birth control and dissemination of birth-control materials while, themselves, covertly enjoying the benefits of family planning.

So much for the logic underlying recent proposals for controlling population growth in the United States. But what is the evidence on which this argument is based? On what empirical grounds is the government being asked to embark on a high-priority program of providing contraceptive services to the poor? Moreover, what, if any, are some of the important issues that the suggested policy raises — what are its social and political side effects? And, finally, is such a policy, even if appropriate for the poor and even if relatively unencumbered by public disapproval, relevant to the problem of population growth in America? If demographic curtailment is really the objective, must alternative policies be considered and possibly given highest priority?

Has Birth Control Been a Tabooed Topic?

The notion that the American public has only recently become willing to tolerate open discussion of birth control has been assiduously cultivated by congressmen and others concerned with government policy on population. For example, Senator Tydings credited Senators Gruening and Clark and President Johnson with having almost single-handedly changed American public attitudes toward birth control. In 1966 he read the following statement into the 28 February *Congressional Record*:

> The time is ripe for positive action. Ten years ago, even five years ago, this was a politically delicate subject. Today the Nation has awakened to the need for Government action.
> This change in public attitude has come about through the efforts of men who had the courage to brook the tides of public opinion. Senator Clark is such a man. Senator Gruening is such a man. So is President Johnson. Because of their leadership it is no longer necessary for an elected official to speak with trepidation on this subject.

A year later, Senator Tydings reduced his estimate of the time required for the shift in public opinion to "3 or 4 years." Senator Gruening maintained that the "ninety-eight distinguished men and women" who testified at the public hearing on S. 1676 were "pioneers" whose "names comprise an important roll which historically bears an analogy to other famous lists: the signers of the Declaration of Independence, those who ratified the Constitution of the United States and others whose names were appended to and made possible some of the great turning points in history." Reasoning from the continued existence of old, and typically unenforced, laws concerning birth control (together with President Eisenhower's famous anti-birth-control statement), Stycos, in a recent article, stated:

> The public reaction to family planning in the United States has varied between disgust and silent resignation to a necessary evil. At best it was viewed as so delicate and risky that it was a matter of "individual conscience." As such, it was a matter so totally private, so sacred (or profane), that no external agents, and certainly not the state, should have anything to do with it.

Does the evidence support such impressionistic claims? How did the general public regard government sponsorship of birth control long before it became a subject of congressional hearings, a National Academy report, and a Presidential Committee report? Fortunately, a question on this topic appeared in no less than 13 national polls and surveys conducted between 1937 and 1966. As part of a larger project concerned with public knowledge and opinions about demographic topics. I have gathered together the original data cards from these polls, prepared them for computer processing, and analyzed the results. The data are all from Gallup polls and are all from national samples of the white, adult population. Here I concentrate on adults under 45 — that is, on adults in the childbearing age group.

The data . . . contradict the notion that Americans have only recently ceased to regard birth control as a tabooed topic. As far back as 30 years ago, almost three-quarters of the women questioned in these surveys actively approved having the *government* make birth-control information available to the married. By the early 1960's, 80 percent or more of women approved overcoming legal barriers and allowing "anyone who wants it" to have birth-control information. The figures for men are similar. The question asked in 1964 — the one question in recent years that did not mention illegality — brought 86 percent of the women and 89 percent of the men into the category of those who approved availability of birth-control information for "anyone who wants it." Furthermore, in judging the level of disapproval, one should bear in mind that the remainder of the respondents, in all of these years, includes from 7 to 15 percent who claim that they have "no opinion" on the subject, not that they "disapprove."

An important difference of opinion corresponds to a difference in religious affiliation. Among non-Catholics (including those who have "no religion" and do not attend church) approval has been considerably higher than it has been among Catholics. Among non-Catholic women, over 80 percent approved as early as 1939, and among non-Catholic men the percentages were approximately the same. The 1964 poll showed that 90 percent of each sex approved. Among Catholics, in recent years about 60 percent have approved, and, in 1964, the question that mentioned neither the government nor legality brought opinions of approval from 77 percent of the women and 83 percent of the men.

Clearly, if birth-control information has in fact been unavailable to the poor, the cause has not been a generalized and pervasive attitude of prudery on the part of the American public. Although public officials may have misjudged American opinion (and may have mistakenly assumed that the Catholic Church "spoke for" a majority of Americans, or even for a majority of Catholics), most Americans of an age to be having children did not regard birth control as a subject that should be under a blanket of secrecy and, as far back as the 1930's, evinced a marked willingness to have their government make such information widely available. It seems unlikely, therefore, that poorer sectors of our population were "cut off" from birth-control knowledge primarily because informal channels of communication (the channels through which most people learn about birth control) were blocked by an upper- and middle-class conspiracy of silence.

What has happened, however, is that pressure groups for family planning, like the Catholic hierarchy they have been opposing, have been acting as self-designated spokesmen for "public opinion." By developing a cause as righteous as that of the Catholics (the "rights" of the poor as against the "rights" of a religious group), the family planners have used the American way of influencing official opinion. Now public officials appear to believe that publicly supported birth-control services are what the poor have always wanted and needed, just as, in the past, official opinion acceded to the notion that such services would have been "offensive" to certain groups. Nonetheless, the question remains of whether or not publicly supported services are actually appropriate to the attitudes and objectives of the poor and uneducated in matters of reproduction. Is the government responding to a mandate from the poor or to an ill-concealed mandate from the well-to-do? If there is no mandate from the poor, the provision of birth-control services may prove a convenience for certain women but is likely to have little effect on the reproductive performance of the poor in general. Let us look at the evidence.

Is There a Mandate from the Poor?

The notion that the poor have larger families than the affluent only because they have less access to birth-control information implies that the poor *desire* families as small as, or smaller than, those of the well-to-do. The poor are simply unable to realize this desire, the argument goes, because of lack of access to birth-control information. The National Academy of Sciences Committee on Population stated the argument very well.

The available evidence indicates that low-income families do not want more children than do families with higher incomes, but they have more because they do not have the information or the resources to plan their families effectively according to their own desires.

The committee, however, presents none of the "available evidence" that "low-income families do not want more children than do families with higher incomes." Actually, my data supply evidence that runs counter to the statement quoted above, both with respect to the desired or ideal number of children and with respect to attitudes toward birth control.

I shall begin with the preferred size of family. A number of national polls, conducted over some 25 years, provide data concerning opinions on ideal family size. In addition, I include tabulations of data from two national surveys on fertility (the "Growth of American Families Studies"), conducted in 1955 and 1960. My detailed analyses of the results of these polls and surveys are given elsewhere and are only briefly summarized here.

· · ·

The data lend little support to the hypothesis that the poor desire families as small as those desired by the middle and upper classes. Within both the educational and the economic categories, those on the lower rungs not only have larger families than those on the higher rungs (at least in the case of non-Catholics) but say they want larger families and consider them ideal. This differential has existed for as long as information on preferred family size in this country has been available, and it persists. It thus seems extremely hazardous to base a major governmental effort on the notion that, among individuals (white individuals, at least) at the lower social levels, there is a widespread and deeply held desire for families as small as, or smaller than, those desired by the well-to-do. No major survey shows this to be the case.

Not only do persons of lower socioeconomic status prefer larger families than the more affluent do, they also generally favor birth control less.

Looking at the educational differential, one finds that, in general, the proportion of those who approve birth control drops precipitately between the college and grade school levels. As far back as the early 1940's, over 80 percent of women and 75 percent of men with some or more college education approved government action on birth control. By 1964, over 90 percent of both sexes approved. By contrast, only 60 percent of men and women with an elementary school education approved in the 1940's, and, despite a rise in approval, there is still a differential. When non-Catholics alone are considered, the educational difference is even more pronounced in many cases.

Turning to economic or income status, one generally finds the same results. The high proportions . . . of women in the highest and next-to-highest economic brackets who, in recent years, have approved birth-control efforts is noteworthy, as is the fact that approximately 80 percent of women in these brackets approved such efforts as far back as the 1930's. On the other hand, men and women in lower income brackets have been slower to approve birth-control policies.

Despite the inverse relationship just described, I may have overemphasized the lesser approval of birth-control programs on the part of persons of lower economic and social status. After all, in recent years approval often has been high even among people at the lowest social levels. Among women with only a grade school education, the percentage of those favoring birth-control programs averaged 73 percent in polls taken between 1959 and 1964; among men at the lowest educational level, the corresponding average was 68 percent. Yet it is undeniably true that throughout the period for which data are available, the people who needed birth-control information most, according to recent policy pronouncements have been precisely the ones who were least in favor of a policy that would make it widely available.

The truth of this conclusion becomes more evident when we move to an analysis of a question asked on the 1966 Gallup poll: Do you think birth-control pills should be made available free to all women on relief who are of childbearing age? This question presents the public with the specific issue that is the focus of current policy—namely, birth control especially for the poor.

It is clear that the overall level of approval drops when specific reference to a poverty-oriented birth-control policy is introduced. The decline is from an average of approximately 80 percent for each sex during the period 1959-64 to 65 percent for men and 71 percent for women in 1966. Of most significance, however, is the fact that the largest proportionate drop in approval occurs among members of the "target" groups themselves—the poor and uneducated. In particular, there is a remarkable drop in approval among men at this socioeconomic level. There is a 42-percent decline in approval among men who have had only a grade school education and a 29-percent drop among those with a high school education. Among the college-educated men the drop in approval is only 6 percent. The results, by income, parallel those by education: there is a 47-percent drop for men in the lowest income group but only a 9-percent drop for those in the highest income bracket. Even if the tabulations are restricted to non-Catholics, the results are essentially the same.

If the ghetto-oriented birth-control policy urged on the federal government meets with limited public enthusiasm, how does the public view extension of that policy to teen-age girls? This question is of some importance because a notable aspect of the pressure for government-sponsored family-planning programs is advocacy of making birth-control information and materials available at the high school level.

The Committee on Population of the National Academy of Sciences urges early education in "family planning" in order to prevent illegitimacy.

> . . . government statistics show that the mothers of approximately 41 percent of the 245,000 babies born illegitimately in the United States every year are women 19 years of age or younger. Thus a large proportion of all illegitimate children are progeny of teen-age mothers. To reduce the number of such children born to teen-age mothers, high-school education in family planning is essential.

Katherine B. Oettinger, Deputy Secretary for Family Planning of the Department of Health, Education, and Welfare, importunes us not to "demand the eligibility card of a first pregnancy before we admit vulnerable girls to family planning services." The Harkavy report states:

> Eligibility requirements should be liberal with respect to marital status. Such services should be made available to the unmarried as well as the married.... Eligibility requirements should be liberal with respect to the age of unmarried women seeking help. This will undoubtedly pose some problems, but they may not be insurmountable. Some publically supported programs are already facing them (for example, in Baltimore).

Representative Scheuer from New York has berated the federal government for not "bringing family planning into the schools." He has cited the "desperate need for family planning by unmarried 14-, 15-, and 16-year-old girls in school [which] is so transparently evident that it almost boggles the imagination to realize that nothing has been done. Virtually no leadership has come from the federal government."

Obviously there is little recognition in these statements that such a policy might engender a negative public response. Yet such a possibility cannot be discounted. The results of the 1966 question "Do you think they [the pills] should be made available to teen-age girls?" suggest that a policy of pill distribution to female adolescents may be viewed by the public as involving more complex issues than the mere democratization of "medical" services . . .

It may be seen that, in general, a proposal for distribution of pills to teen-age girls meets with very little approval. There is more disapproval among women than among men. Even among women under the age of 30, only 17 percent approve; among men in this age group, 29 percent approve. At no age does feminine approval reach 20 percent, and in most cases it is below 15 percent. Furthermore, restriction of the results to non-Catholics does not raise the percentages of those who approve the policy. Most noteworthy is the socioeconomic gradient among men. Whereas 32 percent of college-educated men approve distribution of pills to young girls, only 13 percent of men with a grade school education do. Thirty-three percent of men in the highest income bracket approve, but only 13 percent in the lowest bracket do.

Clearly, the extension of "family planning" to poor, unmarried teen-agers is not regarded simply as "health care." Individuals may approve, in a general way, a wider availability of birth-control information without approving federal expenditure to facilitate a high level of sexual activity by teen-age girls. One suspects that explicit recognition and implied approval of such activity still comes hard to our population, and that it comes hardest to the group most involved in the problems of illegitimacy and premarital conception—namely, the poor and uneducated themselves. The extreme disapproval of a policy of pill distribution to teen-age girls that is found in lower-class groups (particularly among lower-class men) suggests that a double standard of sexual behavior is operative in these groups—a standard that does not allow open toleration of the idea that the ordinary teen-age girl requires the pill, or that a part of her junior high school and high school education should include instruction in its use.

Can "Five Million Women" Be Wrong?

The most widely publicized argument favoring federal birth-control programs, and apparently the one that elected officials find most persuasive, is the claim that there are approximately "five million" poor women "in need" of publicly subsidized birth-control help. I list below some of the principal assumptions upon which this estimate is based—all of which introduce serious upward biases into the evidence.

1. It is claimed that women at the poverty and near-poverty levels desire families of 3.0 children. While this may be true of nonwhite wives at this economic level, it is not true, as we have seen, of white women, who comprise a major share of the "target" group and who, on the average, desire a number of children closer to 4 (especially if Catholics are included, as they are in the "five million").

2. It is assumed by the estimators that 82 percent of all poor women aged 15 to 44 are at risk of conception (that is, exposed sexually), in spite of the fact that only 45 percent of poor women in this age group are married and living with their husbands. In arriving at the figure of 82 percent, the estimators assumed that all women in the "married" category (including those who were separated from their husbands and those whose husbands were absent) were sexually exposed regularly, and that half of the women in the "non-married" category—that is, single, widowed, and divorced women—were exposed regularly. Information is scarce concerning the sexual behavior of widows and divorced women, but Kinsey's data on premarital coitus leads one to believe that the assumption of 50 percent for single women may be high. Among the women with a grade school education in Kinsey's sample, 38 percent had had coitus at some time between the ages of 16 and 20, and 26 percent, at some time between the ages of 21 and 25. Moreover, as Kinsey emphasizes, these encounters were characteristically sporadic.

3. The proportion of sterile women among the poor is assumed to be 13 percent, although the Scripps 1960 "Growth of American Families Study" showed the proportion among white women of grade school education to be 22 percent.

4. No allowance is made for less-than-normal fecundity, although the Scripps 1960 study had indicated that, among women of grade school education, an additional 10 percent (over and above the 22 percent) were subnormal in their ability to reproduce.

5. It is taken for granted by the estimators that no Catholic women would object, on religious grounds, to the use of modern methods, and no allowance is made for objection by non-Catholics, on religious or other grounds. In other words, it is assumed that all women "want" the service. Yet, in response to a question concerning the desirability of limiting or spacing pregnancies, 29 percent of the wives with grade school education who were interviewed in the Scripps 1960 study said they were "against" such limitation or spacing. Among the Catholic wives with grade school education, the proportion "against" was 48 percent, although half of these objectors were "for" the rhythm method. Similar objections among the disadvantaged have been revealed by many polls over a long period.

6. Perhaps most important, the estimate of 5 million women "wanting" and "in need of" birth-control information includes not only objectors but women who are already practicing birth control. Hence, in addition to all the other biases, the estimate represents a blanket decision by the estimators that the women require medical attention regarding birth control—particularly that they need the pill and the coil. In the words of the Harkavy report:

> This may be considered a high estimate of the number of women who need to have family planning services made available to them in public clinics, because some of the couples among the poor and near poor are able to exercise satisfactory control over their fertility. However, even these couples do not have the same access as the non-poor to the more effective and acceptable methods of contraception, particularly the pill and the loop. So, simply in order to equalize the access of the poor and the near-poor to modern methods of contraception under medical supervision, it is appropriate to try to make contraceptive services available to all who may need and want them.

Yet the 1960 Scripps study found that, among fecund women of grade school education, 79 percent used contraceptives. The 21 percent who did not included young women who were building families and said they wanted to get pregnant, as well as Catholics who objected to birth control on religious grounds. As for the methods that women currently are using, it seems gratuitous for the federal government to decide that only medically supervised methods—the pill and the coil—are suitable for lower-income couples, and that a mammoth "service" program is therefore required. In fact, the implications of such a decision border on the fantastic—the implications that we should substitute scarce medical and paramedical attention for all contraceptive methods now being used by poor couples.

In sum, the argument supporting a "need" for nationwide, publicly sustained birth-control programs does not stand up under empirical scrutiny. Most fecund lower-class couples now use birth-control methods when they want to prevent pregnancy; in the case of those who do not, the blame cannot simply be laid at the door of the affluent who have kept the subject of birth control under wraps, or of a government that has withheld services. As we have seen, opinion on birth control has been, and is, less favorable among the poor and the less well educated than among the well-to-do. In addition, the poor desire larger families. Although it may be argued that, at the public welfare level, birth control has, until recently, been taboo because of the "Catholic vote," most individuals at all social levels have learned about birth control *informally* and without medical attention. Furthermore, the most popular birth-control device, the condom, has long been as available as aspirin or cigarettes, and certainly has been used by men of all social classes. When one bears in mind the fact that the poor have no difficulty in gaining access to illegal narcotics (despite their obvious "unavailability"), and that the affluent had drastically reduced their fertility before present-day contraceptive methods were available, one must recognize and take into account a motivational component in nonuse and inefficient use of contraceptives. Indeed, were relative lack of demand on the part of the poor not a principal factor, it would be difficult to explain why such an important "market" for birth-control materials—legal or illegal —would have escaped the attention of enterprising businessmen or bootleggers. In any event, any estimate based on the assumption that all poor women in the reproductive group "want" birth-control information and materials and that virtually all "need" publicly supported services that will provide them—including women with impaired fecundity, women who have sexual intercourse rarely or not at all, women who object on religious grounds, and women who are already using birth-control methods—would seem to be seriously misleading as a guide for our government in its efforts to control population growth.

Moreover, the proposal for government sponsorship takes no account of the possible advantages of alternative means of reaching that part of the "market" that may not be optimally served at present. For example, competitive pricing, better marketing, and a program of advertising could make it possible for many groups in the population who are now being counted as "targets" for government efforts to purchase contraceptives of various kinds. When one bears in mind the fact that an important reason for nonuse or lack of access to contraceptives may be some sort of conflict situation (between husband and wife, adolescent child and parent, and so on), it becomes apparent that the impersonal and responsive marketplace is a far better agency for effecting smooth social change than is a far-flung national bureaucracy loaded with well-meaning but often blundering "health workers." The government could doubtless play an initial stimulating and facilitating role in relation to private industry, without duplicating, on a welfare basis, functions that might be more efficiently handled in the marketplace.

Would the Policy Have Side Effects?

The possible inadvisability of having the government become a direct purveyor of birth-control materials to poverty groups becomes more clear when we consider some of the risks involved in such a course of action.

Even if the goal of reducing family size were completely and widely accepted by the poorer and less well educated sectors of the population, we should not assume that the general public would necessarily view a policy concerned with the means and practice of birth control (in any social group) as it views ordinary medical care—that is, as being morally neutral and obviously "desirable." Birth control is related to sexual behavior, and, in all viable societies, sexual behavior is regulated by social institutions. It is thus an oversimplification to think that people will be unmindful of what are, for them at least, the moral implications of changes in the conditions under which sexual intercourse is possible, permissible, or likely. An issue such as distribution of pills to teen-age girls runs a collision course with norms about premarital relations for young girls—norms that, in turn, relate to the saliency of marriage and motherhood as a woman's principal career and to the consequent need for socially created restrictions on free sexual access if an important inducement to marriage is not to be lost. Only if viable careers alternative to marriage existed for women would the lessening of controls over sexual behavior outside of marriage be unrelated to women's lifetime opportunities, for such opportunities would be independent of the marriage market and, a fortiori, independent of sexual bargaining. But such independence clearly does not exist. Hence, when the government is told that it will be resolving a "medical" problem if it makes birth-control pills available to teen-agers, it is being misled into becoming the protagonist in a sociologically based conflict between short-run feminine impulses and long-run feminine interests—a conflict that is expressed both in relations between parents and children and in relations between the sexes. This sociological conflict far transcends the "medical" issue of whether or not birth-control services should be made widely available.

Actually, the issue of sexual morality is only one among many potentially explosive aspects of direct federal involvement in family-planning programs for the poor. Others come readily to mind, such as the possibility that the pill and other physiological methods could have long-run, serious side effects, or that racial organizations could seize on the existence of these programs as a prime example of "genocide." Eager promoters of the suggested programs tend to brush such problems aside as trivial, but the problems, like the issue of sexual morality, cannot be wished away, for they are quite patently there. There *are* risks involved in all drug-taking, and it is recognized that many of the specific ones involved in long-term ingestion of the pill may not be discovered for many years. No one today can say that these are less than, equal to, or greater than the normal risks of pregnancy and childbirth. Equally, a class-directed birth-control program, whatever its intent, is open to charges of genocide that are difficult to refute. Such a program cannot fail to appear to single out the disadvantaged as the "goat," all the while implying that the very considerable "planned" fertility of most Americans inexplicably requires no government attention at all.

Population Policy for Americans

It seems clear that the suggested policy of poverty-oriented birth-control programs does not make sense as a welfare measure. It is also true that, as an inhibitor of population growth, it is inconsequential and trivial. It does not touch the principal cause of such growth in the United States—namely, the reproductive behavior of the majority of Americans who, under present conditions, want families of more than three children and thereby generate a growth rate far in excess of that required for population stability. Indeed, for most Americans the "family planning" approach, concentrating as it does on the distribution of contraceptive materials and services, is irrelevant, because they already know about efficient contraception and are already "planning" their families. It is thus apparent that any policy designed to influence reproductive behavior must not only concern itself with all fecund Americans (rather than just the poor) but must, as well, relate to family-size goals (rather than just to contraceptive means). In addition, such a policy cannot be limited to matters affecting contraception (or even to matters affecting gestation and parturition, such as abortion), but must, additionally, take into account influences on the formation and dissolution of heterosexual unions.

What kinds of reproductive policies can be pursued in an effort to reduce long-term population growth? The most important step toward developing such new policies is to recognize and understand the existing ones, for we already have influential and coercive policies regarding reproductive behavior. Furthermore, these existing policies relate not merely to proscriptions (legal or informal) regarding certain means of birth control (like abortion) but also to a definition of reproduction as a primary societal end and to an organization of social roles that draws most of the population into reproductive unions.

The existence of such pronatalist policies becomes apparent when we recall that, among human beings, population replacement would not occur at all were it not for the complex social organization and system of incentives that encourage mating, pregnancy, and the care, support, and rearing of children. These institutional mechanisms are the pronatalist "policies" evolved unconsciously over millennia to give societies a fertility sufficient to offset high mortality. The formation and implementation of antinatalist policies must be based, therefore, on an analysis and modification of the existing pronatalist policies. It follows, as well, that antinatalist policies will not necessarily involve the introduction of coercive measures. In fact, just the opposite is the case. Many of these new policies will entail a *lifting* of pressures *to* reproduce, rather than an *imposition* of pressures *not* to do so. In order to understand this point let us consider briefly our present-day pronatalism.

It is convenient to start with the family, because pronatalism finds its most obvious expression in this social institution. The pronatalism of the family has many manifestations, but among the most influential and universal are two: the standardization of both the male and the female sexual roles in terms of reproductive functions, obligations, and activities, and the standardization of the occupational role of women—half of the population—in terms of child-bearing, child-rearing, and complementary activities. These two "policies" insure that just about everyone will be propelled into reproductive unions, and that half of the population will enter such unions as a "career"—a life's work. Each of the two "policies" is worth considering.

With regard to sex roles, it is generally recognized that potential human variability is greater than is normally permitted *within* each sex category. Existing societies have tended to suppress and extinguish such variability and to standardize sexual roles in ways that imply that all "normal" persons will attain the status of parents. This coercion takes many forms, including one-sided indoctrination in schools, legal barriers and penalties for deviation, and the threats of loneliness, ostracism, and ridicule that are implied in the unavailability of alternatives. Individuals who — by temperament, health, or constitution — do not fit the ideal sex-role pattern are nonetheless coerced into attempting to achieve it, and many of them do achieve it, at least to the extent of having demographic impact by becoming parents.

Therefore, a policy that sought out the ways in which coercion regarding sex roles is at present manifesting itself could find numerous avenues for relieving the coercion and for allowing life styles different from marriage and parenthood to find free and legitimatized expression. Such a policy would have an effect on the content of expectations regarding sex roles as presented and enforced in schools, on laws concerning sexual activity between consenting adults, on taxation with respect to marital status and number of children, on residential building policies, and on just about every facet of existence that is now organized so as exclusively to favor and reward a pattern of sex roles based on marriage and parenthood.

As for the occupational roles of women, existing pressures still attempt to make the reproductive and occupational roles coterminus for all women who elect to marry and have children. This rigid structuring of the wife-mother position builds into the entire motivational pattern of women's lives a tendency to want at least a moderate-size family. To understand this point one must recognize that the desired number of children relates not simply to the wish for a family of a particular size but relates as well to a need for more than one or two children if one is going to enjoy "family life" over a significant portion of one's lifetime. This need is increased rather than lessened by improved life expectancy. Insofar as women focus their energies and emotions on their families, one cannot expect that they will be satisfied to play their only important role for a diminishing fraction of their lives, or that they will readily regard make-work and dead-end jobs as a substitute for "mothering." The notion that most women will "see the error of their ways" and decide to have two-child families is naive, since few healthy and energetic women will be so misguided as to deprive themselves of most of the rewards society has to offer them and choose a situation that allows them neither a life's work outside the home nor one within it. Those who do deprive themselves in this fashion are, in effect, taking the brunt of the still existing maladjustment between the roles of women and the reproductive needs of society. In a society oriented around achievement and accomplishment, such women are exceptionally vulnerable to depression, frustration, and a sense of futility, because they are being blocked from a sense of fulfillment both at home and abroad.

In sum, the problem of inhibiting population growth in the United States cannot be dealt with in terms of "family-planning needs" because this country is well beyond the point of "needing" birth control methods. Indeed, even the poor seem not to be a last outpost for family-planning attention. If we wish to limit our growth, such a desire implies basic changes in the social organization of reproduction that will make nonmarriage, childlessness, and small (two-child) families far more prevalent than they are now. A new policy, to achieve such ends, can take advantage of the antinatalist tendencies that our present institutions have suppressed. This will involve the lifting of penalties for antinatalist behavior rather than the "creation" of new ways of life. This behavior already exists among us as part of our covert and deviant culture, on the one hand, and our elite and artistic culture, on the other. Such antinatalist tendencies have also found expression in feminism, which has been stifled in the United States by means of systematic legal, educational, and social pressures concerned with women's "obligations" to create and care for children. A fertility-control policy that does not take into account the need to alter the present structure of reproduction in these and other ways merely trivializes the problem of population control and misleads those who have the power to guide our country toward completing the vital revolution.

The Blacks Cry Genocide

RALPH Z. HALLOW*

Not long ago a family planning center in Cleveland was burned to the ground after militant Negroes had labeled its activities "black genocide." More recently, the antipoverty board of Pittsburgh became the first in the nation to vote down OEO appropriations to continue Planned Parenthood clinics in six of the city's eight poverty neighborhoods. The move resulted from intense pressure and threats of violence by blacks—all males—who have kept the genocide issue boiling since one of the clinics was threatened with fire bombing last fall. Although a coalition of women, black and white, has succeeded in rescuing the program, national officers of Planned Parenthood-World Population fear the Pittsburgh example may encourage black opponents to lay siege to similar programs in other cities. Organized opposition can be found in cities from California to New York, and summer could bring the violence which militant critics of the clinics have threatened.

Although concerted opposition to the Planned Parenthood Association (PPA) programs in the ghettos has centered in Pittsburgh, the issue has been gaining national currency through articles published in *Muhammad Speaks*, the newspaper of the Black Muslims. The author of the articles is Dr. Charles Greenlee, a respected black physician in Pittsburgh who first raised the issue nearly two years ago. Dr. Greenlee contends that the birth control information and "propaganda" of federally financed family planning programs are carried into the homes of poor blacks by "home visitors" and public assistance workers, who allegedly coerce indigent black women into visiting the clinics. Greenlee says, and welfare officials deny, that the intimidation takes the form of implicit or explicit threats that welfare payments will be cut off if the recipient has more children. Thus it is argued, the free clinics constitute "genocide," a conscious conspiracy by whites to effect a kind of Hitlerian solution to the "black problem" in the United States.

Dr. Greenlee's formula for leading his people out of white America's cul-de-sac is:

---

*Reprinted with permission from *The Nation*, Vol. 208 (April 28, 1969), pp. 535-537. Figure deleted.

black babies equal black votes equal Black Power. Recognizing this logic, he said recently on a local television panel discussion, the white power structure is using the neighborhood clinics to "decimate the black population in America within a generation." The Planned Parenthood national office sent a black representative to sit on the panel. The two top white executives of PPA in Pittsburgh decided their presence on the panel would only lend credence to Dr. Greenlee's charges. But, they point out, the neighborhood community action committees have representatives, including blacks, on the local PPA board.

Also arguing PPA's side of the question was Mrs. Frankie Pace, a resident of the city's largest black ghetto, the Hill District, where most of the "action" occurred during the civil disorders last April. Mrs. Pace believes that most black women in poor neighborhoods not only want the clinics but also desperately need such help because they are often ignorant of scientific methods of birth control. (Health department and welfare workers in nearly every U.S. city report that they still occasionally encounter indigent women who believe that urinating after intercourse prevents conception.)

The television panel illustrated the new alliances that have grown up over the "black genocide" issue. Seated next to Dr. Greenlee was Msgr. Charles Owen Rice, who for more than thirty years has enjoyed the reputation of being the liberal's liberal. Always a champion of the cause of labor and more recently of peace and an end to the war in Vietnam, he has nevertheless enunciated a position on birth control that is closer to that of the Vatican than to the more liberal one held by a significant number of priests and lay Catholics in America. He said during the panel discussion that the term "black genocide" is not too strong; for, he observed, it is "passing strange" that no clinics exist in the city's two mostly white poverty neighborhoods. Local PPA officials point out, however, that the predominantly Catholic populations in those neighborhoods have rejected the establishment of clinics in their communities.

PPA supporters also suggest it was no accident that William "Bouie" Haden was the only black leader to whom the Catholic diocese of Pittsburgh recently gave a $10,000 annual grant—to help run the United Movement for Progress, Haden's black self-help group. Haden, a fiery though not so young militant, was quick to pick up Dr. Greenlee's charges of "black genocide" and to force the temporary closing last summer of one of the clinics on his "turf," the city's Homewood-Brushton district. Although about seventy irate black women forced Haden to back off from the issue for a time, in early February he led the forces which, through skillful parliamentary maneuvering, got a divided and confused anti-poverty board to vote down an appropriation to continue the clinics. Although Haden's enemies flaunt his long criminal record, most observers recognize him as a sincere and effective leader who did much to keep Homewood-Brushton cool during the disorders last April.

In spite of his leadership abilities, Haden has only piecemeal support for his "black genocide" charges. Family planning supporters point out that it was the black women in the poverty neighborhoods who demanded that PPA set up a network of neighborhood clinics under the hegemony of the city's anti-poverty board. The women claimed that the PPA center in the downtown area was inaccessible to the indigent whose welfare allowances made no provision for baby-sitting fees and bus fares.

To complicate the issue still further, supporters of family planning programs in the ghettos include such eminent black men of the Left as Bayard Rustin and Dr. Nathan Wright, Jr., who was chairman of the Black Power conference. Writing on "Sexual Liberation" in the Newark *Star-Ledger*, Dr. Wright said the poor—both black and white—are discriminated against sexually and should seek the help of Planned Parenthood.

The term "family planning" is slightly euphemistic; except in the states where it is prohibited, birth control counseling is offered even to unmarried girls under 18, provided there is parental consent and usually if the girl has had one child. Women in the 15-to-19-year age group account for the highest percentage of illegitimate births (40.2 percent for whites and 41.9 for blacks), according to U.S. Public Health Service figures for 1964. Here again, defenders of birth control argue that the clinics help to alleviate one of the grossest hypocrisies practiced by our male-dominated legislatures. Lawmakers, they say, hand down so-called moral standards for American women in defiance of the sexual practices actually prevailing in the society. If young women from enlightened middle-class families are still undergoing unwanted pregnancies and are forced to seek expensive or dangerous abortions, how much worse must it be for the teen-age daughters of the indigent?

Everywhere the statistics are on the side of family planning—at least for those who view them in unideological terms. In New Orleans, for example, where the largest family planning program in the United States has been operating, an indigent female population of 26 percent accounted for 56 percent of all births, 88 percent of illegitimate births and 72 percent of stillbirths. Nationally, the infant mortality rate of blacks is twice that of whites. The United States ranks fifteenth in the world in infant mortality, and there is a surfeit of evidence relating the problem directly to poverty. A study by the U.S. Department of Health, Education and Welfare found that the most effective way to reduce infant mortality is to offer family planning. Finally, of the 5.3 million indigent women in the United States, only 850,000 receive family planning services, and only 30 percent of those who do are nonwhite.

All this, however, means nothing to the black militant and his white allies who believe that Black Power and "poor" power (and the consequent redistribution of wealth they would bring) are threatened by free family planning clinics whose representatives actively seek out black women. Caught in the middle is the indigent American woman who wishes to have the same freedom to choose sex without conception that her middle-class counterpart enjoys.

3

Planning the Metro-Urban Environment?

Urban and suburban America are beset with numerous serious problems. The widespread utilization of rivers and streams for waste disposal has severely affected the quality and quantity of water in many instances. Public support of expressway systems, single-family unit-housing development, and the expansion of consumer credit have combined with extensive use of the automobile to create problems of uncontrolled land use, mass transit tangles, air pollution, and noise. Sheer population growth, coupled with the productive forces springing from technology, has generated staggering problems of waste disposal. And state annexation and tax laws, suburban growth, and wide differentials in income have helped to divide urban and suburban America racially and have rendered it ever more difficult for city governments to cope with their mounting problems.

Many modern metro-urban problems can be traced to a number of sources, most of them closely interrelated. Problems of air, water, transit, housing, and even education are rooted in part in the development of an industrial, technical, and urban society. Further, the solution of these problems has often been hampered by public policy that permits and sometimes even encourages urban sprawl, while preserving antiquated tax, annexation, and other laws. Public attitudes and behavior patterns have, in turn, provided support (or at least resisted change) of continued and even increased suburban spread and reliance upon the automobile. The interrelatedness of these problems is exemplified by the links between annexation laws, housing and transportation policy, suburban behavior patterns, and air pollution.

Many of the problems which plague the metro-urban environment result from the nature of today's decision-making systems. The environment is largely the product of countless decisions made somewhat independently of one another in hundreds of decision-centers. Further, these decisions are often designed with short-run goals and localized values in mind and are made in response to immediate and proximate stimuli. Thus the political system in many ways resembles the uncontrolled market system in which the sum of many rational and purposeful decisions can produce a set of environmental conditions desired by virtually no one. This is not to say that man exercises no control over his environment; he obviously does. The point is that a number of individual decisions, all made with some degree of independence and having some consequences external to the decision-center itself, add up to a set of conditions which may be universally undesirable.

The character of modern metropolitan problems suggests a need to approach problem-solving from a systems perspective. Narrowly conceived, one-dimensional attempts to cope with problems on a piecemeal basis are not only apt to be inadequate to meet society's needs, but may also produce unanticipated, unwanted consequences. Success in dealing with metro-urban problems, therefore, comes more easily when there is careful, systematic analysis of the problems prior to selection of the policy. Such analysis alone cannot insure success, however. The politically atomized character of the metropolitan environment, the nature of the decision-making process, the wide variations in perceptions of "environmental quality," and the enormity of the problems themselves all mitigate against early solution. Nevertheless, adherence to a systems perspective may reduce the uncertainty in decision-making and increase the probabilities for eventual improvement of the metro-urban environment.

The selections in this chapter dramatize some of the physical dimensions of the problems currently facing metro-urban America, emphasizing the realities and difficulties of complex decision-making, and illustrating the need for a systems perspective in defining and developing solutions to these problems. None of the articles display great optimism about man's ability to develop "total solutions" to the physical and planning problems in the metro-urban environment. They do suggest, however, that a combination of a systems perspective, careful planning, and additional knowledge about man and his environment holds promise for some amelioration of current problems.

In the opening selection, the brief excerpts from the report of the President's Council on Recreation and Natural Beauty dramatically portray the grim realities of the urban crisis. These problems include planning, urban sprawl, noise, waste, dirty air and water, and many others.

In the second selection, Mr. Berry notes that society is now beginning to recognize some of the limits of the earth's capacity to provide resources and absorb waste. He discusses some of the causes and characteristics of modern air pollutants, as well as modern techniques for monitoring and measuring them. Mr. Berry describes several matters inherent in problem solution, the most difficult being the fact that there is no one solution. Rather, solutions, like the sources of air pollution themselves, must be many and varied and their implementation slow and costly. Finally, Mr. Berry raises the crucial question of distributing the costs of programs to clean the environment, and concludes that the general public and the customers of the industries who are engaged in the clean-up efforts will most surely pay the bill. Mr. Berry does not predict early doom for the planet, but he argues that there are limits on the time left to redress environmental imbalances.

Reporting on events at a 1969 conference on waste, Mr. Grinstead describes the growing volume and increasingly complex composition of the waste from packaging produced in the United States. He tells of the conflicts and problems, such as the need felt by industry to produce more and better packaging materials in order to satisfy public demand. Other difficulties in the waste problem include the question of who will pay for research on alternative packaging and disposal methods, and what types of disposal are most appropriate for what types of refuse.

In the fourth selection, Mr. Bragdon begins with a rundown on modern sources of noise, both within and outside of the home. He discusses some of the medical implications of noise, such as temporary and permanent loss of hearing and interference with sleep. Additionally, he reports that noise can interfere with other communications, on-the-job performance, and in the case of jet aircraft, property damage. Mr. Bragdon concludes that noise is not a condition natural to man, and that through planning we can indeed reduce it.

The report of the Advisory Commission on Intergovernmental Relations briefly traces the development of modern urban-suburban society, mentions some of the more serious problems which have accompanied this development, and emphasizes the difficulties of devising and implementing remedial programs. Over the past decades, the report notes, there has been a massive migration of people into urban areas so that most Americans are now concentrated in about two hundred metropolitan areas. More recently there has been an exodus to the suburb, and in many areas suburban dwellers now outnumber core city residents. Although these trends have brought many benefits, they have generated serious problems. One of the more serious among these is the abandonment of the central city by the white middle and upper class to the poor and racial minorities. Generally fragmented politically, the metropolitan area is plagued with inadequate tax and decision-making mechanisms, and is frequently characterized by great disparities in the provision of public services from region to region. The report visualizes an even greater metropolitan role in the future for state and federal governments.

In the closing article, Professor Marquis makes an urgent plea for the judicious use of force in altering the environment, and for the employment of a systems perspective. Both natural and human systems are complex, he maintains, and precipitous and ill-advised alteration of one portion of a system can touch off unexpected, unwanted consequences for the larger system. Natural ecosystems are intricate entities and their components interdependent. Massive changes at one point will have repercussions throughout the system. Likewise, in the human environment we have learned to use energy but are still unable to eliminate uncertainty about the probable effects of changed behavior. What is needed for both natural and human environments, Marquis argues, are systems of control that permit the prediction — and avoidance — of unwanted consequences. Such systems rely heavily on information. We need to increase our knowledge of how systems work and what can, or cannot, be controlled. In Marquis' words, "man can deal with uncertainties by seeking to reduce them through greater knowledge." In short, Marquis holds that through the proper combination of knowledge and energy, man can make adjustments in his environment and move toward the solution of problems. But this requires a systems perspective, information, and a balanced use of control.

The Urban Crisis

THE PRESIDENT'S COUNCIL ON
RECREATION AND NATURAL BEAUTY*

Urban Growth

For more than seven out of ten Americans, home is an urban setting—not only the place of residence, but the site of most experience. By the year 2000—a mere 32 years away—nearly nine out of ten Americans will dwell in urban areas.

As a consequence of this increasing urban concentration, cities and their surroundings have become increasingly congested, cluttered, blighted and besmogged. Seldom do they offer an environment to nourish the human spirit. But with the reassertion of natural influence and the imaginative design of his own structures, man can create environments hospitable to his highest aspirations....

More than 134 million of the Nation's 200 million people live in metropolitan areas. By 1980 these areas will, if present trends continue, spread to make room for another 45 million people. Between 750,000 and a million acres will continue to be paved and built upon each year, and the Nation's urbanized land area may increase by 50 percent.

By the year 2000, according to an Urban Land Institute projection, 90 percent of Americans are expected to live in cities. By the year 2000, 60 percent of the American people are expected to be living on only 7 percent of the land, concentrated in the three largest metropolitan areas: One megalopolis reaching from west of Chicago to Maine and down the Atlantic coast to south of Norfolk, a second stretching down California from 150 miles north of San Francisco to the Mexican border, and a third extending the length of the Florida peninsula.

This staggering prospect carries with it the possibility that the metropolitan areas can destroy themselves as decent places to live, owing to an inability to plan and govern on a regional scale.

It seems clear that in these urban agglomerations the problems of air pollution, water pollution, disposal of solid waste, and the destruction of open land will grow to such proportions as to demand radical innovations in planning and governmental techniques and organization....

Sprawl

The impact of America's population boom is felt most heavily in the metropolitan suburbs, which are growing seven times as fast as the central cities. By the mid-1960's a majority of Americans living in metropolitan areas were suburbanites; in 1966 the Bureau of the Census estimated that 60 million Americans lived in metropolitan-area central cities and 66 million in their suburbs.

Typically, this rapid growth is scattered and piecemeal as the fringes of one suburb coalesce with those of the next. The resultant haphazard, leapfrogging

*This selection is composed of excerpts taken from *From Sea to Shining Sea; A Report on the American Environment—Our Natural Heritage* (Report of The President's Council of Recreation and Natural Beauty, Washington, D.C., 1968). It is designed to illustrate the grim realities of the physical dimensions of many of our urban problems.

growth of metropolis is a major threat to the quality of the American environment.

The New York Metropolitan Area's Regional Plan Association has labeled the result "Spread City." A land developer and mortgage banker has described the process to a Congressional committee:

> A farm is sold and begins raising houses instead of potatoes—then another farm. Forests are cut, valleys are filled, streams are buried in storm sewers.
>
> Traffic grows, roads are widened. Service stations . . . hamburger stands pockmark the highway. Traffic strangles. An expressway is cut through and brings cloverleafs which bring shopping centers. Relentlessly, the bits and pieces of a city are splattered across the landscape.
>
> By this irrational process, non-communities are born—formless, without order, beauty or reason—with no visible respect for people or the land. Thousands of small, separate decisions—made with little or no relationship to one another nor to their composite impact—produce a major decision about the future of our cities and our civilization, a decision we have come to label "sprawl."

Sprawl leaves few sizable open spaces in its wake. The distinctive land forms, scenic vistas, and the other happenings of nature that give individuality to an area are erased. The resulting monotonous, homogenized, helter-skelter patchwork surrounds nearly every metropolitan area in the country.

Sprawl stretches out the distances people must travel to work, to shop, to school, to play; adjacent areas are too often unrelated. Sprawl wastes land; a projection by the New Jersey State planning agency suggests that by 2000 one-third of the State's land will be devoted to roads, parking lots, and other transportation facilities. In the confusing, unrelated, amorphous agglomerations that are typical of sprawl it is often difficult for many who live there to feel a sense of community, or a means of participation.

Farm areas often feel the onslaught well ahead of sprawl's physical encroachments. Even before it is "good business" to install pieces of towns on rural acreage, speculation, rising land values and increasing taxes frequently make it unprofitable to farm. The result is a metropolitan area fringe of weed-infested fields and ragged and spotty development—a rural-to-urban transition belt, often 20 miles wide, that is neither town nor country. This is the principal way America's future cities are being created. At every step of the process of subdividing and developing new land for housing, public agencies are involved. Yet neither the individual public agencies nor the individual builders can determine the aggregate result; this country-to-town conversion process is a problem of public responsibility that can be solved only by broad public powers providing both regulation and incentives. . . .

Spillover Pollution

In St. Louis some industries truck refuse across the Mississippi River to Illinois where it is burned in open dumps; the resulting polluted air drifts back across the river to St. Louis.

Boston burns its trash in incinerators that shower soot and ashes on residents of nearby cities. The Boston Metropolitan Planning Commission, facing a critical garbage disposal problem, wants to install additional incinerators with pollution-control filters, but no local government wants them in its backyard.

Atlanta daily dumps tons of poorly treated sewage into the Chattahoochee River, which supplies drinking water for neighboring cities downstream.

In the San Francisco metropolitan area, Marin County—where mountains, bay, and ocean meet just north of the Golden Gate—has some of the most spectacular natural beauty in the Bay Area. People from the entire region go there for recreation. But Marin County is permitting some of its best scenery to be subdivided because its property tax base is inadequate to finance regional parks.

Around each of these metropolitan areas unplanned subdivisions and highway strip developments continue to sprawl over local boundaries and clutter the landscape.

Similar examples of environmental pollution, monotony, and ugliness can be found in every metropolitan area in the United States. In most cases the problems extend across political boundary lines and thus are insoluble by a city or county acting alone. Disposal of wastes and urban sprawl are largely metropolitan regional problems that can only be solved on a regional basis.

Air Pollution

Fly over any metropolitan area in the Nation, with one exception, and you can see plumes from smokestacks or dump fires fouling the air; and the pollution that can be seen is only a small fraction of the whole.

The single exception is the City of Los Angeles. After a 20-year campaign there, stationary sources of air pollution generally are under control. Nevertheless, a murky haze still hangs over the city frequently. Despite its pioneering efforts to control its stationary sources of pollution, Los Angeles still has a serious air pollution problem because of its millions of automobiles.

At its worst, air pollution is fatal. During the 1966 Thanksgiving weekend, for instance, the Public Health Service estimates that 168 persons in New York City died because of an unusually high concentration of pollutants in the air. An atmospheric temperature inversion that weekend held pollutants close to the ground.

Though death in such incidents is the most dramatic effect, air pollution also contributes subtly and seriously to the rising incidence of such respiratory diseases as lung cancer, bronchitis, and emphysema. Beyond that it stings eyes, is offensive to smell, and blankets cities with murky gloom. It can shorten the life of everything it touches. It can kill and stunt trees, gardens, and crops. It can soil clothing, smudge buildings, and even peel paint and corrode machinery.

Pollution Sources and the Management Gap: The Nation's 90 million cars, trucks and buses cause the largest share of air pollution; industries that burn coal and oil are responsible for most of the rest. The major industrial polluters include pulp and paper mills, iron and steel mills, oil refineries, smelters, chemical manufacturers, and power and heating plants. Aircraft also contribute to the problem. For example, the Federal Aviation Administration estimates that on a typical day some 35 tons of pollutants are spewed over the National Capital area from planes landing and taking off at Washington's National Airport.

Across the Nation, the U.S. Public Health Service estimates that a total of more than 140 million tons of pollutants a year are dumped into the atmosphere—nearly

1,500 pounds for each American—and that every U.S. city has an air pollution problem serious enough to require careful and regular investigation, whether or not its citizens can see or smell the pollutants.

Although it is technically practical and economically feasible to control most stationary sources of pollution, few communities have done so. There is an imperative need for air quality management programs organized on a regional basis. . . .

Water Pollution

Clean water is beautiful to look at and delightful to walk beside and play in. A fountain in a city, a brook in a suburb, a spring in a wilderness all enhance their surroundings. But America's growing population and industry are dumping increasing torrents of wastes into the streams, lakes, and bays that once were clean and clear.

The problem is particularly acute in the major rivers that flow through the hearts of metropolitan areas. Waterborne wastes destroy beauty and make water-related recreation undesirable or impossible. The Potomac, the Hudson, and the Mississippi illustrate the problem. The Potomac's most serious pollution is in precisely the reach of the river with greatest potential for enjoyment by the 2½ million residents of the Washington, D.C., Metropolitan area. As the Potomac slowly flows through the Nation's Capital, its load of silt, filth, and acid from farms, mills, and mines blends with discharge from overloaded sewers to nourish an algae bloom and a summer stink that rises from the river for miles below the metropolis. The Hudson, from Albany to Manhattan, is an open sewer. Scavenger eels, one of the few animals that can live in waters loaded each day with 200 million gallons of raw sewage and the effluent of dozens of factories, have been known to attack sanitary engineers taking water samples. The Mississippi, at St. Louis, is so polluted that test fish placed in a sample of river water diluted with 10 parts of clean water die in minutes. . . .

Thermal pollution, caused by discharge of water at high temperatures from powerplants, also is cause for increasing concern as the number of nuclear powerplants along ocean and river shorelines increase.

Electric power generation has doubled every 10 years since 1945. The rate of increase continues to jump so that some analysts estimate that the doubling time for increase in demands may now be as short as five years. More moderate estimates give 10 years to double the power demands. Either are staggering increases.

About 70 percent of the industrial thermal pollution load in the United States today is caused by the steam electric power industry. Powerplants are now discharging into United States waterways 50 trillion gallons of heated water a year, in some cases with devastating effects on the environment and aquatic life.

By 1980, the power industry will use one-fifth of the total fresh water runoff of the United States for cooling and is predicted to spew forth 100 trillion gallons of heated discharge. . . .

Waste

Into American homes flows a steady stream of groceries and gadgets. Out of them flow cans and cartons, bottles and broken toys and bric-a-brac. This solid waste includes 48 billion cans (250 per person), 26 billion bottles and jars (135 per person), and 65 billion metal and plastic caps (338 per person) a year. These and demolished buildings, worn-out appliances, and the other residues of affluence total more than 2,000 pounds per person per year — more than 5 pounds a day for each American.

Not only is solid waste increasing in volume, its characteristics are changing. Accumulation of nonreusable containers is a difficult part of the problem. The continuing trends toward nonreturnable bottles and new types of disposable paper products add to the problem.

Tin cans will rust and disintegrate in time, but aluminum and glass are more permanent and some containers made of new kinds of plastic are possibly even more durable. Many are not consumed completely even by incineration; their litter on the landscape can be expected to remain indefinitely. The development of naturally disintegrating containers offers promise and should be encouraged.

Nationwide, collection and disposal of garbage and other solid waste cost an estimated $3 billion in 1967, and this was accomplished by methods little improved over those of 25 years ago. Although salvage industries do $5 to $7 billion worth of business a year, they use only a small part of the Nation's total waste. The great bulk, which is neither salvaged nor recycled for reuse, has a vast potential for littering the landscape. Two other results of improper waste management are air pollution from burning of refuse, and water pollution by seepage from dumps. Population growth, increasing amounts of refuse per person, shrinking numbers of acceptable disposal sites, and archaic technology combine to make solid waste management an urgent environmental problem in many metropolitan areas.

Yesterday's solution was to dump "outside the city limits," on unused land at the edge of town. But in today's metropolis, the merging of the suburbs leaves little room for dumps; one result is that too often they are located where they destroy out-of-the-way areas of natural beauty, such as stream valleys and marshes. . . .

Littering, a common sign of urban blight, is an expensive habit, costing the Nation's taxpayers nearly $½ billion a year. New York City, alone, spends $10.5 million — one fourth of its Park Department budget — to keep its parks and beaches clean. The Forest Service and National Park Service spend $4 million a year for sanitation and litter removal. Litter is increasing each year, fouling city neighborhoods and countryside alike, causing fire hazards and public health problems, and drastically reducing enjoyment of the environment. . . .

Signs and Noise

Façades of professionally designed commercial buildings are ruined by latter-day addition of variegated signs, and both the architecture and the message get lost. The skylines of many cities are invaded with out-of-place displays of garish neon and flashing lights, which often have a blighting effect. Even street benches lose their functional simplicity when made to frame a commercial sign. Corporate and small business publicity has wallpapered the urban scene, seldom directing its art to the enhancement of the community.

The clutter is not limited to private signs. Cities cannot control their own official signs, generally posted with a conspicuous lack of coordination or taste by a multitude of public authorities. Traffic safety, as well as appearances, can be improved through the elimination of tension and confusion caused by a jumble of identification, warning, and directional signs.

Sounds are an integral part of our urban life. The parade, the concert in the park, the street peddlers, the clanging of a cable car, all belong to the exciting history of the city. Sounds have intensified in this industrial age to a point where they now constitute a form of pollution of the urban environment. A quiet atmosphere is recognized as the sign of a pleasant community; sounds have become noise. The din in the streets, in the skies, and often within buildings, reduces efficiency, frays nerves, dampens dispositions, and according to medical studies, is insidiously reaching deafening levels. Aside from public health and economic productivity, the quality of life is affected by noise, especially when added to all the other forms of stress associated with life in the city. . . .

The Chemistry and Cost
of Contamination:
Perspectives on Polluted Air — 1970

R. STEPHEN BERRY*

We are making a fast transition into a society in which many people recognize the environment as the finite medium in which we live, and not as a limitless source and sink.

Let me summarize the present state — the physical, biological and legal aspects of the pollution problem — and point out a few examples.

Sources of air pollution can be classified expeditiously as (1) power and heat generation, (2) industrial processes, (3) waste incineration and other waste disposal processes, and (4) transportation. The first and last of these sources have characteristic and moderately well-studied patterns of emission. Power and heat generation is still primarily achieved by burning coal, oil or gqs. The best-identified pollutant from this class of sources is of course sulfur dioxide; others from the same sources include solid particulate and nitrogen oxides. Transportation, meaning automobiles and trucks and jet airplanes burning hydrocarbon fuels, is responsible for carbon monoxide, hydrocarbons and their oxidation products, nitrogen oxides and solid particulate, especially lead. Waste incineration produces particulate and nitrogen oxides under any circumstance, and carbon monoxide if it is improperly done. Each type of industrial processing source has its own pattern of pollutants, almost as characteristic as a fingerprint.

The prospect for the next few years is an increasing flood of air pollution from all these sources. The world's annual sulfur dioxide production doubled between 1940 and 1965 and will more than double between 1970 and 1990. The number of automobiles is increasing fast enough that by 1980 the trend toward lower pollution

*Reprinted by permission of Science and Public Affairs, the Bulletin of the Atomic Scientists. Copyright © 1970 by the Educational Foundation for Nuclear Science. From the *Bulletin of the Atomic Scientists* (April 1970), pp. 2, 34–41. Figures deleted.

(from the use of control devices) will be reversed. Per capita solid wastes are increasing two to four per cent each year, and if present policy is not changed, part of this waste will appear as air pollution.

Brown and Gray Cities

The pollution patterns of various cities and even neighborhoods differ considerably. Some cities, like Eugene, Oregon, with its kraft paper plant, or Gary, Indiana, the victim of steel mills and coking ovens, derive most of their pollutants from a single industry. Larger cities, however, generally fall into one of two basic classes, which I call the brown air cities and the gray air cities. Brown air cities derive a very high proportion of their pollution from automobiles. In relatively young cities, such as Los Angeles or Denver, the morning air is visibly brown from nitrogen dioxide, produced in the early traffic rush. The older, gray air cities, such as New York or Chicago, depend heavily on the burning of coal or oil for space heating, and derive their electric power largely from the same fuels burned in generating stations in or near the cities. This burning produces vast quantities of particulate. So much particulate is produced each morning from coal or oil burning that the air has a gray color, rather than the brown of nitrogen dioxide. These two types of cities have to be dealt with somewhat differently.

Pollutants can be classified usefully in several ways other than by source. For purposes of analyzing the problem, we may categorize pollutants according to how well they are now monitored. Moderately reliable methods are available for measuring sulfur dioxide concentrations continuously; it has recently become possible to monitor carbon monoxide on a continuous basis also. The technical difficulties associated with such monitoring are due primarily to the fact that the pollutants occur in very small quantities, one to 100 parts per million for carbon monoxide, and a hundredfold less for sulfur dioxide. Hence one needs methods of high sensitivity and high specificity to avoid interference. Nitrogen oxides and "total oxidant" levels can also be measured with moderate ease, but with some ambiguity about what one is measuring. Particulate is measured on an intermittent basis by filtering the material from large volumes of air, or continuously by an opacity method that is unfortunately influenced by particle size. The content of the particulate is rarely investigated systematically or regularly, except to determine the combustible fraction. More selective or convenient particulate monitors are appearing, but only a few laboratories, particularly of the U.S. Public Health Service, have done extended monitoring studies of individual hydrocarbons, of nitrogen oxide and nitrogen dioxide separately, and occasionally of other species such as hydrogen fluoride that tend to be associated with specific kinds of sources.

Electron Analyzer

All in all, we do now have effective continuous monitors for at least one characteristic substance from power and heat generation and from transportation. More general monitors, applicable to gaseous pollutants from a wide range of industrial processes, will probably appear on the commercial market within the next year or two. For example, an electron impact analyzer has been developed at the National Bureau of Standards and will probably be a prototype for a monitoring device.

Particulates and droplets still require batch analyses, and normally are restricted to analyses for heavy elements and a few specific compounds. Hydrocarbons could be monitored automatically and frequently by gas chromatography. As yet, systematic hydrocarbon measurements have been carried out at the research level, rather than as routine monitoring.

In all probability, the course of pollution control has been influenced by the ease with which various species have been monitored. For example, systematic and automatic on-site analyses are not available for carcinogenic hydrocarbons such as benzo-a-pyrene, or for phenols, or for lead. None of these pollutants has been the focus of a control campaign, or of extended low-level toxicological studies. Until recently, carbon monoxide analyses could not be done on a continuous automatic basis, especially in the road-level sites where they would be most useful. Now, with monitors available, standards for air quality are being established with regard to carbon monoxide. Sulfur dioxide, the easiest common pollutant gas to monitor, is the standard villain and the target for most grass roots antipollution campaigns, as well as the first gas for which regional air quality standards have now been proposed. Perhaps if the differential infra-red monitor for carbon monoxide now coming into use had been available a few years before the colorimetric sulfur dioxide monitor, automotive pollution would be a much smaller problem today.

Recognizing the dependence of control strategy on input data should prepare us for future surprises. The field is still young enough that significant new pollutants or components in pollutant-generating cycles continue to come to light. In photochemical smog, peroxyacetylnitrate (PAN) was discovered in 1960 and identified as a major irritant despite its very low ambient concentrations. Other peroxyalkyl-nitrates were recognized at the same time. Then, eight years later, the peroxyaryl-nitrates such as peroxybenzylnitrate turned up in smaller concentrations, but proved to be far more irritating.

Effects on Health

The relationship of air pollution to health is of course the nub of the problem and in some ways its most difficult aspect. Systematic public health studies of the effects of pollution are still rather rare, and, with a few important exceptions, the medical profession has not rushed to make these studies.

Several studies looked for correlations of cancer with air pollution. The case for such a correlation with cancer of the lung is not a strong one now. On the other hand, a recent study including several other types of cancer found significant correlations of mortality, particularly in gastrointestinal cancer, with chronic exposure to sulfur dioxide and nitrogen dioxide. I estimated from the results of this study that a five-fold reduction in Chicago's average annual sulfur dioxide concentration (with all other variables held constant) would reduce the number of deaths from cancer by about 800 per year.

Statistical studies and physicians' observations have coupled bronchitis and emphysema with pollution. Increases in the sulfur dioxide concentrations correlate well with increased degree of illness in cases of chronic bronchitis, when these increases are accompanied by increases in particulate levels. As yet, the acute effects on human health of atmospheric sulfur dioxide without particulate, at present ambient levels, are not known. However it is almost impossible to conceive of a realistic situation in which we would encounter sulfur dioxide without particulate pollutants. This point is currently important because studies of sulfur dioxide alone have sometimes been misinterpreted in the press. Evidence is growing that exposure for 24 hours to about 0.2 parts per million of sulfur dioxide, with particulate present, represents a recognizable danger to health.

Carbon monoxide levels are high and are overwhelmingly due to motor vehicles. Concentrations are of course highest along crowded arterial streets and highways, especially at times of day when cars accelerate and decelerate in the speed range up to 40 miles per hour. The monoxide levels now exceed 30 parts per million occasionally and exceed 15 parts per million (ppm) very often for periods of eight hours or more in heavy traffic areas. The toxicity and general health effects for such carbon monoxide levels are subject to some dispute. New York aims for no eight-hour averages as high as 30 ppm and no more than 15 per cent of the eight-hour averages to exceed 15 ppm. Some changes in judgmental abilities and motor control have been reported from carbon monoxide levels of 30 ppm. It has been suggested that four to six hours of exposure to this concentration is equivalent, in terms of the oxygen-carrying capacity of the blood, to being at an altitude of 6,000 feet, without acclimating.

High CO Level

Clearly the carbon monoxide levels are not so high that people collapse on city streets from lack of oxygen. However they are high enough in selected places — tunnels, for example — to worry seriously about direct toxic effects. And, apart from the direct effects, one presumes that driving an automobile requires some skill and alertness, particularly in traffic, but the monoxide levels suggest that this may not be the case. Apparently, there are no studies as yet of possible correlations of carbon monoxide levels and automobile accident rates.

Sometimes air pollution has been the clear cause of injury and death. Called by the sardonic euphemism of "episodes," documented examples of those shameful incidents have occurred in the United States, Mexico, France, England and Japan. The "episode" that occurred in November and December of 1962 was quite remarkable in that it was recognized in the United States, England, Holland, Germany and Japan. The worst in terms of demonstrated mortality was the London "killer smog" of 1952: a conservative estimate puts the number of excess deaths from this one "episode" at 3,500 to 4,000, due to the pollutants that accumulated during the four days of the incident. Other estimates run to 8,000 or more.

Focusing attention on "episodes" is useful both because it does arouse public sentiment, and because it can be the basis for a reasonable expedient control strategy. However men have literally made the atmosphere nonviable in at least one place. The industrial city of Yokkaichi, Japan, is so badly polluted that its inhabitants were officially urged to move elsewhere.

One naturally wonders whether places such as Los Angeles will become uninhabitable. At present, it appears that people do build up some resistance to exposure to ozone; one noxious component in the atmosphere of brown air cities. Perhaps we can adapt to the entire complex of pollutants of photochemical smog, so that people can continue to move to Los Angeles, provided they condition themselves. Unfortunately, there is no indication of a build-up of resistance to the sulfur oxides from coal burning. In fact, sulfur dioxide may be radio-mimetic, causing damage to nucleic acids.

Control Strategies

Pollution abatement and air management strategies differ, depending on what the pollutants are and on the time scale of the control program. The easiest program to implement is usually one designed to control "episodes" by reducing peak pollutant concentrations for a few hours or days. This kind of program obviously represents the smallest perturbation of the society. Reducing chronic pollutant levels is usually a slow and moderately costly process; even the conversion of a single large boiler from one fuel to another may require an entire season.

The health problems and control strategies for gray air cities, brown air cities and cities polluted by single industries obviously differ. As yet, no critical short-term incident has been identified in which large numbers of people died from the photochemical smog of brown air cities. Brown air is more a source of severe chronic discomfort than of acute incidents of increased mortality. By contrast, most of the severe "episodes" occurred in gray cities, at times when sulfur dioxide and particulate levels were high. Yet people have tolerated chronic gray air conditions for hundreds of years with little more than grumbling.

The obvious Machiavellian inference is that in gray air cities, the public would probably be molified with abatement programs designed only to deal with incidents of dangerously high levels of sulfur dioxide and particulate. In brown air cities, we would have to reduce the chronic level of automotive pollutants below some intolerance level determined largely by our ability to adapt to these substances. In industrial areas, we would have to control odors and obnoxious visible stack products such as foams or sewage fumes. In fact, some major pollution control programs have in part taken this form. Such programs of expediency and minimum perturbation may be quite sinister, insofar as they sometimes pre-empt more fundamental approaches. But expedient programs may be necessary to save thousands of lives, because we may not get something better into effect before the next killer smog comes along.

A classic comedy situation arose when the New York City Council prohibited garbage burning—obviously a simple way to reduce air pollution quickly. Unfortunately no one had checked to see that other means were available for disposing of the garbage. Another example emphasizes the folly of the expedient approach. William Stanley, former Director of the Air Pollution Control Department of Chicago, often said: "Sure, I know how to get rid of air pollution from garbage-burning tomorrow; dump the garbage in the river."

What are the alternatives to the fast and expedient approach I have treated so cavalierly? We should examine these rather carefully; it may be that the cures are as bad as the disease or worse. In looking at ways to handle the air pollution problem, and some other problems too, we have to examine the effects of the cures and, eventually, the goals and values.

The complexities of trash and garbage disposal are easy to recognize as soon as one is sensitized to them. One quickly realizes that a reasonable control strategy must deal with collection and disposal problems of solid and liquid wastes, as well as with the incineration problem. Other areas of air pollution abatement may involve more subtle interactions, or sometimes interactions about which we can only speculate. It may be, for example, that sulfur dioxide from coal burning acts as an inhibitor for formation of photochemical smog from automotive pollutants. No one knows whether this actually occurs, but on chemical and observational grounds, it is a possibility we must examine. The answer may have a strong influence on the strategy of pollution control in gray air cities, at least for intermediate times of five to 20 years. This influence operates as follows: at the moment, it looks considerably easier to achieve control of the emission from coal (or oil) burning than of automotive emissions. If the two pollution systems, from coal burning and from automobiles, do not interact, then the strategy of choice is obviously to work in two stages, solving the easier problem first. This way we would get rid of the bulk of the sulfur dioxide and particulate from coal or oil as fast as possible. On the other hand, if sulfur dioxide were really helping to keep gray air cities free of photochemical smog, then the best strategy might be to reduce coal-burning and automotive pollutants together, even if this procedure meant removing sulfur dioxide slower than we would with a two-stage strategy.

No One Solution

The problems of pollution abatement are partly technological, partly economic and partly political. Let me explore one example in which engineering, economics and public pressure all have clear roles in determining the strategy, but for which there is no single clear solution. This is the problem of pollutants from coal-burning electric power plants. There are at least four possible directions for the electric power industry: improving the fuel quality, removing the pollutants (primarily sulfur dioxide and particulate), switching to gasified coal or re-siting the plants. Each has its own gains, its own alternative ways for implementation, and its own time scale.

Improving fuel quality normally means switching from coal containing about three per cent sulfur or more to coal with 1.5 per cent sulfur or less. This is probably the method most available. One can expect a 50 to 70 per cent reduction in sulfur dioxide this way. The low-sulfur coal costs two to six dollars per ton more than high-sulfur coal, and cannot be used in all furnaces. Presently, only dry-ash, and not "wet bottom" or slag-tap, furnaces are adapted for the high-melting ash of low-sulfur coal. Furthermore the amount of fly ash is approximately inversely proportional to the sulfur content in much coal, so that either greater precipitator capacity must be installed or more particulate will come out the stack. Partial desulfurization is another potential tool, but still presents formidable technical problems. With low-sulfur coal from either source, the net gain is a reduction by a factor of two or three in sulfur dioxide output, per ton of coal. However electric power requirements are predicted to increase by a factor of five by 1990, and 40 per cent of this power will be generated by coal burning. Hence the use of low-sulfur coal is at best a short-term expedient for badly polluted cities. Burning gas or low-sulfur oil is a possibility for short-term relief, but the supplies of both these fuels are limited.

Several chemical methods of removing sulfur dioxide from stack gas are either available or will become available in the near future. Most of these methods produce a by-product suitable for sale: sulfuric acid, elemental sulfur or ammonium sulfate, for example. The net cost to the company for the operation is estimated to be between $2.50 and $0.35 per ton of coal, and removes 90 per cent or more of the sulfur dioxide. One process with no by-product, based on reaction of sulfur dioxide with dolomite, has already been used at the Union Electric Company in St. Louis (with considerable problems) and in Lawrence, Kansas (with more success).

Any or all of these processes could almost surely be available very soon if a major engineering task force—a micro-NASA—were put to work on them. At the moment, effort is highly fragmented. The Electric Research Council is working at a leisurely pace on one, and industries in the gas-cleaning business are each trying to develop their own process with what in-house capability they may have. Two or three years ought to be a sufficient time for the development, engineering and installation of chemical controls, if the problem were treated as a national goal and the attack upon it were implemented accordingly.

Mine-mouth gasification is a possible direction but it will be at least another 18 months before the pilot plant stage is complete. It will probably be at least three to five years before even the best-situated coal mines could start supplying gas to electric power plants. Much of the technology is known already in Europe but to be competitive with American coal, the developers would have to develop designs and methods of their own.

Still further in the future is plant re-siting and power transmission by super-conducting transmission lines. Generating stations have lifetimes of 40 years or more; many large operating plants still have long useful lives. However the projected demand for electric power means we need many new plants. Presumably some of the new plants will replace existing facilities in polluted cities, and not merely supplement them. Moreover, in terms of use of natural resources, it may be sensible for many of the new power stations to burn high-sulfur coal, collect the sulfur oxides and convert them to salable by-products. The only serious limitation on this strategy will be the problem of the carbon dioxide that will be produced.

Other, still more exotic, methods to generate electric power also lie on the horizon as possibilities. Probably they will eventually be needed, but until there is strong motivation to work them out, they will remain exotic.

Let us assume that electric power companies will eventually reduce their pollution. Which course they choose will be a function of costs and of public pressure, as it appears in public policy. If public pressure is great enough, they may have to commit themselves to a mixed strategy, with short-term, intermediate, and long-term, abatement measures. For example, a relatively inexpensive short-term approach is complete or partial conversion from coal or high-sulfur oil to low-sulfur oil or coal—or, where it is available in sufficient quantity, to gas. The intermediate time range might be handled by chemical recovery of sulfur oxides from the flues, with high-sulfur fuel as the principal fuel. The long-term part of the solution might be construction of power plants at the mine sites, with all the technology for sulfur oxide and carbon dioxide collection built into the new plants.

Strategies

Whatever changes we choose to make, somebody has to pay. A basic problem with direct implications for our strategy of implementation is simply "Who should pay?"

I shall put off the question of punitive actions for the moment, because pollution is an area where punishment is only part of a strategy to achieve an end, and is never defensible for vengeance, that is, as an end in itself.

Who should pay? Who can be made to pay? The general public, which we can equate with those who presumably benefit from a clean environment, is one group. In many cases, probably in most cases, the "customers" of the polluter may be made to bear the costs. This includes the tenants of an apartment converting its furnace from coal to gas, as well as the buyers of steel from a company that installs precipitators. Utilities can, under existing law, pass the costs of capital equipment directly on to their customers; in fact they are entitled to obtain profit on this equipment. Hence the electric power rates will presumably go up as power companies install pollution control equipment. Operating costs cannot as readily be passed on as higher rates; there is a time lag because of the regulatory process for utility rates and the problem of determining what may be a fair profit. Another important situation, in which the polluter could be expected to bear part of the cost rather than pass it on to his customers, is the case of one polluting industry in a field, in which the other competitors are under no pressure to spend money on pollution control. The polluter, forced to control emission, must raise prices, cut other costs or work on a smaller profit margin until he has paid for his control measures. This case is probably more the exception than the rule. A third situation where the polluter could be made to pay for the privilege of polluting or for the cost of pollution control is the case of the private automobile.

Until last year's change in attitude, it was ridiculous to think a polluting industry would voluntarily control its pollution and bear the costs. Now that pollution control is becoming socially acceptable or even desirable, voluntary and self-supported abatement begins to look less like a laughably naive policy. However, no one has yet polled a company's stockholders to see whether they would let the cost of pollution control be absorbed in their dividends. It would be amusing to try.

Essentially, then, we can expect the costs of pollution control to be borne by the public or by the customers. A strict theory of benefits would say, in most cases, that the general public is the principal recipient of the benefits, so that public money should pay the costs. This could take the form of fast tax write-offs (which now operate), direct subsidies, or low-cost loans underwritten by the government; the form is not particularly relevant here. A theory based on harm, which seems to be the choice of some of the recent entrants to the anti-pollution campaign, would put the costs on the polluter. However, I hope the foregoing argument makes it clear that this would usually amount to passing the costs on to the polluter's customers. If expedience and speed, rather than benefits or harm, were the prime consideration, public financing would probably be the method of choice. Theories based on costs, especially in the broad sense used by most economists in this field, are roughly equivalent to a theory of harm. Cost theories have the difficulty that the inferences one draws are terribly sensitive to how broadly one defines costs, and how one deals with the valuation problems of health and aesthetics. At the present time there is another difficulty; the society is, in effect, trying to develop pollution management programs while it is changing its entire assessment of harm, costs and values. What still seems like a small cost to one part of American society has been re-evaluated now by another segment as a high cost, or a severe harm.

Polluters Pay

One other basis of judgment, my own current favorite, is one of negligence. This view, like the cost theory, has the danger of being all things for all men, when applied to pollution. However I see it as putting part of the responsibility for improvement on the negligent polluter, and part on the public for tolerating the muck we live in. Furthermore I see strong reason to use methods that get things done as soon as possible, especially when these things involve major research and development. The implication of this view is that we should spend substantial amounts of public money for air pollution control, but it also implies that each polluter should carry a significant share of the effort and costs of solving his own specific problems. We simply cannot wait for the coal industry to find economic ways of desulfurizing or gasifying goal, or for the steel industry to take voluntary initiative in developing effective controls for coking operations.

Let us grant that there is finally some public sentiment for change; how might governments and polluters now deal most effectively with the problems of abatement? Pollution problems will not go away spontaneously; we have some 800 years of historical precedent to make this assumption.

For the short term, roughly the next 20 years, we can afford to treat pollution problems as if they were primarily technical and administrative. We need new ways, far faster and more effective than those we have, to develop pollution control technology. We must develop and implement programs of pollution management to reduce the hazards of the environment that we are so rapidly making hostile. But it is terribly important to recognize and accept that the problem of environmental pollution is fundamentally neither technical nor administrative. The problem is far deeper and more difficult; it is really a problem of the goals and aspirations, of the manner of life of the human species. We shall return to this aspect in the final section.

Let us examine the administrative problems first. Several viewpoints which suggest themselves are based on whether one considers pollution and its control a matter of benefit, of blame, or of negligence. In effect, these different views imply different relative amounts of carrot and stick. To analyze the abatement problem, we also must consider the secondary effects of any pressure we apply, the public's degree of impatience, the inertia of polluters and the technological time scale. Whatever the approach, it is important to keep in mind that the goal is pollution abatement, or better, re-balancing technological benefits against the quality of our environment.

Interpreting pollution problems in terms of blame implies that the pressures for change should be more punitive than persuasive. Fines, taxes, jail and injunctive closure of plant operations have all been suggested or used. The concept of a pollution tax is popular in some quarters, particularly in connection with theories based on cost. Unfortunately, if my analysis is correct, in most cases where a pollution tax would be applied, the cost would be passed on to the polluter's customers who would have to pay this cost. In other words, the poor customer would pay for the privilege of letting his vendor pollute. The pollution tax would only be effective in situations where the polluter could not or would not pass the tax on to his customers. It is not at all clear that enough examples of this kind exist to make a general pollution tax effective or desirable. An exception is the private automobile; one could tax effluent from automobiles by taxing the fuel or, with inspections, the vehicles, and then use this money to pay for the development of lead-free gasoline refineries and catalytic muffler reactors, for example.

Pollution taxes are an indirect way of achieving an end. Proponents of such taxes have argued largely by showing how they would work successfully, without examining the alternative ways they might operate. In particular, the assumption is usually made that the effluent fee will drive the polluter into reducing his effluent. The obvious alternative is that he will pay the fee and pass it on to his customers, or simply absorb the fee. The closest thing to evidence on this in America comes from fines for pollution. Here, the chronic problem has been the difficulty of making the fines large enough to be punitive. In general, pollution fines have been notoriously ineffective as a device to reduce pollution; they are simply absorbed in operating costs. The landlord raises rents a little to pay the fines for [a] dirty coal furnace, rather than raising them enough to pay for conversion to oil or gas. I fear that effluent taxes would operate the same way.

In terms of real remedies, injunctive closure has been a much more effective force than a fine, particularly with industrial processes. Personal penalties, such as jail sentences, are another possibility. Thus far, we cannot judge their effectiveness. At one time, incidentally, air pollution in London was a capital crime.

If taxes, fines and jail sentences are the sticks, then subsidies, low-interest loans, tax benefits and technical assistance are the carrots that we could offer. A benefit theory makes these all reasonable possibilities: the public wants to get rid of pollution, so the public is the customer that should pay. This approach certainly appears at first sight to be the most efficient, in terms of overcoming the inertia of the polluters. It has not really been tried on a large scale, except in London. There, it was very effective recently in implementing smoke control program.

Cost-benefit analysis, at least in its more simplistic forms, seems inappropriate and possibly dangerous now for pollution and environmental problems. Apart from the usual difficulties of valuation, it may be too early. At this time, many harmful effects of pollution are just being demonstrated; we can expect to learn much more about effects of pollution on health in the next few years. It would be judicious to act now from a medically conservative position, using correlation studies, such as those of sulfur dioxide and particulate matter with morbidity and mortality, to define the strictest standards and goals, both long- and short-term, that our technology allows. In time, when we have a clearer understanding of the medical picture, we should consider a cost-benefit approach and a revision of the standards.

Now let us examine the technological aspect. One approach opened by the Air Quality Act of 1967, but not yet exploited widely, is the use of federal mission-oriented research and development money. True, the National Air Pollution Control Administration (NAPCA) has started in this direction by awarding money for research and development of air management methods: some 350 grants will be awarded in 1970 for these purposes. The NAPCA budget, however, is modest. A typical program within NAPCA, that of the Process Control Engineering Division, is doing some in-house research on one method of sulfur oxide removal, cooperates with other groups to study several other specific control methods, and is beginning to study the pollution problem more broadly, by trying to determine where research is needed.

Task Forces Needed

A different and more vigorous tack is available, and has been suggested in various forms. I shall state it in the way I like best: we could create strong, well-funded and highly directed task forces to solve specific technological problems of environmental management. These micro-NASA projects would be natural devices to move much faster than we now do with the development of chemical methods for removing pollutants from stack gases, with coal gasification, with developing automobiles and other, perhaps radically different transportation systems that produce far less pollution per passenger-mile or per passenger-trip. Industrial participation in these projects is clearly very desirable; once developed, the new technologies have to be produced and supplied to society. However we can expect, judging from the situation with which we are now wrestling, that industry alone will not ordinarily support major programs to do this engineering, at least not at a sufficiently rapid pace. We learned from NASA how fast a whole new technology can be created, developed, engineered and applied. We could use the space program as our model, learning from it what to do and what not to do, to solve many of the specific technical problems of environmental management that we can now define as precisely as John Kennedy defined the goal of putting men on the moon.

The National Laboratories have been suggested as natural locations for these task forces. This seems eminently reasonable to me. Programs could be developed in which in-house teams of broadly-trained scientists and engineers could work with larger groups of specialists on loan or leave from industries. Presumably the success of each task force would destroy the need for its existence. Moreover it looks as if we have enough major problems of research, development and engineering in environmental control to justify long-term support for continuing versatile in-house groups that would give the generalist's viewpoint in each new task force. University programs are starting to appear, from which these "environmentalists" can hopefully be drawn.

Clear solutions to some of the immediate outstanding technical problems would do much to resolve our critical pollution problems, at least on an intermediate time scale. Financial inducements in the form of tax credit or direct subsidies would equally well induce major polluters to develop and install the devices, and adopt the control methods that our task forces would presumably produce. This is admittedly the approach of an impatient man, and I concede to being guilty of impatience. I would like to persuade many others to be as impatient as I am.

At the same time that we try to solve well-defined technical problems, we can look at the harder, more ill-defined problems of consumption of raw materials, goods and energy, the problems of environmental management that we are learning to recognize. These are problems that deserve careful, scholarly investigation. We cannot expect to achieve a basic solution of the solid waste problem, or the urban transportation problem, or the problem of restoring a dead lake to some still-undefined "healthy" state, by a crash program. They are the long-term problems that require that we consider the effects of each proposed solution. Recognition of these as deep-seated problems is symptomatic of a technological society just realizing that it must pay the piper. Programs in universities and national laboratories have started to appear with advertised intentions to deal with these grand-scale problems, and a little federal money may be available, even in these times, to support them.

At this time, the most hopeful possibilities for relief seem to lie in the Federal Air Quality Act of 1967. The definition of Air Quality Control Regions, with precisely defined standards of air quality, in terms of specific ambient pollutant levels and time-schedules, represents a broader, clearer and more direct approach to air quality management than any this country has ever seen before. Taking these steps was extremely important, but the most critical step of all is the one we now confront: adopting implementation procedures. Here is where the aroused and — presumably — informed public, with its newly-awakened concern for the environment, can help determine the quality of the air it breathes.

Ultimate Catastrophes

Let me move on to an apocalyptic note. We almost surely can mange the environment, and maybe clean it, for another 20, perhaps even 50 years. It is virtually certain that we cannot do this indefinitely, the way we now live. All sorts of cataclysms await us. In air pollution, the increasing concentration of carbon dioxide is a popular favorite. There is a reasonable possibility that there will be enough carbon dioxide in the atmosphere in 2020 to create a greenhouse effect, melt the polar icecaps and inundate the coastal cities. Certainly the carbon dioxide concentration is rising just a bit less than one ppm per year, or about 0.3 per cent per year. Not surprisingly, opposed to the hot-world people (those who believe that carbon dioxide will warm up the earth) is a group of cold-world people, who believe that the increasing opacity of the upper atmosphere, due to particulate matter, will reduce the amount of sunlight absorbed by the earth and ultimately cause a new ice age. It has even been suggested that we use these opposing effects and balance the carbon dioxide and particulate in the atmosphere to keep our climate temperate.

I myself have tried my hand at the game of cataclysms by examining the rate at which we consume energy, and comparing this rate to the rate at which we absorb energy from the sun. If we are successful in developing the underdeveloped nations and in maintaining the growth of the developed nations, then in two or three hundred years, we will be spending energy as fast as we absorb it. One rather clear conclusion of this estimate, albeit a far-reaching one, is that we can look forward to our grandchildren and great-grandchildren living with some sort of energy rationing.

Another favorite apocalypse of my own is due to the world-wide appearance of lead in the atmosphere. Present levels are supposedly well below industrial toxic levels, but only by about a factor of three. However statements to this point are usually carefully worded to say that the chronic effects of very low doses are not known. One of the effects of chronic lead poisoning is to make its victims stupid. I sometimes think we have passed that critical threshold.

At the risk of repeating the most popular platitude of 1969, I want to point out again that we must understand and select a balance between the benefits of our technology and the benefits of a clean environment. We can have both, at least for a time, but we must recognize the costs. For the next 50 years or so, we can afford the price of clean air and water. Public sentiment at the moment even suggests that perhaps we shall soon be willing to pay it. Until 1969, just the opposite seemed the case. We can see this by comparing the death rate from the worst air pollution "episodes" with an excess death rate (i.e., available by existing means) that we know American society has tolerated. The death rate in Vietnam has been between 20 and 40 per 100,000 per week. This is just about the death rate in the London smog of 1952, and is roughly 10 times that of November 5 to 11, 1969, in Chicago. In plain words, we have been killing ourselves with air pollution, but only at a rate that society seems willing to sustain. The new concern has come well before pollution-caused mortality has reached a disaster level. Let us take sensible advantage of this period of grace.

No Deposit No Return

ROBERT R. GRINSTEAD*

Each family in the United States discards, on the average, a ton of empty packages each year. Some of these are made of paper and decay quickly; some are plastic and uncorrodable and imperishable. These may outlast all other monuments of our civilization. Some empty packages are burned in municipal incinerators, adding to air pollution; many simply litter roads, streams, beaches, and parks. Taken together, the empty cans, bottles, boxes, and bubble-packs that we discard are creating a mountain of trash which is beginning to exceed the available space for disposal.

This situation stimulated the gathering of some 300 representatives of government, industry and academia at the First National Packaging Wastes Conference in San Francisco on September 22 to 24, 1969. The co-sponsors of the conference, the U.S. Bureau of Solid Wastes Management, the Packaging Industry Advisory Committee, and the University of California at Davis, succeeded in assembling a surprising variety of points of view and professional expertise. During the two-and-a-half day session, economists described the size and shape of the problem. Corporation executives outlined the contributions of packaging manufacturers. Scientists and engineers reported on technical developments. Public officials pleaded for immediate solutions. Even psychologists and publicists discoursed on the motivation of people to take individual action to reduce the packaging waste disposal problem.

San Francisco's ingenious, albeit controversial proposal to ship its trash off to the wilds of Northern California made the city an appropriate locale for the gathering. As Mayor Joseph L. Alioto told the gathering in his official welcome, San Francisco is undecided about what to do with its trash, and his best wishes to the conference therefore bore a note of special urgency.

The Bulk of Cities' Trash

The size and character of the packaging disposal problem were outlined to the

*Reprinted from ENVIRONMENT (November 1969), pp. 17-23. Copyright © 1969 by Committee for Environmental Information. Figures deleted.

conference by economists Eric B. Outwater and Arsen Darney, Jr. A significant aspect of the problem, Darney told them, is that since nearly all of the packaging material is discarded by that well-known character, the individual consumer, or by the retailer who serves him, the packaging waste disposal problem is virtually synonomous with the municipal trash disposal problem. Some 60 million tons are created in the U.S. each year, just about one ton per family. While this represents only about one-third of the average municipal pickup, most of the remainder is made up of similar materials, mainly newspapers and reading matter, plus miscellaneous metal, glass, and plastic discards. Wet garbage, lawn clippings, and other yard debris actually account for only twenty to thirty percent of the total.

Delegates listened intently to Leonard Stefanelli, President of the Sunset Scavenger Company of San Francisco, who unburdened himself on the woes of the modern day scavenger operator. Where once upon a time rags, bottles, paper, and numerous other items could be salvaged at a profit from the trash pickups, not even newspapers were valuable now, complained Stefanelli, and corrugated paper board was the only significant reclaimable item.

Listeners winced a bit at Stefanelli's criticism that the continually changing materials—the pride of the packaging industry—contributed still further to his troubles in developing efficient salvage procedures.

Salvage problems are not the only cause for concern, however. Speakers who followed listed several factors as contributors to the increasing packaging waste disposal problem.

Rapidly rising quantities. Packaging wastes are increasing at the rate of six percent a year, against a one percent increase in population.

More complex materials. Use of composite materials, such as laminates, metallized paper and plastics, and paper products containing a variety of impregnated chemicals is rising. This seriously impedes attempts to salvage materials for reuse.

Greater variety of materials. This is particularly true of plastics, but the aluminum beer can is also a conspicuous example.

Increasing damage to the environment. Because most waste dumps are poorly managed, they contribute significantly to pollution of nearby streams, and, where burning is practiced, to pollution of the atmosphere.

Decreasing disposal space. Most cities dispose of trash in open dumps, which require substantial amounts of land. Increasing scarcity of land, particularly in urban areas, worries most large cities, many of which have gone or are seriously considering going to other methods.

Increasingly stable materials. The requirements of resistance of the package to rough treatment, weathering, and the action of its contents have led to materials which are simply more resistant to breakdown.

Taken together, this impressive array of trends clearly foreshadows rising costs of disposal for packaging wastes. At the present time the bulk of this cost is mainly in the collection from the individual houses or businesses. Hugh Marius of the Sanitation Department of New York City told delegates that that city's collection costs averaged $27 per ton, or about $50 per garbage can per year. Sanitary landfill disposal added only $2 to this, but New York is rapidly running out of fill space. Conversion to incinerators is under way, but this will up the disposal tag from $2 to $5 per ton. Marius also pointed to a problem which has mushroomed in his city within the last few years: the abandoned car, of which 50,000 were hauled off that city's streets in 1969 alone.

Who Will Pay the Costs?

Industry spokesmen sparked a major controversy in this initial session with statements that since the consumer was the one who created the waste, he should therefore bear the burden of additional costs to dispose of it. Consumers, they maintained, demand increasing convenience, service, and attractiveness in their purchases, and the industry has had to respond to these demands. Housewives demand, for example, that baby food come in jars instead of cans, according to Virgil Wodicka, a Hunt-Wesson Foods executive, and the industry has had to comply.

Arrayed against these views were those of a number of speakers, led by Alfred Heller of the conservationist organization California Tomorrow. They reminded the industry that much packaging material also serves as advertising matter, and is not of any special help to the consumer in carting his purchase home. The so-called "bubble" package, in which a small hardware (or similar) item is embalmed in a half a square foot or so of cardboard and an equal spread of transparent plastic, was cited as one example.

Both points of view appeared to have merit, the rapidly increasing volume of material being a result of both demands by consumers for convenience and attempts by manufacturers to outdo their competitors. Numerous speakers during the following sessions, including industry spokesmen, agreed that manufacturers should undertake serious efforts to both reduce the amount of material and to increase the ease of disposing of it after use.

Not so easily resolved was the companion question of where to obtain the revenue to pay for the increased disposal costs. Suggestions came in all shades, from simply taking it directly from the consumer by increases in collection fees to taxes of various sorts on the manufacturer of the package itself. Industry delegates voiced the expected alarm at the prospect of another encroachment of government regulatory power, but Congressman P. N. (Pete) McCloskey of California's Eleventh District warned them, at a luncheon address, that the packaging industry could not stand idly by in the face of a mounting problem such as this. He called on the industry to take some initiative in developing solutions to the disposal of its products. Congress, he said, was in the process of rearranging its priorities, and was becoming more concerned about such things as pollution and waste disposal. Should it decide the problem was getting out of hand, Congress would most likely focus its interest on the source of packaging material, the manufacturer.

Similar thoughts were offered by Congressman Henry Reuss of Wisconsin. Reuss pointed to the already considerable federal involvement through research funds to provide for better methods of disposing of solid wastes.

Irving Bengelsdorf, Science Editor of the Los Angeles, California, *Times,* provided the final word at the last session of the meeting. He chided the packaging industry for shrinking from federal taxation to pay for waste disposal, while at the same time asking for federal money to finance research in the field. He suggested the possibility of an industry-wide research effort to seek new answers to the waste problem.

Packaging Industry Developing Solutions

Having heard about all of the problems connected with disposing of packaging wastes, the conference turned to possible solutions. Engineers and scientists provided some interesting glimpses of developments on the way.

Paper. The largest single component of the packaging business is paper products, of which about half is corrugated board. G. K. Provo of the Crown-Zellerbach Corporation pointed out that something like twenty percent of this board is now recycled—that is, returned to the manufacturing process—as is a good deal of other paper scrap. For the most part, however, this is mainly production scrap or clean boxes obtained from business consumers. Some fibreboard is salvaged from municipal refuse, but by and large the paper component of this stream of waste goes to the dump. An obvious solution to much of the problem is therefore the reclamation of more of this waste paper.

Metals. Tin cans, according to Dr. L. P. Gotsch of the American Can Company, are on the way out. The aluminum can has already appeared, and steel producers are switching to a chrome- and resin-coated steel can. This will be much more acceptable to the steel mills when it appears as scrap.

Glass. Glass technologists have been experimenting with various ideas for using scrap glass, some of which were described by E. R. Owens of the Owens-Illinois Glass Company. These include incorporation of the scrap glass into vinyl floor tiles, insulation, and other construction materials.

One of the most fascinating projects underway was described by Clemson College's Professor Samuel Hulbert who, with the support of the U.S. Bureau of Solid Wastes, has developed a glass material which decomposes upon contact with water. Hulbert has also come up with various coatings which protect the material from moisture until the coating is cracked or broken, after which the bulk of the material decomposes into silica and other natural minerals. In large quantities, however, these breakdown products may also be difficult to dispose of.

This development illustrates one of the dilemmas of the waste engineer, namely that "improvements" in disposability often merely transform the problem into a different one. In this case, should beer bottles end up being flushed down the sink instead of being tossed into the garbage can, the problem will simply be transferred from the garbage dump or incinerator to the sewage plant.

Conservationists also may view such a development with mixed feelings, since anything which speeds up the decomposition of bottles tossed out along the roadsides runs the risk of encouraging exactly this method of disposal.

Plastics. Although a relatively small part of the waste problem, the plastic component is growing rapidly, and no simple means of salvaging plastic waste for reuse is on the horizon. The Dow Chemical Company's T. B. Becnel pointed out that the industry is concentrating on efficient means of incineration as a means of disposal. Plastics are both a desirable and an undesirable component of trash which is to be incinerated. Because of their relatively high fuel value, plastic materials improve the incineration of trash and garbage mixtures. But some plastics, mainly the vinyl types, liberate extremely corrosive hydrogen chloride when burned. This leads to increasing maintenance costs and requires highly efficient cleaning-up equipment for the stack gases.

Most of the developments, under close scrutiny, struck some observers as nibbles at the problem of packaging waste disposal. The efforts of the packaging industry, while significant, are directed either at the wastes generated in their own operations, or at nominal reductions in size or complexity of the mounting volume of packaging material. Few schemes seemed likely to be able to cope with the immediate problem: how to dispose of the mushrooming output of packaging waste now threatening to engulf the nation's cities.

Squeeze or Burn?

The two most promising approaches for handling the total waste stream seem to be incineration or some sort of compaction-plus-dumping. Development of the latter idea has been carried to its highest stage by a Japanese firm, which presented a film describing its process at the conference. In their scheme, raw garbage is compressed into a block under a pressure of 3,000 pounds per square inch. At this point, they claim, the resulting block is sterile and sufficiently dense to use for building blocks or for disposal in the ocean. As an added precaution, the blocks are usually encased in chicken wire plus concrete or asphalt. Just how much compressed garbage can be absorbed in construction uses is not clear, and ocean disposal will no doubt be limited to coastal areas. Nor has the long-term stability of the blocks been proven. Nevertheless, some experts see this as an immediate, though possibly limited, solution to the solid waste disposal problem.

Incineration can also deal with the entire output of trash and garbage, Elmer Kaiser, a professor of engineering at New York University, told delegates. He stressed that, from an engineering standpoint, incineration is a highly developed operation. While utilized currently for only about ten percent of the municipal waste load in the U.S., incineration seems likely to be the next candidate as open dumps and landfills disappear before increasingly rigid air pollution codes and spiralling land costs. Most urban refuse has a fuel value about half that of coal, and as a bonus, some power can be generated to help pay the tab. Yet to be answered, however, is whether increasing use of incineration in urban areas may necessitate stricter codes on stack gas emissions, raising costs another notch.

Unfortunately, incineration does not provide a complete solution, since the residue usually constitutes about one-third of the weight of the trash fed in. This residue, however, is sterile, makes good landfill, and is much more amenable to various salvaging schemes than the raw garbage.

The rather substantial amounts of residue from incineration processes lead to nagging suspicions that in time even this may become a disposal problem. The concept of total reclamation of all solid wastes, or at least of packaging wastes, was therefore clearly on the minds of many of those in attendance. It appeared as a kind of mirage, however—a vision of something to come in the distant future. Nevertheless, a number of speakers referred to the problems involved in greater salvage of wastes as technically feasible but at present economically unacceptable.

Trends

It is probably too much to expect a gathering of 300 individuals from as diverse a set of backgrounds to agree on many details of how to manage a problem of this size. Yet it seemed that some consensus had developed in three general areas as the meetings concluded.

First, the individual consumer appears to be a key factor in finding solutions to the waste problem. Professor P. E. McGauhey, of the University of California, Berkeley, Sanitary Engineering Laboratory, cautioned delegates that solutions to the waste disposal problem must be acceptable to the citizen. Other speakers generally agreed that the individual must be convinced that the sloppy and in-efficient disposal methods in use today carry an increasing cost to the environment. He must be persuaded that he would be better off paying these costs now in the form of increased municipal trash disposal rates or in a little extra effort in segregating his own trash, than later on in the form of polluted streams, smoggy skies, and blighted countryside.

Second, considerable effort is still needed on the technical front, not only to minimize the amount of packaging and the difficulty of disposing of the complex materials in use, but also to develop better methods of collecting, sorting, cleaning, and disposing of the waste itself. Efforts of the federal agencies charged with the task of developing better solutions to the disposal problem, while heroic, are pitifully small. Congressman Reuss underlined this point when he compared the $15 million spent by the U.S. Bureau of Solid Waste Management on research and demonstration plants to the $300 million spent by the Department of Defense on chemical and biological warfare research. This, Reuss maintained, indicated a serious misplacement of our priorities.

Finally, both the private and the public sectors of the economy must work together. The packaging industry must scrutinize its own operations to minimize the magnitude of the problem. But industry of all sorts may have contributions to make through research—perhaps contracted for with government agencies—directed at the salvage problem. The federal government has a major role to play through provision of this research money. But both it and lower levels of government can also be useful in careful use of the taxing power to encourage use of readily disposable materials, and to encourage placing of a value on preservation of the environment.

Noise — A Syndrome of Modern Society

CLIFFORD R. BRAGDON*

Urban noise occurs around the clock. Garbage trucks announce the arrival of the day. In apartments, the sounds of the neighbor's children, pets and television pierce the morning silence. On the way to work, general traffic din and the cacaphony of building construction and street repair projects continuously assault the ears. The work environment is another auditory experience. Noise has been recognized for years as a problem in factories. Now general office design, with its expansive glass areas, open spaces, narrow partitions and hard acoustic surfaces, enclosing typewriters, telephones air conditioners and business machines, may create noise exceeding industrial levels.

Home offers little refuge when the urban dweller returns in the evening. Our heating-ventilating systems, plumbing and home appliances hiss, chug, hum, swish and grind indoors while the walls of the house or apartment building only partially subdue the roar of automobile and air traffic from outside, making us aware in mind and body that noise is an ever present part of our contemporary urban life.

It is becoming increasingly clear that noise is an environmental pollutant comparable to air and water pollution. Already, noise in metropolitan areas sometimes surpasses standards for maximum noise levels established for industrial workers. Expanding population, expanding technology and expanding industry foreshadow greater noise to come.

We tend to think of noise mainly as a general nuisance and to react by simply clapping our hands over our ears to shut out the nuisance when it becomes unbearable. We do this literally as individuals and figuratively as communities with ordinances against specific noises such as automobile horns.

A better understanding of the rising noise level, its known effects, and the possible hazard of a continuing increase is needed. We will then be better able to assess the importance of noise in weighing the benefits and costs of technological innovations which contribute additional noise and to consider what steps, if any, we want to take to reduce this environmental pollutant.

One man's music is another man's noise. This is one of the difficulties in the way of a more scientific approach to noise. Noise cannot be understood by considering physical properties alone; it also has a subjective basis. In fact, for all practical purposes, noise can be defined as unwanted sound. The sound of roaring motors may be part of the fun to drag racers; the same sound is noise to people living by the side of the road.

Sound is measured from a base called the "threshold of hearing." This is the weakest atmospheric pressure from sound waves that can be detected audibly by a young ear under ideal listening conditions. The units of sound measurement are decibels. As the number of decibels goes up from the threshold of hearing, the sound intensity or loudness increases exponentially—that is, a twenty decibel sound is ten times louder than a ten decibel sound; a thirty decibel sound is ten times louder than a twenty decibel sound, and so on. The table below gives a series of noise sources, the level of sound they produce in decibels and the relative change in sound intensity or loudness as the decibels increase.

Generally speaking, the louder or more intense a noise is, the more annoying it is. Yet two sounds of equal intensity do not necessarily have the same effect. A patterned sound is less annoying than one that is random — particularly if the random noise is sudden and unfamiliar.

Noise Levels

Noise Source	Decibels	Relative Change in Sound Energy
Threshold of Hearing	0	1
Whispering	30	1,000
Conversation	60	1,000,000
Food Blender	80	100,000,000
Heavy Traffic	100	10,000,000,000
Jet Aircraft	120	1,000,000,000,000

A high pitched sound is more annoying than a low pitched sound. Thus, it is important to consider not only the decibels, which express pressure or loudness but also the cycles per second, which express frequency or pitch. With frequency as with intensity, the effect of noise differs depending on its regularity or irregularity. A pure tone which vibrates at the same frequency till it ceases is less irritating than "white noise" which is a random mixture of frequencies.

Frequencies are usually expressed in eight "octave bands." Each band represents the doubling of the cycles per second. 37.5 to 75 cycles per second is one octave band; 75 to 150 cycles per second is another and so on up to 4800 to 9600 cycles per second. Above 20,000 cycles per second, the frequency is up where (as Flanders and Swan have it)

> "The ear can't hear as high as that
> But it ought to please any passing bat."

There are differences of opinion about permissible occupational noise levels. The American Academy of Ophthalmology and Otolaryngology states that at present our knowledge of the relations of noise-exposure to hearing loss is much too limited for us to propose safe amounts of noise exposure. However, the Academy recommends noise-exposure control and tests of hearing if there is habitual exposure to continuous noise at eighty-five decibels at a frequency of 300 to 1200 cycles per second. The British Medical Society recommends hearing conservation measures when noise intensity exceeds 85 decibels in the frequency range of 250-4,000 cycles per second. The U.S. Air Force recommends ear defenders when personnel are exposed to 85 decibels in the 300-4800 cycle per second frequency range.

Some industrial standards simply set the amount of hearing loss which will permit a worker in a noisy industry to collect compensation. In California, the

State Department of Industrial Relations requires ear protection if a worker is exposed for more than five hours a day to ninety-five decibels or more above 300 cycles per second. The American Standards Association has suggested some permissible daily quotas of exposure to noise which they suggest should protect a worker from hearing loss. Over an eight-hour working day, they suggest a limit of eighty-five decibels at any frequency above 700 cycles per second.

In the Soviet Union, it is recommended that industrial noise levels should not exceed seventy decibels.

Only recently has there been concern about entire urban areas as well as occupational environments. As Dougherty and Welsh have commented:

> The saving quality heretofore has been that community noise has been a short-term exposure as compared to an 8 hour day period in industry. As the power use of both home and street increases, steps must be taken to limit the noise output. Otherwise, total timed exposures will exceed industrial standards, standards that actually rely on regular audiograms to prevent severe hearing loss.

Effects of Noise on Health

Health — as defined by the World Health Organization — is not simply the absence of disease but more comprehensively, physical, mental and social well-being. To assess the total effect of noise on health, both direct physical effects and less direct mental and social effects must be considered.

The Organ of Corti, located within the cochlea of the inner ear, is the site of hearing loss induced by noise. Damage to the Organ of Corti impairs the hearing function. The noted audiologist Joseph Sataloff describes the process in this way:

> Sound induced motion of the fluid in the cochlea induces shearing and bending movements of the hair cells in the Organ of Corti, which, in turn, result in electrical stimuli transmitted by the auditory nerve. Prolonged and excessive noise eventually produces deterioration and, finally destruction of hair cells, and thus disrupts the sound transmission mechanism.

A short exposure to intense noise may result in a temporary loss in hearing acuity, from which the ear recovers, usually within twenty-four hours. This is called a temporary threshold shift; it changes the individual's threshold of hearing from that base line at which we begin to measure decibels to a threshold that may exclude whispering (thirty decibels) or even conversation (about sixty decibels). With more severe exposure to noise or with repeated exposure, recovery of the threshold is not complete and a permanent threshold shift — a permanent hearing loss — remains.

The early stages of deafness are frequently unnoticed because loss of hearing occurs first in the upper frequencies, above the 3000 cycles per second level that is essential to clear understanding of the spoken word. We tend to have difficulty in understanding speech before we realize that we are losing our hearing. It is possible for audiometric examination to reveal up to a forty per cent hearing impairment in both ears without such deterioration being detected subjectively.

It seems reasonable to suspect a definite relationship between a temporary and a permanent threshold shift at the onset of hearing loss. A test was devised for predicting the magnitude of a permanent threshold shift, based on the temporary threshold shift experience at the beginning of exposure, but this has recently been challenged by Dr. Joseph Sataloff.

Defects in hearing may be the most common significant disability in the United States, with noise the probable primary cause. The American Mutual Insurance Alliance estimates that between five and six million members of the work force suffer enough auditory impairment to make hearing of speech difficult. Research by Dr. Aram Glorig indicates that approximately six million men have work conditions potentially damaging to hearing.

As for the general population, a recently published report by the Public Health Service suggests that 6,500,000 persons have impaired hearing in one or both ears. The Save Your Hearing Foundation believes that hearing disability involves over 15,000,000 persons. Data indicating the extent and degree of hearing loss for the general population cannot be considered comprehensive because surveys have been conducted only on specific population and age groups. Nevertheless, hearing loss is generally recognized as the major hazard of a noisy environment.

In Western civilization it has been taken for granted that some hearing loss normally occurs with the aging process independent of environmental factors. However, the possibility that this hearing loss is in part the cumulative result of "ordinary" noise in our life is suggested by some revealing work by Dr. Samuel Rosen with the Maaban tribe of Sudan. In this environment, except for tribal celebrations and domestic sounds, community noises generally remain under forty decibels. Dr. Rosen investigated 541 tribespeople ranging in age from ten to ninety and found neither the progressive elevation of blood pressure nor the high-tone hearing loss which occur with aging to varying degrees in most individuals in Western civilization.

It is possible that one or more conditions other than noise, which correlate with age in Western society but not in the Sudan might be the major factor in Western loss of hearing. Atherosclerosis and hypertension are two such possible conditions. Dr. Roy Sullivan warns that findings such as Dr. Rosen's should be interpreted "with caution, in light of cultural, hereditary, diet and other environmental differences between the two societies." More recent work by Dr. Rosen indicates that actual loss of hearing, beginning with the young adult, may be an indicator of later atherosclerosis and heart disease.

The physiological effects of noise are not limited to the ear, although little is known about the relationship of other mechanisms to health. A Soviet study cited in a recent United Nations report indicates that long-term exposure to intensive high-frequency noise produces numerous temporary shifts in the activities of the central nervous and circulatory systems. Muscular tension, increased heart and respiratory rates and contraction of the arterioles (minute arteries) have been noted. Peripheral constriction of the blood vessels persists as a normal response to repeated moderate noises, according to several sources, although some adaptation occurs.

Noise is a stress; one which is often intense, repetitive or of long duration. The body responds to stress with a variety of hormonal and neurological mechanisms. It is believed that some of these responses, when prolonged or repeated, may contribute to the development of progressive psychosomatic disease, or may worsen such disease after it has developed. Noise may therefore sometimes be a factor in such diseases as peptic ulcer and essential hypertension. However, plausible as it may be to assign noise a role in a number of health problems, only in the case of deafness has a direct relationship been proved.

There are a number of ways in which noise interferes with our daily activities and thus may indirectly affect our health and well being.

Interference with Sleep

Depth, continuity and duration of sleep all affect its recuperative value and all may in turn be affected by noise.

A recent summary of sleep research states:

> Sleep deprivation experiments have demonstrated that the lack of sleep alone can produce deterioration in behavior — even symptoms like those of psychosis — and that sleeplessness is accompanied by biochemical changes in the body. It may not be surprising that sleep loss, even relatively mild, should exacerbate the symptoms of psychotic patients.

Current studies indicate that the phase of sleep characterized by rapid eye movements is the dream stage, and is the most essential. It occurs predictably four or five times each night and accounts for twenty to twenty-five per cent of adult sleeping time. A generalized excitable state may develop if rapid eye movement (REM) sleep is disrupted. In experiments depriving humans of REM sleep, certain psychological changes were observed which suggested that more serious disturbances were impending.

Sleep deprivation experiments with cats show that they become excessively hungry, eat abnormal amounts of food, and are continually restless and sexually hyperactive.

Little research has been undertaken specifically to assess the role of noise in upsetting human sleep, but it is known that the REM sleep phase can be disrupted by noise. Dr. Rosen, commenting on current sleep studies at the Stanford Research Institute, indicates that the electroencephalographic (brain wave) patterns of sleeping subjects can be radically altered by sound without the subject awakening.

Some research has been done in the U.S.S.R. on the relationship of noise to sleep in general.

> When noise is at a level of fifty decibels ... falling asleep is a lengthy process (one and a half hours) and there are fairly short intervals of deep sleep (one hour) followed, on waking, by a sense of fatigue accompanied by palpitations. The level of thirty-five decibels can be considered as the threshold for optimum sleeping conditions, since at this level it takes only twenty minutes to fall asleep and the period of deep sleep lasts from two to two and a half hours.

A thirty-five decibel standard for night noise was also recommended in the *Final Report on Noise* presented in 1963 to the British Parliament. The British survey recorded a noise level of 49-61 decibels on main residential roads during night hours. Even residential roads with only local traffic had 45-53 decibels and minor roads had 43-49 decibels. Noise levels in parks, courtyards and gardens in residential areas well away from traffic were no lower than 41-46 decibels.

Exterior community noises can be reduced by about 10-25 decibels when they penetrate a dwelling. Even with this reduction, the level of noise within homes on some of these roads would frequently exceed the recommended thirty-five decibel standard.

Interference with Communication

Auditory communication often alerts us to possible danger; when noise interferes with communication it may be hazardous. For example, accidents sometimes occur because a driver does not hear an ambulance siren or does not hear it soon enough. This may be the result of traffic noises or may be because he has turned on his radio, his heater or his air conditioner. Emergency vehicle accidents may be due to man's increasing inability to hear and to sort out the various noises which surround him and to distinguish important sound messages from background noises which mask the message. Auditory messages compete for perceptual recognition just as do visual messages.

The effect of noise interference on conversation may not be dramatic; unheard speech, unlike an unheard siren, is not likely to send a man to the hospital. Yet speech communication is a basic human tool and we are affected when intruding noises make it difficult for us to talk together. We find it hard to relax as well as to converse. Behavioral responses such as frustration and increased anxiety may result from the simple fact that background noises have made conversation difficult.

For easy listening, ninety-seven per cent of the spoken words should be heard correctly. Listening becomes fatiguing when ninety per cent or less of the words are heard. Although most speech sounds are below 3000 cycles per second, in order to hear speech completely it is essential to hear all sounds in the frequency range from 200 to 6000 cycles per second. The higher frequencies are found in the consonant sounds which are the primary determinants of intelligibility.

When background noise approaches 80 decibels, it causes a significant decline in hearing accuracy. Maximum permissible levels of background noise have been established, known as speech interference levels (SIL). The SIL index is based on averaged decibel readings for frequencies in three octave bands (600–1200; 1200–2400; 2400–4800 cycles per second). One study indicates that, while telephone conversations are nearly unimpaired with an SIL of 55–65 decibels, they are impossible at an SIL reading over 75 decibels. A 65–75 decibel SIL barely permits conversation with raised voices when the speakers are more than two feet apart. An SIL of less than 55 decibels is desirable in an office.

Interference with Performance

Research on noise in industry has dealt with its effect on performance as well as its effect on hearing, and has generally shown the ability of industrial workers to do specific tasks unaffected by noise. Most of these studies were based on short-term exposure to noise.

In recent years performance experiments have been broadened to include multiple task analysis and mental as well as physical tasks. These new studies suggest that the conclusion that performance is unaffected by noise needs to be reevaluated, although some results are contradictory, and we still have inadequate information about performance when noise is sustained over a long period.

Performance is least affected by expected noise. In situations where noise occurs unexpectedly, and is unfamiliar to the perceiver there is a greater tendency for work efficiency to be altered. To a degree, we subjectively adjust to noise when it develops a familiar pattern.

Some evidence suggests that as noise reaches higher decibel ranges, particular skills are affected. In tasks requiring continuous attention there are increases in errors and in failures to notice unexpected events if noise is above ninety decibels. When noise becomes extremely intense—above 120 decibels—performance is severely curtailed unless protective hearing devices are worn. Beside noticeable pain and damage to the unprotected ear, there are many unpleasant body sensations. These sensations may include vibrations in the head, movement of air in the nose, loss of equilibrium, and vision disturbance.

If performance is defined simply as the ability to complete a task while exposed to noise, without consideration for associated stress, the total effect of noise will not be appreciated.

Property Damage

People living in the vicinity of an airport have complained of damage to their homes as well as interference with sleep and the general nuisance of subsonic aircraft noise. The introduction of the supersonic aircraft with its attendant sonic boom has produced a tremendous increase in property damage complaints.

These have been caused by flights of the relatively small military supersonic planes. The giant supersonic transport (SST) which is still in the process of development would present a greater sonic boom problem, and for this reason, the SST may be limited to intercontinental flights. Secretary of the Interior Udall recently appointed a scientific committee to look into the effects of sonic booms from the SST. The sonic boom and other problems of the SST were discussed by Dr. Kurt Hohenemser in the April and September 1966 issues of *Scientist and Citizen* and are brought up to date with another article in [the March 1968] issue. They will therefore not be discussed in detail here.

Economics of Noise

The cost of noise in dollars has been measured in only a few cases.

☐ During the past fifteen years, industrial workers have been awarded approximately fifteen million dollars for noise-induced hearing loss. Workers in noisy industries are now making noise costly to employers before, rather than after hearing loss is sustained. For example, the Steel Workers' contract stipulates that employees required to work in abnormal environments receive compensatory pay. Intense noise is one such abnormal work stress which can cost management an additional five to ten cents per man hour.

☐ Current law suits for health and physical damage, principally from subsonic jet aircraft noise involve claims for more than two million dollars in damages. For example, ten families have sued the city of Los Angeles for $400,000, contending that they have suffered permanent hearing damage and emotional disturbance from jets at the Los Angeles International Airport.

☐ Sonic boom claims presented to the U.S. Air Force during the fiscal years 1956–1967 amounted to almost $20 million. Approved claims, with money actually awarded however, amounted to only $1.3 million. In Southwestern France more than $400,000 has been awarded to satisfy property damage claims to area residents due to flights of the Mirage IV supersonic bomber.

The economic benefits of reducing environmental noise have not been studied. They are difficult to measure, as are the added pleasure, health and comfort of a quieter environment.

Is Noise Necessary?

In other ages as well as in other cultures, man's sense of hearing may have been keener. Without artificial light, man necessarily depended more extensively on observations by ear. Today's emphasis on visual perception has tended to diminish our awareness of the auditory character of our environment, and our auditory sense has tended to atrophy. We do not seem to realize that noise is not an inherent condition of existence, and have become permissive toward noise.

Certainly other parts of the world besides the Sudan, where Dr. Rosen studied the quiet life of the Maaban, have less noisy environments than does the United States. A United Nations report shows that noise pollution, like air pollution, is common to the industrialized nations. The pertinent question, then, is whether a rising noise level is the inevitable accompaniment of increasing industrialization.

While it might be conceded that a highly industrialized country tends to be noisier than a less industrial country, a particular level of noise is no more inevitable than a particular level of air pollution. It is essentially a question of cultural values. Do we want a quieter environment? How much are we willing to pay for it? West Germany, among other industrialized European nations, seems to be more concerned about noise than this country and has taken steps toward its control and abatement. In Switzerland, a Federal Anti-Noise Commission has been empowered to establish both day and night noise level maximums in various populated areas. Unlike U.S. courts, Swiss courts have fully backed the legality of such control.

It is not, of course, a simple matter of buying a given amount of quiet for a given amount of money. It is a matter of establishing what importance noise control and noise abatement have relative to the other values of our urban civilization. It is a matter of making choices. In the case of the SST we may have to decide whether we want the added speed enough to accept the sonic booms.

If quiet is valued highly, city planners may begin to consider noise as a criterion in all land use and transportation proposals; architects may reject a satisfying visual design unless it is also a satisfying auditory design. In fact, "audiocation" could become a helpful adjunct to the present beautification movement which now considers our environment only in visual terms.

There is presently little government attention to noise control on local, state or federal levels. If effective citizen demand requires a change, government agencies may encourage noise abatement technology, or even hold back the introduction of new technology until it meets noise pollution control standards.

However, if communities consider the interference of noise with sleep, communication and work performance and its possible effects on health and well being as an acceptable price to pay for unrestricted technological development, our cities will continue to get louder as they get bigger and more "advanced."

Metropolitan Needs and Government Performance

ADVISORY COMMISSION ON INTERGOVERNMENTAL RELATIONS*

Great cities have given way to metropolitan areas as the centers of American life. To many observers, the emergence of the modern metropolis is a cause for concern as much as for celebration. Metropolitan development confronts, and helps to create, a long agenda of problems that can be solved only by public action. The agenda includes providing public investments and services to keep pace with population growth and changing needs, rebuilding the older urban centers, eliminating the inequities of social and economic segregation, and offering equal opportunities for all to share in the benefits of urban life.

This array of urban problems has been widely recognized but subject to varying interpretation. A fundamental issue, whether governments are capable of dealing with these problems, is often slighted. Thus social critics, noting the contrast between splendid new suburban homes, an abundance of high-powered cars, and recurrent crises in such areas of public responsibility as education and water supply, conclude that there is a striking imbalance in national priorities. Galbraith, in *The Affluent Society,* attributes this curious urban blend of private splendor and public squalor to a national folklore that assigns high value to private production, with a corresponding neglect of important public investments. If the American public assigned higher priority to government undertakings, presumably government would respond with vastly improved programs.

While public attitudes are surely important factors influencing government performance, a more searching examination of the state of public business in metropolitan America will reveal that the organization of government also has much to do with current inadequacies. Even where demands for improvement are voiced

* Reprinted from Advisory Commission on Intergovernmental Relations, *Metropolitan America: Challenge to Federalism* (Washington, D.C.: U.S. Government Printing Office, 1966), pp. 1–11. Footnotes deleted.

loudly and persistently, governments in urban areas often seem unable to hear or to respond. To meet the needs of a metropolitan age, it is essential to remove obstacles within the system of government itself. Efforts to arouse public awareness and concern for urban problems are unlikely to produce tangible results unless there are channels for transmitting this concern to government, and unless government is equipped to take effective action in response.

Urban Growth and Services

The rapid pace of metropolitan expansion poses one significant set of challenges to local government. The great majority of people and economic activities in the United States are now concentrated in over 200 metropolitan areas, and virtually all future growth is expected to take place within these areas. Inside metropolitan areas, however, growth does not take a concentrated form but tends to spread well beyond the established cities into fringe territory. By now, more than half the metropolitan population lives outside the central cities. This pattern of growth imposes major new service demands on local governments in outlying areas, many of which have never before had to cope with the pressures of sudden population increase.

President Johnson outlined the national magnitude of the urban growth challenge in his 1965 message to Congress on the cities:

> Our new city dwellers will need homes and schools and public services. By 1975, we will need over 2 million new homes a year. We will need schools for 10 million additional children, welfare and health facilities for 5 million more people over the age of 60, transportation facilities for the daily movement of 200 million people, and more than 80 million automobiles.
>
> In the remainder of this century—in less than 40 years—urban population will double, city land will double, and we will have to build in our cities as much as all that we have built since the first colonist arrived on these shores. It is as if we had 40 years to rebuild the entire urban United States.

Urban growth is a complex process requiring a wide variety of public and private resources. The expansive pattern of urban development in the United States means, first, that a large supply of land is needed to accommodate increases in population and economic activity. In fact, the need for urban land tends to grow at a faster rate than population increase. In the New York metropolitan region—defined broadly to include several contiguous metropolitan areas in New York, New Jersey, and Connecticut—the population is expected to grow from 16 million in 1960 to 22 million in 1985. If recent trends in land development continue, the urbanized land area will more than double during the same period, growing from 2,400 square miles in 1960 to 5,200 square miles in 1985. In other parts of the country, as well, the increase of population requires more than a proportional commitment of fringe land to urban development.

There is no shortage of land in the United States. Even the densely populated eastern seaboard contains abundant reserves of open land that can be used for urban expansion. Problems arise in making this land suitable for urban living. Highways and other transportation channels must be provided to make fringe areas accessible to the core cities and to metropolitan job centers. Schools, water supply, parks, hospitals, utilities, local roads, and shopping centers are all needed to serve a growing population. In the New York region, the necessary public service investments alone will cost an estimated $16,800 for each new household. The high public cost of servicing urban growth has tempted many local governments to provide inadequate levels of service or to rely excessively on facilities supplied by private land developers. Thus, one of the major shortcomings in water supply and waste disposal is the continued reliance on private wells and individual septic tanks in communities where the growing density of population calls for public water and sewage systems. Local governments often supply services haphazardly and only after crises have developed. Where local land regulation is inadequate, potential sites for parks, schools, and public buildings may be taken for private development before the community can act to acquire them. Housing, shopping centers, and industry may destroy irreplaceable natural resources by leveling woodlands, polluting streams, and filling in wet lands so that natural drainage patterns are interrupted and flooding becomes a problem.

The plight of suburbanites can easily be exaggerated. Despite crabgrass and faulty septic tanks, most new residents of the suburbs enjoy good living conditions. But public expectations are rising quickly. Many government officials as well as private developers have sensed increasing dissatisfaction with the quality of the new environment being built in the suburbs and are seeking ways to build better communities.

Social and Economic Disparities

Other metropolitan problems are more ominous than the inadequate services of newly developing suburbs. Metropolitan growth in the United States is producing patterns of racial and economic segregation, with severe consequences for disadvantaged groups, for the communities where they are concentrated, and ultimately for the entire urban society. While large numbers of people have been moving from the older central cities to the suburbs, others have been moving from rural areas into the central cities. Since World War II, there have been vast migrations of southern Negroes, Puerto Ricans, and people from Appalachia to the great cities. And while more prosperous groups were moving to the suburbs to find better housing, many earlier residents of the cities remained — some because they preferred to live in the central cities, many because they could not afford the cost of a suburban house. Within the suburbs, there has been further segregation as different builders produced new one-class communities with housing entirely in a particular price range. Local government policies have had a hand in limiting the range of families who can afford to live within their borders. Because of the high cost of providing public services for new residents, many communities have made use of zoning and other land development controls to hold down population growth and to exclude middle and lower income families whose modest houses would not yield enough in property taxes to cover their service costs. In addition, racial discrimination on the part of builders, real estate brokers, and mortgage institutions has reinforced economic segregation with direct policies of racial exclusion.

As a result of this combination of forces, low-income families, broken families, the elderly, the unemployed, and Negroes are concentrated in the central cities of most large metropolitan areas. This segregation can lead to cultural isolation of disadvantaged groups from the rest of society. Current interpretations of urban poverty stress the self-reinforcing character of the culture of poverty in which economic deprivation leads to low levels of aspiration and destroys incentives for self-improvement. Concentrations of poor people lead also to improverished governments, unable to supply services to people who are particularly dependent on government help. People in the central cities need many kinds of government services: welfare, education, health, police, and fire protection. Yet the tax resources of these cities are limited by the very nature of their population. With the loss of middle and upper income families, as well as industries and retail firms, the central cities have been increasingly unable to raise sufficient tax revenue for their mounting service needs.

Thus the social disparities between suburban and central city communities give rise to economic and fiscal disparities as well. Tax-poor governments provide inferior services for their citizens and deny them significant opportunities to participate in the benefits of metropolitan life. As James B. Conant has noted, the great disparities between public education in the slums and in the suburbs are incompatible with the American ideal of equal opportunity for all. Educating slum children is far more difficult than educating middle-class children; yet many schools in wealthy suburbs spend $1,000 per pupil annually and provide a staff of 70 professionals per 1,000 students, while slum schools are likely to spend only half as much and to provide 40 or fewer professionals per 1,000 pupils. The low level of education and other public services that the poor receive is closely related to the pattern of urban development and to its impact upon government finances.

Other detrimental consequences result from suburban growth that serves privileged groups and excludes the poor. Where residential choices available to the poor are sharply restricted, public programs that involve relocation of low-income families create severe hardship for them and retard progress toward national housing goals. Relocation for urban renewal and highway construction is one of the most troublesome elements of these programs. The disappointing results of much relocation, occasioned by the shortage of housing that low-income families can afford, have created increasing opposition to the rebuilding of central cities and the construction of needed public works.

Metropolitan Interdependence

Underlying many metropolitan problems is the failure of governmental institutions to come to grips with the growing interdependence of people and communities within metropolitan areas. As urban settlement spreads across lines of local jurisdiction, the cities and suburbs together come to comprise a single integrated area for living and working. People look for housing and employment within a broad region circumscribed more by the convenience of commuting and by personal preferences than by local government boundaries. The existence of a metropolitanwide housing and job market is, in fact, the basis for defining metropolitan areas. In the definition of the U.S. Bureau of the Budget and the Bureau of the Census, "the general concept of a metropolitan area is one of an integrated economic and social unit with a recognized large population nucleus."

The detailed criteria used in defining "standard metropolitan statistical areas" (SMSA's) provide further insight into the integrated character of these areas. Each area must contain at least one city of 50,000 inhabitants or more, or "twin cities" with a combined population of at least 50,000. The metropolitan character of the county containing the central city or cities is established by determining that the county is a place of work or residence for a concentration of non-agricultural workers. The specific conditions that must be met include a requirement that at least 75 percent of the labor force must have nonagricultural occupations, and other tests concerning population density and job concentrations. In New England, the components of metropolitan areas are cities and towns rather than counties. Outlying counties (cities and towns in New England) are considered part of the metropolitan area if they meet either of the following tests:

(1) If 15 percent of the workers living in the county work in the county where the central city is located; or

(2) If 25 percent of those working in the outlying county live in the county where the central city is located.

If the information concerning these two requirements is not conclusive, other kinds of information are considered: reports of newspaper circulation, the extent to which residents of outlying areas maintain charge accounts in central city retail stores, official traffic counts, and other indicators of central city-suburban interaction.

Metropolitan areas are integrated in other ways, as well. Local communities share many kinds of natural resources used for urban living: water supplies, drainage basins, recreation areas. They also share many manmade facilities that cut across local boundaries, such as highway and utility systems, and many other facilities that serve large segments of the metropolitan population, such as airports and commercial centers. These forms of interaction, together with the metropolitan character of housing and employment markets, create a broad area of common interest. The optimum use of shared facilities and resources calls for a high level of cooperation and for coordinated action by interdependent communities.

The policies of any one community typically have considerable impact in other parts of the metropolitan area. If one locality fails to control air or water pollution, its neighbors suffer. This principle was illustrated recently when Nassau County, which borders New York City, demanded that New York put its mosquitoes under surveillance. The public works commissioner of Nassau County charged that swarms of mosquitoes from the city had been invading Nassau territory: "Mosquitoes have no respect for boundary lines or home rule," he complained.

The effects of local action (or inaction) that spread into other communities have come to be known as "spillovers." They are very common in metropolitan affairs and often consist of indirect effects. Thus, suburban communities that succeed in excluding the poor impose considerable burdens on other communities where the poor are concentrated. Spillovers can also be beneficial to neighboring localities. Effective traffic control or public health measures benefit people outside a city or town as well as local residents. Spillovers usually imply disparities between tax and service boundaries. Thus the residents of central cities may be taxed to provide services that are important to the suburbs as well as to themselves. Or suburbanites may be taxed to clean up polluted streams that flow into neighboring territory. In all these cases, people who do not live in a particular jurisdiction nevertheless have a strong interest in its performance of government functions.

The prevalence of spillovers constitutes a strong case for cooperation in metropolitan areas. Metropolitan service needs also provide compelling arguments for joint action. In such fields as water supply and sewage disposal, the cost of service per household can be reduced dramatically in large-scale operations by joint agreement of local governments. Similarly, areawide transportation systems—highways, public transit—require joint planning if they are to provide needed service at reasonable cost.

Despite the evident and important benefits of cooperative action in metropolitan areas, many local governments continue to go it alone. The realities of functional interdependence in metropolitan areas are in conflict with concepts of home rule that predate the age of metropolitan growth. Home rule in the contemporary metropolitan setting has often led to local isolation and conflict, to the detriment of the metropolitan population at large. Each community, in pursuing its own interests, may have an adverse effect on the interests of its neighbors. A major task for government in metropolitan areas is to develop policies consistent with the integrated character of the modern metropolitan community. Federal policies are guided increasingly by an awareness of this need, as President Johnson emphasized in his message on the cities:

> The interests and needs of many of the communities which make up the modern city often seem to be in conflict. But they all have an overriding interest in improving the quality of life of their people. And they have an overriding interest in enriching the quality of American civilization. These interests will only be served by looking at the metropolitan area as a whole, and planning and working for its development.

Governmental Obstacles

The fundamental metropolitan problem is not that there are difficulties in supplying public services or ameliorating social and economic disparities. It is that governments in metropolitan areas are often unable to cope with these issues. The system of local government in the United States has many achievements to its credit, but, like any social system, it also has its disadvantages. Within metropolitan areas, many important issues of public policy can no longer be handled by local communities acting alone; their small areas of jurisdiction are inadequate for either administering areawide services or resolving areawide problems.

The close ties of people and businesses to one another in metropolitan areas have no parallel in government. While social and economic relationships have shifted to an enlarged metropolitan scale, governments and the loyalties they inspire have remained local. As Roscoe Martin has put it:

> The metropolitan area has no capital, courthouse, or city hall, no corporate existence, no body, no soul, no sense of being, indeed no being in any concrete meaning of the term. Al Smith was from the sidewalks of New York, not from the sidewalks of the New York-Northeastern New Jersey standard consolidated area.

Metropolitan areas are governed not only by traditional cities, towns, and counties, but also by a wide variety of special districts that overlap other boundaries. The complexity of local government can be illustrated by listing the array of local jurisdictions responsible for Park Forest, a suburb of Chicago, as of 1956: Cook County, Will County, Cook County Forest Preserve District, village of Park Forest, Rich Township, Bloom Township, Monee Township, Suburban Tuberculosis Sanitarium District, Bloom Township Sanitary District, Non-High School District 216, Non-High School District 213, Rich Township High School District 227, Elementary School District 163, South Cook County Mosquito Abatement District.

Fragmentation of this kind may appear to bring government "closer to the people," but it compounds the difficulties of achieving coordination within metropolitan areas. Political responsibility for government performance is divided to the point of obscurity. Public control of government policies tends to break down when citizens have to deal with a network of independent governments, each responsible for highly specialized activities. Even where good channels are developed for registering public concern, each government is so circumscribed in its powers and in the area of its jurisdiction that important metropolitan action is virtually impossible for local goverments to undertake. If a few governments are prepared to agree on joint measures or coordinated programs, their efforts can be blocked by others that are unwilling to cooperate.

Local governments, fragmented as they are, nevertheless keep the metropolis running. They operate the schools, maintain the streets, take care of police and fire protection. But when issues of metropolitanwide importance arise—such as commuter transportation, water supply, or racial and economic segregation—people must turn to other channels for action. As Robert Wood has pointed out, an "embryonic coalition" of metropolitan leaders tends to emerge to tackle areawide problems. These leaders—politicians, editors, businessmen, labor leaders—operate informally and outside the regular structure of government, as they attempt to prod government into action. They lack the requirements for effective policymaking: an adequate institutional base, legal authority, direct relationships with the metropolitan constituency, and established processes for considering and resolving issues as they emerge.

When important public issues can only be handled informally and outside government channels, it is time to review the system of government in metropolitan areas and to regard the shortcomings of this system as major problems in themselves. Norton Long has set the problems of metropolitan areas in this political context:

> The problems of the metropolis are important, but not because of flooded cellars or frustrated motorists, nor because they seriously threaten the viability of the metropolitan economy. They are important because they are symptomatic of the erosion of the competence of local government. . . . The threat of the eroded central city and the crazy-quilt triviality of suburbia is the threat to destroy the potential of our maintaining and reconstructing meaningful political communities at the local level. What has been treated as a threat to our physical well-being is in reality a threat to our capacity to sustain an active local civic life.

The Federal System and Metropolitan Issues

With local governments often unwilling or unable to meet metropolitan needs, the Federal and State Governments have taken on increasing responsibilities for metropolitan welfare. The State role ranges from financial aid to local governments to direct State operations in metropolitan areas, such as highway building, and State establishment of special metropolitan authorities responsible for such functions as water supply and port development. The Federal role consists mainly of financial assistance for programs administered by State or local government. The number and size of Federal-aid programs have been growing at a striking rate: there are now more than 70 Federal-aid programs that directly support urban development, as well as a number of other kinds of Federal aid available to local governments in metropolitan areas.

State and Federal programs are helping to cope with many metropolitan needs, but they also raise troublesome political and governmental issues. Federal and State participation in metropolitan affairs greatly complicates the already fragmented governmental scene. Activities of all three levels of government now function in close juxtaposition, subject to an extremely complicated web of Federal, State, and local laws and administrative regulations. In the course of supplying needed help, Federal and State programs threaten to push the confused governmental situation closer to a state of chaos. Coordination of efforts is a prime requirement for effective government action in metropolitan areas; yet the problems of coordination are compounded by the addition of higher levels of government to the fragmented local scene.

There is an implicit danger that greater reliance on Federal and State action in metropolitan areas may be a form of political abdication in which local governments wash their hands of difficult responsibilities and pass the buck to higher levels. This approach would lead to waning local influence over policies and programs that have significant local impact. Thus it is important to find ways of administering State and Federal programs within a system of democratic control in which metropolitan citizens can shape the programs that operate in their own areas.

Local communities in search of financial aid have turned mainly to the Federal Government rather than the States. The rural orientation of State legislatures has been well documented, and is only now changing to reflect recent reapportionments. For a number of reasons, the cities have found a more sympathetic hearing in Washington than in the State capital. In seeking Federal aid for urban problems, cities have tended to bypass the State and deal directly with Washington. A pattern of intergovernmental relations has developed in which cities and towns in metropolitan areas pursue largely independent policies, with a minimum of inter-local cooperation, but many engage in numerous direct dealings with the Federal Government. The State role has been lagging far behind both local and Federal activity. Yet the States occupy critical positions within the American federal system and possess the power and resources to strengthen local capacities and stimulate greater cooperation within metropolitan areas.

The new intergovernmental relationships also pose more fundamental issues for the future of the American federal system. Minimizing State participation in urban affairs is tantamount to removing State influence from a critical range of domestic issues. The federal system of the United States involves a division of powers between the States and the Federal Government. The States have created a further division by delegating powers to the local governments they have established. If the State role in this partnership is weakened, the ramifications may be far reaching. Without active State participation, it is doubtful whether local government can be reorganized to perform more effectively in metropolitan areas; the localities derive their powers from the States and need State authorization for structural reforms. More broadly, the State role in metropolitan affairs must be considered in terms of the philosophy of the federal system. The division of authority between the States and the Federal Government has served the country well in the past and has helped to safeguard the values of representative and responsible government. Basic changes in the system of intergovernmental relations should not be undertaken lightly or permitted to occur by default.

Poor coordination and conflicts of interest among governments often block effective action to deal with metropolitan problems. Changes in the structure of government within metropolitan areas, and innovations in relations among the Federal Government, the States, and local communities are needed to overcome these obstacles. The complex federal system of the United States, however, is rich in possibilities for adaptation to meet the changing circumstances of metropolitan growth. With sufficient imagination and effort, the resources of the federal system can be brought effectively to bear on the urban problems that challenge our age, just as previous generations found ways of adapting the federal system to deal with other national challenges.

Ecosystems, Societies, and Cities

STEWART MARQUIS*

Man has long harbored the delusion that sheer application of energy, of mechanical force, brings control over nature. Only now is he discovering that the gross application of force leads to unintended consequences that reverberate throughout natural systems, sometimes even to reversing or offsetting the effect of the original force. Man is also discovering that this applies not just to natural systems but to the social and artifact systems which are part of them.

Thus man has wrought major changes in natural ecological systems by altering land forms and water courses, by building complex artifact systems from natural substances, by drawing on huge stores of energy reserves, by developing settlements called cities. All this he has done—to bring mechanical-force technology

*"Ecosystems, Societies, and Cities" by Stewart Marquis is reprinted from *American Behavioral Scientist,* Volume XI, No. 6 (July/August 1968), pp. 11-16, by permission of the Publisher, Sage Publications, Inc. Footnotes deleted.

to bear on reducing the uncertainties of human survival. But in doing so he has upset the naturally-stabilized ecological systems he is part of and replaced them with social and artifact systems which are not naturally stabilized, but are up to him to manage. Moreover, in his efforts to reduce individual uncertainties, he has disturbed the social certainties developed over centuries of human social organization, as well as the natural certainties developed over millenia of evolution. In short, man is now faced with the management of ecosystems, parts of which are artifactual and social, his own creation. In this situation he finds a new technology is needed.

Looking at what is unique to man makes it hard to understand and cope with what seem to be purely human problems. Because, by focusing on human behavior and organization — whether social, economic, or political — we leave out all the rest of nature, including the physical, chemical, biological, and ecological aspects of man and his societies. We see people and their artifacts not only as dominant, which they are, but as separate, which they are not. Studying human societies in rural areas or smaller settlements does not usually lead to such anthropomorphic distortion, because there it is only too obvious how closely linked are human tribes, farms, and villages to all the rest of nature. . . .

Natural Ecosystems

The natural ecological system, or ecosystem, includes all natural organisms and substances within a given space or area. It incorporates both the community of populations of various animal and plant organisms and protista and the various inorganic substances such as air, water, and soil. This means including man as one species in the community of species, and his artifacts as one category of natural substances. It also means concentrating on the natural relationships between and among people, their artifacts, natural organisms, and natural substances.

Natural ecosystems are complex, interdependent, highly organized systems. Their many organisms and substances are linked together in complex networks, making up a mosaic of feedback loops by which changes in any one part of a network will have repercussions in many other parts of that network. Natural ecologists deal extensively with food-chain networks, in which green plants use solar energy to transform inorganic materials into complex organic molecules; the plants are eaten by animals; the animals burn organic molecules to release energy for work; and both plant and animal materials are further broken down by decomposers, the inorganic materials being returned for further photosynthesis. Thus, natural ecologists speak about the cycling of materials through the ecosystem and the one-way flows of energy, from solar to stored chemical energy, to release for biological work, and thence to conversion into thermal energy which is no longer useful for work.

This suggests that we can analyze natural ecosystems as sequences of states that change over time. Obviously it takes energy to perform the work of changing the various states of organisms, substances, and ecosystems from one form to another. This work, in turn, is constrained by organization to given types and locations. Thus, we can use the *energetic* concepts of work, energy, and power as measures of dynamic states, and of the processes of change within ecosystems.

The *organetic* concepts of organization, structure, matter, and system can be used to describe the stable states which constrain energetic behavior. The network organization of complex natural ecosystems thus determines their stability, with this ecosystem structure exercising passive, built-in constraints on the performance of work. Today, these energetic and organetic concepts are being applied not only to physical systems, as in physics and chemistry and engineering, but also to natural systems, as in biology and ecology.

All the stabilized constraints exerted by ecosystem networks establish relative certainties for ecosystem structure and behavior. Thus natural ecosystems that have evolved over centuries have generally reached climax states, in which the naturally-stabilizing network constraints control the impact of normal disturbances coming from outside the ecosystem. These climax states are steady states, since natural ecosystems are open systems with inputs from, and outputs to, their environments.

Within a stable ecosystem, each organic species has established itself in an "energy-niche," in which it has access to certain sources of energy, either directly from the sun (as for green plants) or indirectly through eating or absorbing energy which plants have bound into complex organic molecules. Such a climax eco-system thus tends to have fairly stable species populations and food-chain net-works. But stability, in a naturally-evolved ecosystem, is also dependent on com-plex interdependencies between many different organic species. Hence there are "multiple organic pathways" for dealing with disturbances that threaten stability in the ecosystem.

Stable ecosystems can, however, be profoundly disturbed by major inputs of energy of organic materials rich in bound chemical energy, or of organisms made up of such molecules. For example, competition and conflict to obtain the new energy can have repercussions throughout the system, as various organisms seek it for performing their normal kinds of work. New energy inputs also act directly to upset the stable pattern of energy-niches among existing organisms, the pattern of food-chain networks, species populations, and so on.

Some natural ecosystems fluctuate within established thresholds caused by fresh inputs of energy that occur periodically. Sometimes this may be seasonal, reflecting the variations of solar energy and other conditions, while others may fluctuate with tides. Variable ecosystems are often found at the borders between more stable ecosystems, such as at the seashore or the forest fringe. A fluctuating ecosystem can nevertheless offer periodic opportunities for some new species to break into food-chains and energy-niches. Howard Odum suggests that early man took advantage of such opportunities.

Up to now, the natural evolution of ecosystems, communities, and societies has been far more dependent on the slow change of passive, built-in constraints resid-ing in complex networks of food-chains than on the adaptive behavior of any one species. What has favored their stability has been the multiplicity of organic species with their huge numbers and vast biomass. Obviously the more massive stabilities of land forms, water cycles and watercourses, airflows and climate, have been contributing factors. In any case, the patterned behavior of groups or societies of given species, like insects or birds, has become closely fitted to their niches within ecosystems. Man, as another such organic species, started out just as closely interdependent with all other species in the ecosystem.

But in the case of man, and a few other species, an experiment in nature has been taking place in which the possibilities of adaptive learning behavior are being tested to the utmost. In cities, we see that men have learned to apply vast energy resources by taking over the ecosystem niches, territories, and current solar energy inputs of a variety of species and multitudes of individual organisms. In the city, man flaunts his freedom from a scarcity of current solar energy by devoting huge areas to other purposes, letting solar energy go to waste. For his current supplies he draws instead on the growth of crops in other regions. In addition, man has learned how to find, extract, and use new energy supplies for human purposes — mainly to decrease his uncertainties about his individual survival needs for food, clothing, and shelter.

Human Societies

The society man builds can be looked at as a special kind of complex, inter-dependent system. Just as do natural ecosystems, human societies maintain their stability through complex mosaics of networks of feedback loops, so that changes in one part of the network will have repercussions in many other parts. Just as for the natural ecosystems, society and its many social organizations have evolved as a way of coping with scarcity and the competition of other species using the same energy sources.

But despite the similarities, human society is not an ecosystem, since it includes only one species and none of the natural substances. Nor does man control the natural ecosystem of which he and his society are merely a part, though a dominant one.

Man's dominant position has come primarily because of his entry into a new energy-niche, one never before occupied by any organic species on earth. By learning to use the stored energy of fossil fuels, first for heat and then later for mechanical work, he ceased being dependent on current solar energy. He could now draw on the solar energy of past centuries, long since converted into organic materials and stored in the form of coal, oil, and natural gas.

Because of this, man has been able to alter the energetics and organetics of major portions of the earth's land surface. He has progressively reduced the sus-tenance-survival uncertainties of major segments of the human population of the earth. Indeed, he seems to be approaching the time when his applications of me-chanical force will take him from conditions of energy and material scarcity to conditions of affluence.

On the other hand, during centuries of earlier evolution men were but minor components in massive natural systems and hence they did not have to worry about whether or not their actions would affect ecosystem stability and survival. But now they seem to have traded their ancient uncertainties for a whole new set, arising from their disturbed social and ecological systems.

Firstly, men are still plagued by uncertainty, because only some men have benefited from the new assurance of survival while others have not. Hence there is growing competition and conflict among them about energy and material resources, about the territories they are found in, and about the technologies by which to apply them. These uncertainties will no doubt continue until not just some, but most, of the human species is assured of individual sustenance-survival. Secondly, uncertainties have arisen because of the constantly revolutionizing effect of new resources, technologies, products, production processes, occupational skills, and education. They have made older social organizations and modes of individual behavior inadequate and useless. What have long seemed to be relative certainties in human social relations — built into codes of ethics and morality, consolidated in custom and law, central to philosophy and religion — begin to seem inappropriate to conditions of relative abundance and affluence.

Man discovers now that he cannot use his huge new energy resources nor his hardware technologies to cope with his new social uncertainties. For here he is no longer dealing with the killing off or modification of other species and the taking over of their territories or niches. Here he is dealing with the modification, exploitation, or elimination of other human societies, or even other members of his own society. Man's new technology has brought major differences of living standards around the world, so that the energy and material requirements of different cultures and subcultures have seemed to grow markedly different. But these differences, and the growing awareness of differences, have become major sources of conflicts between human societies and between groups within societies. In applying to these conflicts the old energy resources and technology, namely force and the threat of force, man has discovered that in some cases they don't really work because they virtually insure his own extinction. Or else they directly contradict the older inhibitions, built into his stable societies, which now forbid him to treat other humans as he once treated other species. Man must learn to cope with the uncertainties of other people and other societies as he did on a much smaller scale when he took the first steps toward developing stable organizations, communities, and societies by incorporating potentially competitive groups into larger groups. What he has not yet discovered is how to do this at the worldwide scale now required.

System Control

There is nothing new about the idea of complex systems in nature or society. To say that natural organisms and substances exist in complexity and mutual dependence has also been accepted as true, but not very useful. If we know of no practical way to deal with complexities, we may be much better off to ignore them, limiting our concern to the much simpler problems that can be dealt with pragmatically, or we may not get started at all.

Much of our human application of mechanical-force technology in the past can be thought of in these terms. Faced with the need to act on specific uncertainties, men proceeded to do so without concerning themselves about the analysis or control of surprise repercussions. They cleared or drained land, they dammed rivers, pumped water, crushed ore and formed metal. In these and many other ways they used energy to perform work that would lessen the immediate uncertainty. They ignored repercussions or "externalities" that might deeply affect the larger ecosystems, or else assumed they would be dealt with by nature or other men.

But now time is running out. Partly some concern has been forced on us because there are simply more of us, and our mutual dependence is much greater than it was in the past. But partly our concern comes from a greater knowledge of what repercussions may occur, since repercussions are only unexpected if we lack the equipment with which to expect them.

One result of our concern is that we are beginning to have methods for controlling repercussions. This is because our new tools also enable us to understand more fully the consequences of how force is used. Thus the burden of our newer technology will be to deal with the selective use of force, whether by nature or man. Indeed, we are finding this principle just as important to our fuller understanding of the natural processes as it is of the social. We are barely beginning to comprehend the significance and complexity of controlled force in biological and ecological systems.

What we are suggesting here is hence not a completely new and different technology, but an extended one, built on the same basic principles as those already being applied in the natural sciences. This means that our new tools for understanding will be based on our fundamental energetic-organetic concepts. To these we must add new concepts which will not be separate and different from those used in past technologies, but grow directly out of them.

Now then, if the power to alter natural ecosystems by force does not bring control, what does? Norbert Wiener coined the term "cybernetics" to refer to "control and communication in the animal and the machine." We suggest here that control deals with the directing of energy into specific kinds of work for specific purposes at specific times and locations—that is, with the selective application of force. Energy, expressed as sheer capacity for work, does not bring this kind of control; only information does that.

As we have seen, some constraints of work behavior are exercised by the passive, built-in interdependencies of complex network systems. The special kind of organization needed to control complex systems will be referred to as cybernetic-organetics. It includes not only the organetic concepts of organization, structure, and system, as applied to control structures and systems, but also the cybernetic concepts of control, information, communication, and management. Up to now technology has rested mainly on energetic-organetic concepts, dealing with the application of energy to perform work. Now we will begin to talk about a cybernetic-organetic technology and the application of information and structure to exert selective control of force.

Obviously, we are still concerned with the control of energetic-organetic systems because it is the natural ecosystems that are disturbed and out of control. To rectify this, man is now entering the development of the fuller technology of ecosystem management. This involves control by design-and-construction of components, by synthesis-and-assembly of subsystems, and by monitoring-and-regulation of components, subsystems, and overall ecosystem. Management of this kind, for human purposes, means a kind of concern about goals that has not usually been part of energetic-organetic technology, where the goals were taken as given by nature or man. Now we are talking about how to deal with systems within which goals and purposes are generated and changed, and how these, in turn, affect priorities and set the bases for evaluating system performance.

We get some inkling of the nature of cybernetic-organetic technology from many of the terms already used here. Man has begun to be much more selective and discriminating in his applications of mechanical force in terms of the design, construction, and operation of such complex artifact systems as telephone and electric power networks, missiles, space vehicles, and computers. His newly developing science and technology of control relies a great deal on detailed information about controlled systems and the missions he expects them to perform. For the present, much of this new technology deals more with the organetics of information than with the organetics of control structures or of systems that control or are controlled. Much of it is also for relatively simple physical systems, which are carefully defined so as to exclude any social, economic, or political components and subsystems.

As Stafford Beer suggests, man's attempts to control complex systems still tend to have some of the earmarks of applying brute mechanical force to maintain stability and achieve system goals. Thus there are still major implications of the need to force man's notions of organization and stability and to fight off the constant threat of chaos and randomness. Perhaps this is becoming less true of complex physical systems. But it is still true of most human efforts to manage social and ecological systems.

The first need, here, is for better information. That is, if information provides capacity for control, then man's principal need is for more precise and accurate information about the systems to be controlled and the potential ways to control them. To begin with, he needs information that will clarify what he can control or influence, and what he cannot. Also needed is a great deal more information about the natural stabilities or certainties he can draw on as he builds or rebuilds, or regulates, or learns to live with, complex networks of natural, social, and artifact systems. Toward this end man will be interested in how to design major segments of ecosystems, assemble segments together into ecosystems, and regulate those ecosystems to better satisfy human goals. He will want to develop models of ecosystems that enable him to evaluate the stability of ecosystem behavior, its sensitivity to various disturbances, and the reliability of its many parts. It means that he will want most to develop ecosystem models that illuminate the potentials of policy, design, and control for achieving human goals.

Man can deal with uncertainties by seeking to reduce them through greater knowledge. He can hope to learn the probabilities or risks, which will better enable him to plan and act, exerting selective control. But he can also deal with uncertainties by turning them into certainties, or at least by increasing the probabilities of certain desired outcomes, decreasing risks. Whichever means of control he selects will entail expenditures of energy. He can use energy to organize materials into wanted products, and to see that they get distributed to those who want them. He can use energy to eliminate organisms that compete with him for energy or that threaten him with disease. He can use energy to store food and other materials against times of shortages. He can use energy to keep other people from stealing his goods. All these energetic-organetic actions do not so much decrease uncertainty as they increase certainty.

So man copes with his uncertainties through organetic means. He organizes materials into tools by which he can bring other energy to bear in performing desired work. He organizes other species into forms and locations that will produce food and fibers for his use. He organizes himself and other people into social organizations which focus the work of many on the achievement of common or complementary goals. And he organizes his observations, measurements, and experiments into concepts and images that provide information capacity for the control of energetic-organic systems.

But our major contention here is that man must learn to understand and work with nature, of which he is a part. This means that he must learn to build his artifact and social systems into close interdependence with the stabilizing natural controls. It also means that the much-needed cybernetic-organic technology must be built on some fundamental concepts about the natural structure of controls. Sound control will depend on learning to model the structures of systems and controls so that we can deal more precisely with the matchings or mis-matchings between the structures of energetic-organic systems and those of cybernetic-organic systems — plus the structures of our information about both. Much of current control technology is couched in terms of indeterminacy and probability, which may be necessary at this stage. But it will probably not be adequate for the kind of control that is needed. Perhaps this will come when man recognizes the stable patterns and relative certainties in nature on which his controls must depend, and adds these to the instabilities and uncertainties he now sees in the social and artifact systems created by man.

Cities

The human city is a comparatively new type of ecosystem in nature. In a sense, it is only a partial ecosystem, since it contains no significant numbers of green plants carrying on the photosynthesis to produce food and fibers for human consumption. Thus, the basic relationship between a city and its surrounding region is that photosynthesis takes place in the region, producing organic materials which are eaten and respired there, but also producing food materials which are shipped into the city for consumption by urban people. By applying mechanical force, man has created an ecosystem with relatively little photosynthesis, lots of respiration by people and their artifacts, major alterations in natural ecosystems, and growing problems of ecosystem disturbances.

As unique human-dominant ecosystems, cities might be looked at as evolutionary experiments in the ability of one species to create and control its own ecosystems. At this point in time we cannot say whether or not the experiment will succeed or whether or not cities will prove to be stable ecosystems. What we can say is that most of them are not stable now.

The question is whether or not the human-dominant ecosystem can achieve some steady-state condition in relation to the flow of energy and the cycling of materials — or at least a steady state whose transient disturbances or variations get damped out, or which man can control. Urban characteristics have been changing so fast that it seems impossible, without some more fundamental form of analysis, to say whether or not there is some climax steady-state situation for cities. What we need to know is whether or not specific city ecosystems have internal tendencies to remain stable within the same basic operating range, wherein controlling processes tend to eliminate disturbances. Or do we assume that they tend to move on to some new steady-state, under the influence of major disturbances? At this point it is not at all clear whether or not man himself is a major disturbance that keeps his ecosystems out of control, through the revolutionary effects of technological change.

By now man has disturbed or eliminated most of the natural stabilizers of many natural ecosystems, most of all in cities. To cope with the uncertainties of natural phenomena, he has tried to substitute the hardware of buildings for protection from the elements, pipes and sewers for water flow and waste disposal, wires and pipelines for energy and fuel flows, other wires and streets and rail lines for communication. He has tried to substitute the "software" of social organizations — firms, agencies, associations, families — to cope with other natural uncertainties.

Now man is finding that these synthetic man-made artifacts and organizations do not bring stable control but begin to lead into more and more disturbance. Thus, a philosophy of non-control (laissez-faire), which once supported the competitive development of mechanical-force technology, no longer works. But neither do strenuous efforts at control by the most powerful men, those who control the major energy resources. And they are today's contradictory climate of "laissez-*me*-faire" but "control-the-other-guy."

A further source of disturbance comes from the city itself as a system. Obviously, people who live at bare subsistence levels do not require very much energy and materials. If they live as minor components in natural ecosystems, they and their societies can usually persist even through major disasters. Being interdependent with other species in the primarily natural ecosystems, they have a variety of energy reserves. But if such people live in cities, any major crisis, whether natural or economic or political, can lead to epidemic or famine. Living in cities, they are dependent mainly on other humans, on artifact systems run by humans, and on the continual transporting by humans of organic materials into the city, and waste materials out.

Indeed, much of the energy and material requirements of cities goes to establish and maintain complex social and artifact systems needed to cope with an ecosystem that is "out of kilter," or always on the edge of being so. That is, they are needed for coping with the stresses, the crises, the instabilities that mark an ecosystem which has lost its natural stabilizing factors.

We might say that human-dominant ecosystems, especially cities, are made up of massive artifact structures and massive human social organizations. These replace the great species variety, organism numbers, and total biomass that support stability in the natural ecosystem. All of which becomes evident when we think of establishing and maintaining an ecosystem inside a space vehicle. In it will be man and a few other organisms — plus a lot of hardware including emergency back-up replacements, lest some critical artifact system should fail. In a similar fashion, man's one-crop agricultural areas are much more vulnerable to crises from outside disturbances (drought, disease, or insects) than are the richly-varied ecosystems of the tropical rain forest, the coral reef, or even the natural prairie grasslands.

Within a city, man himself has created a situation where he must either return to the natural stabilizers, develop new ones, or design some combination by which he can gain and maintain control of himself, of his social and artifact systems, and the natural ecosystem he is part of. It seems very unlikely that he can construct adequate control systems out of hardware and people, ignoring the rest of nature. More likely he will have to find ways of combining the strengths of natural constraints with newer forms of social and artifact control structures.

Controlling Ecosystems, Societies, and Cities

We are not suggesting here that mechanical-force technology is bad, that it was in some sense a mistake for man to have developed and applied it, or that we should now seek to halt or prohibit its further development. What we do suggest is that there is much more to a scientific approach to cities than the innovations of cybernetics, information theory, computer hardware, and decision-making theories. True, scientific analysis can aid in decision-making, provide better information, enable us to handle huge masses of data. But these are secondary to what science can add to our bases for understanding ecosystems, societies, and cities. It is especially true of the new insights it can afford us into casual relationships in human problems.

We are therefore suggesting that a much more sophisticated approach to complex systems is now required. System control of this kind might include measures to regulate the pace of technological change or measures to slow down or even stop the application of specific technologies. But such limits would be highly selective constraints. They would be used where undesired effects outweigh desired effects, or where no other known method of control would minimize or modify an especially undesirable effect.

Obviously what we suggest here is something different from the social planning or social engineering of which many are speaking and writing today. We are suggesting the planning and engineering of complete ecosystems, including man and his doings as critical parts. But we are suggesting still more strongly the need to deal with the complex interdependencies between lesser systems—the social, the artifactual, the natural—as they function in the larger ecosystem. The means to achieve this may involve large measures of social engineering, since we are suggesting that these problems must be dealt with by men, through their social systems. But the matters to be dealt with go far beyond the social.

Lancelot Law Whyte suggests some of the difficulties here, when he points out that greater physical power adds to man's ability to destroy more than to his ability to build. Thus, mechanical-force technology has heightened social unrest and military might, but not the methods for integrating society. This is because formative processes require time in the organization of complex systems, including control systems, while such systems can be destroyed almost instantaneously.

Whyte also suggests that man's positive human tendencies and his personal relations are inherently divergent, producing variety and novelty. This means that positive tendencies cannot easily converge in a unified, common purpose. Cooperation in a human community is most effective when brought to bear against some obstruction limiting all its members, to eliminate some enemy or problem.

This raises profound questions about whether or not men will in fact develop the cybernetic-organetic technology of control they must now develop in concert. Presently, most destructive power is controlled by those still deluded by the possibilities of mechanical force—whether applied to air pollution, Vietnam, or urban slums. Nor is the understanding and discrimination required for ecosystem control typical of management, whether in large-scale business, industry, government, or the military. Certainly it is not yet true of those who manage city ecosystems.

Perhaps ours is a transitional period in which man will have to prove his ability to live in tune with what he cannot manage, and to manage more effectively what he can control.

But it may also be true that man will not learn to combine natural with human control. If he does not, then this experiment in adaptive behavior, in settlement patterns, in organic species, will have proven a failure. The rest of nature will undoubtedly proceed with other experiments.

4

Contamination
of the Land

Man's contamination of the land is much the same story as his contamination of the air and water, and his cluttering of the cities. Man has cut the land to shreds to uncover mineral deposits. He has covered large portions of it with rubbish. He has carved it up for financial gain. He has ripped large holes in it with machines and bombs. And he has covered it with chemicals and deadly radioactive materials.

As in despoiling the air, the water, and metropolitan areas, much of what man has done has been other than intentional or thoughtless ecological rape. A lot of contamination has been unanticipated or at least unwanted, resulting from activity designed to improve some aspect of human life. When DDT was first used, its long-term effects on the ecology were unknown. When lands were stripped of their forests the consequences of impending erosion were yet to be realized. Food manufacturers and distributors, can and bottle industries, consumers, and municipalities who dispose of rubbish all do what they do without the slightest intent of contaminating the land. Similarly, the Atomic Energy Commission and the farmers, though they know they are contaminating the land, are not pleased with the results of their activity. They, too, would prefer to avoid the secondary effects of their undertakings.

These facts underscore two major causes of the environmental crisis. First, values often conflict. Recreation and conservation interests, both with good intentions, clash over such questions as the development of the Mineral King area in California for recreational purposes. Likewise, transportation and conservation interests, again both with good intentions, clash over the development of an airport in the Florida Everglades. Second, decision-making is so decentralized that ecologically sound planning of a comprehensive order becomes virtually impossible.

The selections in this chapter illustrate the foregoing two points: that values often clash and that decision-making systems and human behavior are at the root of many environmental problems. In the first selection, Mr. Egler maintains that the problem associated with pesticides in the human environment arises not from a lack of scientific knowledge, but from human behavior. Pesticides have clearly done a great deal of good for mankind. But there have also been dysfunctional consequences of their use by agriculturalists who have had only short-run benefits in mind. Mr. Egler points out that the loosening of just a single thread in the ecosystem can, in some cases, lead to a much greater unraveling.

In the second article, Marjory Douglas tells how the Everglades have already been altered through incremental exploitation for private gain. Her description, however, of the recent success of conservationist interests in halting the development of a huge airport there shows that growth and development need not always win out over ecological values.

In describing the battle between conservation and recreation forces over development of a recreation site in the Mineral King area, Mr. Hano vividly illustrates the conflict between two well-intended and legitimate values, and the role played by government agencies in determining the fate of the land. To the conservationists, the development of a highway into the area will mean permanent ruin of the natural condition of the land. To their opponents in this struggle—the Disney interests, the U.S. Forest Service, agencies of the California state government, California political figures, and a host of business groups—development will mean millions of dollars.

In the final selection, Professor Gilmour sketches the vast array of interests and interest groups involved in public land policy. The interests—conservationist, cattle, sheep, mineral, and timber—all play a significant role in the formation of public land policy and, as can be expected, bring to the policy process a wide range of values and goals. Some of these interests tend upon occasion to fragment internally; given the growing pressure on land resources, the conservation interests, for example, find themselves on opposite sides of some issues. Professor Gilmour's thesis is that just as the interests are many and varied, so are the values embodied in public land policy.

Pesticides — In Our Ecosystem

FRANK E. EGLER*

The problem of pesticides in the human environment is 95 per cent a problem — not in the scientific knowledge of pesticides, not in the scientific knowledge of the environment—but in the scientific knowledge of human behavior. The problem has come into existence because of a revolt of an intelligent minority against the growing pseudo-scientific technology of our age, a revolt in which the knowledgeable scientists are peculiarly silent. In recognition of such problems as this, Professor Loren Eiseley, historian and philosopher, writes of the need for "an enlightened campaign not only against apathy but—what is worse—an apparently organized stupidity in areas where that attitude is most unbecoming."

This paper will be primarily an inquiry into pertinent aspects of that 95 per cent portion, the sociological. Concerning the remaining 5 per cent, the scientific knowledge of pesticides and of the environment, and of the interrelationships of the two, is rapidly advancing and readily available in the literature. . . .

*Reprinted with permission from the American Scientist, Vol. 52 (March 1964), pp. 110-136. Abridged and footnotes deleted.

Pesticides have probably existed ever since the first cave dweller by the side of the sea noticed that salt water, flung far in a storm, killed plants; and then used that knowledge to effect the intentional killing of plants. Other pest killers were found, and exploited.

The tempo, the variety, and the effectiveness of pesticides, could they be graphed, would appear like our own human population curve, the rate of increase itself increasing. DDT was first synthesized in 1874; its insecticidal properties were not discovered until 1939. During World War II, research in chemical warfare was enormously stepped up. The chemists searched for chemicals by which man could kill man, his crops, his livestock.

From these indubitably sinister origins developed the post-World War II pesticide industry. It was found that what poisoned man also poisoned insects. It was found that some substances could kill insects, without killing man, at least immediately. It was found that, with pests so controlled, crop production burgeoned and yields per acre shot up. The race was on. Farmers produced more. Farm prices were supported, while excesses were stored, given away, or destroyed. And with it, the pesticide industry mushroomed. Synthetic pesticide production in the United States was 124,259,000 lb. in 1947. It soared to 637,666,000 lb. in 1960. It is still soaring, as chemicals ever more effective are synthesized to combat the forms of life that have developed immunities to the present chemicals. The wholesale value of these products is now stated as being close to 400 million dollars. The big chemical concerns have much at stake. Monsanto Chemical's business in agricultural chemicals (which includes chemical fertilizers) reportedly has had an average growth rate of about 20 per cent annually over the last decade. Dow Chemical's business in this field showed a moderate but still healthy growth at 12 per cent a year. Stauffer Chemical's volume in agricultural chemicals, comprising 18 per cent of its total sales, approximated 40 million dollars in 1961, more than double the 1962 figure. Hercules Powder's farm chemicals volume has tripled in the last decade. And American Cyanamid derives 17 per cent of its over all sales from agricultural chemicals. Sales of pesticides in 1962 revealed a slow down in growth rate, but still an increase over 1961. To the hopes and plans of the industry, this is but a small beginning, as they eye the underdeveloped countries, with their unfertilized and pest-ridden croplands, their proliferating human populations, and the toll of human disease. It is understandable, if not forgivable, that those whose ecological nonsophistication is restricted to a simple equation involving "more food – for more people – with less disease – today" should look upon themselves as the saviors of mankind, and should look upon the profits of the pesticide industry as a moral and righteous source of private profit.

If this degree of ecological nonsophistication shall prove to have been insufficient for the good of mankind, then the fault lies not only with industry, but with the science which has failed to produce and to communicate the proper knowledge, and with the society that has failed to educate its citizenry and that tolerates the offending industries.

In the years before 1962, many scientists were expressing great concern as to the side-effects, the indirect effects, and the long-term effects of these pesticides, not only on the target organisms themselves, but on other organisms, as the pesticides moved through the environment, interacting among themselves, following food chains as predator ate predator, and acting upon man himself, as in cancer-producing substances, in ways most difficult to document in a factual manner.

The struggling scientists, however, were ridiculed or ignored or silenced in a variety of ways, even by their own colleagues, and especially by the chemical industry and by its chief disciples in the U.S. Department of Agriculture and the Food and Drug Administration. In any event their work was not entirely lost to society. There came a change.

The years 1962 and 1963 are so completely dominated by one person and one book that historians of the future may well refer to this period as the Carsonian Era of "Silent Spring" (1962). With initial appearance of excerpts of the book in the June *New Yorker* magazine, the world has been treated to the most absorbing and instructive body of scientific and pseudoscientific literature it has ever known. There has been defense and counter-defense, a focusing upon minutiae, distortion, innuendo, bias, claims of emotionalism themselves written with extreme and apparent emotion. The book rose to the Best Seller lists, and stayed there for months. With it all, I seriously wonder how many of the most vocal have really read the book! I have made it a point to ask everyone who expresses a strong opinion about it to me, whether he has really read the book. The replies unfortunately were never taped by modern recorders. In all truthfulness, I here report that I have yet to find the pro-pesticide man who admits to reading the book. (Maybe this statement will elicit affirmative replies—but, after all, a year and a half has passed.) The case is typified by the Director of Research of a large chemical manufacturer who, when asked about the book, stammered apologetically that he really had not read it; he tried; several times; but he just could not bring himself to read it. It is abundantly clear from some of the anti-reviews, that the reviewers themselves really had not read it through. They read into it what they feared to find, what the anti-chemical alarmists said they had found. In short, they criticized it for what they *thought* was in it. One of the most interesting reviews that has come to my attention is that of Dill, *et al.* (1963), in which quotations from anti-Silent Spring reviews are paired with and refuted by quotations from the book itself.

Another milestone was reached on May 15, 1963, with the Report of the President's Science Advisory Committee, published by the White House. This Report did not alter the pesticide picture as Rachel Carson had portrayed it. It vindicated that picture, and lent a stature to it that one person alone, even Dr. Carson, could not have given.

The story of pesticides in 1962–1963 is that of the angry, emotional, and sales-conscious reaction of the industry and of its disciples in government agriculture, abetted albeit innocently by the obsessively scientific, not that of the cool and calm progress of scientific knowledge through a democratic society....

Some Strands of the Human Ecosystem Web

The web of the human ecosystem—the web in which persistent pesticides have been introduced at certain points by man and have ramified throughout the web so extensively as to be causing a "revolution" in all those strands that are collectively to be called the "environment" of man—this web is a highly complex phenomenon. It is not only more complex than we think. It is more complex than we *can* think. Nevertheless, there are certain strands, and certain combinations of strands, which are sufficiently integrated into themselves to have attained a certain distinctness in our scientific thinking and action. *That they are thought to be completely independent of the rest of the ecosystem is precisely at the root of the entire pesticide-ecosystem problem.* I refer specifically to those fields of science and technology (often involving more of the latter than the former) known as agriculture, forestry, horticulture, and certain aspects of medicine. Through these four fields runs a common strand, that of entomology. It is entomology which has spawned the field of "Pest Control." There is no phrase in this entire paper which is more loaded with emotionalism than this. It sets up a great evil; then destroys it. It creates both the dragon, *and* St. George. (The fire ant was not a pest until the commercial sprayers told the believing Department of Agriculture that it was.) It is the web-strand-crossings of entomology-agriculture, entomology-forestry, entomology-horticulture, and entomology-medicine (where insects have been the vectors of disease) that have served as *the four major focal points for the entry of pesticides into the human ecosystem, and the spread therefrom.* They are worth further consideration.

Agriculture is the basis of our food supply. It is the hope of our burgeoning populations, even though we now grow too much, store too much, give away too much, destroy too much. Any threat to agriculture is couched in alarmist terms, and immediately arouses alarmist reactions in the general public. There is no question that our agriculture is dependent upon the use of chemical pesticides, even as there is no question that what the ecologist is asking for is a gradual reduction in the use of broad-spectrum persistent chemicals, and a gradual increase in various biological means of control that affect the target organism alone. On the other hand, agriculture is one of the most non-ecological of these fields, and agriculturists are some of the most non-ecological of these technicians. We must realize that agronomists are a one-species-oriented people. Their efforts are to plough, plant, and harvest the greatest crops at the least cost, within one year or even several months. In their training and in their thinking, they are strangers in time and space to the complex ecosystem. They want a simplified, if highly unstable environment.

Agriculture is extremely effective in communicating to the general public through its "extension services." The relationship between them and ecosystem ecology does not always express compatibility. Ian McMillan (in *The Condor,* 1960) says that ". . . Extension Services, more than any other forces, are responsible for this (unwise) land-use picture. What they have done, however innocently, is to encourage and advise toward maximum, immediate, economic exploitation of the land, without regard for end results. They have demonstrated and advocated only that which is most profitable economically. I have never noted any real concern for conservation of the future. Through their influence and tutelage we have, on the local level, a leadership of prosperous ignoramuses." A specific instance of problems of this kind is indicated in a release by the Connecticut Area Citizens for Biological Control (1963).

Forestry has certain things in common with agriculture, even though the time-scale for growing timber crops is far greater. Insect damage takes enormous toll of our forest resources. Insecticides "control" (but rarely eradicate) those insects. The costs of that damage in terms of the costs of insecticide control present irrefutable, sound, and logical arguments for the widespread use of pesticides—as long as only two strands of the web are considered. On the other hand, foresters can be remarkably ignorant of other strands, of the ramifying effects of wildlife changes within the forest, of long-term reactions from the loss of nitrogen-fixing "pest plants" such as alder. Silvics, as an ecological science and as the foundation of silviculture, is as undeveloped as classical "ecology." So-called control of the gypsy moth is one of the most informative case histories in this forestry-entomology ganglion. This restricted picture is presented admirably by Worrell (1960) in a tightly documented essay that links this forest economist with an Ivy League university and a respected conservation organization. We all recognize the gypsy moth as an unmitigated nuisance which should certainly be controlled without affecting the rest of the ecosystem. But, even in this rigid cost-benefit study, there is no figure for the timber losses involved, for areas where the timber value is often the least important of all ecosystem values, and where other effects in the ecosystem are simply not considered. It is an illuminating study.

Horticulture and bug control are congenial bed-fellows. He who has picked Japanese beetles endlessly off his roses, and who needs only go to the nearest supermarket to pick up a can of "harmless" (to himself) spray that will "kill everything" (he does not want), is easily convinced. I am not saying that these pesticides should never be used by the homeowner. I am only saying that they should be used wisely, that the too-fine print should be read, that alternate means should be used whenever and as soon as available. It is wisest not to drive 80 miles an hour on glare ice, even for an emergency, if alternate means are available. And it is even wiser to avoid, or not to create, such emergencies. Horticulturists and horticultural societies have been easily wooed to marriage with pesticides. They themselves are generally laymen with no professional training in any of the sciences. Too often they are gullible to the blandishments of the quick-kill-salesmen of pesticide hucksters. Frankly, I believe industry has a point when it says that the collective effect of all the homeowners putting pesticides in the ecosystem is infinitely worse than of the agriculturists. Agriculture, watching its profits, cannot afford a 5 per cent increase in pesticide use unless absolutely necessary for its immediate crop. But the home owner, finding that one spritz "works," will give 900 per cent more for good measure, often with arms and legs bare, and mouth wide open. I know the reactions of these new ex-city suburbanites, especially in town meetings when voting on gypsy moth control and when whipped into fear by the vested interests of the local agricultural experiment station. It is here, more than anywhere else, where one sees a corrosive contradiction between science and a democracy, a democracy of human beings who are apathetic, or credulous, or both. One mosquito bite where they cannot scratch in public, one fuzzy-wuzzy caterpillar on a darling baby threatening his health, and they soon turn into lawn lizards or barbecue pit vipers, which in all scientific seriousness I consider two of the most dangerous races of wildlife which can vote to affect vast areas of forest land far beyond their own quarter-acre lots.

Professional horticulturists often abet this situation. It is my sober opinion that the peak of ecological ignorance is attained in those too-numerous instances where it is recommended that one part of a garden not be sprayed, so as to protect the beneficial insects. It is, of course, reassuring to realize that these people are aware that beneficial insects exist. It is, however, very difficult to accept their implication that nature was so created for man that bad insects will go where they can get killed, and good insects where they will thrive, not to mention the intelligence of the chemicals themselves to stay where they are put, and not move past the garden wall in ground water, surficial runoff, and in the bodies of other animals in the food chain, and not react with other chemicals to form more critical compounds.

Medicine comes into our discussion from three vantages: insect-borne diseases, the field of nutrition, and pollen-caused allergies. All three may be heavily dominated, directly and indirectly, by industry.

Insect-borne diseases strike terror in the heart of man. Pesticides strike the insect-borne diseases. Ergo, pesticides are marvelous. There is no question that lives saved from malaria by DDT spraying are to be reckoned in the millions. For example, the population of Madagascar, which had been stationary for many years, doubled in a dozen years following the initiation of an antimalaria campaign. I suppose this is "good." In terms of a two-strand science, pesticides and human disease form a most successful combination. An excellent recent expression of this non-ecologic view was contributed a few months ago by Thomas Jukes (1963), formerly nutritionist and biochemist of American Cyanamid.

Nutrition itself has been the battle ground between the powerful food industry, and those who are concerned about pesticide residues in their diet. The food industry in turn has heavily invaded some of our campuses. Furthermore, the trade organizations of this industry have been extremely effective in distributing literature in saturation campaigns. Of "the genius of the American food industry," we are endlessly reminded. I have had such literature forwarded to me from strange places, small town libraries, local nature centers, school teachers. With it all, as is true in this entire field, the companies themselves keep as pure as possible. It is difficult to pinpoint the corporate source of trouble.

Allergy, as a medical field, is closely related for our purposes to the control of ragweed with herbicides. Ecosystematically speaking, ragweed control is an absurdly simple procedure. The plant is a pioneer, growing only on bare soil, not growing where it is crowded out by other plants. In croplands, it is controlled by known farming procedures. On roadsides, it is only increased by such spraying, as spraying kills its competitors as well as it, while it disappears when the rubble strip at the side of the road is itself removed by better road design. Nevertheless, this two-strand part of our ecosystem has developed to preposterous dimensions, to be mentioned [later in] this paper. Much of the "action" arises in the industry-sustained weed control conferences. My acquaintance with the public health sections of these conferences leads me to say that two groups of people attend them, M.D.s who are concerned about the pollen counts in the atmosphere but who have absolutely no knowledge about ragweed as a component of plant-communities, and commercial sprayers. The latter teach the former, and woe betide any mere botanist who dares to rear his head on the simple botanical facts of ragweed life.

In addition to forestry, agriculture, horticulture, and medicine, three other pesticide-land parts of the ecosystem are deserving of mention: wildlife, ranges and pastures, and right-of-ways and roadsides. All three of these are suffering from a lack of ecosystematic sophistication, often within their own ranks, most certainly on the part of public and other scientific groups who should be supporting them.

In behalf of wildlife, it is understandable that wildlife agencies should be the leaders in opposing unnecessary introduction of persistent broad-spectrum pesticides into the ecosystem. Wildlife is one of the first to suffer, often conspicuously and continuously so. The original fears of these agencies have been amply documented by a continuing barrage of scientific studies confirming not only actual kills, but pesticide movements through the food chains to affect every stage in the reproduction cycles of animals far removed from those initially affected. In this role, the U.S. Fish and Wildlife Service has taken a lead, and should be commended. On the subject of kills, I continue to be disgusted at the outraged replies of the non-ecologic opposition. They often represent the "Big Stiff" school of thought. Unless they have a cold corpse before them, they belittle the effect. And even if they do, they call it an "accident." It seems impossible to convince these people that nature disposes of dead bodies far quicker than they can find them. Simple reflection should indicate their errors. Assume, for example, a bird that raises six nestlings, such as the common chickadee. At the end of the season, that bird population will be 400 per cent greater. Yet by the next nesting season, the population will be the same; 75 per cent will have died. Who has seen a dead chickadee, or one in the process of feeding a predator? Now take a pesticide which destroys 90 per cent of that remaining population, and you have a population imbalance which can be extremely critical. Even worse, an empty habitat will drain into it birds from surrounding areas, very possibly to be killed by the persistent pesticides. The crime is compounded. On the matter of bird populations, there is still another highly unscientific and illogical approach by those to whom . . . well, I am not sure what has gone wrong, except that I am highly interested in this aberrational thinking and cannot explain it away to the credit of the parties involved. I refer to the misuse being made of the figures from the National Audubon Society Christmas Bird Counts (Nat. Aud. Soc. 1963). These Bird Counts are taken each winter at the Christmas season (when most birds have gone south). They are essentially number-counting outings by amateur bird watchers. Through the years, better places have been found by more birders. (Hence, higher counts.) It is quite true that some of these increased counts may be of significance to population scientists. For example, more herring gulls (more garbage in our harbors); more blackbirds (more grain crops); higher counts (more human counters). All these factors would have to be weighed carefully. What disturbs me (or amuses me—I am not sure which is the greater reaction) is the way non-ecologists are using these counts as scientific "data," to be treated statistically, in support of their pesticides-don't-harm arguments. I recall being in the audience during one public pesticide debate, when these counts were brought up by an able industry representative, and ably refuted by the opposition. On the platform after the debate, the industry representative seemed conspicuously alone, so I went up to him and, according to my usual policy, told him I was extremely interested in everything he had to say. He took the comment as a compliment, did not recognize my face (I try to keep it unknown), never asked for my name, never asked for my opinion, and discussed at some length his own views. I still feel confused, but I suspect that he believed "numbers" do not lie. They are "data." They can be treated statistically, to give infallible conclusions. I could only feel—as I do with so much of the mathematical turbulence in my own field of plant ecology—that the concepts and the methods are indeed flawless; and that all may depend on arbitrary subjective and personal elements in the very first steps of the methodology, often hidden from the observer himself, if not manipulated by a subconscious "wishful wisdom." The mind of man is still the determining factor, and not the electronic computer, which only feeds on what is given it. It cannot answer questions that it is not asked.

On the range lands of this country, the cattle and sheep industry play dominant roles. Zoicides have played dominant roles in predator control, often leading to unanticipated disruptions of the ecosystem. These extremely virulent poisons are not only carried through the food chain to still other animals. Man is learning the hard way what a good ecologist could have told him in the first place, that irruptions of rodents and rabbits are part of this ecosystemic upset. One of the clearest recent studies on this subject is that of Niering, Whittaker and Lowe (1963) in the cactus country near Tucson. In this case, it took two outside ecologists to see at once what local specialist-researchers had long been missing—that persistent cattle grazing had totally upset the original ecosystem, resulting in a new, and to a great extent irreversible, ecosystem without cactus reproduction and with more rodents. Since the land in question is a national heritage, for cactus, not cows, it remains to be seen whether this ecologic knowledge is applied without delay by those who guard our national heritages. The case has some points in common with my study of the role of fire, kinds of fires in producing, maintaining, and destroying the Everglades of Florida.

Another facet of range land management is associated with invading brush and with brush control. The role of pre-whiteman fires in conditioning the original grasslands is gradually being accepted (Humphrey, 1962) over the edapho-climatic climax jargon of an American ecology fast becoming obsolete (or so I hope). "Brush control" was heavily dominated by the aerial herbicide sprayers, and non-ecologic scientists were quite vocal in their researches on "kill" of woody plants. We hear less about that these days. Strangely, I hear more of bulldozing, and mechanical means of ripping out the unwanted plants, in recent years. Without hesitation, I say that such techniques of brush control indicate a woeful lack of ecological knowledge of the nature of plant-communities and of vegetation management. I do not say that alternative and successful methods could be applied at once; I do say that they need research by ecologists, and not by agronomists, physiologists, sprayers, or engineers.

With right-of-ways and roadsides—occupying more of our country than all six New England states put together—I have been peculiarly involved in this field of Right-of-way Vegetation Management as long as anyone in the nation. It is 95 per cent a human social problem, and 5 per cent a botanical problem, as I have amply demonstrated in various publications. The botanical solution rests on vegetation situations which are all too obvious to intelligent observers of the outdoors, and yet are contrary to certain tidy textbook and armchair theories on "plant succession" that old-time American-ecologists just hate to discard. Complications on the human social scene are formidable. Herbicide manufacturers and spray contractors are extremely effective. Highway and utility engineers know but two kinds of plants: "grass" which does not grow up; and "brush" which does. (I remember the time that I failed to convince an otherwise intelligent engineer that a shrub would not grow up into a tree.) The world's most colossal corporation, American Telephone and Telegraph, which spent 3.5 million dollars in eight years unwisely spraying 200,000 acres in one subsidiary alone, runs the largest industrial research laboratory in the world, Bell Telephone Laboratories. Yet, to my most recent knowledge, they have not one investigator evaluating the ecological results of this spraying on the vegetation! Their philosophy, as that of many other companies with which I have dealt in many capacities is that "they have the weeds," "herbicides are good for weeds," so "we use herbicides—as the salesman tells us, because he should know." A new chapter appears to open in 1962 with the formation of Right-of-way Resources of America. The founder of the organization aimed to bring together the leading scientists in the field, as a research and advisory committee. The organization has served very efficiently in communicating scientific knowledge to various citizen groups. On the other hand, it has shown certain weaknesses—typical of such scientific groups—which are anything but complimentary to the scientific fraternity. It remains to be seen whether scientists, even though the "best" in their field, have the knowledge, the courage, and the freedom, to present a united front to the public—even though industry, with a minute fraction of that knowledge, has presented an overwhelming front to the public for years.

There are two other strands in the human social ecosystem that play, or could play, significant roles. I refer first to the citizen groups dealing with the conservation of natural resources, and second our universities collectively referred to as "academia."

Conservation organizations are maturing rapidly in recent years. It is perfectly true that many of them can trace their historical origins to specialist interests, sometimes encumbered and overcast with a sickly sentimentality. On the other hand, these citizen organizations are rapidly enlarging their interests to include all strands of the ecosystemic web. The more critical ones have already attained to a degree of ecologic sophistication, in acceptance of factual knowledge, in keeping abreast of legislation activities, in communicating to the general public, far superior to that of their confreres in academia. Although the record is still spotty, and surprising blunders still occur, I feel that the greatest hopes lie in this direction. It may be unwise to single any one out for mention. If I were to judge by the number of references in my files, and by the absence of instances that I consider ecologically and sociologically unsound, I believe I would give top honors to the National Audubon Society. The academic world unfortunately too often knows this group only from its bird-feeding bird-counting members. That field known as the "conservation of natural resources" is coming closer and closer to an "applied ecosystem ecology."...

Conclusion

The scientific awareness of the problem of pesticides in the human environment is not new. For example, Lyle Thorpe, Director of the Connecticut State Board of Fisheries & Game, has told me of his concern, during the World War II spraying of Pacific islands, when he found large dead lizards soon after such spraying. Nevertheless, coordinated scientific and social concern within the sphere of general ecology is very largely a post-Silent Spring phenomenon since mid-1962.

As a scientific subject, the phenomenon lies in the field of general ecology, here often called ecosystematics to distinguish it from minor and obsolescent fields that may also carry the name "ecology."

What has developed . . . is not only the feebleness of an existing science of ecology, but also the rather disturbing inability for needed ecologic research to be carried out by both government and universities. Furthermore, there is the very disturbing inability of this ecologic knowledge to communicate itself to other parts of the human ecosystem once it does exist. And finally, there is the even more disturbing flood of literature supported by specialist-"experts" who speak from their one-strand vantages on the ecosystem web. What shows up especially and incontrovertibly is the non-existence of suitable teaching and research in our universities.

In the light of this undesirable situation, I trust that somewhere, somehow, an Institute for the Study of Ecosystem Ecology will arise, with sufficient intelligence, money and energy to carry on research and to communicate that research throughout our society. It might be affiliated with a university. It might be affiliated with a government agency, although both our state (with few exceptions) and our federal governments are themselves split into specialist groups, and lack the coordinating power of a Department of Natural Resources, or of Ecosystem Ecology. To date, only a lone woman, and a special White House panel, have shown the necessary scientific sophistication.

In our human ecosystem, the dislocation of one strand of this web, though possibly for the short-term good of that strand and of its shortsighted and narrow-minded custodians, can result in adverse readjustments through the whole web. The entire integrated ecosystem of life on earth is being weighed in the balance.

Victory in the Everglades

MARJORY STONEMAN DOUGLAS*

After a violent controversy between conservationists and the promoters of a huge jet airport in the Everglades, peace descended in Florida at last in November 1969. On Thanksgiving Day, President Nixon announced that he had made his personal decision that the jetport could not be built at that site. It was peace of a sort, because a landing strip for jet planes, already built, was allowed to function only so

* Reprinted with permission from *Interplay* (March 1970), pp. 8–11.

long as it was proved, after 90 days, that it did not destroy wildlife, pollute or contaminate its environment and threaten the water supply of the Everglades National
Park and the lower West Coast of Florida. The first few jets began to land at the training airport in January 1970, after a contract, carefully stating the restrictions, was
signed between the Federal government, the State of Florida and the Dade County
Port Authority. It was agreed also that after another jetport site had been approved,
the training strip would be moved.

It was the greatest victory yet won in the United States by national and local
conservation organizations and concerned individuals everywhere, with the support of the major national magazines, newspapers, TV and radio, against the exploitation by large private interests of our valuable and dwindling natural resources.

To the great aviation interests the Florida Everglades, with the Everglades
National Park at its southern tip, looks, from a flying airplane, like an old wet carpet.
To many Florida businessmen and newcomers it seems only a vast stretch of empty
land waiting to be used to bring more people and more money into the state of
Florida. But to conservationists and scientists, that great central region from
Okeechobee to Cape Sable is the source of wildlife and sea life and the whole
water supply of the region so that it can truly be called the heart and life of all
South Florida.

The conflict over the Everglades jetport developed long after the Dade County
Port Authority first decided that it needed a much larger airport, far away from
urban areas and the rising complaints of residents against plane noise. By 1967,
the Federal Aviation Administration had approved the Port Authority's search for a
site with a planning grant of $500,000. The Authority floated a bond issue of $52
million, of which $44 million was to go to build a jetport at some undesignated site,
preferably in Dade County. Nine different places, some as far away as the Bahamas,
were studied and declared impractical. Comments from the Port Authority indicated
that they were considering Collier County as a location. The Everglades were not
mentioned.

In 1967 Joseph Browder, a Miami radio man and member of the Tropical Audubon
Society, the local chapter of the National Audubon Society, was startled to hear, at
a meeting of the Port Authority, that the jetport was likely to be built in eastern
Collier County in the general area of the Big Cypress. The Big Cypress is a swamp
north of the Tamiami Trail on the edge of the Everglades and the location of a
Mikasuki Indian hunting ground with several villages. He called this to the attention
of the National Audubon Society, which was the group which first stopped the killing
of Everglades birds by plume hunters for the New York millinery trade, with a
Federal act. It was instrumental in establishing the Everglades National Park in
1947. They were assured by the Port Authority that every precaution would be taken
by jetport planners to protect the wildlife and the water supply of the Park, which
lies immediately to the south. Conservationists ruefully admit now that their fears
had been soothed by the reassurance of the Authority so that they did not begin their
active protest until 1968.

Demands from the Superintendent of the Everglades National Park to know
exactly how the Port Authority meant to protect the Park from the jetport, and its
inevitable surrounding development of hit-or-miss urban sprawl, were met by the

reply that they meant to build only one training strip to be run by a crew of not more than ten men.

Then Robert Padrick, chairman of the Central and Southern Florida Flood Control District, discovered that the Port Authority planned to cut a four-lane highway from Miami to the jetport straight through the Everglades, a highway hardly necessary if the Port Authority meant what it said about the single training strip. It was soon made clear that the Port Authority all this time had been quietly buying up land for a 39-square-mile jetport right there.

Representatives of many state and national conservation societies—Gerri Souci of New York, for the Eastern branch of the Sierra Club, Joseph Browder, now representing the National Audubon Society, Superintendent Raferty of the Everglades National Park, the representative of the Florida Fish and Wildlife Service—got together at once to try to force a public confrontation with the Port Authority. It would be required to reply publicly and in writing to 119 questions about the jetport, compiled and edited by the Florida National Resources Board. The answers sent back by the Port Authority were so vague, evasive and unsatisfactory, generally consisting of the phrase "under study," that the idea of a public confrontation was given up as useless. The general attitude of the Port Authority to the whole question was that these protests against a multi-million-dollar project by people who were only "alligator lovers and bird watchers" were not important enough to be bothered with.

Conservationist Fears Confirmed

In April 1969, the Department of Federal Transportation announced an appropriation of $200,000 for a multi-million-dollar high-speed transportation system to the jetport. In May, after a meeting in Naples, a Collier County businessman revealed that the Port Authority expected to build around the jetport an urban complex for heavy industries, the devastating effect of which would be exactly what the conservationists had most feared.

They learned then, if they had not learned it before, that the Port Authority had no intention of trying to keep even the vague promises they had made to safeguard the Everglades National Park and the water supply of the lower West Coast.

At this point, exhausted conservationists would have given in to despair except that new men, like Dan Paul, an attorney, joined them with bolder plans for fighting the increasing threat. Twenty-two national conservation organizations throughout the United States joined forces to bring the fight to Washington.

In June, they appealed to Senator Jackson of the Senate Committee on Interior Affairs who, with Senator Nelson, held a series of hearings on the threat to the Park by the proposed jetport. As a result, Secretary Hickel of the Department of the Interior ordered a study of the jetport's effect on the environment by Dr. L. B. Leopold of the Department of the Interior, aided by Arthur Marshall, Field Coordinator of the U.S. Fish and Wildlife Service. At the same time, the National Academy of Science began making its own study of the situation.

By late August the word began to leak out that both reports were completely adverse to the jetport. And for the first time, the Port Authority began to realize that they might be forced to abandon their plan. Ex-Secretary of the Interior Stewart Udall was hired by them to make a third environmental study. It was also reported that the Metro Commission of Dade County was so impressed by the evidence against that jetport site that they had begun negotiations with the State Cabinet of Florida to trade it for land elsewhere. Governor Kirk suggested that the port be moved to Palm Beach.

The Dade County Port Authority compounded the confusion by issuing a series of statements to the local press, in varying but less lofty tones of voice. They said they had acted in good faith with the approval of the Federal government, by which they meant the support of the Federal Aviation Administration; that they had already spent $13 million and hated to see that money go to waste; that they were sure something could be done so that the Everglades National Park would not be damaged, although they never said what; and they insisted that conservationists had delayed so long before making their first protests that the land for the jetport had already been acquired before the Port Authority learned there would be objections. This in the face of the fact that the Port Authority had bought up the land with what would seem to be deliberate secrecy.

By September 3, 1969, the fight was taken by the coalition of national conservation societies to the highest governmental levels in Washington. Secretary of the Interior Hickel held a series of meetings with Secretary of Transportation John Volpe to try to come to some agreement that would save the Park. He was increasingly irritated by the Port Authority's arrogant assumption that what they said was above question: this in the face of the adverse scientific reports, including that by Stewart Udall, which advocated moving the jetport.

The Media Enter the Fray

Suddenly the pages of many of the most important national newspapers and magazines burst forth with articles and photographs on the dangers to the Everglades National Park: *Life, Time, Newsweek,* the *New York Times,* the *Christian Science Monitor,* the *Audubon Magazine,* with much pro-Park talk on national radio and TV hookups. The general public was increasingly aroused.

Secretary Hickel found that he and Secretary Volpe could not reach an agreement on the removal of the jetport site. He therefore took the issue directly to President Nixon for his personal decision, who announced on Thanksgiving Day that the jetport was not going to be built on the Everglades site. That was that.

Work on the training strip that had brought the roar of bulldozers to the Mikusaki Indian villages and the planes to the very edge of the ancient Square Ground, scene of the immemorial Green Corn festival with its religious rites, was at once stopped. A compromise was reached by the signing of the contract stating the terms by which another jet site must be searched for by the Port Authority, the Everglades land already acquired disposed of, and what part of the expenses the Federal government was prepared to pay. If, after 90 days, the training strip was found to pollute or contaminate the environment and affect the water supply, it was to be discontinued at once. It would be moved permanently when another jetport site was found.

There is an apprehension among the embattled conservationists, elated as they are by the President's epoch-making decision, that the Port Authority may still hope to retain the jetport site by insisting that no other possible site can be found. It is quite evident that the coalition of national conservation societies, created for this emergency, as well as thousands of priviate citizens and many Florida organizations, especially the newly formed "Friends of the Everglades," are prepared to bring an unrelenting vigilance to the protection of the great region.

A Watery Eden Lost Forever

There is, of course, no question that the unique and remarkable Everglades can ever be restored to what it was in the 5,000 years of its development since the last of the risen sea water ran off at the beginning of the last Polar Ice Age.

Then the fresh water from Florida's great average rainfall flowed south through lakes and creeks into Okeechobee, from which, in rainy seasons, the excess water spilled out eastward through the Loxahatchee Slough to the Atlantic, westward slowly through the meandering Caloosahatchee, but chiefly flowed, as fast as four miles an hour, down the long curving course of the Everglades to the delta of the Ten Thousand Islands. The whole region, with the bristling sawgrass which sprang up to make it a true river of grass, was then an example of one of the most perfectly balanced natural engineering systems in the world. In dry times the fresh water glades were protected from the constant pressure of salt sea water by the rock rims of both coasts. In rainy seasons the excess fresh water flowed over natural dams, the rapids and rocks in the short rivers. Where the fresh water flowed into the salt, at the tip of Florida, astronomical quantities of tiny sea creatures were spawned, to move out to enrich the teeming Florida seas. Early man and early animals lived well throughout the Everglades then, never disturbing that wonderful, life-giving balance.

It was only the American, who, as late as 1906, first brought the threat of destruction to this system of the Glades. That was the year when Governor Napoleon Bonaparte Broward, having campaigned on a promise to drain the Everglades and create an "Empire of the Sun," sent the first dredge to digging a canal up the north New River at Fort Lauderdale, to Lake Okeechobee.

The history of the Everglades since then has been one of change and encroachment by the pressure of population, since boom days, into south Florida. The jungles south of the Lake were cut down so that vast vegetable and sugar cane fields spread and burn up the 30-foot-deep rich peaty-muck accumulated in the first 5,000 years. By the year 2000 the soil will be gone, mined out by vegetable growers. The fresh water dams in rivers, blown up for transportation, no longer prevented the encroachment of salt water, which has crept in everywhere, requiring that the well fields of growing East Coast cities be moved farther toward the Glades.

More canals were built: the St. Lucie canal from the Lake eastward, the lovely Caloosahatchee ruined by another. To keep the water table at the right level for vegetable growers around the Lake, billions of gallons of fresh water were discharged from the Lake and eastward into the Atlantic. At Stuart, the excess fresh water killed off the salt water fish in the protected inland waterways. There were complaints that there was not enough water for East Coast cities. In 1947 the Everglades National Park was established in the lower Glades.

The Army Engineers' development of a system of canals and pumps and dikes, making three great water conservancy areas for the East Coast counties, managed to cut off the vital flow of water to the Everglades National Park, thus creating a situation of great and immediate danger. Water in abundance was allowed to flow into the Park only after the conservationists' protests had an effect in Washington. Water standing in the conservancy basins, like a series of lakes, still evaporates under the Florida sun almost as fast as it can be run in. This problem has not yet been solved, along with that strange one—the surplus of fresh water in Lake Okeechobee allowed to run in billions of wasted gallons east and west into the Atlantic and the Gulf of Mexico.

A "Thirteen Million Dollar Education"?

It has been argued that the Everglades has been so changed that nothing that happens to it matters. That is an impossible belief. The Everglades are still there, if battered. The porous rock is there that holds water like a reservoir, as well as the Lake. The Florida rains and hurricanes bring their great supply of fresh water, in cycles of wet and dry. Despite the statement of some officials that the cities are threatened with water shortages, it is not unreasonable to demand wise replanning without waste, to insure water enough for all the people and cities that can be supported by South Florida, along with farms, industries, wildlife, sea life, wilderness and recreation areas and the Everglades National Park. This can be done only if the Everglades region is considered to be a related whole, one and indivisible.

Perhaps, after all, the great jetport controversy may be considered a $13 million education, if it has brought wisdom about the Everglades to millions of people, including the President of the United States.

Protectionists vs. Recreationists —
The Battle of Mineral King

ARNOLD HANO*

Mineral King Valley, located within the northern tip of the Sequoia National Forest, 228 miles northeast of Los Angeles, is a serene-appearing place. Backpackers come each summer to hike over the ridgeline into the wilderness beyond. Fishermen angle for trout in 20 emerald lakes that sparkle in hanging basins above the valley floor. A tiny community of cabin dwellers move back into their shingled shacks to escape the heat of the San Joaquin Valley towns below the Sierra's western slopes. In winter, snows sometimes bury the cabins until nothing is visible but white-mantled peaks and lonely evergreens, and the only sound is a coyote's howl. . . .

*From *The New York Times Magazine* (August 17, 1969), pp. 25+. © 1969 by The New York Times Company. Reprinted by permission. Edited.

The valley is public land, 1,500 acres in all, superintended by the U.S. Forest Service. Its magnificent ski bowls and its dependable snow pack from fall to spring have long been eyed by skiers and resort operators. Back in 1949, the Forest Service invited developers to submit proposals to turn the valley into a year-round recreation resort. But no bids were received; the problem of constructing a new access road to the valley appeared too difficult and too expensive.

By 1965, however, when bids were again invited, interest had grown mightily, and so had Southern California's ski population. A major ski resort was badly needed; this time six developers submitted plans. One bid was approved late in 1965. The bidder, Walt Disney Productions, was granted a three-year permit to develop its master plan. Now Disney's master plan has been approved by the Forest Service, accompanied by cries of anger and anguish from such traditional protectors of the primitive scene as the Wilderness Society, the National Parks Association and the litigious Sierra Club.

Nor is opposition restricted to these groups. The public has become involved. Bumper strips have begun to appear in California—"KEEP MINERAL KING NATURAL." College youngsters talk of taking their militant tactics to the Sierra hills, threatening "lie-downs" in front of the highway bulldozers to come. Letter writers, urged on by Sierra Club chapters, are pressuring Congress to help block the development. The temptation is to call this a conservation battle, but because both sides claim to be conservationists, let me try two other words—recreationists and protectionists.

At Mineral King, Walt Disney Productions intends to build a $35.3-million, year-round resort to accommodate skiers in winter and such warm-weather activists as hikers, swimmers, fishermen and campers the rest of the year. An Alpine Village will be built on the 7,800-foot-high valley floor, with five-story hotels, restaurants and shops. Twenty-two ski lifts and gondolas will rise to the magnificent skiing surfaces, 3,000 and 4,000 feet above the valley. An enclosed lift will take the hungry tourist to a restaurant midway up one peak, and the more ambitious, or less vertiginous, to another eatery, at an 11,100-foot summit. In winter there will be skiing, skating and skibobbing. Novice skiers will see their mistakes on a closed-circuit TV screen via taped replay. In summer, the valley turns into a wonderland of gurgling streams, limestone caves and grassy meadows; rugged trails to sightseeing points will permit the viewer to spot, 30 miles at a distance, Mount Whitney, America's highest peak below Alaska.

Plans have been drawn for skating rinks, heated swimming pools, horse corrals, a chapel, a theater and a five-acre sublevel parking structure for visitors' cars. A cog-assist electric railway will transport visitors from the nine-level parking facility, cut into a natural swale, to the village, a mile and a quarter up the valley. If all had gone well, construction of a new 20-mile access road, to replace the steep goat path and reduce the two-and-a-half hour trip to 35 minutes, would have begun early next year, at a cost to California taxpayers of more than $1-million a mile. And if all had continued well, Disney hoped to collect its first $1.25 (or maybe $1.50) parking fee in December, 1973. By 1978, the resort expected to attract nearly a million persons a year, to sleep up to 3,300 each night and to accommodate as many as 8,000 skiers on its slopes at one time. All this in a valley not much more than two miles long and a mile and a quarter wide.

The protectionists are aghast. They believe that the construction of the Disney development and the access road will overcrowd and desecrate the tiny valley, pollute air and streams and compromise outdoor values. They point to the official designation of Mineral King (the Sequoia National Game Refuge) and decry the plundering of a game refuge by private development with, they say, the likelihood that wild animals and their habitats will be abused. Finally, they charge that the planned access road, now blocked by the Federal injunction, must pass through nine miles of the Sequoia National Park and violate national park values. . . .

Michael McCloskey, new executive director of the Sierra Club, emphasizes the probable damage to trees along the road from auto pollutants that will coat trunk, branch and leaf. "Smog has poisoned trees in the hills around Los Angeles," McCloskey points out. "Those trees are not protected by national law. These trees are." Protectionists do not pretend that the situation will be as bad as that of Los Angeles, where an inversion layer keeps contaminants from being blown away. Sierra winds will blow most of the smog away. Most, but not all. Morison R. (Jim) James, supervisor of Sequoia National Forest, in referring to the 20-mile access route leading up to Mineral King, says: "On a hot August day, you can see the smog and haze climb up the canyon from below, even now. To some extent, this will be compounded by all the cars climbing the new road."

In reply to protectionists' arguments, both Disney and the U.S. Forest Service — landlord of Mineral King — issue a general demurrer: no pollution, no erosion, no desecration, no threat to a single sequoia, no alienation of public land or of public trust. Forest Service officials insist that the designation of the area as a national game refuge in no way affects its right to put the land to other use. The Forest Service runs its land under a "multiple-use" philosophy, assigning to each area a use or a variety of uses that seems best adapted to that area. The uses are five in number — water and watershed management, timber, grazing, wild life and recreation. Understandably, this often leads to conflict between "users." Loggers see forestland as construction material; watershed people see the same trees as necessary to prevent runoff. Concessionaires want to build hot dog stands where prairie dogs make their homes. At Mineral King, the Forest Service has decided that the valley can best be used for recreation.

Recreationists see in Mineral King a piece of primitive land once practically inaccessible and now about to be made available for the playtime pursuits of thousands of Southern Californians. . . .

The Disney people and the Forest Service are not unaware of esthetic and ecological considerations. Robert B. Hicks, an economist hired to run the Mineral King project by Walt Disney personally, before Disney's death in December, 1966, is adamant that the natural beauty of the area will remain unblemished, and that the numbers of visitors will not unduly tax the small valley's dimensions.

The Disney staff has received 37 awards for its past work in wilderness conservation. Walt Disney was a life member of the Izaak Walton League and—the observer is gently reminded—was elected in 1955 an honorary life member of the Sierra Club. . . .

Project Manager Hicks brings to his job excellent credentials. An economist, he also holds a degree in engineering. He is a one-time resident of Visalia, 55 miles east of Mineral King, so he knows the area. He has skied for more than 20 of his 47 years. He is a friend of Willy Schaeffler, director of ski events at the 1960 winter Olympics, who serves as Disney's ski consultant. The two men often ski Mineral King, learning what they can of the slopes.

Hicks spends other time visiting service clubs in Southern California, speaking to Rotary, Kiwanis and the like, softly selling the Disney plan, armed with slides of the area as it now looks and as Disney artists foresee it. He devotes a few minutes of his presentation to "correcting the misstatements of the press."

One such "misstatement" is the inclination to prejudge the Mineral King project as a transplanted Disneyland—cute, colorful, supercalifragilisticexpialidocious and out of keeping with the rugged setting of the High Sierra. Nothing so infuriates the Disney people. Says Hicks: "It is unfair to think that Disney did a good job at Disneyland, but will do a bad job elsewhere. Why not assume this project will be just as appropriate for Mineral King as Disneyland was for the recreation needs of Anaheim?"

To the Disney side of the debate have come a cluster of politicians, including U.S. Senator George Murphy, Gov. Ronald Reagan and past Gov. Edmund G. (Pat) Brown; civic groups; state and Federal agencies; local newspapers; local business-men. The Disney project will be big business, not only for Disney. The Forest Service will receive back from the Disney operation an estimated $300,000 the first year, graduating to $600,000 by Year 5—1978—based on a percentage of receipts. The building of a $23-million road is a pork barrel of much succulence. The influx of tourists means money to the gateway cities in the San Joaquin Valley below. The city of Visalia, astride a freeway that runs north from Los Angeles, is the capital of Tulare County; county officials are fairly slavering over what they expect to be $500-million in taxes, payrolls and the like within 10 years after the project opens its doors. Tulare County is afflicted by high unemployment; Pat Brown, while he was Governor, wangled $3-million from the Federal Government toward the cost of the new road because it will run through this economically depleted area.

Not that crassly fiscal advantages are the only considerations of politicians. Friendship may be another consideration. George Murphy, Ronald Reagan and Walt Disney were close personal friends. Before he left office, United States Senator Thomas H. Kuchel, long identified as a champion of wilderness, strongly endorsed the Mineral King project in words the Disney people circulate whenever the debate begins: "If we fail to develop selected areas such as Mineral King, the 50 million people who will be in California before the end of this century will spill over the sides of the coastal cities and ravage the Sierra with unplanned and undirected enthusiasm for the vanishing outdoors.". . .

Within the valley are two creeks—Monarch and Kaweah—that merge to form the east fork of the Kaweah River, one of the major watering sources of the San Joaquin Valley farmlands below.

Monarch Creek is a young stream, still carrying glacial debris as it cuts through the valley floor. It is, in fact, one of the ongoing architects of the valley, a jubilant stream that kicks up its heels once in a while. When Monarch Creek becomes bored with its old channel, it changes course and begins to carve out a new direction. Disney and the Forest Service cannot countenance such initiative that might one day send Monarch Creek waters tumbling through the lobby of a new hotel. "Disney will put the stream into a permanent channel," explains W. S. (Slim) Davis, chief of recreation for the National Forests of California, "and keep it there."

Does Forester Davis approve of this tampering with nature?

Davis chuckles, "Let's say, we'll complete nature's job sooner."

It is this chuckle that chills protectionists, the sound of smug man maneuvering nature at his whim. "That's typical of the Forest Service," says the Sierra Club's McCloskey. "'Nature doesn't know what it is doing. We know better.'"

Protectionists point out that glaciers and streams, without the help or hinderance of man, created Mineral King. The valley knows how to survive its own catastrophes, but it is defenseless before man's. Mineral King has lived through flood, volcanoes, glaciers, changeable streams and storms, not for just a century, but for 20,000 centuries. Avalanches this winter tore out several thousand trees. To the protectionists, this is nature's way. The trees will grow back. Once, millions of years ago, giant sequoias covered most of the Northern Hemisphere. Then the Ice Age swept all before it, except for a few pockets in the west slopes of the Sierra Nevada. Only here, in all the hemisphere, did giant sequoias survive. Today their offspring live, growing and vigorous. The sequoias have lived through the Ice Age. Can they live through the Disney Age?

Strictly speaking, it is not the Disney development that threatens Sierra vegetation, but the proposed access road. Mineral King has been saved from human hands, for the large part, because of its inaccessibility. . . .

In 1890, when the Sequoia National Park was established, Mineral King, though ecologically a part of the park, was not included, because of the miners. The national park system does not take in land where commercialism exists, and where man's works are as evident as they were at Mineral King, in the form of the primitive road and a few cabins.

Mineral King became, instead, part of the less sacrosanct national forest reserve. But all about it lay the Sequoia National Park, and to get to Mineral King, you had to cross the park.

In 1945, the Forest Service began to look on the area as a possible winter resort. Naturally the problem was access, and the solution was to persuade the state of California to allocate the funds for a new road. But with the migration of Americans to California, at the end of the war, the state had road-building projects enough. No state money was available when the Forest Service asked for bids from private developers in 1949, and no private developer would build a road with his own money.

In 1960, Walt Disney inquired whether the Forest Service might not again be putting the land out to bid. In 1965, a prospectus went out, and six developers responded. Even before the Disney bid was selected, the California Legislature voted to add the Mineral King road to the state highway system. After Disney was picked, the pace continued to accelerate. Funds came from Federal and state coffers.

But there remained one final step before road building could begin. The Forest Service and the Park Service had still not agreed on the road's nine miles through the Sequoia National Park. The Forest Service is part of the Department of Agriculture; the Park Service is part of the Department of Interior. Historically, these two giant Federal departments have not got along well; on this project, friction has been pronounced. The Park Service, custodian of the area through which this part of the road must run, has been traditionally more protective of the natural elements than has the Forest Service. In this instance, the major question has been whether the Sequoia National Park's giant sequoias will be endangered by the road.

Nature lovers were concerned that numbers of sequoias would be cut down to make room for the road. This fear appears groundless. California highway engineers have come up with a route that will not touch a single sequoia. Another fear remains. Will road construction, with its removal of eight million cubic yards of soil, its cuts and fills and subsequent runoff, undermine the giant trees' root structures?

The answer may depend on how carefully the California Division of Highways builds its road. Large cuts presuppose large fills, which can ravel and run off, and erode the drainage channels below. In these drainage ways many of the giant sequoias stand. If cuts are kept small, and roadbuilders immediately replant vegetation to stabilize the soil, the runoff problem is mitigated somewhat.

And the care the highway division takes may depend on the money available. It has $23-million to do the job. One consultant engineer privately estimated that building such a road properly, meeting esthetic and ecological criteria, will run closer to $45-million. Protectionists fear that, if he is right, the road will prove to be a hasty job, with much runoff and devastating soil disturbance.

There are 103 sequoias along the road right-of-way, of which 45 are said to be in a position of "possible jeopardy." But not only the sequoia is in danger. The last three miles of new road within the national park will be through thick stands of redwood, incense cedar, fir and pine.

Asked what would happen here, a Disney official said, "We will avoid the redwoods."

"How about the others?"

"We'll chop 'em down."

Perhaps the most concentrated felling of trees will occur just where the road ends, at the proposed new parking facility, below Mineral King Valley. Trees by the hundreds will be axed, to make room for cars by the thousand.

So the question is not whether there will be physical change in the area leading to Mineral King, or in Mineral King itself. The question is, how much? The question is not whether there will be disruption in the valley, but how severe? Such questions, of course, are as answerable as asking how high is up: "It is all a matter of philosophy," says Jim James. "The development will change the looks of the valley.

I'd be a fool to deny it. But it will not *ruin* the looks of the valley. It will be an acceptable change."

It depends on what you are looking at and looking for. Certain changes in Mineral King would be welcome. The development of cabins on the valley floor is today a hodgepodge of groaning slats and shattered shingles. The Disney people tell visitors that the use of pit toilets (and the bushes) by cabin dwellers and summer campers and the presence of a horse-renting stable have contaminated the river below so that it is unfit for human drinking.

Yet all this is easily changed, as the Sierra Club's Mike McCloskey points out. "A little enforcement by the Forest Service would keep the place clean." Nor does McCloskey think the river is that contaminated. "A recent park report says the water quality is excellent for fish. It can't be very polluted."

The problem at Mineral King is that recreationists and protectionists look at the same thing with different eyes. One sees public land unused and considers it a waste. The other sees the same public land unused, and considers it preserved. One sees the tampering with nature, and considers it necessary. The other sees the tampering with nature, and imagines a biotic community jeopardized. One views ski slopes and wild animals, in that order. The other views wild animals and ski slopes, in that order. One seeks immediate gratification for himself; he wolfs down pleasures and seeks out more. He is hedonist, recreationist. The other defers his gratifications, saving them for later generations. He is puritan, protectionist. The recreationist at Mineral King says: "Look beyond the ridges; there are still nearly two million acres of adjacent wilderness. What's wrong with using this tiny piece of land, this mere 1,500 acres, this less than one-tenth of 1 per cent of all the national forest land in California?" The protectionist sees population growing and public land shrinking, and he wonders where it will ever stop.

The recreationist sees public land put to use; the protectionist sees it put to auction. In California alone, 46 ski areas have been built on national forest land; throughout America, the figure is nearly 200. The only thing unique—say the recreationists—is that the Disney resort will be better than any other. The only thing unique—say the protectionists—is the magnitude of the Disney development.

One wonders, today, whether the Forest Service does not secretly agree that the proposed development is a wee bit bigger than the service originally conceived. The Forest Service prospectus, calling for bids, speaks of a development "conservatively estimated at $3-million." The Disney investment will be $35.3-million. The Forest Service prospectus suggests accommodations for "at least" 100 overnight visitors. Disney plans to bed down 1,505 the first year, and 3,310 by 1978. The prospectus calls for parking 1,200 autos; Disney's nine-level facility will handle 3,600 cars the fifth year, with plans for two supplemental parking lots in case of overflow crowds.

Do these quantum jumps give the Forest Service occasional twinges concerning the ability of the tiny valley to absorb such a crush of visitors and installations? Forest Service recreation specialist Peter J. Wyckoff says: "I'm not worried about the winter and skiing. But in the summer the country is fragile and overuse could easily destroy it." Mike McCloskey testifies to the fragility: "At this high elevation, the growing season is short, and vegetation has a tenuous hold on life. Only a narrow balance of conditions allows vegetation to thrive here. Upset the balance, and you destroy that hold on life."

So the Forest Service must know it has taken a chance.

The Sierra Club has also worried that the Disney development would trigger similar developments in the area. Even Disney had been concerned, remembering how—in Bob Hicks's words—"honky tonks and beer parlors" had sprung up on private land all around Disneyland, giving the area a cheap and garish look. Hoping to avert this at Mineral King, Disney had bought up the small parcels of private land near the site of its proposed development to insure unified control of the area. But a parcel of 160 acres within the boundary of the Sequoia National Forest, near the town of Silver City, five miles west of Mineral King, remained in other private hands.

Early in 1969, the Tulare County planning department approved an application for construction of a residential and commercial community on this 160-acre site, the Seaborn-Wells project. The development would include a 30-unit motel, a 72-unit lodge, 20 condominiums, 48 single-family units, a gas station, a swimming pool, stores and a restaurant. All virtually cheek by jowl with Mineral King.

Now the Forest Service finds itself in an embarrassing position. On one hand, it endorses development on *public* land by a private investor—the Disney organization. On the other, it finds itself opposed to development of *private* land by a private investor—the Seaborn-Wells people.

"We are against a development of this magnitude in the valley," says Jim James, and he is talking about Seaborn-Wells, not Disney. "It competes with the idea we have of the total capacity of the place." Jim James spoke to the Tulare County board of supervisors, and in May Seaborn-Wells was turned down. But Seaborn-Wells will now appeal.

If Seaborn-Wells wins its appeal, the Forest Service will institute condemnation proceedings to buy the land. But 160 acres in this area of suddenly inflated real-estate values could cost as much as $2-million. All this should have been taken care of before the Forest Service put Mineral King out for bid in 1965; the 160 acres could have been bought up for a song.

The Sierra Club fears of "piggy-back" developments were further confirmed in June when plans were announced for the construction of a 12,000-acre resort at Three Rivers, gateway to Mineral King.

Withal, the Forest Service has emerged as something less than heroic. In its Mineral King prospectus in 1965, the service estimated the cost of the new access road at $5-million. It missed by $18-million. When asked about this discrepancy, the Forest Service explained: "We were using 1953 cost figures." This is the service that superintends 186 million acres of public land.

Something else is needed. We all have suffered too long over Federal and state abuse of public land. Dams in the Grand Canyon; oil wells drilled in the Santa Barbara channel that seep tar over the golden beaches of Southern California and murder birds and sea life in the bargain; state tidelands in Maryland slickered away from the people and given to a real-estate developer; now, Mineral King.

You can't blame Disney or his ilk. That is the nature of the beast. But someone or something must keep a check on development; somebody must say: "All right, that's enough. Any more and the place bursts at the seams." When Disney's Bob Hicks was asked: "How come you've got a chapel in your plans? Isn't that the beauty of Mineral King—that you don't need to get inside a building to commune with God?" he answered: "I agree. I don't see the need. Somebody threw it in." The problem won't be getting Disney to leave out things, but to keep it from throwing in more. Yet there is nobody to keep it from throwing in more. The Forest Service is, by law, that check, but a Disney official says with contempt: "Our standards are higher than the Forest Service's."

What we have at Mineral King is another absentee landlord. It is easy enough to be offended by the Disney project, and its threat to the ecology of Mineral King. Something is going to be taken forever from Mineral King—nature with the bloom of creation upon it. In its place, Disney will leave another pleasure palace, for Southern Californians, who have more pleasure palaces per capita than any other people in the world. So it is easy for the protectionist to take his potshots at the Mineral King development.

But more significant is how government landlords—Park Service, Forest Service and the like—continue to allow massive violations of public land. Yellowstone National Park—our oldest national park—is today a chaos of urbanization within a bewildered wilderness. Yosemite National Park is so overcrowded, a trip becomes more drudgery than pleasure. The scars to the terrain of our national forests, left by indifferent loggers, turn public land into festering sores.

What can be done? The President's new Cabinet-level Environmental Quality Council might help, though its first action—to suggest further oil drilling in the Santa Barbara channel—boggles the minds of protectionists in the coastal cities of California. What is truly needed is a Federal Department of Conservation, to protect all our natural resources—to handle pollution of air, water and land; to study population growth; to establish public-land policy; to meet recreation needs without disturbing wild-life ecology. All the parts tied together in one department, not sundered among a half-dozen.

As for Mineral King, the whole struggle may be past history. It is not likely the Sierra Club will win a permanent injunction against the development, although the granting of a temporary injunction may force Disney to postpone its opening. Even the most optimistic conservationists know the score—Progress always beats Protectionism. It is less likely that the Forest Service will now suggest to Disney: "Look, this is a great pleasure palace you have designed, but perhaps the valley can't take it. Can't you cut it back—leaving out the theater, the chapel, the closed-circuit TV, the restaurant on the summit, a few hundred parking spaces? Can't the people swim in the lakes; do we need heated pools? Can't it be a *modest* development, with five or six ski lifts, not 22; with two slopes for skiing, not five?"

But it is too late. The Forest Service will not sacrifice $300,000 the first year, and $600,000 the fifth year. Such money justifies its existence, come budget time. Mineral King has subtly changed in Forest Service eyes, from a remote and lovely alpine valley to a playground with turnstiles.

Perhaps, then, the truest value of Mineral King is that it stands as the latest crass example of abuse of public land by the very agents to whom we entrust that land. One wonders how long America must tolerate such stewardship.

Private Interests and Public Lands

ROBERT S. GILMOUR*

Corporations, conservationists and associated private beneficiaries of the federal domain have long been regarded as influential, perhaps the most influential of those who decide on disposal and use of public land resources. That private interests participate in nearly all administrative and legislative decisions affecting the timber, forage, mineral, water, wildlife and recreational resources on public lands is taken for granted.

Traditionally, conservation groups have been viewed as pitted in a continuous, stag-like battle with private economic interests to check wholesale despoilation and plundering of forests, parks and wild lands. As early as 1895, John Muir and his newly formed Sierra Club opened a vigorous campaign against loggers and stockmen who "invaded" the Yosemite Valley. The continuation of that fight is still recognizable, in other sectors, fully three-quarters of a century later. Antedating even Muir's famous efforts in the Far West, John A. Warder founded the American Forestry Association in 1873 to challenge "cut-and-get-out" loggers of the East and Midwest. But in this century the traditional picture of embattled conservationists and land users often obscures or miscomprehends a more complex reality involving shifting alliances of numerous governmental as well as nongovernmental participants. Indeed, conservation societies have more than once found themselves on opposite sides of intense resource-use controversies. Some, such as the American Forestry Association, have been torn from within, experiencing the heft of industry memberships. Also, private interests are involved in different types of policy-making processes, regardless of whether the site of decisional power is Congress or the Executive Branch. Before examining the processes further, our attention is first directed to the participating private organizations, their goals, capabilities and political roles in public lands politics. No two interest groups hold precisely the same perspectives on the value of available land resources or identical claims to land use, but areas of common interest are identifiable and mutually understood within each of these private organizations.

Conservation-Recreation Groups

Specific organizational objectives advanced by groups in this general category range from wilderness and natural resource preservation to large-scale develop-

*Reprinted with permission from Current History (July 1970), pp. 36-42. Footnotes deleted.

ment of public land areas for mass recreation. Most do have one important feature in common: they serve no special economic purposes nor do they attempt to claim economic benefits for their members. There are exceptions, of course. The American Ski Association and the Outboard Boating Club of America, among others, clearly represent commercial recreation interests with definite economic stakes in land policy outcomes.

Groups of this sort participating most regularly in public lands decisions since World War II were the Izaak Walton League of America, the National Audubon Society, the National Wildlife Federation, the Sierra Club, the Wilderness Society, and the Wildlife Management Institute. This list is by no means exhaustive; nevertheless these are the organizations public lands officials and congressmen "expect" to become active when conservation values are at stake.

During the 1960's, newer groups of this type have also become frequent participants in policy-making. Among these are the Sport Fishing Institute, the Save-the-Redwoods League, Ducks Unlimited, and Friends of the Earth. Clearly, several of these groups have more specialized objectives than a general conservation society such as the Izaak Walton League. Accordingly, their participation has been selective.

Also important to conservation-recreationist goals, and to political contests involving those goals, has been support rendered by lobbying organizations with broad-gauged interests such as the A.F.L.-C.I.O., the Farmer's Union, the General Federation of Women's Clubs, the National Association of Soil Conservation Districts, and the National Grange—recruited by conservationists as a means of enhancing their coalitions and demonstrating their breadth of appeal.

Conservation and recreation associations vary considerably in their numerical strength and their organizational divisions as well as in their specific objectives. The venerable Izaak Walton League of America and the National Audubon Society in 1970 had, respectively, 55,000 and 100,000 individual memberships in several hundred local chapters throughout the country. Each organization supports representatives in Washington to sustain lobbying activities, although its main headquarters are elsewhere.

National Audubon maintains an extensive staff of over 50 professionals in New York City where the society produces its handsomely tailored and politically sensitive magazine, *Audubon*. The Wilderness Society, which has tripled in size during the 1960's—to 60,000 members—has no subsidiary units. It does engage a highly active Washington staff of 25 persons to promote the preservation of federal wild areas and to inform members, regularly, of its progress and setbacks. The rapidly expanding National Wildlife Federation has a full-time staff of 21 to coordinate the activities of 8,600 local chapters and 480,000 associate members.

The Sierra Club, once a Far Western regional organization, has rapidly extended both its interests and its membership to the East. Sierra Club headquarters remain in San Francisco, but there is now a New York City staff of nine and a Washington contingent of two. The club is almost invariably represented at important intergroup conservation meetings and congressional hearings held in Washington, not to mention those conducted in the West. The Wildlife Management Institute is the only national conservation group distinguished by substantial backing from private industry. Even so, the institute's goals and actions vis-à-vis divisive issues such as wilderness and wild rivers preservation are seldom compatible with those of the organized economic interests.

In most political controversies, national conservation and recreation organizations have found ready agreement according to the generally shared objectives of protecting natural resources on the remaining federal wild areas from industrial exploitation and developing more and better recreational facilities in existing multiple-use areas. But as the pressure for additional public facilities increases, a growing stress between preservation and recreation values and their organized expression appears to be inevitable. Tensions of this sort have already become evident when organizations representing mechanized recreationists—skiers, motor boat enthusiasts and auto campers—have broken ranks with the traditional alliance. For example, the Outboard Boating Club of America submitted lengthy statements to Congress in the late 1950's and early 1960's opposing the proposed Wilderness Preservation Act in much the same terms as those employed at the time by various economic interests also opposed to the bill.

Uneasy Partnerships

Historically, conservation-recreation groups have maintained an uneasy partnership with the United States Forest Service (Department of Agriculture) and the National Park Service (Department of the Interior) in many political contests. This accord does not withstand jurisdictional disputes between these two agencies, such as their struggle for the Oregon Dunes in the early 1960's. Conservation associations typically side with the Park Service, indicative of tensions inherent in the Forest Service's concept of multiple-use management. Conservationists have generally been even less enthusiastic about the operative multiple-use principle in the Bureau of Land Management (Department of the Interior).

In some of the controversies, such as the dispute over the wilderness preservation in its early stages, allied conservationists have opposed all three of these federal bureaus and, in this case, the Interior Department's Bureau of Indian Affairs in addition. In relation to land-managing agencies, conservation and recreation groups are not unlike economic interests concerned with public lands in wanting, as former Forest Service Chief Richard McArdle put it, "to bolt down one particular use over large areas . . . priority over all other uses."

Economic Interests

Because of the diversity of corporate enterprise permitted on the public domain, the specialized interests of economic associations active in land politics are more varied and numerous than those of conservation and recreation groups. Nonetheless, each of these national organizations has the definite purpose of enhancing the conditions of access, exploitation and development of forest resources by its members. Most may be roughly classified according to the general types of resources—timber, forage, minerals and water power—most important to commercial operations of the companies and individual entrepreneurships they represent.

Privately owned wood lots continue to supply the major proportion of raw material for American forest products. But industrial dependence on the national forests, forest lands controlled by the Bureau of Land Management and forests on Indian reservations has increased steadily during the past decade. Representing the expanded resource needs of loggers, saw mill operators and forest products manufacturers are three large and consistently active national associations. Two of these, the American Paper Institute (A.P.I.) and the American Pulpwood Association, have their central offices in New York City. Both maintain continuous contact with the third and largest organization of this type, the National Forest Products Association (N.F.P.A.), located in Washington, D.C. The American Pulpwood Association has some 350 corporate members; the A.P.I. and N.F.P.A. each are federations of more than a dozen state and regional associations.

Subsidiary divisions of each national group, and individual corporations as well, participate in legislative and administrative decisions through their testimony at congressional hearings and through their informal meetings with congressional committee chairmen, with other congressmen, and with officials in the Departments of Agriculture and the Interior. Often this participation is the result of encouragement and guidance from the national organizations' leadership.

Similar organizations articulate the interests of ranchers and stockmen utilizing the forage resources of the public range and the national forests and grasslands. The National Wool Growers Association, established in 1865, and among the oldest organized economic interests, represents approximately 20,000 members in 28 divisions. Even larger is the American National Cattlemen's Association, a confederation of 150 organizational members—40 state and 110 regional—which claims to represent 300,000 ranchers and breeders. Although these organizations have been heavily involved in resource policymaking, not confining themselves to grazing issues alone, neither maintains its headquarters in Washington.

Associations concerned primarily with the exploitation of mineral wealth (metals, petroleum and other subsurface resources) have not generally organized or confederated their lobbying activities beyond the state and regional level. One exception is the American Mining Congress, established in 1898, and currently maintaining a staff of 40 full-time employees in offices near the Capitol. The A.M.C. represents over 600 domestic mineral producers and seldom fails to advocate their interests during legislative contests concerning the application or change of the mining laws. A comparable national group representing oil and natural gas interests is the American Petroleum Institute. However, the A.P.I. has been no more active in public conservation disputes than such regional associations as the Independent Petroleum Association and the Western Oil and Gas Association.

Individuals and companies with a stake in the development of water resources for electric power or reclamation purposes have also organized strong local and regional groups, but most of these are affiliated with the National Water Resources Association (N.W.R.A.). The Association has 5,000 members in 18 Western states and maintains a staff of five in Washington, D.C. Formerly known as the National Reclamation Association, the N.W.R.A. has long had a strong relationship with the Bureau of Reclamation in the Department of the Interior.

A diversity of forest-use goals among the several types of organized economic interests generates remarkably few intergroup conflicts, notwithstanding occasional disputes over the application of the mining and mineral leasing laws. General compatibility of their economic objectives with the prevailing Agriculture and Interior Department policies of multiple use of resources encourages the formation of loose intergroup coalitions across industry lines. Very often these are formed to defend the status quo of access to public domain resources and to counterclaim the persistent and increasing demands of conservationists. Consequently, interest group representatives in both coalitions regularly anticipate the performance of mediating or negotiating roles by those in relevant positions of governmental authority.

Capabilities and Political Roles

The home office location of many national interest organizations is indicative of an important facility for sustained access to federal policy-making—physical proximity to the arenas of legislative and administrative power. Maintenance of well established staff headquarters in Washington promotes the development of interpersonal relationships, often of many years standing, between leading representatives of these associations and their governmental counterparts. Moreover, a confederal organization, common to most national groups, enables them to develop similar relationships with federal administrative officers in the field as well as nation-wide communications networks to transmit politically relevant information and for the activation of widespread popular support or demonstrations of economic impact. Not all the organizations discussed above have the advantages of these facilities, but those that do not have such facilities tend to ally themselves on a temporary or permanent basis with national associations situated more favorably for protracted legislative or administrative contests.

Other facilities of access and influence are less evenly distributed. For example, preservation and conservation groups continued to gain advantage from the prevailing myth of the "ravaging interests" long after the era of untrammeled land exploitation was substantially curtailed by congressional acts and tightened administrative regulations. Most conservation associations have also been able to exploit the surge of interest in outdoor recreation and the consequent popular demand for protection of publicly owned scenic and natural areas. Yet the sustained influence of these groups appears to be limited to the extent that they can arouse membership support in response to crises. This accentuates the strategic advantage in regularized instigation of conflict situations in order to avoid mass membership apathy and decline.

Economic organizations are less subject to cyclical variations in membership size and interest, primarily because they are better able to provide, consistently, both political and nonpolitical advantages important to the corporate lives and profits of their members. Although economic groups find it difficult to generate mass popular support for their policy stands, they are in a position to explain and justify resource claims in the language of national and local economic health. They are often successful in gaining support for this stance among national associations of more general economic purpose, organizations such as the National Association of Manufacturers, the Chamber of Commerce of the United States and the American Farm Bureau Federation.

Considering the diversity of their institutional objectives and stakes in political contests to decide the outcomes of public land issues, economic and non-economic groups severally perform remarkably similar roles. Functioning as advocates for specific organizational goals, national interest group participants in land resource policy-making act as originators of new proposals to modify existing resource allocations, as coalition and alliance builders among organizations with compatible needs, and as bargainers with competing groups and with officeholders in the Executive Branch and Congress. Obviously, private groups might not perform all these roles in the same decision-making situation, nor do all occupy equally advantageous positions for the performance of each role in different policy contests.

Lobby-Sponsored Legislation

As originators of ideas for statutory change in public land administration, organized resource users are probably even more prolific than the federal managers. Certainly interest groups are less constrained in their drafting efforts in that they need not endure the delays and reverses of formal legislative clearance in the Executive Branch. This is not to suggest that all interest group bills submitted to Congress are favorably acted upon or even seriously considered. Most are given the courtesy of an introduction by a friendly congressman and then pigeonholed. Of course the same may be said of many executive proposals for new legislation, but the percentage of successes by federal bureaus is much higher than that of their client groups. Nonetheless, private associations have originated proposals that were later elevated as important public lands issues by congressional committees, and some were enacted as law.

After World War II, livestock and wool growing organizations offered a series of grazing bills which were successively initiated for congressional consideration by the Committees on Agriculture and on Interior and Insular Affairs. All but one of these bills were defeated by the concerted opposition of conservationists, the Forest Service, and members within the congressional committees themselves. The single exception, the Granger-Thye Act of 1950, succeeded to passage after extensive alterations were imposed on the original draft.

While grazing disputes were still in progress, a similar effort to change national forest administration was made by conservation and outdoors associations. Congressional hearings were held in both House and Senate on proposals initiated by conservationists to earmark forest receipts—moneys from timber sales and grazing fees—for construction of recreation facilities. None of these bills was successful, but the concept of a special fund for recreation, land acquisition and development was later sponsored by the Outdoor Recreation Resource Review Commission and by President John F. Kennedy. This type of fund became the prime feature of the Land and Water Conservation Act of 1964. Of all public lands bills originated by national interest groups since 1950, the wilderness preservation bill was unquestionably the most significant in terms of the intergroup conflict it generated, its eventual success, and its lasting aftereffects. Drafted by the Wilderness Society in 1956 and supported by a coalition of conservation and recreation organizations, the bill was finally passed in 1964.

It should be stressed that interest-group drafts of new statutory provisions have very little chance of precipitating issue contests unless they are singled out for sponsorship by the chairman or ranking member of a jurisdictionally relevant congressional committee, or unless they are supported by Executive Branch participants and approved in the legislative clearance process. Neither is likely unless the originating group can demonstrate the agreement of other specialized interests on behalf of its proposals, or better yet, can show widespread popular support for the measure. Both possibilities place a premium on the consummation of strong and articulate coalitions, lending impetus to congressional or executive elevation of an issue and promoting an effective legislative campaign. The same may be said of groups wishing to maintain a status quo position so that claims pressed by coalitions attempting to change the existing allocation of resources may be halted or at least modified.

Loose intergroup coalitions are most commonly formed to initiate or respond to an emergent issue for the duration of one legislative contest. Others are formally maintained on a more permanent basis. The Citizens Committee on Natural Resources is such an alliance, which has long been active among conservation groups. It operates as an information and communications center for its members, undertaking independent lobbying activities as well. Similarly, several of the national timber production associations maintain a formal alliance known as the Forest Industries Council. The Council is directed by a board consisting of the presidents and executive secretaries of the American Pulpwood Association, the American Paper Institute, and the National Forest Products Association. This board meets frequently to consider what positions should be adopted and actions taken on pending or anticipated policy-making situations or disputes. Both these formal coalitions frequently send representatives to appear at congressional hearings and at other legislative bargaining sessions. Each has full-time staff representatives in Washington. These alliances are also active in efforts to muster coalition unity and support during periods of intense controversy over the interests of their members.

In competitive situations, allied groups confronted with the prospect of statutory changes viewed as detrimental to their members typically act as bargainers on behalf of amendments to modify or eliminate the adverse effects of such measures. The medium of exchange in transactions arrived at is most generally a pledge of support for the amended bill by the bargaining coalition, or at least a reduction of that coalition's efforts to defeat the bill outright. Such bargains are not normally consummated as formal agreements. Nor are coalesced groups sponsoring or supporting the resource allocation changes at stake in positions to deal with their opponents directly. Rather, bargains introducing alterations in proposed legislation are negotiated by intermediaries in positions of governmental authority— federal land managing agencies and departments, Budget Bureau officials, and senior members of the congressional committees on Agriculture or Interior—each performing roles as mediators or interest brokers.

Policy Processes

Students of natural resource politics frequently view policy outcomes in this field as the self-interested pronouncements of cozy elites, each involving a federal

executive agency, congressmen and senators on a particular committee or sub-
committee, a private association, and a relatively homogeneous local constituency.
These "subsystems" or "subgovernments" are understood to hold a near monopoly
on policy within the carefully circumscribed jurisdiction of each. Material conflicts
between private interests are thus said to be avoided, indeed, excluded. In describing this "most important political reality" of land and water politics, Professor Grant
McConnell reports:

> Where dramatic conflicts over policy have occurred, they have appeared
> as rivalries among public administrative agencies, but the conflicts are more
> conspicuous and less important than the agreements among these systems.
> The most frequent solution to conflict is jurisdictional demarcation and estab-
> lishment of spheres of influence. Logrolling, rather than compromise, is the
> normal pattern of relationship.
> The success of logrolling and settlement by jurisdictional demarcation
> depends heavily on the exclusion of substantial parts of the population and of
> important interests and values from *all* these systems . . .

Political scientist Theodore J. Lowi carries the analysis further to suggest that

> most contemporary public land and resource policies . . . are characterized
> by the ease with which they can be disaggregated and dispensed unit by
> small unit, each unit more or less in isolation from other units and from any
> general rule.

In a word, these policies and the processes which offer them are "distributive" in
character:

> These are policies that are virtually not policies at all but are highly individ-
> ualized decisions that only by accumulation can be called a policy. They are
> policies in which the indulged and the deprived, the loser and the recipient,
> need never come into direct confrontation.

Understandably, such a policy-making process is made possible by a political
"pork barrel" filled with "unrelated items." What's more, the barrel is presumed to
be infinitely large.

No doubt public land policy of the nineteenth century was arrived at in much the
manner described by these analysts—add to the mix a healthy dose of incom-
petence and corruption. Just as certainly the "distributive" politics of public land
resources continued well into this century. Some public lands decisions continue
to be made according to this model but overwhelmingly public resource use is
now determined in a process regularly referred to as "pluralism." It is not that the
"subsystems" or "subgovernments" have atrophied. On the contrary, they have
been expanded to include additional federal bureaus, congressional committees
and subcommittees, additional and contentious national interest groups, the communications media in its various forms, and an increasingly heterogeneous collection of state and local actors—political executives, agencies and private groups.

Political pluralism is characterized by competition among interest groups and
other actors for the same stakes or resources, bargaining among these parties to
each decision, and compromised outcomes offering a middle ground solution that

"satisfies everyone a little bit but no one entirely." Carried on within the structural frameworks offered by legislative and administrative procedures, this was precisely the kind or process that could be observed in nearly all major—and minor—public lands decisions of the past two decades. Just to name a few, the Granger-Thye Grazing Act of 1950, the Multiple-Use Mining Act (1955), the Multiple-Use and Sustained-Yield Act (1960), the Wilderness Preservation Act (1964), the Land and Water Conservation Act (1964), and the Wild and Scenic Rivers Act of 1968 were all the much compromised results of pluralist politics. During the same period, defeats of the Echo Park and Ramparts Dams and cancellation of the South Florida Jetport adjacent to the Everglades National Park were rather clearly the results of formerly "distributive" arenas turned highly competitive.

As the prevailing nineteenth century fiction of superabundant resources gives way to the reality of scarcity and over-capacity demand in the twentieth century, as commercial organizations and conservationists gain greater capacity for political action, and as the interconnectedness of all natural resources is more widely understood, it is to be expected that public lands policy-making will entail even greater involvement of private groups and more intense conflict. It also seems likely that the "individualized decisions" of the past may be reaggregated in omnibus packages now common to several policy areas.

5

Contamination
of the Water

Clean water is perhaps the most critical of all natural resources. Without it man sickens and dies, crops wither, fields become barren, and the earth becomes un-inhabitable. In his search for quality of life, man has come to rely upon water for many purposes less directly related to survival. The rivers, lakes, and oceans have been transformed into highways of commerce which facilitate trade and economic activity. The waterways and oceans have seemed to be limitless reservoirs for the dilution of domestic and industrial wastes and ideal places to discharge the heated output of electrical generating plants. As sources of additional food the oceans have frequently been considered to be potential beds of non-renewable resources capable of promoting a high standard of living for any foreseeable growth in the world's population. Water has provided man with one of the more stimulating ex-amples of natural beauty and has increasingly become a highly valued recreational source.

Through their importance and availability, water resources have significantly contributed to the environmental crisis. Great cities and industrial plants have grown beside navigable streams, lakes, and natural harbors. The cities and plants have poured billions of gallons of effluent into the waterways, turning them into little more than open sewers and massive cesspools. Rather than sources of natural beauty waterways are all too frequently aesthetic insults and health hazards. Fish, once an important source of food, are often so contaminated by DDT and mercury and other noxious chemicals that they are unsafe to eat. Harbors, beaches, and streams have frequently become so coated with oil carelessly spilled or poured upon their surface that wildlife has been destroyed, recreational use has become impossible, and in some cases rivers have become fire hazards. The spewing into the waterways of millions of tons of nutrients from city sewer systems, detergents, and run-off from fertilized farms, and the increasing level of heat in streams from power plants (thermal pollution), have made many bodies of water virtually unin-habitable by wildlife and have stimulated the growth of algae to the point that many lakes are rapidly dying. Thus, clean water, so essential for a quality of life and even for life itself, may be a disappearing resource unless immediate corrective actions are undertaken.

The ability of the political system to respond effectively to the need for clean water is severely restricted by the physical dimensions of the water system. Waterways do not respect legal and political jurisdictions. The pollution by a local industry or a single city has significant effects on rivers, lakes, and oceans many miles away from the source of the damaging discharge. Much pollution of our water results from the cumulative effect of many small and, in themselves, relatively unimportant sources of contamination. Therefore, it is frequently difficult to identify clearly the activity in need of control. Moreover, the affected legal jurisdiction may have no authority over the polluter, and the administration of controls is both costly and difficult.

Control of the quality of water is complicated by the traditional system of water distribution and sewage disposal in America. This system is fragmented and diffuse. Much of the responsibility for water control is held by small special-purpose districts with limited resources and legal powers. The attempts of these agencies to protect water quality, with or without state and national aid and pressures, are constrained by a number of factors. Water law tends to be rigid and slow to change to meet new environmental conditions. There is still a lack of necessary technological information and financial resources. Administrative inertia is substantial, and powerful groups often find it in their self-interest to block significant changes in the system. Public awareness of the scope of the problem is limited, and many attitudes, such as the widely held belief that clean water should be a "free" resource, militate against vigorous governmental activity.

The problem of clean water has reached crisis proportions. It is intimately related to today's total ecological crisis. The political system must develop ways and means to protect this resource from further deterioration in order to insure the maintenance of the quality of life. The theme of this chapter is that the pollution of water is a major component of the environmental crisis. Present political structures, decisions, and attitudes are still inappropriate to deal effectively with the problem. The articles in this chapter describe the scope and significance of the problem, the major sources of the current threat, the implications for the nation and the world of continued deterioration in the quality of water, the general political response, and the prospects for effective action.

In the opening article, Peter Schrag describes the appalling deterioration of Lake Erie and the streams that flow into it. He details the major sources of the destruction of this body of water and specifies some of the activities being undertaken, as well as those that must be added, to reverse the trend toward environmental decay. Arguing that commitment is necessary to preserve the Lake, Schrag expresses doubt that the present level of commitment is adequate to the task.

Gene Bylinsky approaches the problem of water pollution from a broader perspective. He surveys the major configuration of the problem and its major causes and consequences. Evaluating and critically appraising governmental activities designed to control water pollution, he concludes that, "Unless pollution abatement is undertaken in an imaginative and systematic manner, the 'war' against dirty rivers may be a long, and losing campaign." Optimism over early significant progress, he contends, would be ill-founded.

Professor Rienow focusses attention on the pollution of the seas and documents the deterioration of water quality and the destruction of the resources the seas could provide. Vividly describing the wanton destruction of the seas, he calls for new and more vigorous approaches to the problem. The seas present a particularly ticklish situation in policy design because the ecological effects must be taken into account not only by individual nation states but also by the larger international community.

In the final selection, Professor Molotch presents one of the more dramatic threats to clean water — the spilling of oil onto our waterways and beaches. He traces the political and interest group ties which make this particular example of environmental despoilation possible and which have hampered any serious attempt to prevent its recurrence. The political system, as he sees it, is ill-suited to the needs of environmental protection. The political system and the power relationships within it need reordering to protect the ecology from the activities of persons primarily committed to financial reward.

Life on a Dying Lake

PETER SCHRAG*

North Central flight 940. We take off to the west from the Detroit Metro Airport, turn left in a large loop around the city, and emerge over the crotch of the Detroit River where the patterned effluent spills into the waiting blue water of Lake Erie. *Two weeks before the final countdown for Apollo 11, the supreme $24-billion apotheosis of American technology; the greatest thing, Richard Nixon will say, since the creation.* The brown waters hug the western shore, and beyond, through the thin haze from the Michigan stacks, the ore carriers cut white wakes to feed the factories. We cross the rectilinear fields of Pelee Island and pass Pelee Point on the Ontario shore to the north. Less than 150 miles to the south is Wapakoneta, Ohio, where the first man to set foot on the moon was born.

Man is destroying Lake Erie. [Says the report from the Federal Water Pollution Control Administration.] Although the accelerating destruction process has been inadvertent, it is as positive as if he had put all his energies into devising and implementing the means. After two generations the process has gained a momentum which now requires a monumental effort to retard. The effort must not only be basin-wide and highly coordinated; it must be immediate. Every moment lost in allowing the destruction to continue will require a longer, more difficult, and more expensive corrective action.

Prosaic language from Washington: eutrophication, secondary treatment, nutrient removal, algal blooms, biological oxygen demand. There is little romance in a sewage plant, and none in the technicalities of oxygen depletion, thermal stratifica-

*Copyright © 1969 by Peter Schrag. Reprinted from OUT OF PLACE IN AMERICA, by Peter Schrag, by permission of Random House, Inc.

tion, or discharge of organic wastes. But the destruction of a lake is not merely a technical or a political problem. To think of it is to think of all America, of our love-hate relationship with our technology, about our ambivalence about who we are and what we are, about the Hudson and the Missouri, about the Santa Barbara Channel and nuclear bombs, about defoliation in Vietnam and DDT-poisoned fish in Michigan—about all the things we value, often in contradiction—in our past and our future.

As the plane descends over the murky waters along the Cleveland shore, the brown edging the blue, I have to imagine kids I know, kids like Corky Divoky years ago, scanning the skies for hawks and heron, or walking the ice in the winter, and now confronting the public servants of the draft board and the crusade for freedom in Asia. I hear the reminiscences of old men, telling fish stories about walleye and whitefish and blue pike, species that have all but disappeared. How much, you ask, setting down at Hopkins Airport, is this worth; how much is romance and senti-mentality about a fading past, how much the price of progress, how much the com-fortable guilt of safe men who can attack pollution as an undisputable evil (or war, or technology itself) while languishing in their benefits?

Some thirteen million people live in the basin of this lake, 90 per cent of them on the American side, the rest in Ontario, the polluters and the polluted, perpetrators and victims, all of them dependent on a body of water that, according to the best evidence, is not yet dead but in danger. They drink its water, swim on its beaches, eat its fish, and sail from its harbors. At the same time, they, their cities, and their factories each day dump, leak, pipe, or drop into the lake several hundred million pounds of sewage, chemicals, oil, and detergents fouling beaches, killing wildlife, and imperiling the water itself. Sometimes you can smell and taste it as it comes out of the tap, sometimes you can see it on the beaches and often in the rivers—the Maumee, the Auglaize, the Ottawa—but most significantly, you fear, not what al-ready exists, but what might—and could—happen if the process continues.

In parts of the western end of the lake, the blue-green algae, which thrive on the excess of nutrients from sewage, turn blue water to a murky green and accumulate in heavy mounds on the shore; in Sandusky, once one of the largest freshwater ports in the world, a large fishing industry has been reduced to a couple of opera-tors who truck their low-grade catch to Georgia (where, apparently, people are still hungry enough to buy it); and in Cleveland, the industrial stream called the Cuya-hoga River is pronounced a fire hazard, a declaration that sounded hyperbolic until, last June, the oil on the river began to burn, damaging two bridges.

Cleveland's two fireboats travel the river periodically, hosing oil off docks and pilings so that the inflammable ooze will slowly make its way downstream and into the lake. At the same time, a broken city main is dumping twenty-five million gallons of raw sewage into the river each day. Periodically, the main is repaired, and now the city, with a $100-million bond issue voted last fall, is preparing to improve col-lection and treatment for its entire system and for the neighboring communities that it serves. (Cleveland, incidentally, may also be one of the few municipalities in the world that chlorinates its lakefront beaches so they will be safe for swimming.) But when it comes to pollution of the lake, Cleveland is more a victim than a culprit. Cleveland fouls its own nest with its dirty river and its inadequate sewage system, while Detroit, which dumps the waste of a huge industrial population into the Detroit River, stocks Lake Erie. Approximately 65 per cent of the oxygen-depleting wastes in the lake come from Detroit; 9 per cent from Cleveland. "When it comes to polluting the main part of the lake," said a researcher at the U.S. Bureau of Commercial Fisheries, "Cleveland's hardly on the map."

And yet, in a way, everything is on the map. Everything contributes to, and suffers from, the condition of the lake: people in five states and a Canadian province — hundreds of towns and cities from Toledo to Buffalo: Akron, Erie, Cleveland, Lorain, Conneaut, Ashtabula. The federal government has identified 360 sources of industrial waste — power plants, steel mills, chemical companies, food processors, rubber companies. During every heavy rain, flooding sewers and silt spill into the lake, and even in normal periods silt and fertilizers and pesticides drain into its tributaries. But the greatest polluters may be the city sewage systems themselves. The federal government has estimated that with existing treatment facilities, the cities along the lake discharge effluent equal, in its composition and effects on the lake, to the raw sewage from a population of 4,700,000 people. Some cities are providing secondary treatment, some primary, some none at all. Lake Erie has been called a huge cesspool, an appellation that has at least marginal accuracy. What is absolutely accurate is the statement that in the past fifty years pollution has substantially altered the ecology of the lake, and that it has made the lake far older than its years.

The word, among the scientists, is eutrophication — the process of aging. All lakes grow old as they collect run-off and materials from the surrounding shores. Over thousands of years they eventually accumulate enough silt from erosion and organic materials to turn them into marshes and, finally, into dry land. In Lake Erie man has accelerated that process with his wastes and sewage. An excess of nutrients, primarily phosphates and nitrates, has produced great growths of algae in the water and impaired the oxygen supply, especially in the deeper water during the summer — and especially at the western end, which is hit hardest by the excrement from Detroit. (Biological degrading of the nutrients requires oxygen; when the nutrients are too heavy the oxygen becomes depleted.)

Mayflies, which once grew in huge numbers in the western, the shallowest, end of the lake, and which provided a food supply for fish — cisco, blue pike, walleye, and other species — have declined; the water has been taken over by sheepshead, carp, and other types that are tolerant of low-oxygen conditions and whose eggs can survive the accumulation of sediments at the bottom. Some species that have surmounted changes in food supply and depleted oxygen now take longer to reach maturity. (The total volume of fish caught in the lake each year is as large as ever, but the catch is worth only half of what it was ten years ago; most of the fishing is now done by Canadians.)

On occasion there have been duck kills, flights of birds which have landed on oily water and never flew again, either (it is assumed) because the oil destroyed the birds' natural protection against the water, or because they were poisoned. (There has been some serious talk in recent years about oil drilling in the lake. So far the derricks of the Canadian Pacific Oil and Gas Company, which have been erected on the Ontario side of the lake, are producing only natural gas.) There is also a possibility that the algae, under certain conditions, can manufacture their own poisons, endangering wild life—and possibly human life.

Because the lake is relatively shallow, there is hope that once the rate of pollution is retarded (hopefully, but not certainly, through improved sewage treatment), the lake, with proper oxygen circulation, can recover, spilling its wastes into Lake Ontario and, ultimately, into the Atlantic. The certainty of that recovery and the effectiveness of the measures now being planned (which, among other things, include the removal of phosphates before effluent is discharged into the lake) are still matters of debate—and of time. What is not a matter of debate is that in the past fifty years, Lake Erie has aged 15,000 years.

Barry Commoner, a Washington University (St. Louis) biologist, who has long been concerned with the abuses of technology, writes:

> The lake is threatened with death. . . . Since the area was first settled, Lake Erie has been increasingly burdened with organic wastes and with inorganic nutrients that the lake's algae convert to organic materials. These organic materials would long ago have asphyxiated most of the lake's living things had it not been for the peculiar power of Iron III [an iron compound called ferric iron] to form insoluble complexes with the materials of the bottom mud. The protective skin of Iron III has held the enormous accumulation of potential oxygen-demanding material in the muddy bottom of the lake. But this protective skin can remain intact only so long as there is sufficient oxygen present in the water over the mud. For many years this was so, and the layer of Iron III held the accumulating mud materials out of the lake water. But a serious oxygen depletion now occurs in the summer months. As a result, the protective layer of Iron III has begun to break down—exposing the lake to heavy impact of the accumulated algal nutrient long stored in the mud. If the process continues, we may face a sudden biological cataclysm that will exhaust, for a time, most of the oxygen in the greater part of the lake water. Such a catastrophe would make the lake's present difficulties seem slight by comparison.

The fear is that under existing conditions, Erie could, without warning, turn into a huge swamp. Among the officials of the Federal Water Pollution Control Administration (FWPCA), which is charged with enforcing pollution control measures, Commoner is regarded as a prophet of gloom, a false Cassandra who is trying to frighten people. Nonetheless, FWPCA paraphrased Commoner's statement in its own report on the lake. "Some of that," said one FWPCA official, "was a little exaggerated. We know that the Iron III tends to break down and to release nutrients from the bottom, but there hasn't been any cataclysm, and there's not going to be one."

And yet, perhaps, that's not the issue—shouldn't be the issue. The trouble with conservation is that it has always been a matter of calamities and cataclysms. In the confusion of state, local, and federal anti-pollution responsibilities, there is always a large measure of sympathy for the company or the city that has to spend money for better treatment facilities, for the corporate taxpayer who might move somewhere else, for the time it takes, for the problems involved. The questions are thus always questions of resources, of priorities, of urgency and time. How much are fish worth? What's the value of a duck? What is the relationship between defoliants in Vietnam (or the price of automobiles in Detroit) and an acid discharge on the Cuyahoga or the Maumee?

If a major corporation can increase its earnings $60-million a year by raising prices, then is the expenditure of $18-million for new waste-treatment facilities at its plant in Cleveland something to brag about? How much passion and effort are required by the hypothetical impairment of a municipal water supply? ("The time's going to come," said an angry conservationist in Cleveland, "when they won't be able to put any more chlorine into the drinking water. What the hell are they going to do then?") And to what extent is water or air pollution a problem that only the comfortable can afford? The kids from Cleveland's Hough ghetto (and many others) rarely worry about swimming from polluted beaches; for them and their parents, urban pollution has other, more virulent forms. Their problem, among other things, is rats, not fish.

In the meantime, life on the lake goes on. In most places the problem is invisible; in others it becomes part of the background, an element of lore, like a volcanic mountain on a South Sea island. "People come here expecting to see a swamp," said a Cleveland newspaper reporter. "But there isn't any." On the west side of Catawba Island, near Sandusky, the cabin cruisers and the yawls luxuriate in their elegant marinas, and on the northern tip the Chevies back their trailer-borne runabouts onto concrete ramps for a few hours of fishing or a cruise to Put-in-Bay. At Huntington Park, just west of Cleveland, a kid pinches his toe on the beach and asks whether there's a species of crab that lives only in polluted water; and in Sandusky, Tony DeMore, one of the few remaining commercial fish operators on the American side, stands on his wharf and complains that the problem isn't pollution but overfishing and inequitable regulations that permit Canadians to haul what Americans have to throw back. *"Now they're stocking the lake with coho salmon like they did Lake Michigan to bring the sport fishermen back, but they're driving out the small fish. If Lake Erie had been meant for big fish, the big fellow up there would have put 'em in. It wasn't pollution that drove the fish out. It was ... nature. If somebody doesn't pull the coho out, they'll take over the lake."*

On the Cuyahoga River, twice each day, the excursion boat *Goodtime II* takes tourists on a run of the industrial sites; a tape-recorded spiel piped over the *Goodtime*'s loud speakers describes the adjacent activities of the Great Lakes Towing Co., U.S. Steel, Republic Steel, Sherwin-Williams Paint, National Sugar Refining, and Standard Oil. (No word about waste discharges, about the phenols and oils and acids that ooze into the river. "If you fall in," they say along the river, "you won't drown, you'll decay.") On summer evenings at the foot of the river, on the flats off Front Street, the customers of Fagan's Beacon House sit at their tables just above the ooze listening to Dixieland, drinking beer, and watching the ships go by. It is, they say in Cleveland, one of the places "where everybody goes."

The lake is a presence, a landmark, an opening in the undifferentiated Midwestern landscape, a hole in the world. Every day the ships come through the seaway—the French, the Swedes the Norwegians—unloading their cargoes on the city piers. In Vermilion, the lagoon, despite its murky surface, its oil slicks, and its junk, becomes a backdoor roadway to space. One ties his boat to the cleats in the back yard and takes the folks on a Sunday cruise; in Sandusky an octogenarian Negro sits on a pier with one of his twenty-one children, casting for sheepshead or carp or whatever cares to bite. The lake is not large, yet large enough to be infinite. It offers its lore of ships and waves and weather, the summer storms that drift across the water, driving the waves into the narrow beaches, perpetuating sailor stories and quarrels about which can be worse, the lakes or the Atlantic. Thus there are legendary events and records of disaster: huge steamboats that went down in flames, taking their immigrant passengers with them, Commodore Perry in 1814, Indians in their silent canoes.

The lake is life: Euclid Beach and Cedar Point, Catawba and Sandusky Bay, amusement parks, boats for hire, elegant summer houses tree-shielded from the curious roadway, beach-club privacy, and breakwaters spiny with the antennae of fishing poles. The beer cans collect between the rocks of the jetties, and behind them ragged rubber tires, twigs, and oily cartons undulate against the stones. A CLEAN BEACH IS A FUN BEACH reads a sign posted two hundred yards from Cleveland's own outfall of sewage. "Why can't we have swimming in Lake Erie?" the mayor asks his commissioner of public utilities, and so the water around the beaches is fenced in with heavy sheets of Dacron anchored to the bottom, the chlorine is piped in, and the black workmen rake the accumulated algae into little piles. On July 4 the beach is dedicated to safe swimming. "I have this vision," says a smart mouth. "The mayor arrives in a helicopter and climbs down a rope ladder onto the algae, while the Cleveland Orchestra plays 'Shifting Sands.'"

Who controls this environment? Whose rights are invested in it? The mayor—in this case Carl B. Stokes of Cleveland—is accused of being more interested in creating an image through waterfront chlorination projects than in attacking the fundamental problems. After the Cuyahoga fire, he begins legal action to make the state enforce its own anti-pollution standards against the industries on the river (and perhaps to put a little pressure on the corporate managers); the state, in turn, accuses the mayor and the city of lagging behind in their own anti-pollution efforts: "It is obvious," said an official of the Ohio Health Department, "that Cleveland itself is a major contributor to the problems of the Cuyahoga River and that a major clean-up cannot be accomplished until the city corrects its own faults."

All the states claim that their industries are in compliance with state health and pollution regulations, which simply means that each year they issue a few admonitions, ask the corporations what efforts they propose to make, and let them continue to operate. "All they're doing," someone said in Cleveland, "is licensing the polluters. It seems that it's impossible for anyone to be in violation." (To which the federal people reply that industry is making more progress with waste-treatment than the cities.)

The buck is supposed to stop at the federally conducted enforcement conferences. Under the club of federal authority, all the states in the lake region—Indiana, Ohio, Michigan, New York, and Pennsylvania—have committed themselves to upgrading their municipal waste-treatment facilities to the point where 80 per cent of all phosphates are removed from sewage effluent before it is discharged into the lake. (Some cities are already behind schedule and have received extensions.) Detroit and Cleveland, among others, are building new plants and collection facilities, using local, state, and a little federal money. At the same time, their officers are angry at the paltry federal contribution. While Detroit is scheduled to spend $159-million and Cleveland has voted its $100-million bond issue for better treatment and collection, the federal government spends barely more than $200-million a year on pollution research and development for the entire nation. "The federal people are the biggest hypocrites in the bunch," said a Detroit official. "They go around the country making speeches. Maybe if they made as much noise about getting us more money as they do about dirt, we'd be able to move a little faster." The reply from Washington: "The people who are polluting are responsible."

So far, the lake has been unaffected, and there is doubt that even after the scheduled projects are completed they will be sufficient. In New York State, a Health Department advisory committee of scientists was asked the question: Will phosphate removal retard eutrophication in Lake Erie? The answer, in simple words: Don't expect too much. Nonetheless, FWPCA has committed itself to the process as a necessary first step: phosphates, which come largely from detergents, say the FWPCA technicians, are essential to the growth of algae and plankton, so (because it is relatively easy) phosphates will be removed. No one has yet figured out what to do with the phosphates once they are precipitated out. They will be trucked to . . . where? (Nor is it certain that nitrates, which flood into the lake from agricultural fertilizers, and other sources, are not major factors in eutrophication.)

"The scientists can raise all sorts of questions," says Murray Stein, who is charged with FWPCA's enforcement work. "It doesn't mean they aren't good questions, but every day's delay in studying means time lost forever. You can only hope." (In Ontario, the Water Resources Commission, which has its own problems, speaks about a "breakthrough" in sewage treatment—a chemical-physical process that is said to remove nutrients more effectively and cheaply than existing methods. But the process, so far, has only been tried under experimental, not operational, conditions.)

The FWPCA has estimated that it will cost $1.1-billion in pollution control projects to arrest the process of eutrophication in the next twenty years. Some critics believe the figure is far too low, and a few believe that the job is already impossible, that the lake may already be too far gone.

Who controls this environment? Whose rights are affected, whose life? The issue of pollution creates its own bureaucracies, its own inertia, its own zones of indistinct responsibility. Even though there are federal laws dating back to 1899 that prohibit the dumping of oil and refuse into navigable waters, and even though the various states have established their own regulations, there has never been—in the memory of federal officials—one suit or one criminal proceeding against a polluter. "Pollution law is a little like antitrust law," a federal official tells you. "It's hard to establish a connection between discharges and damage." (Two weeks ago, the Interior Department began to show signs of impatience with the polluters. For the first time since the 1965 Water Pollution Control Act was passed, the government threatened to take court action against private corporations and municipalities that pollute

Lake Erie and other bodies of water. Among those cited in the government's announcement were three steel companies — James & Laughlin, U.S. Steel, and Republic — and the city of Toledo.)

Whose rights are affected, whose environment is it? "Every year there's more talk," says David Blaushild, a Cleveland automobile dealer who heads a group called Citizens for Clean Air and Water. "The governor and the mayor come to the conferences, and make speeches, and go home, and the pollution goes on. You don't have to study anymore. You can smell and see it. It's time to file lawsuits. Why should people take this crap?"

Does the individual have a constitutional right to clean air and water? "It's going to take a disaster to wake people up," Blaushild says. "If this generation doesn't do it, the next generation won't know any better. They'll think that swimming in filth is the normal thing to do. They'll think the moon is supposed to be yellow. They'll think they're breathing clean air and drinking clean water, because they won't know any better." Blaushild writes the Cleveland science museums to ask why they don't take a stronger position against industrial polluters. (Among their trustees are directors of several local corporations.) One of them answers that Blaushild, by selling Detroit's products, has his own share of responsibility.

Who controls this environment? Pollution, pesticides, fallout. The world's experience with nuclear tests has begun to create a wholly new concept of civility and community. In a strange way pollution became a problem by analogy: we learned, for example, that the same ecological processes that concentrate strontium-90 in bones concentrate DDT in fish, that contamination in one place jeopardizes life in others. A bomb test in New Mexico kills infants in Mississippi and Alabama; pesticides on Michigan farms poison fish in distant lakes; sewage from Detroit fouls beaches in Ohio. One can respond cheaply by lamenting the fix that science and technology have gotten us into, but a bumper sticker proclaiming SAVE LAKE ERIE pasted barely a foot above a smoky automobile exhaust is more an illustration of the problem than a solution.

The burden of moral compromise symbolized by Hiroshima and Nagasaki will not be lifted by building a new sewer system in Detroit, however necessary that system may be. Technological amelioration of one facet of environmental destruction can be no more than a surrogate for continued acceptance of its larger and more catastrophic forms. Can one take seriously an organization whose interest in conserving fish is unmatched by a position on the ABM?

The questions are backwards: how much civility can we afford after we have paid for Vietnam? For the car? For our missiles? Can we sustain a decent welfare program despite the war? Can we clean the river without jeopardizing the profits of industry? Because we are trying to satisfy a new, though still unclear, sense of community with old priorities, evasion is inevitable. Which is to say that a professed commitment to protect an environment that ends with a squabble over sewer taxes is no commitment at all. The issue of pollution can produce a paranoid fanaticism just like every other; no one has died from swimming on a contaminated beach on Lake Erie or from drinking its water. Yet somehow, if we cannot distinguish between fanaticism on behalf of a distant generation and that which defends immediate returns and private ends we have simply lost our claim to live.

As Barry Commoner wrote in *Science and Survival:*

> The environment is a complex, subtly balanced system, and it is this integrated whole which receives the impact of all the separate insults inflicted by pollutants. Never before in the history of this planet has its thin life-supporting surface been subjected to such diverse, novel, and potent agents. I believe that the cumulative effects of these pollutants, their interactions and amplification, can be fatal to the complex fabric of the biosphere. And because man is, after all, dependent on part of this system, I believe that continued pollution of the earth, if unchecked, will eventually destroy the fitness of this planet as a place for human life.

If the greatest thing since the creation is worth twenty-four billion clams, how much is the creation worth?

The Limited War on Water Pollution

GENE BYLINSKY*

To judge by the pronouncements from Washington, we can now start looking forward to cleaner rather than ever dirtier rivers. The Administration has declared a "war" on pollution, and Secretary of the Interior Walter J. Hickel says "we do not intend to lose." Adds Murray Stein, enforcement chief of the Federal Water Pollution Control Administration: "I think we are on the verge of a tremendous cleanup."

The nationwide campaign to clean up ravaged rivers and lakes does seem to be moving a bit. For the first time since the federal government got into financing construction of municipal sewage plants in 1956, Congress has come close to providing the kind of funding it had promised. Assuming the Budget Bureau allows Interior to spend all of the $800 million appropriated for the current fiscal year, that will come to almost two-thirds as much as all the federal funds invested in the program so far. There are other signs that the war is intensifying. Under the provisions of the Water Quality Act of 1965 and the Clean Water Restoration Act of 1966, federal and state officials are establishing water-quality standards and plans for their implementation, to be carried out eventually through coordinated federal-state action. Timetables for new municipal and industrial treatment facilities are being set, surveillance programs are being planned, and tougher federal enforcement authority is being formulated. Without waiting for these plans to materialize, Interior is talking tough to some municipal and industrial polluters, with the possibility of court action in the background.

* Reprinted from the February 1970 issue of Fortune Magazine. This article has appeared in a book, *The Environment: A National Mission for the Seventies,* published by Harper and Row.

Even with all this, however, the water-pollution outlook is far from reassuring. Although the nation has invested about $15 billion since 1952 in the construction of 7,500 municipal sewage-treatment plants, industrial treatment plants, sewers, and related facilities, a surprising 1,400 communities in the U.S., including good-sized cities like Memphis, and hundreds of industrial plants still dump untreated wastes into the waterways. Other cities process their sewage only superficially, and no fewer than 300,000 industrial plants discharge their used water into municipal sewage plants that are not equipped to process many of the complex new pollutants.

Since the volume of pollutants keeps expanding while water supply stays basically the same, more and more intervention will be required just to keep things from getting worse. Within the next fifty years, according to some forecasts, the country's population will double, and the demand for water by cities, industries, and agriculture has tended to grow even faster than the population. These water uses now add up to something like 350 billion gallons a day (BGD), but by 1980, by some estimates, they will amount to 600 BGD. By the year 2000, demand for water is expected to reach 1,000 BGD, considerably exceeding the essentially unchanging supply of dependable fresh water, which is estimated at 650 BGD. More and more, water will have to be reused, and it will cost more and more to retrieve clean water from progressively dirtier waterways.

Just how bad water pollution can get was dramatically illustrated last summer when the oily, chocolate-brown Cuyahoga River in Cleveland burst into flames, nearly destroying two railroad bridges. The Cuyahoga is so laden with industrial and municipal wastes that not even the leeches and sludge worms that thrive in many badly polluted rivers are to be found in its lower reaches. Many other U.S. rivers are becoming more and more like that flammable sewer.

Even without human activity to pollute it, a stream is never absolutely pure, because natural pollution is at work in the form of soil erosion, deposition of leaves and animal wastes, solution of minerals, and so forth. Over a long stretch of time, a lake can die a natural death because of such pollution. The natural process of eutrophication, or enrichment with nutrients, encourages the growth of algae and other plants, slowly turning a lake into a bog. Man's activities enormously speed up the process.

Too Much Demand for Oxygen

But both lakes and rivers have an impressive ability to purify themselves. Sunlight bleaches out some pollutants. Others settle to the bottom and stay there. Still others are consumed by beneficial bacteria. These bacteria need oxygen, which is therefore vital to self-purification. The oxygen that sustains bacteria as well as fish and other organisms is replenished by natural aeration from the atmosphere and from life processes of aquatic plants.

Trouble starts when demand for dissolved oxygen exceeds the available supply. Large quantities of organic pollutants such as sewage alter the balance. Bacteria feeding upon the pollutants multiply and consume the oxygen. Organic debris accumulates. Anaerobic areas develop, where microorganisms that can live and grow without free oxygen decompose the settled solids. This putrefaction produces foul odors. Species of fish sensitive to oxygen deficiency can no longer survive. Chemical, physical, and biological characteristics of a stream are altered, and its water becomes unusable for many purposes without extensive treatment.

Pollution today is very complex in its composition, and getting more so all the time. In polluted streams and lakes hundreds of different contaminants can be found: bacteria and viruses; pesticides and weed killers; phosphorus from fertilizers, detergents, and municipal sewage; trace amounts of metals; acid from mine drainage; organic and inorganic chemicals, many of which are so new that we do not know their long-term effects on human health; and even traces of drugs. (Steroid drugs such as the Pill, however, are neutralized by bacteria.)

A distinction is often made between industrial and municipal wastes, but it is difficult to sort them out because many industrial plants discharge their wastes into municipal sewer systems. As a result, what is referred to as municipal waste is also to a large extent industrial waste. By one estimate, as much as 40 per cent of all waste water treated by municipal sewage plants comes from industry. Industry's contribution to water pollution is sometimes measured in terms of "population equivalent." Pollution from organic industrial wastes analogous to sewage is now said by some specialists to be about equivalent to a population of 210 million.

The quality of waste water is often measured in terms of its biochemical oxygen demand (BOD), or the amount of dissolved oxygen that is needed by bacteria in decomposing the wastes. Waste water with much higher BOD content than sewage is produced by such operations as leather tanning, beet-sugar refining, and meat-packing. But industry also contributes a vast amount of non-degradable, long-lasting pollutants, such as inorganic and synthetic organic chemicals that impair the quality of water. All together, manufacturing activities, transportation, and agriculture probably account for about two-thirds of all water degradation.

Industry also produces an increasingly important pollutant of an entirely different kind—heat. Power generation and some manufacturing processes use great quantities of water for cooling, and it goes back into streams warmer than it came out. Power plants disgorging great masses of hot water can raise the stream temperature by ten or twenty degrees in the immediate vicinity of the plant. Warmer water absorbs less oxygen and this slows down decomposition of organic matter. Fish, being cold-blooded, cannot regulate their body temperatures, and the additional heat upsets their life cycles; for example, fish eggs may hatch too soon. Some scientists have estimated that by 1980 the U.S. will be producing enough waste water and heat to consume, in dry weather, all the oxygen in all twenty-two river basins in the U.S.

Designed for a Simpler World

How clean do we want our waterways to be? In answering that question we have to recognize that many of our rivers and lakes serve two conflicting purposes—they are used both as sewers and as sources of drinking water for about 100 million Americans. That's why the new water-quality standards for interstate streams now being set in various states generally rely on criteria established by the Public Health Service for sources of public water supplies. In all, the PHS lists no fewer than fifty-one contaminants or characteristics of water supplies that should be controlled. Many other substances in the drinking water are not on the list, because they haven't yet been measured or even identified. "The poor water-treatment plant operator really doesn't know what's in the stream—what he is treating," says James H. McDermott, director of the Bureau of Water Hygiene in the PHS. With more than 500 new or modified chemicals coming on the market every year, it isn't easy for the understaffed PHS bureaus to keep track of new pollutants. Identification and detailed analysis of pollutants is just beginning as a systematic task. Only a few months ago the PHS established its first official committee to evaluate the effects of insecticides on health.

Many water-treatment plants are hopelessly outmoded. They were designed for a simpler, less crowded world. About three-fourths of them do not go beyond disinfecting water with chlorine. That kills bacteria but does practically nothing to remove pesticides, herbicides, or other organic and inorganic chemicals from the water we drink.

A survey by the PHS, still in progress, shows that most waterworks operators lack formal training in treatment processes, disinfection, microbiology, and chemistry. The men are often badly paid. Some of them, in smaller communities, have other full-time jobs and moonlight as water-supply operators. The survey, encompassing eight metropolitan areas from New York City to Riverside, California, plus the State of Vermont, so far has revealed that in seven areas about 9 per cent of the water samples indicated bacterial contamination. Pesticides were found in small concentrations in many samples. In some, trace metals exceeded PHS limits. The level of nitrates, which can be fatal to babies, was too high in some samples. Earlier last year the PHS found that nearly sixty communities around the country, including some large cities, could be given only "provisional approval" for the quality of their water-supply systems. Charles C. Johnson Jr., administrator of the Consumer Protection and Environmental Health Service in the PHS, concluded that the U.S. is "rapidly approaching a crisis stage with regard to drinking water" and is courting "serious health hazards."

Clearly, there will have to be enormous improvement in either the treatment of water we drink or the treatment of water we discard (if not both). The second approach would have the great advantage of making our waterways better for swimming and fishing and more aesthetically enjoyable. And it is more rational anyway not to put poisons in the water in the first place. The most sensible way to keep our drinking water safe is to have industry, agriculture, and municipalities stop polluting water with known and potentially hazardous substances. Some of this could be accomplished by changing manufacturing processes and recycling waste water inside plants. The wastes can sometimes be retrieved at a profit.

Dispensing with Bacteria

Even if phosphorus pollution from fertilizers and detergents were entirely eliminated—an unlikely prospect—phosphates from domestic and industrial wastes would still impose a heavy load upon rivers and lakes. As population and industry grow, higher and higher percentages of the phosphorus will have to be removed from effluents to keep the algae problem from getting worse. The conventional technology being pushed by the federal water-pollution war cannot cope with phosphorus, or with many other pollutants. But there are advanced technologies that can. Advanced water treatment, sometimes called "tertiary," is generally aimed at removal of all, or almost all, of the contaminants.

One promising idea under investigation is to dispense with the not always reliable bacteria that consume sewage in secondary treatment. Toxic industrial wastes have on occasion thrown municipal treatment plants out of kilter for weeks by killing the bacteria. "We've found that we can accomplish the same kind of treatment with a purely physical-chemical process," says a scientist at the Robert A. Taft Water Research Center in Cincinnati.

In this new approach, the raw sewage is clarified with chemicals to remove most suspended organic material, including much of the phosphate. Then comes carbon adsorption. The effluent passes through filter beds of granular activated carbon, similar to that used in charcoal filters for cigarettes. Between clarification and adsorption, 90 per cent or more of the phosphate is removed. The carbon can be regenerated in furnaces and reused. Captured organic matter is burned. Carbon adsorption has the great additional advantage of removing from the water organic industrial chemicals that pass unhindered through biological secondary treatment. The chemicals adhere to the carbon as they swirl through its complex structure with millions of pathways and byways.

A Product Rather than an Effluent

Other treatment techniques are under study that make water even cleaner, and might possibly be used to turn sewage into potable water. One of these is reverse osmosis, originally developed for demineralization of brackish water. When liquids with different concentrations of, say, mineral salts are separated by a semipermeable membrane, water molecules pass by osmosis, a natural equalizing tendency, from the less concentrated to the more concentrated side to create an equilibrium. In reverse osmosis, strong pressure is exerted on the side with the greater concentration. The pressure reverses the natural flow, forcing molecules of pure water through the membrane, out of the high-salt or high-particle concentration. Reverse osmosis removes ammonia nitrogen, as well as phosphates, most nitrate, and other substances dissolved in water. Unfortunately, the process is not yet applicable to sewage treatment on a large scale because the membranes become fouled with sewage solids. Engineers are hard at work trying to design better membranes.

New techniques are gradually transforming sewage treatment, technically backward and sometimes poorly controlled, into something akin to a modern chemical process. "We are talking about a wedding of sanitary and chemical engineering," says David G. Stephan, who directs research and development at the Federal Water Pollution Control Administration, "using the techniques of the chemical process industry to turn out a product—reusable water—rather than an effluent to throw away." Adds James McDermott of the Public Health Service: "We're going to get to the point where, on the one hand, it's going to cost us an awful lot of money to treat wastes and dump them into the stream. And an awful lot of money to take those wastes when they are going down the stream and make drinking water out of them. We are eventually going to create treatment plants where we take sewage and, instead of dumping it back into the stream, treat it with a view of recycling it immediately—direct reuse. That is the only way we're going to satisfy our water needs, and second, it's going to be cheaper."

Windhoek, the capital of arid South West Africa, last year gained the distinction of becoming the first city in the world to recycle its waste water directly into drinking water. Waste water is taken out of sewers, processed conventionally, oxidized in ponds for about a month, then run through filters and activated-carbon columns, chlorinated, and put back into the water mains. Windhoek's distinction may prove to be dubious, because the full effects of recycled water on health are unknown. There is a potential hazard of viruses (hepatitis, polio, etc.) being concentrated in recycling. For this reason, many health experts feel that renovated sewage should not be accepted as drinking water in the U.S. until its safety can be more reliably demonstrated.

Costs naturally go up as treatment gets more complex. While primary-secondary treatment costs about 12 cents a thousand gallons of waste water, the advanced techniques in use at Lake Tahoe, for instance, bring the cost up to 30 cents. About 7½ cents of the increase is for phosphorus removal. Reverse osmosis at this stage would raise the cost to at least 35 cents a thousand gallons, higher than the average cost of drinking water to metered households in the U.S. Whatever new techniques are accepted, rising costs of pollution control will be a fact of life.

A Perfect Marriage for Sludge

Ironically, these new treatment techniques, such as removal of phosphorus with chemicals, will intensify one of the most pressing operational problems in waste-water treatment—sludge disposal. Sludge, the solid matter removed from domestic or industrial waste water, is a nuisance, highly contaminated unless it's disinfected. The handling and disposal of sludge can eat up to one-half of a treatment plant's operating budget. Some communities incinerate their sludge, contributing to air pollution. "Now in cleaning the water further we are adding chemicals to take out phosphorus and more solids," says Francis M. Middleton, director of the Taft Center. "While we end up with cleaner water, we also end up with even greater quantities of sludge."

Chicago's struggle with its sludge illustrates some of the difficulties and perhaps an effective way of coping with them. With 1,000 tons of sludge a day to dispose of, the metropolitan sanitary district has been stuffing about half of it into deep holes near treatment plants, at a cost of about $60 a ton. The other half is dried and shipped to Florida and elsewhere where it is sold to citrus growers and companies producing fertilizers for $12 a ton—a nonprofit operation. Vinton W. Bacon, general superintendent of the sanitary district, says this state of affairs can't continue. "We're running out of land. Not only that, but the land we're using for disposal is valuable. And even it will be filled within two years."

Bacon is convinced he has an answer that will not only cut costs but also solve disposal problems indefinitely while helping to make marginal lands bloom. Bacon's scheme, tested in pilot projects in Chicago and elsewhere, is to pump liquid sludge through a pipeline to strip mines and marginal farmland about sixty miles southwest of Chicago. "We put the sludge water through tanks where it's digested," Bacon says. "Then it can be used directly without any odor or health dangers. It's the perfect marriage. That land needs our sludge as much as we need the land. Most astounding, even acquiring the required land at current market prices, taking in the cost of a twenty-four-inch, sixty-mile-long pipeline, the pumps, reservoirs, irrigation equipment, and manpower, the cost would still come to only $20 a ton. We could build a pipeline 200 miles long and still not run higher costs than with our present system."

An aspect of water pollution that seems harder to cope with is the overflow of combined sewers during storms. A combined system that unites storm and sanitary sewers into a single network usually has interceptor sewers, with direct outlets to a stream, to protect the treatment plant from flooding during heavy rains. But in diverting excess water from treatment plants, interceptor sewers dump raw sewage into the waterways. Obviously, this partly defeats the purpose of having treatment plants.

So bad are the consequences of sewer overflow that some specialists would prefer to see part of the federal money that is being channeled into secondary treatment go into correction of the combined-sewer problem instead. But more than 1,300 U.S. communities have combined sewers, and the cost of separating the systems would be huge. The American Public Works Association estimated the cost of total separation at $48 *billion*. The job could be done in an alternative fashion for a still shocking $15 billion, by building holding tanks for the overflow storm water. Still another possibility would be to build separate systems for sewage and to use existing sewers for storm water. The federal war on water pollution discourages construction of combined sewers but strangely includes no money (except for $28 million already awarded for research and development) to remedy the problem of existing combined-sewer systems.

Slicing Up Rivers

The General Accounting Office recently surveyed federal activities in water-pollution control and found some glaring deficiencies. The G.A.O. prepared its report for Congress and therefore failed to point out that in some of the deficiencies the real culprit was Congress itself. Still largely rural-oriented, Congress originally limited federal grants for construction of waste-treatment facilities to $250,000 per municipality. The dollar ceiling was eventually raised, but was not removed until fiscal 1968. In the preceding twelve years about half of the waste-treatment facilities were built in hamlets with populations of less than 2,500, and 92 per cent in towns with populations under 50,000.

In drafting the legislation that provides for new water-quality standards, Congress again showed limited vision, leaving it up to the states to decide many important questions. Each state is free to make its own decisions on pollution-control goals in terms of determining the uses to which a particular stream or lake will be put. Each state is to decide on the stream characteristics that would allow such uses — dissolved oxygen, temperature, etc. Finally, each state is to set up a schedule for corrective measures that would ensure the stream quality decided upon, and prepare plans for legal enforcement of the standards.

It would have been logical to set standards for entire river basins since rivers don't always stay within state boundaries. What's more, there were already several regional river-basin compacts in existence that could have taken on the job. But with the single exception of the Delaware River Basin Commission, of which the federal government is a member, the government bypassed the regional bodies and insisted that each state set its own standards. Predictably, the result has been confusion. The states submitted standards by June 30, 1967, but Interior has given full approval to only twenty-five states and territories. It has now become the prickly task of the Secretary of the Interior to reconcile the conflicting sets of standards that states have established for portions of the same rivers.

Some states facing each other across a river have set different standards for water characteristics, as if dividing the river flow in the middle with a bureaucratic fence. Kentucky and Indiana, across the Ohio from each other, submitted two different temperature standards for that river: Kentucky came up with a maximum of 93° Fahrenheit, while Indiana wants 90°. Similarly, Ohio set its limit at 93°, while West Virginia, across the same river, chose 86°. Up the river, Pennsylvania, too, decided on 86°. One reason for such differences about river temperature is that biologists don't always agree among themselves about safe temperatures for aquatic life. At one recent meeting in Cincinnati, where federal and state officials were attempting to reconcile the different figures for the Ohio, the disagreement among biologists was so great that one exasperated engineer suggested, "Maybe we should start putting ice cubes at different points in the river."

A Failure of Imagination

The biggest deficiency in the federal approach is its lack of imagination. Congress chose the subsidy route as being the easiest, but the task could have been undertaken much more thoughtfully. A regional or river-valley approach would have required more careful working out than a program of state-by-state standards and subsidies, but it would have made more sense economically, and would have assured continuing management of water quality.

A promising river-valley program is evolving along the Great Miami River in Ohio. The Miami Conservancy District, a regional flood-control agency, began two years ago to explore the concept of river management. The Great Miami runs through a heavily industrialized valley. There are, for instance, eighteen paper mills in the valley. Dayton, the principal city on the river, houses four divisions of General Motors and is the home of National Cash Register. To finance a three-year exploratory program, the Miami Conservancy District has imposed temporary charges, based on volume of effluent, on sixty plants, businesses, and municipalities along the river. These charges amount to a total of $350,000 a year, ranging from $500 that might be paid by a motel to $23,000 being paid by a single power-generating station.

With this money, plus a $500,000 grant from the Federal Water Pollution Control Administration, the district has been looking into river-wide measures that will be needed to control pollution even *after* every municipality along the river has a secondary treatment plant. (Dayton already has one.) The district's staff of sanitary engineers, ecologists, and systems analysts has come up with suggested measures to augment the low flow of the river as an additional method of pollution control. The Great Miami's mean annual flow at Dayton is 2,500 cubic feet a second, but every ten years or so it falls to a mere 170 cubic feet a second. To assure a more even flow, the Miami District will build either reservoirs or facilities to pump ground water, at a cost of several million dollars. The cost will be shared by river users. District engineers are also exploring in-stream aeration, or artificial injection of air into the river to provide additional dissolved oxygen. The state has set an ambitious goal for the Great Miami—to make the river usable "for all purposes, at all places, all the time."

To meet this goal, the district will introduce waste-discharge fees, which will probably be based on the amount of oxygen-demanding wastes or hot water discharged. Will these amount to a charge for polluting the river? "No," says Max L. Mitchell, the district's chief engineer. "Charges will be high enough to make industry reduce water use."

Federal money would do a lot more good if it were divided up along the river-basin lines instead of municipality by municipality or state by state, with little regard for differences in pollution at different points in a basin. To distribute federal funds more effectively, Congress would have to overcome its parochial orientation. Also, Congress should be channeling more funds into new waste-treatment technologies and ways of putting them to use. Unless pollution abatement is undertaken in an imaginative and systematic manner, the "war" against dirty rivers may be a long, losing campaign.

Santa Barbara: Oil in the Velvet Playground

HARVEY MOLOTCH*

Santa Barbara seems worlds apart both from the sprawling Los Angeles metropolis a hundred miles further south on the coast highway and from the avant-garde San Francisco Bay Area to the north. It has always been calm, clean and orderly. Of the city's 70,000 residents, a large number are upper and upper-middle class. They are people who have a wide choice of places in the world to live, but they have chosen Santa Barbara because of its ideal climate, gentle beauty and sophistication. Hard-rock Republicans, they vote for any GOP candidate who comes along, including Ronald Reagan and Max Rafferty, California's right-wing Superintendent of Public Education.

Under normal circumstances, Santa Barbarans are not the sort of people who are accustomed to experiencing stark threats to their survival, or arbitrary, contemptuous handling of their wishes. They are an unlikely group to be forced to confront brutal realities about how the "normal channels" in America can become hopelessly clogged and unresponsive. Yet this is exactly what happened when the Union

*Reprinted from *Ramparts* (November 1969), pp. 43-51. Copyright Ramparts Magazine, Inc., 1969. By Permission of the Editors. Figures deleted.

Oil Company's well erupted in the Santa Barbara Channel last January, causing an unparalleled ecological disaster, the effects of which are still washing up on the local beaches.

In the ensuing months it became clear that more than petroleum had leaked out from Union Oil's drilling platform. Some basic truths about power in America had spilled out along with it. The oil disaster was more than simply another omen for an increasingly "accident-prone" civilization. Precisely because it was an accident — a sudden intrusion into an extremely orderly social process — it provided Santa Barbarans with sharp insights into the way our society is governed and into the power relationships that dictate its functions.

Across the political spectrum in Santa Barbara, the response has been much the same: fury. Some, including persons who never before had made a political move in their lives, were led from petition campaigns to the picket line and demonstrations, to the sit-down, and even to the sail-in. The position they finally came to occupy shows that radicalism is not, as experts like Bruno Bettelheim have implied, a subtle form of mental imbalance caused by rapid technological change or by the increasing impersonality of the modern world; radicals are not "immature," "undisciplined" or "anti-intellectual." Quite the contrary. They are persons who live in conditions where injustice is apparent, and who have access to more complete information about their plight than the average man, giving them a perspective that allows them to become angry in a socially meaningful way. In short, radicals are persons who make the most rational (and moral) response, given the social and political circumstances. Thus, as recent sociological studies have shown, radical movements like SDS draw their memberships disproportionately from the most intelligent and informed members of their constituent populations.

Optimistic Indignation: Government by the People

For over fifteen years, Santa Barbara's political leaders attempted to prevent the despoilation of their coastline by oil drilling in adjacent federal waters. Although they were unsuccessful in blocking the leasing of *federal* waters beyond the three-mile limit, they were able to establish a sanctuary within *state* waters (thus foregoing the extraordinary revenues which leases in such areas bring to adjacent localities). It was therefore a great irony that the one city which had voluntarily exchanged revenue for a pure environment should find itself faced, in January of 1969, with a massive eruption which was ultimately to cover the entire city coastline with a thick coat of crude oil. The air was soured for many hundreds of feet inland, and tourism — the traditional economic base of the region — was severely threatened. After ten days, the runaway well was brought under control, only to erupt again in February. This fissure was closed in March, but was followed by a sustained "seepage" of oil — a leakage which continues today to pollute the sea, the air and the famed local beaches. The oil companies had paid a record $603 million for their lease rights, and neither they nor the federal government bore any significant legal responsibility toward the localities which those lease rights might endanger.

The response of Santa Barbarans to this pollution of their near-perfect environment was immediate. A community organization called "GOO" (Get Oil Out!) was established under the leadership of a former state senator and a local corporate executive. GOO took a strong stand against any and all oil activity in the Channel and circulated a petition to that effect which eventually gained 110,000 signatures and was sent to President Nixon. The stodgy Santa Barbara News-Press (oldest daily newspaper in Southern California, its masthead proclaims) inaugurated a series of editorials, unique in their uncompromising stridency and indicative of the angry mood of the community. "The people of the Santa Barbara area can never be repaid for the hurt that has been done to them and their environment," said a front-page editorial. "They are angry—and this is not the time for them to lose their anger. This is the time for them to fight for action that will guarantee absolutely and permanently that there will be no recurrence of the nightmare of the last two weeks...."

The same theme emerged in the hundreds of letters published by the News-Press in the weeks that followed and in the positions taken by virtually every local civic and government body. Rallies were held at the beach, and GOO petitions were circulated at local shopping centers and sent to sympathizers around the country. Local artists, playwrights, advertising men, retired executives and academic specialists from the local campus of the University of California executed special projects appropriate to their areas of expertise.

A GOO strategy emerged for an attack on two fronts. Local indignation, producing the petition to the President and thousands of letters to key members of Congress and the executive, would lead to appropriate legislation. Legal action against the oil companies and the federal government would have the double effect of recouping some of the financial losses certain to be suffered by the local tourist and fishing industries while at the same time serving notice that drilling in the Channel would become a much less profitable operation. Legislation to ban drilling was introduced by Senator Alan Cranston in the U.S. Senate and Representative Charles Teague in the House of Representatives. Joint suits for $1 billion in damages were filed against the oil companies and the federal government by the city and county of Santa Barbara (later joined by the State of California).

All of these activities—petitions, rallies, court action and legislative lobbying—expressed their proponents' basic faith in "the system." There was a muckraking tone to the Santa Barbara protest: the profit-mad executives of Union Oil were ruining the coastline, but once national and state leaders became aware of what was going on and were provided with the "facts" of the case, justice would be done.

Indeed, there was good reason for hope. The quick and enthusiastic responses of the right-wing Teague and the liberal Cranston represented a consensus of men otherwise polar opposites in their political behavior. But from other important quarters there was silence. Santa Barbara's representatives in the state legislature either said nothing or (in later stages) offered only minimal support. Most disappointing of all to Santa Barbarans, Governor Ronald Reagan withheld support for proposals which would end the drilling.

As subsequent events unfolded, the seemingly inexplicable silence of most of the democratically-elected representatives began to fall into place as part of a more general pattern. Santa Barbarans began to see American democracy as a very complicated affair—not simply a system in which governmental officials carry out the desires of their constituents once those desires become known. Instead, increasing recognition came to be given to the "all-powerful Oil lobby"; to legislators "in the pockets of Oil"; to academicians "bought" by Oil and to regulatory agencies that lobby for those they are supposed to regulate. In other words, Santa Barbarans became increasingly ideological, increasingly sociological and, in the words of some observers, increasingly "radical." Writing from his lodgings in the Santa Barbara Biltmore, the city's most exclusive residence hotel, an irate citizen penned these words in a letter published in the local paper: "We the People can protest and protest and it means nothing because the industrial and military junta are the country. They tell us, the People, what is good for the oil companies is good for the People. To that I say, Like Hell! . . . Profit is their language and the proof of all this is their history."

Disillusionment: Government by Oil

From the start, Secretary of Interior Walter Hickel was regarded with suspicion, and his publicized associations with Alaskan oil interests did little to improve his image in Santa Barbara. When he called a halt to drilling immediately after the initial eruption, some Santa Barbarans began to believe that he would back them up. But even the most optimistic were quite soon forced to recognize that government policy would indeed confirm their worst fears. For, only one day later, Secretary Hickel ordered a resumption of drilling and production—even as the oil continued to gush into the Channel.

Within 48 hours Hickel reversed his position and ordered another halt to the drilling. But this time his action was seen as a direct response to the massive nationwide media play then being given to the Santa Barbara plight and to the citizens' mass outcry just then beginning to reach Washington. Santa Barbarans were further disenchanted with Hickel and the executive branch both because the Interior Department failed to back any legislation to halt drilling and because it consistently attempted to downplay the entire affair—minimizing the extent of the damages and hinting at possible "compromises" which were seen locally as near-total capitulation to the oil companies.

One question on which government officials systematically erred on the side of Oil was that of the *volume* of oil spilling into the Channel. The U.S. Geological Survey (administered by the Department of the Interior), when queried by reporters, produced estimates which Santa Barbarans could only view as incredible. Located in Santa Barbara is a technological establishment among the most sophisticated in the country—the General Research Corporation, a research and development firm with experience in marine technology. Several officials of the corporation made their own study of the oil outflow and announced findings of pollution volume at a minimum of *ten-fold* that of the government's estimate. The methods which General Research used to prepare its estimates were made public. The Geological Survey and the oil interests, however, continued to blithely issue their own lower figures, refusing to provide any substantiating arguments.

Another point of contention was the effect of the oil on the beaches. The oil companies, through various public relations officials, constantly minimized the actual amount of damage and maximized the effect of Union Oil's cleanup activities; and the Department of the Interior seemed determined to support Union Oil's claims. Thus Hickel referred at a press conference to the "recent" oil spill, providing the impression that the oil spill was over at a time when freshly erupting oil was continuing to stain local beaches. When President Nixon appeared locally to "inspect" the damage to beaches, Interior arranged for him to land his helicopter on a city beach which had been thoroughly cleaned in the days just before, thus sparing him a close-up of much of the rest of the county shoreline, which continued to be covered with a thick coat of crude oil. (The beach visited by Nixon has been oil-stained on many occasions subsequent to the President's departure.) Secret servicemen kept the placards and shouts of several hundred demonstrators at a safe distance from the President.

The damage to the "ecological chain," while still of unknown proportions, was treated in a similarly deceptive way. A great many birds died from oil which they had ingested while trying to preen their oil-soaked feathers—a process Santa Barbarans saw in abundant examples. In what local and national authorities called a hopeless task, two bird-cleaning centers were established (with help from oil company money) to cleanse feathers and otherwise minister to injured wildfowl. Spokesmen from both Oil and the federal government then adopted these centers as sources of "data" on the extent of damage to the bird life. Thus, the number of birds killed by oil pollution was computed on the basis of the number of fatalities at the wildfowl centers. It was a preposterous method and was recognized as such. Clearly, the dying birds in the area were provided with inefficient means of propelling themselves to these designated centers.

At least those birds in the hands of local ornithologists could be confirmed as dead, and this fact could not be disputed by either Oil or Interior. This was not so, however, with species whose corpses are more difficult to produce on command. Several official observers at the Channel Islands, a national wildlife preserve containing one of the country's largest colonies of sea animals, reported sighting unusually large numbers of dead sea lion pups on the oil-stained shores of one of the islands. Statement and counter-statement followed, with Oil's defenders (including the Department of the Navy) arguing that the animals were not dead at all, but only appeared inert because they were sleeping. In a similar case, the dramatic beaching in Northern California of an unusually large number of dead whales—whales which had just completed their migration through the Santa Barbara Channel—was acknowledged, but held not to be caused by oil pollution.

In the end, it was not simply the Interior Department, its U.S. Geological Survey and the President who either supported or tacitly accepted Oil's public relations tactics. The regulatory agencies at both national and state levels, by action, inaction and implication, effectively defended Oil at virtually every turn. In a letter to complaining citizens, for instance, N. B. Livermore Jr. of the Resources Agency of California referred to the continuing oil spill as "minor seepage" with "no major long term effect on the marine ecology." The letter adopted the perspective of Interior and Oil, even though the state was in no way being held culpable for the spill. This tendency was so blatant that it led the State Deputy Attorney General, Charles

O'Brien, to charge the state conservation boards with "industry domination." Thomas Gaines, a Union Oil executive, actually sits on the state agency board most directly connected with the control of pollution in Channel waters.

Understandably enough, Secretary Hickel's announcement that the Interior Department was generating new "tough" regulations to control off-shore drilling was met with considerable skepticism. The Santa Barbara County Board of Supervisors was invited to "review" these new regulations and refused to do so in the belief that such participation would be used to provide a false impression of democratic responsiveness.

In previous years when they were fighting against the leasing of the Channel, the Supervisors had been assured of technological safeguards; now, as the emergency continued, they could witness for themselves the absence of any method for ending the leakage in the Channel. They also had heard the testimony of Donald Solanas, a regional supervisor of Interior's U.S. Geological Survey, who said about the Union platform eruption: "I could have had an engineer on that platform 24 hours a day, seven days a week and he couldn't have prevented the accident." His explanation of the cause of the "accident"? "Mother earth broke down on us." Given these facts, Santa Barbarans saw Interior's proposed regulations—and the invitation to the County to participate in making them—as only a ruse to preface a resumption of drilling.

Their suspicions were confirmed when the Interior Department announced a selective resumption of drilling "to relieve pressures." The new "tough" regulations were themselves seriously flawed by the fact that most of their provisions specified measures (such as buoyant booms around platforms, use of chemical dispersants, etc.) which had proved almost totally useless in the current emergency.

The new regulations did specify that oil companies would henceforth be financially responsible for damages resulting from pollution mishaps. Several of the oil companies have now entered suit (supported by the ACLU) against the federal government, complaining that the arbitrary changing of lease conditions deprives them of rights of due process.

Irritations with Interior were paralleled by frustrations encountered in dealing with the congressional committee which had the responsibility of holding hearings on ameliorative legislation. A delegation of Santa Barbarans was scheduled to testify in Washington on the Cranston bill to ban drilling. From the questions which congressmen asked them, and the manner in which they were "handled," the delegates could only conclude that the committee was "in the pockets of Oil." As one of the returning delegates put it, the presentation bespoke of "total futility."

At this writing, six months after their introduction, both the Cranston and Teague bills, though significantly softened, lie buried in committee with little prospect of surfacing.

Disillusionment: Power Is Knowledge

The American dream is a dream of progress, of the efficacy of know-how and technology; science is seen as both servant and savior. From the start, part of the shock of the oil spill was that such a thing could happen in a country having such a sophisticated technology. The much overworked phrase "If we can send a man to the moon . . ." took on special meaning in Santa Barbara. When, in years previous, Santa Barbara's elected officials had attempted to halt the original sale of leases, "assurances" were given by Interior that such an "accident" could not occur, given the highly developed state of the industry. Not only did it occur, but the original gusher of oil spewed forth completely out of control for ten days, and the continual "seepage" which followed it remains uncontrolled to the present moment—seven months later. That the government would embark upon so massive a drilling program with such unsophisticated technology was shocking indeed.

Further, not only was the technology inadequate and the plans for stopping a leak, should one occur, nonexistent, but the area in which the drilling took place was known from the outset to be extremely hazardous. That is, drilling was occurring on an ocean bottom known for its extraordinary geological circumstances—porous sand lacking a bedrock "ceiling" capable of restraining uncontrollably seeping oil. Thus, the continuing leakage through the sands at various points above the oil reservoir cannot be stopped, and this could have been predicted from the data known to all parties involved.

Another peculiarity of the Channel that had been known to the experts is the fact that it is located in the heart of earthquake activity in a region which is among the most earthquake prone in the country. Santa Barbarans are now asking what might occur during an earthquake; if pipes on the ocean floor and casings through the ocean bottom should be sheared, the damage done by the Channel's thousands of potential producing wells would devastate the entire coast of Southern California. The striking contrast between the sophistication of the means used to locate and extract oil and the primitiveness of the means to control and clean its spillage became extremely clear in Santa Barbara.

Recurrent attempts have been made to ameliorate the continuing seep by placing floating booms around an area of leakage and then sending workboats to skim off the leakage from within the demarcated area. Chemical dispersants of various kinds have also been tried. But the oil bounces over the booms in the choppy waters, the workboats suck up only a drop in the bucket, and the dispersants are effective only when used in quantities which constitute a graver pollution threat than the oil they are designed to eliminate. Cement is poured into suspected fissures in an attempt to seal them up. Oil on the beaches is periodically cleaned by dumping straw over the sands and then raking it up along with the oil which it has absorbed. The common sight of men throwing straw on miles of beaches, within view of complex drilling rigs capable of exploiting resources thousands of feet below the ocean's surface, became a clear symbol to Santa Barbarans. They gradually began to see the oil disaster as the product of a system that promotes research and development in areas which lead to strategic profitability—without regard for social utility.

This kind of subordination of science to profit came out more directly in the workings of the Presidential committee of "distinguished" scientists and engineers (the DuBridge Panel) which was to recommend means of eliminating the seepage under Platform A. When the panel was appointed, hopes were raised that at last the scientific establishment of the nation would come forth with a technologically sophisticated solution to the problem. Instead, the panel—after a two-day session and after hearing no testimony from anyone not connected with either Oil or the Interior Department—recommended the "solution" of drilling an additional 50 wells under Platform A in order to pump the area dry as quickly as possible. One member of the panel estimated that the process would take from 10 to 20 years. Despite an immediate local clamor, Interior refused to make public the data or the reasoning behind the recommendations. The information on Channel geological conditions had been provided by the oil companies (the Geological Survey routinely depends upon the oil industry for the data upon which it makes its "regulatory" decisions). The data, being private property, thus could not be released—or so the government claimed. For Union Oil itself has given a clearance to the public release of the data. In this way both parties are neatly protected, while Santa Barbara's local experts remain thwarted by the counter-arguments of Oil/Interior that "if you had the information we have, you would agree with us."

Science played a similarly partisan role in other areas of the fight that Santa Barbarans were waging against the oil companies. The Chief Deputy Attorney General of California, for example, complained that the oil industry "is preventing oil drilling experts from aiding the Attorney General's office in its lawsuits over the Santa Barbara oil spill." Noting that his office had been unable to get assistance from petroleum experts at California universities, the Deputy Attorney General stated: "The university experts all seem to be working on grants from the oil industry. There is an atmosphere of fear. The experts are afraid that if they assist us in our case on behalf of the people of California, they will lose their oil industry grants."

At the Santa Barbara campus of the University, there is little oil money in evidence and few, if any, faculty members have entered into proprietory research arrangements with Oil. Petroleum geology and engineering is simply not a local specialty. Yet it is a fact that oil interests did contact several Santa Barbara faculty members with offers of funds for studies on the ecological effects of the oil spill, with publication rights stipulated by Oil. It is also the case that the Federal Water Pollution Control Administration explicitly requested a U.C. Santa Barbara botanist to withhold the findings of his study, funded by that agency, on the ecological effects of the spill.

Most of these revelations received no publicity outside of Santa Barbara. The Attorney's allegation, however, did become something of a state-wide issue when a professor at the Berkeley campus, in his attempt to refute the charge, actually confirmed it. Wilbur H. Somerton, professor of petroleum engineering, indicated he could not testify against Oil "because my work depends on good relations with the petroleum industry. My interest is serving the petroleum industry. I view my obligation to the community as supplying it with well-trained petroleum engineers. We train the industry's engineers and they help us."

Santa Barbara's leaders were incredulous about the whole affair. The question—one which is asked more often by the downtrodden sectors of the society than by the privileged—was posed: "Whose university is this, anyway?" A local executive and GOO leader asked, "If the truth isn't in the universities, where is it?" A conservative member of the state legislature, in a move reminiscent of SDS demands, went so far as to demand an end to all faculty "moonlighting" for industry. In Santa

Barbara, the only place where all of this publicity was appearing, there was thus an opportunity for insight into the linkages between knowledge, the university, government and oil — and into the resultant non-neutrality of science. The backgrounds of many members of the DuBridge Panel were linked publicly to the oil industry. DuBridge himself, as a past president of Cal Tech, served under a board of trustees which included the president of Union Oil and which accepted substantial Union Oil donations.

While "academic truth" was being called into question, some truths not usually dwelt on by Oil's experts were gaining public attention. In another of its front-page editorials, the News-Press set forth a number of revealing facts about the oil industry. The combination of output restrictions, extraordinary tax write-off privileges for drilling expenses, the import quota, and the 27½ per cent depletion allowance creates an artificially high price almost double the world market price for a comparable product delivered to comparable U.S. destinations. The combination of available incentives creates a situation where some oil companies pay no taxes whatsoever during extraordinarily profitable years. In the years 1962-1966, Standard Oil of New Jersey paid less than four per cent of its profits in taxes, Standard of Cailfornia less than three per cent, and 22 of the other largest oil companies paid slightly more than six per cent. It was pointed out again and again to Santa Barbarans that it was this system of subsidy which made the relatively high cost deep-sea exploration and drilling in the Channel profitable in the first place. Thus the citizens of Santa Barbara, as federal taxpayers and fleeced consumers, were subsidizing their own eco-catastrophe.

The Mechanisms of Deception

The way in which federal officials and the oil industry frustrated the democratic process and thwarted popular dissent in Santa Barbara is hardly unfamiliar. But the upper-middle-class nature of the community, and the sharp features of an event which was a sudden disruption of normality, make it an ideal case for illustrating some of the techniques by which the powers that be maintain the status quo.

The first of these has been described by Daniel Boorstin as the technique of the "pseudo-event." A pseudo-event occurs when men arrange conditions to simulate a particular kind of event so that certain prearranged consequences follow as though the actual event had taken place. Several pseudo-events took place in Santa Barbara. From the outset, it was obvious that national actions concerning oil were aimed at freezing out any local participation in decisions affecting the Channel. Thus, when the federal government first called for bids on a Channel lease in 1968, local officials were not even informed. Further, local officials were not notified by any government agency in the case of the original oil spill, nor (except after the spill was already widely known) in the case of any of the previous or subsequent more "minor" spills. The thrust of the federal government's colonialist attitude toward the local community was contained in an Interior Department engineer's memo released by Senator Cranston's office. Written to the Assistant Secretary of the Interior to explain the policy of refusing to hold public hearings prior to drilling, it said: "We preferred not to stir up the natives any more than possible."

The Santa Barbara County Board of Supervisors turned down the call for "participation" in drawing up new "tougher" drilling regulations precisely because they knew the government had no intention of creating "safe" drilling regulations. They refused to utilize "normal channels," refusing thereby to take part in the pseudo-event and thus to let the consequences (in this case the appearance of democratic decision-making and local assent) of a non-event occur.

There were other attempts to stage pseudo-events. Nixon's "inspection" of the Santa Barbara beachfront was an obvious one. Another series of such events were the congressional hearings set up by legislators who were, in the words of a well-to-do lady leader of GOO, "kept men." The locals were allowed to blow off steam at the hearings, but their arguments, however cogent, failed to bring about legislation appropriate to the pollution crisis. Many Santa Barbarans had a similar impression of the court hearings regarding the various legal maneuvers against oil drilling.

Another technique for diffusing and minimizing popular protest evidenced in the Santa Barbara affair might be called the "creeping event." A creeping event is, in a sense, the opposite of a pseudo-event. It occurs when something *is* actually taking place, but when the manifestations of the event are arranged to occur at an inconspicuously gradual and piecemeal pace, thus avoiding some of the consequences which would follow from the event if it were immediately perceived to be occurring.

The major creeping event in Santa Barbara was the piecemeal resumption of production and drilling after Hickel's second moratorium. Authorization to resume *production* at different specific groups of wells occurred on various dates throughout February and early March. Authorization to resume *drilling* of various groups of new wells was announced by Interior on dates from April 1 through August. Each resumption was announced as a particular safety precaution to relieve pressures, until finally on the most recent resumption date, the word "deplete" was used for the first time in explaining the granting of permission to drill. There is thus no *specific* point in time at which production and drilling were re-authorized for the Channel—and full resumption still has not been officially authorized.

A creeping event has the consequence of diffusing resistance by withholding what journalists call a "time peg" on which to hang the story. By the time it becomes quite clear that "something *is* going on," the sponsors of the creeping event (and the aggrieved themselves) can ask why there should be any protest "now" when there was none before, in the face of the very same kind of provocation. In this way, the aggrieved has resort only to frustration and the gnawing feeling that events are sweeping by him.

A third way of minimizing legitimate protest is by use of the alleged "neutrality" of science and the knowledge producers. I have discussed the "experts" and the University. After learning of the collusion between government and Oil and the use of secret science as a prop to that collusion, Santa Barbarans found themselves in the unenviable position of having to demonstrate that science and knowledge were not, in fact, neutral arbiters. They had to prove, *by themselves*, that continued drilling was not safe; that the "experts" who said it was safe were the hirelings, directly or indirectly, of oil interests; and that the report of the DuBridge Panel recommending massive drilling was a fraudulent document. They had to show that the university petroleum geologists themselves were in league with the oil companies and that information unfavorable to the oil interests was systematically withheld by virtue of the very structure of the knowledge industry. This is no small task. It is a long and complicated story, and one which pits lay persons (and a few academic renegades) against an entire profession and the patrons of that profession. An illustration of the difficulties involved may be drawn from very recent history. Seventeen Santa Barbara plaintiffs, represented by the ACLU, sought a temporary injunction against additional Channel drilling at least until the information utilized by the DuBridge Panel was made public and a hearing could be held. The injunction was not granted, and in the end the presiding federal judge ruled in favor of what he termed the "expert" opinions available to the Secretary of the Interior. Due to limited time for rebuttal, the disorienting confusions of courtroom procedures, and also perhaps the desire not to offend the Court, the ACLU lawyer could not make his subtle, complex and highly controversial case that the "experts" were partisans and that their scientific "findings" followed from that partisanship.

A fourth obstacle was placed in the way of dissenters by the communications media. Just as the courtroom setting was not amenable to a full reproduction of the facts supporting the ACLU case, so the media in general—due to restrictions of time and style—prevented a full airing of the details of the case. A more cynical analysis of the media's inability to make known the Santa Barbara "problem" in its full fidelity might hinge on an allegation that the media were constrained by fear of "pressures" from Oil and its allies. Metromedia, for example, sent to Santa Barbara a team which spent several days documenting, interviewing and filming for an hour-long program—only to suddenly drop the project entirely due to what is reported by locals in touch with the network to have been "pressures" from Oil. Even without such blatant interventions, however, the full reproduction of the Santa Barbara "news" would remain problematic.

News media are notorious for the anecdotal nature of their reporting; even so-called "think pieces" rarely go beyond a stringing together of proximate events. There are no analyses of the "mobilization of bias" or linkages of men's actions with their pecuniary interests. Science and learning are assumed to be neutral; regulatory agencies are assumed to function as "watchdogs" for the public. Information contradicting these assumptions is treated as an exotic exception.

The complexity of the situations to be reported and the wealth of details needed to support such analyses require more time and effort than journalists have at their command. Their recitation would produce long stories not consistent with space limitations and make-up preferences of newspapers, or with analogous requirements within the other media. A full telling of the story would tax the reader/viewer and would risk boring him. The rather extensive media coverage of the oil spill centered on a few dramatic moments in its history (e.g., the initial gusher of oil) and a few simple-to-tell "human interest" stories such as the pathetic deaths of the sea birds struggling along the oil-covered sands. With increasing temporal and geographical distance from the initial spill, national coverage became increasingly rare and sloppy. Interior Department statements on the state of the "crisis" were reported without local rejoinders as the newsmen who might have gathered them began leaving the scene. While the Santa Barbara spill received extraordinarily extensive national coverage relative to other controversial events, this coverage nevertheless failed to adequately inform the American public about a situation which Santa Barbarans knew from first-hand experience.

Finally, perhaps the most pernicious technique of all because of the damage it does to the social conscience, is the routinization of evil. Pollution of the Santa Barbara Channel is now routine; the issue is not whether or not the Channel is polluted, but *how much* it is polluted. A recent oil slick discovered off a Phillips Oil platform in the Channel was dismissed by an oil company official as a "routine" drilling by-product which was not viewed as "obnoxious." That about half of the oil currently seeping into the Channel is allegedly being recovered is taken as an improvement sufficient to preclude the "outrage" that a big national story would require.

Similarly, the pollution of the moral environment becomes routine; it is accepted as natural that politicians are "on the take," "in the pockets of Oil." The depletion allowance remains a question of percentages (20 per cent or 27½ per cent), rather than a focus for questioning the very legitimacy of such special benefits. "Compromises" emerge, such as the 24 per cent depletion allowance and the new "tough" drilling regulations, which are already being hailed as "victories" for the reformers. Like the oil spill itself, the depletion allowance debate becomes buried in its own disorienting detail, in its pseudo-events and in the triviality of the "solutions" which ultimately come to be considered as the "real" options. Evil is both banal and complicated, and each of these attributes contributes to its durability.

The Mechanisms of Change

What the citizens of Santa Barbara learned through their experience was that the parties competing to shape decision-making on oil in Santa Barbara do not have equal access to the means of "mobilizing bias." The Oil/Government combine had, from the start, an extraordinary number of advantages. Lacking ready access to media, the ability to stage events at will, and a well-integrated system of arrangements for achieving their goals (at least in comparison to their adversaries), Santa Barbara's citizens have met with repeated frustrations.

Their response to their relative powerlessness has been analogous to that of other groups and individuals who, from a similar vantage point, come to see the system up close. They become willing to expand their repertoire of means of influence as their cynicism and bitterness increase. Letter writing gives way to demonstrations, demonstrations to civil disobedience. People refuse to participate in "democratic procedures" which are a part of the opposition's event-management strategy. Confrontation politics arises as a means of countering official events with "events" of one's own, thus providing the media with stories which can be simply and energetically told.

Thus, in Santa Barbara, rallies were held at local beaches; congressmen and state and national officials were greeted by demonstrations. (Fred Hartley of Union Oil inadvertently landed his plane in the middle of one such demonstration, causing a rather ugly name-calling scene to ensue.) A "sail-in" was held one Sunday with a flotilla of local pleasure boats forming a circle around Platform A, each craft bearing large anti-Oil banners. City hall meetings were packed with citizens reciting demands for immediate and forceful local action.

A City Council election held during the crisis resulted in a landslide for the Council's bitterest critic and the defeat of a veteran councilman suspected of having "oil interests." In a rare action, the News-Press condemned the local Chamber of Commerce for accepting oil money for a fraudulent tourist advertising campaign which touted Santa Barbara (including its beaches) as completely restored to its former beauty.

One possible grand strategy for Santa Barbara was outlined by a local public relations man and GOO worker, who said, "We've got to run the oil men out. The city owns the wharf and the harbor that the company has to use. The city has got to deny its facilities to oil traffic, service boats, cranes and the like. If the city contravenes some federal navigation laws [which such actions would unquestionably involve], to hell with it. The only hope to save Santa Barbara is to awaken the nation to the ravishment. That will take public officials who are willing to block oil traffic with their bodies and with police hoses, if necessary. Then federal marshals or federal troops would have to come in. This would pull in the national news media."

This scenario has thus far not occurred in Santa Barbara, although the continued use of the wharf by the oil industries has led to certain militant actions. A picket was maintained at the wharf for two weeks to protest the conversion of the pier from a recreation and tourist facility into an industrial plant for the use of the oil companies. A boycott of other wharf businesses (e.g., two restaurants) was urged. The picket line was led by white, middle-class adults — one of whom was a local businessman who, two years earlier, was a close runner-up in the Santa Barbara mayoralty race.

Prior to the picketing, a dramatic Easter Sunday confrontation (involving approximately 500 persons) took place between demonstrators and city police. Just as a wharf rally was breaking up, an oil service truck began driving up the pier to make a delivery of casing supplies for oil drilling. There was a spontaneous sit-down in front of the truck. For the first time since the Ku Klux Klan folded in the '30s, a group of (heavily) middle-class Santa Barbarans was publicly taking the law into its own hands. After much lengthy discussion between police, the truck driver and the demonstrators, the truck was ordered away and the demonstrators remained to rejoice over their victory. The following day's News-Press editorial, while not supportive of such tactics, was quite sympathetic, which was noteworthy given the paper's longstanding bitter opposition to similar tactics when exercised by dissident Northern blacks or student radicals.

A companion demonstration on the water failed to materialize. A group of Santa Barbarans was to sail to the Union platform and "take it," but choppy seas precluded a landing, and the would-be conquerors returned to port in failure.

It would be difficult to predict what forms Santa Barbara's resistance will take in the future. A veteran News-Press reporter who covered the important oil stories has publicly stated that if the government fails to eliminate both the pollution and its causes, "there will, at best, be civil disobedience in Santa Barbara and at worst, violence." In fact, talk of "blowing up" the ugly platforms has been recurrent — and it is heard in all social circles.

But just as this kind of talk is not entirely serious, it is difficult to know the degree to which the other militant statements are meaningful. Despite frequent observations about the "radicalization" of Santa Barbara, it is difficult to determine the extent to which the authentic grievances against Oil have been generalized into a radical analysis of American society. Certainly an SDS membership campaign among Santa Barbara adults would be a dismal failure. But that is too severe a test. People, particularly basically contented people, change their world-view very slowly, if at all. Most Santa Barbarans still go about their comfortable lives in the ways they always have; they may even help Ronald Reagan win another term in the state house. But I do conclude that large numbers of persons have been moved, and that they have been moved in the direction of the radical left. They have gained insights into the structure of power in America not possessed by similarly situated persons in other parts of the country. It can be a revealing shock to experience an event first-hand and then to hear it described, and distorted, by the press and the government. People extrapolate from such experiences to the possibility that official descriptions of other events may be similarly biased and misleading. And when these questions arise, deeper ones follow. As a consequence some Santa Barbarans, especially those with the most interest in and information about the oil spill, while still surrounded by comfort and certainty, have nevertheless come to view power in America more intellectually, more analytically, more sociologically—more radically—then they did before.

Manifesto for the Sea

ROBERT RIENOW*

Jeremiah, as he wailed "There is sorrow on the sea; it cannot be quiet," was seemingly but drawing a literary backdrop for his lamentations. Even he could not have anticipated that one day the mighty oceans would be literally the subject of despair.

The myth of great and unfathomable seas—a limitless frontier of exploitation—lies at the base of the legal and political regime that marks man's historic relationship to those seas. We still intone with Byron:

> Roll on, thou deep and dark blue ocean, roll!
> Ten thousand fleets sweep over thee in vain;
> Man marks the earth with ruin—his control
> Stops with the shore.
>
> —Childe Harold

And because we are mesmerized by the endless beating of the eternal waves into agreeing with the poet that the seas are invincible, we admit, long after it is thoroughly outmoded, the doctrine of res nullius. Even as we maul and poison the

*"Manifesto for the Sea" by Robert Rienow is reprinted from American Behavioral Scientist, Volume XI, No. 6 (July-August 1968), pp. 34-37, by permission of the Publisher, Sage Publications, Inc. Footnotes deleted.

oceans, destroying the delicate chains of life so intricately assembled, we stubbornly cling to the doctrine that the sea is big enough to absorb the assorted blows of man, individually and collectively.

We have not yet adjusted our thinking to the mastery of technology. Because the seas could gulp a schooner and all hands aboard without a belch, we forget that a loaded 200,000-ton oil tanker is an indigestible item. Because a liner or two could spew their slops overboard with impunity, we have come to believe that we need put no limits on the filth that we pipe to the depths. Because the once-pure oceans are seemingly illimitable, we make them the dumping grounds for the hottest by-products of our atomic age, a deadly assortment of long-lasting radioactive wastes.

Yet because these premises are false, a critical urgency has arisen. Hundreds of conglomerate nations, pressed by burgeoning, hungry populations, are now attacking the seas with the full vigor of unrestrained technological prowess. If we would save them and their resources from death, we must soon cease the abuse and establish a new protective regime of law not yet imagined by man—a law able to combat the massive destructive powers which humanity has come to possess.

Our entire philosophy is contrary to our need. It is the ancient, worn-out credo of "inexhaustible" resources, the myth which has so grossly impoverished our once rich resource base. But in the case of the seas, the myth has been multiplied a thousand times.

Indeed, we use the seas not only as a soporific against the reckoning that our fecundity and industrial productivity must surely impose upon us, but as a glittering promise beyond anything we have yet known. Predicts Dr. William A. Nierenberg, Director of Scripps Institution of Oceanography, in an outburst of optimism: "We're learning more and more about food chains and we know the oceans could yield enough protein on a sustained basis to feed 30 *billion* people."

Not only unlimited food, such as it may be, will be seined from the ocean's depths, but minerals will be mined, oil tapped on its floor, and great underseas cities glimmer through its watery aisles, cloistered havens for our unwanted millions. Dr. Donald F. Hronig, Science Adviser to the President, summarized these bullish prophecies by concluding that "The ocean is big business right now, and the rate it's going, it's reasonable to expect it will become an even bigger business in the years ahead."

This frontier legend of the seas paints a pristine, limitless, and romantic cornucopia of the deep. With oceanographers chafing in the lead to generate the enthusiasm, we are regaled with fabulous statistics. There are 1.5 trillion tons of manganese nodules pimpling the ocean floor, enough minable phosphate material off the coast of Mexico to last, at present rates of consumption, for 4000 years, and enough oil to fill 25% of the entire oil production of the world.

This, then, is our image of the sea—a prodigally bounteous, untamed frontier bursting with potential riches for all. The myth is founded on public ignorance of a type foreboding of tragedy. It is abetted by a less than honest assessment by the sea's fervent exploiters. Minerals and oil may be there in untold quantities, but the dangers to men, and the pollutive destruction of the waters in obtaining them, are never stressed. As for the sea harvest of food which is depended upon to stave off the famines to come, the fatuity of such predictions is that they ignore completely the nature and delicacy of the sea's life chains. And there is no note taken of the fact that the productive part of the sea is largely on its fringes—the continental shelves, the bays and estuaries. The wide expanse of the sea is ecologically a watery desert.

"Preserving habitat for salt-water fish requires controlling the development of tidelands, tidal bottoms, and all the fringing brackish water habitat. This is the part of the sea called the *estuarine zone.* The word estuary as used here describes any of the protected coastal areas where there is a mixing of salt and fresh waters, including all the tidal rivers, marshes, tideflats, lagoons, bays, and shallow sounds," explains John Clark, writing for the American Littoral Society. "Two out of every three species of useful Atlantic fish," he adds, "depend in some way upon tidal lands and the shallowest of our bays for their survival. Even oceanic fish often have complex life cycles which bring them into coastal bays, lagoons, and tidal rivers at tiny young stages of their lives."

It has been estimated that 90% of the salt-water fish are taken in shallow coastal waters. More importantly, the parts of the ocean bordering the land are the fertile environment in which flourishes the plant growth on which bait fish, shellfish, shrimp, and plankton all thrive. "The richest coastal marshes produce ten tons of plant stuff per acre per year—more than six times the amount (one and one-half tons) of wheat produced per acre, on a world average."

Even the undersea farming that excites the imagination of some scientists is planned to take place in the estuaries, coastal swamps, and shoreline areas. Dr. John H. Ryther of Woods Hole Oceanographic Institution points out that the productivity of the one and one-fourth million acres of mangrove swamps in the Philippines, if applied to the raising of milkfish in ponds, would in itself produce a tonnage of protein food equal to the present fish harvest of the entire United States. Aquaculture is designed to be practiced near the shores.

Yet it has been made evident that the seas are most shockingly vulnerable to the insults that stem from the activities of man in the very place where man and ocean meet. The traditional "accepted" use of coastal waters for the outfalls of municipal and industrial sewage systems is now seriously questioned, as the wastes mount geometrically. "In recent years," says a team of scholars, "many have realized that, although the oceans contain an almost limitless supply of diluting water, other beneficial and economically important uses of the near-shore ocean waters must be considered when an ocean outfall is designed for the disposal of sewage."

Up to now the pollution of harbors, bays, and estuaries has been carried to the point of hazard or nuisance on the basic assumption that the tidal scrubbing would be effective. We are, indeed, with our overburden of wastes and our identification of coastal waters with the vast expanse of the oceans, destroying an environment which is at the same time both separate from the seas and yet highly interdependent. The multiplication of people and their industries is fast rendering barren the most fruitful part of the seas. "Coastal and estuarine regions of the sea which receive large amounts of organic wastes often produce sulfides from the bottom sediments in concentrations so high that animals and plants inhabitating these environments are damaged seriously."

Direct outfalls may make of a bay or harbor a disease-ridden and noisome thing, as in the town of Winthrop Harbor in the Boston vicinity. There, the fascinating and profitable array of life forms that marks a seacoast was suffocated by an overwhelming growth of sea lettuce, feeding on the ingredients of the raw sewage that was being dumped in ever greater quantities from the North Metropolitan Sewer near Deer Island.

As we continue to pollute each of our 22 watersheds, all the vast quantities of inland wastes are added to the coastal burden of pollution. All up and down the coasts, each river spills its accumulated filth and contaminants at its mouth, in volumes that even the indefatigable tide cannot overcome. With river valleys the choice habitation of man, it follows that the rivers provide the plumbing system for most of mankind, and the coastal waters of the seas become an elongated septic tank. The Thames estuary is today a notorious sewer. The domestic industrial effluents of a million people pour down the estuary of the once-lovely River Tyne. Should you consult the engineering manuals rather than the travel folders, you will find, instead of a lyric description of the sunrise over Hawaii's famed Kailua Bay, the less savory discussion of the sewage daily discharged into it. You will be enlightened by the figures of sewage burden from Nanaimo and the sulfate discharge of the 700-ton-a-day mill into the Northumberland Channel of the North Pacific. Yet the time is close at hand when the very odor alone of such waters will force the tourist agencies (albeit for a different reason) to join the ecologists and engineers in their mounting concern for the debauchment of the world's bays.

Added to the befoulment by sewage and industrial effluents, we now face the swelling floods of thousands of concoctions of pesticides and herbicides which drain constantly down into the rivers' mouths. It was the late Lloyd Berkner, eminent scientist and dean of the Dallas Graduate Research Center, who first called attention to the lethal effects of these pesticidal compounds on the floating diatoms of the sea, manufacturers of 70% of the oxygen in the air we daily breathe.

Long-lasting DDT is particularly deadly to fish life. "The Interior Department reveals that one part of DDT in one billion parts of water kills blue crabs in eight days." Yet this vicious and discredited pesticide, which has proved to be all but eternal in its toxicity and is peculiarly lethal to aquatic life, is flushed off the watersheds of every major farming country without restraint into the most productive areas of the world's oceans. Pomeroy et al. mention the depredation visited upon mullet *(mugil cephalus)*, menhaden *(brevoortia tyrannus)*, and the commercial shrimps *(penaeus spp)* which enter the marsh creeks in spring and spend most of the summer feeding there.

Many of the pesticides, indeed, were particularly "formulated to combat terrestrial arthropods—spiders, insects, etc., distinguished by their jointed feet and limbs, segmented bodies, and horny skeletons. In other words, what selective toxicity is built into these pesticides is directed to the arthropods. Unfortunately, it happens that a number of our most valuable marine food species, including lobsters, crabs, and shrimp, are also hapless arthropods." It has also been found that some varieties of plankton important in the diet of oysters and clams are especially vulnerable to minute concentrations of herbicides, much smaller concentrations than are employed for the extensive weed control programs upstream.

As if sewage, industrial effluents, and pesticidal-herbicidal compounds were not enough, our civilization makes still another death-dealing assault upon the nurseries of the seas. The fallout from nuclear explosions that spreads itself about the earth in the falling rain also gathers in the watersheds' drainage, collecting finally in the estuaries along with the wastes that spill out of uranium mills, dribble from atomic installations, and find their way from industrial and medical applications to the outfalls on the banks. Thus, the Severn, the Blackwater, Britain's Solway Firth, as well as the seas off the Irish and Netherland coast, are causing increasing concern because of their growing concentrations of radioactive wastes. Over the short period of six years there has been a progressive and measurable increase of Strontium 90 and Cesium 137 in the coastal water, fish, mussels, and shrimps in the North Sea.

These are but examples; the threat is universal. A careful evaluation by a team of scientists repeats that "Future additions of *significant amounts* of radionuclides to the estuarine and marine environment, whether accidental or intentional, will almost certainly occur in a variety of climatic, geographic, and geologic areas.

As if this steadily advancing radiation of our seafood nurseries were not fast enough, we are still (after more than twenty years of waste disposal research) directly dumping our radioactive poisons into our coastal seas. "A Canadian report states that more than 16,000 drums, each containing 55 gallons of low-level waste, were dumped off the coast of California from 1946 to 1957. At Harwell (U. K.) contaminated solid waste, consisting of building material, protective clothing, laboratory equipment, animal remains, etc., is first reduced in volume as much as possible, and subsequently either stored or discharged into the sea. The total volume of this waste amounts to approximately 3200 cubic feet per week, weighing about 29 tons."

The pressure for this kind of sea disposal of radioactive wastes becomes intense as one ponders the fantastic estimates for the future. "In the United States, it is estimated that the nuclear power industry will have produced three thousand million curies of radioactivity in 27 million litres of solution by 1970, and 60 thousand million curies in 1.1 billion litres of solution by the year 2000." The safety of these disposal arrangements, which has the support of a body of scientists, has been founded on a pair of assumptions: that there are "deeps" where the lethal debris will remain isolated, and that what escapes will be greatly diluted.

Both assumptions are currently challenged. Many experts hotly argue that our research as to the circulation, mixing, and sedimentation in the deep sea is pitifully inadequate. Russian scholars are most doubtful about the current practices. Nicolas Gorsky, a member of the U.S.S.R. Geographical Society, notes the vertical mixing or circulation described by Professor Zubov which "ventilates the deep layers of the ocean and also raises to the surface a layer rich in nutrient phosphates and nitrates, forming a basis for abundant life. But this process will bring death if pernicious radioactive solutions from the waste products of the atomic industry accumulate in the ocean depths."

More important, Professor Gorsky describes another similar phenomenon known as "upwelling." Because of winds, currents, or the relief of the ocean bed, deep, cold layers of water, laden with nutrients, come to the surface and lap the continental slope or the submerged banks. This phenomenon is especially marked on the Atlantic coast of North America, the California coast, and the western coast of both South America and Africa.

The regions where upwelling occurs are exceptionally rich in plant and animal life, including fish. If the water rising to the surface should be contaminated with substances dissolved out of radioactive wastes it will mean the end of the highly productive fisheries in these regions.

Indeed the Russian conclusion is that it is impossible to isolate or localize the poisoning of the seas. Even if the currents and movement of the water did not focus on the shores, the concentrating factor in the oceanic food chains is itself a competent countervail to dilution. Thus, in the central Pacific Ocean, "plankton were found to contain on the average nearly 500 times the general water concentration of fallout activity. An examination of the fish of the German bight coastal area shows that the radioactivity level remains constant even when nuclear tests decrease."

We cannot register all the land-based insults to the ecosystems of the seas. But there is one more we must note: the threat from off-shore and shore-based oil drilling operations as well as by the still very inadequately policed regulation of oil spillages, accidental and deliberate, from ocean-going vessels. Thus there exists an insensate and unremitting strangulation of the world's bays and estuaries wherever demographic and economic growth press the shores. Against all this assorted mindless aggressiveness of man, smugly ensconced behind the legal embattlements of the nation-state, the seas are wholly defenseless, open to their ultimate death. The sole item of concern over Earth's oceans has, to date, centered on the traditional, barnacle-encrusted, primitive doctrine of the freedom of the high seas. This outworn manifesto is comprised of: "(1) freedom of navigation; (2) freedom of fishing; (3) freedom to lay submarine cables and pipelines; and (4) freedom to fly over the high seas."

All of these are exploitive rights; they do not pretend to tackle the preservation of the common seas or the ecological realities concerning their survival as living elements in a world suddenly drenched in an outpouring of pollution, poisons, and petroleum. At our breakneck and improvident pace, we now face the eventual destruction of our most productive asset of the future for lack of laws to protect it. "The catchy phrase 'Freedom of the Sea'" remarks Edward W. Allen, "bespeaks a noble concept, that is, if applied with noble aspirations, but it can be a deceptive cliché if utilized to conceal ignoble motivations." The day when a tide could scrub the estuaries clean and there still existed interminable miles of lonesome beaches, when the seas could absorb our ecological insults, is long past.

When will we come to grips with the exploding issue of marine pollution? We have grappled tentatively with the question of the rights of co-riparians in an international drainage basin to a proper share of whatever water is of acceptable quality. It is asserted that "there are principles limiting the power of states to use such waters without regard to injurious effects on co-riparians."

Hopefully, there are few defenders today of the Schooner Exchange doctrine — the principle invoked by Attorney General Harmon in the Rio Grande dispute of 1895 — that the jurisdiction of a state within its territory is exclusive and absolute and susceptible only of self-imposed limitations. In contradiction, what a nation does with its rivers, states Griffin, is subject to the legal rights of each co-riparian state in the drainage basin. "No international decision supporting any purported principle of absolute sovereignty has been found."

It is some advance to formally recognize that the seas are an international drainage basin of which all littoral states are "co-riparians." For on ecological principle alone (however the legal precedents direct) the well-being of the seas as a living, productive ecosystem for the benefit of the community of nations is wholly dependent on what happens to the margins and the land masses.

However, at present we concede jurisdiction over marginal seas on grounds of defense to littoral states because we still assume their stake is superior to that of the community of nations. The international approval of the continental shelf doctrine and the adoption of the convention of Fishing and Conservation of the Living Resources of the Sea give an authority to coastal states also on the basis that they have a primary interest.

Thus the primary legal interest continues to be exploitive; it is a matter of staking out national claims under the misleading guise of "conservation." The direction of American concern is evident from this budget extract: Out of an annual total of $462.3 million for United States federal marine science spending, $191.6 is for national security, $49.2 for fisheries development and seafood technology, and but $9.5 million for pollution abatement and control.

The present flabby attitude of the nation-states, that condones the destruction of coastal waters by the drainage of poisons and pollutants, is a malignant threat to the welfare of the seas and therefore to the welfare of mankind. It is imperative that we develop a modernized legal regime that affords protection to the maritime interests of the community of states as a whole. This objective calls for the international regulation of watersheds with the family of nations viewed as co-riparians.

A. P. Lester, British barrister, while assessing the rights of riparians to clean water, noted that "state responsibility for extraterritorial damage to the territory of another state has been based upon the concepts of neighborship, abuse of rights, and international servitudes." None of these principles in its traditional garb is adequate to the preservation of the physical integrity of the sea against the destructive forces and wastes of twentieth-century industrialism.

If Grotius in his day could find a common stake of all the riparians to the water of a river, certainly we today must recognize the valid claim of the family of nations to productive coastal waters and estuaries. Having identified the fringes of the seas as the vital element in the seas' well-being, and the growing dependency of all of mankind on the future harvest of the oceans, one must readily conclude the superior claim of the international community to the ecological health of coastal waters.

Unless we want to be faced with the globe-enveloping spectre of a dead and stinking ocean, we are faced with the task of somehow evolving an international regime of oceanic stewardship. Besides international controls of pollutants and of the use of rivers and estuaries, such a regime would embody a creative application of the legal principle of servitudes, under which sovereign jurisdiction over rivers would yield to the prescriptive rights of the family of nations to a viable system of seas.

There is little time left to debate the juridical niceties. Already the chlorinated hydrocarbons (DDT, its cousins and derivatives) have traveled the biological waterways and concentrated in the complex oceanic food chains, so that not only is every species of fish used by man contaminated, but the carnivorous birds who feed on seafood are in real trouble. Biologists report that the last twenty remaining pairs of Bermuda petrels are dying out for want of fertility of eggs because of DDT; their extinction is forecast within ten years. The peregrine falcon is now extinct as a breeding bird along the east coast of the United States. Ducks, geese, and gulls are often so loaded that their eggs are "hot."

The irony is that man, who is the source of all this poisoning, is himself the end of these many varied food chains; he eats the choice large fish who have concentrated the poisons from algae all the way up, and he thus becomes the final residuary of the very lethal concoctions he has created to use on other life. Indeed, it should be evident that he cannot long continue in such folly without jeopardizing his own existence.

What we need now is an entirely new manifesto of the sea built not, as in the past, on legal limitations alone, but constructed primarily on the ecological realities of a sick sea in what may be fatal crisis.

6

The Future and the
Environmental Crisis

The selections in the preceding five chapters illuminate the causes and nature of many of the problems which contribute to the current ecological crisis and demonstrate how these relate to the political system. Some environmental problems have resulted from crass abuse and exploitation; others have emerged unintentionally from purposeful activities in various areas of policy. In many instances, damaging strip mining, the pollution of the air and water, the scattering of litter across the countryside, and the senseless, random butchery of the landscape for lucrative, residential, industrial, and commercial purposes have reflected a rampant "I got mine, damn the consequences" syndrome. Such exploitation and rape of the public interest has been permitted or even encouraged in many cases by unholy alliances of self-interest and weak-willed decision-makers operating within a confused pluralistic political system.

At the same time, some aspects of the environmental crisis have resulted from such well-intended activities as the design of transit systems, the production of power, and the control of disease and pests. Frequently, the activities have created harmful effects because the benefits appeared to outweigh the undesirable consequences. In other cases, the consequences were not at first known. And in still others, the costs of eliminating the negative effects were too high, the planning was poor, or there was a failure to make full use of available information and technology.

The many components of the environmental crisis stem from the interaction of a number of factors. The major causes of urban air pollution, for example, are the automobile and industry. But there are secondary causes as well, such as the development and sunk costs of transit systems; human behavior patterns; local, state, and federal government relations; consumer credit (which permits the deficit purchase of automobiles); the multiplicity of governments in urban areas; the location policies of business and industry; state laws concerning annexation; and many others.

The population problem provides another example. The current crisis of population growth is the result of decisions made without concern over the ramifications of population itself. Decisions are made by people in millions of centers regarding family planning, medicine, pesticide use, factory location, transit artery placement, and housing. The "population problem," therefore, is not really a discrete problem;

rather, it is a "consequence" of policy made in other areas on the basis of other considerations.

Like the cause, the cure of the environmental crisis is complicated and elusive, and faces formidable scientific, administrative, and political barriers. First, no single ecological problem can be solved independently and apart from consideration of others. Population, for example, can not be controlled unless it is considered as a variable in the planning processes within such areas as medicine, public health, agriculture, economics, and civil liberties.

Second, we often lack the scientific information or rationality necessary to solve existing problems or to predict outcomes, and thus cannot anticipate and avert new problems. We were not aware until fairly recently, for example, of the implications of extensive use of DDT; or the internal combustion engine; or the impact of noise on physical and psychic health. Prediction might have helped us avoid such problems, but once they exist, protected by habit, they are still more difficult to solve and the challenge to science is still greater.

Third, the nature of decision-making in the United States militates against problem solution. Literally thousands of decision-makers make millions of decisions in thousands of decision-centers. Decisions are made in the context of scarce resources and conflicting pressures. More often than not, they are made in response to immediate and localized stimuli. The result is often the creation of new problems or the aggravation of old ones.

Fourth, political support for broad-scale attack on environmental problems is often fleeting or lacking. Environmental quality is in some ways a "style" issue. It concerns us only when the more basic needs of employment, food, and shelter are satisfied. In other words, the perception of environmental problems as salient issues may be in part a function of affluence. It has been argued that one must be rather well off to become deeply committed to the elimination of air or water pollution. This means that public support for an attack upon environmental problems may be undercut by a sudden increase in the importance of issues related to war or economic distress.

Fifth, there may be intolerable ideological costs associated with pollution control. We may be reluctant or even completely unwilling to undertake improvement programs that restrict individual or corporate prerogatives regarding family planning, factory location, or modes of travel.

Finally, there is the problem of preferences among values. Different individuals and groups want different things. Some are more concerned about clean air than jobs; others prefer jobs. Some want vehicular access to mountain or lake parks; others want to keep automobiles out and the wilderness pristine for hunting and fishing. Thus, even with perfect and evenly distributed information on conditions, problems, prospective solutions, and so forth, people will want different things and will interpret and use information in distinct ways because they have had different experiences and have developed different sets of values which serve as cognitive screening devices. Related to this, of course, is the fact that even collective goals change with time. This means that a society may develop new goals and wants before it can mobilize men and materials to satisfy old ones.

These circumstances form the context in which the political decision-makers *must operate in their search for substantially sound and politically viable solutions to environmental problems.*

What, then, are the prospects for improving the condition of the environment, for avoiding an eco-catastrophe? We have in the past made incremental gains on many fronts. We have cleaned some rivers and increased the effectiveness of family planning programs. And coupling the apparent growth of public awareness and concern over man's future on earth with a growing body of knowledge about our environment, we are sure to make even more advances in environmental improvement in the future. But at the same time, we are likely to continue to make some of the same kinds of mistakes which we have made in the past; and decision-making will probably remain decentralized and rather myopic. Thus, anything approximating a total solution can be only a pipe dream; the search for a utopian environment can lead only to frustration and disillusionment.

The articles in this sixth and final chapter touch in various ways on the future. In the opening article, Professor Commoner again reminds us of the nature of the environmental crisis. Although past increases in the size of the population attest to the earth's capacity to absorb the effects of increased human activity, the environment remains rather delicately balanced and in some cases even the slightest intrusions can upset this balance. As examples of the complex and interrelated character of current patterns of human activity, Professor Commoner cites the relation of fertilizer use to urban sewerage treatment processes, and the relation of any possible future use of electric automobiles to current policies and plans for electrical power generation and distribution. Professor Commoner suggests that many dimensions of the environmental crisis result from the precipitous use of technological advances and concludes that environmental problems will not respond to scientific solution but require instead hard choices in the social and political sphere.

In the second selection, Luther Carter sketches some developments on the legal front in the drive to redress environmental abuses. Environmental problems, he notes, generally involve value conflict and disagreement over the proper use of environmental resources; such controversies are finding their way into the courts with increased frequency. Carter briefly describes a number of cases which have recently come before the courts. Law schools have begun to introduce environmental courses in their curricula. And the growing possibility that the courts will entertain pleas of citizens who complain about the "rape" of the public trust — and decide in their favor — is sure to spur legislative and executive decision-makers into giving greater consideration to environmental questions in future planning. Typically, the courts are beginning to respond, Carter points out, to the needs felt by society.

Following Mr. Carter, Edwin Dale explains that one of the hard facts of economic life is that pollution cannot be reduced through a trimming of work or production output. Instead, he continues, we must use technology itself to control pollution, and the development of appropriate technology can be facilitated through taxes and use of the police powers.

In the fourth selection, Professor Caldwell asserts that law and institutions tend to lag behind social and technological change, and that in these times of extremely rapid change, society's ability to handle its problems is diminishing. We can no longer afford to permit the future to be shaped largely by random decision processes and undirected forces of change. The basic environmental problem today, Professor Caldwell says, is not a runaway technology, but man's misuse of it. This misuse is supported by widespread lack of information and by actual misinformation. Much of our behavior is governed by "mind-stopping" cliches. Thus, it is necessary for changes in attitudes to precede changes in policy. As excessive and dysfunctional cognitive baggage, Professor Caldwell cities several beliefs which, in our opinion, are morally repugnant and which may well prove suicidal. These include the notions that: "(1) speculation in land values is a legitimate way to 'windfall' wealth, (2) government must help enterprise, but not attempt to control it, (3) growth (especially economic growth) is an absolute good, (4) people have a right to do as they please with their property, and (5) government by judges is preferable to government by administrators." Professor Caldwell suggests that changes are needed in the structure of American government, that individuals in education, business, and industry should join in the effort to avoid ecological disaster, and that perhaps the key to change lies in new systems of belief.

In the next selection, the editors of this volume paint a rather pessimistic picture of our capacity to cope, in any massive sense, with environmental problems. Several facts of political life lead us to this conclusion; these include the decentralization of decision-making, American myth systems, and the nature of environmental problems themselves. Man may avoid extinction, but he is likely to take the action necessary to do so only when problems reach truly crisis proportions and are recognized as such by the population at large, opinion molders, and the political leadership at all levels of government. That is the fundamental challenge.

In the final article, Professor Ogden points up three basic modes of action which he believes should direct man's effort to avoid ecological disaster. First, research and teaching must continue. New knowledge must be developed and large numbers of citizens must be made aware of basic ecological principles. Second, we must, through political processes, put available knowledge and technology to work to improve environmental quality. And finally, and perhaps most fundamentally, man must restructure his value system. He must exercise restraint in his use of technology to alter and interrupt natural processes and systems. Man, in short, must learn to accept change and to live with nature.

Nature under Attack

BARRY COMMONER*

The proliferation of human beings on the surface of this planet is proof of the remarkable suitability of the terrestrial environment as a place for human life. But the fitness of the environment is not an immutable feature of the earth, having been developed by gradual changes in the nature of the planet's skin. Living things have themselves been crucial agents of these transformations, converting the earth's early rocks into soil, releasing oxygen from its water, transforming carbon dioxide into accumulated fossil fuels, modulating temperature and tempering the rush of waters on the land. And in the course of these transformations, the living things that populated the surface of the earth have, with the beautiful precision that is a mark of life, themselves become closely adapted to the environment they have helped to create. As a result, the environment in which we live is itself part of a vast web of life, and like everything associated with life is internally complex, and stable, not in a static sense, but by virtue of the intricate play of internal interactions.

On a small scale, the dependence of environmental stability on the nice balance of multiple biological processes is self-evident. A hillside denuded of vegetation by fire and thus lacking protection against the erosion of heavy rains previously afforded by the canopy of leaves and the mat of roots can quickly shed its soil and lose its capability to support plants and harbor animals. And on this scale, the threat of thoughtless human interventions is equally self-evident; we have long since learned that brutal lumbering or greedy exploitation of the soil can permanently alter the life-supporting properties of a forest or a once-fertile plain. On this scale, too, we know, from the wastelands that surround our smelters, or from the disappearance of shellfish in a polluted estuary, that human ingenuity is rapidly creating new and more devastating hazards to the stability of the environment. We also know of numerous specific risks to particular living components of the biosphere—that DDT threatens to wipe out the birds of prey; that industrial wastes kill off a river's game fish; that sewage renders a beach unusable.

Such small-scale and specific assaults on the living environment illuminate the basic principles that govern the impact of human intrusions on the environment: (1) Because of the complex network of interactions in the environment an intrusion in one place may exert its main effect in a distant locale. Massive nuclear weapons have often been exploded on isolated Pacific islands. But, because of the peculiarities of the lichen-caribou-man food chain on which they depend, it has been the Eskimos and Lapps living in the Arctic Circle that are most seriously affected by worldwide fallout generated by these blasts. (2) Food chains and nutritive metabolism constitute a kind of biological amplifier which can enormously intensify an originally weak intrusion on the environment. Thus, DDT sprayed at a low concentration accumulates in plankton, is further concentrated in the fish that feed on plankton, ultimately reaching a peak concentration in the birds that prey on fish. In this way DDT becomes several-hundredfold concentrated in the osprey and the

*Reprinted from the Columbia FORUM, Spring 1968, Volume XI, Number 1. Copyright 1968 by The Trustees of Columbia University in the City of New York.

eagle, which fall accidental prey to our war on insects. (3) Like any other system comprised of complex feedback cycles, an ecosystem tends to oscillate (witness the well-known interacting cycles of wolf and rabbit populations). And like other oscillating processes, an ecosystem can be driven into self-accelerating changes, and to ultimate collapse, by over-stressing at a particularly vulnerable point. Thus over-fertilization of surface waters can so accelerate the growth of algae as to deplete the oxygen content (in the dark hours) so that the algae themselves die and pollute the water. These principles tell us what is required for the stability of the environment in which we live and for its continued suitability as a place for human life. The system must accommodate itself to the stresses placed upon it in such a way as to maintain the internal processes which account for its stability.

How has the living environment been faring under these stresses? Where has the system managed to accommodate itself and achieve a new, if different, but stable balanced state? What stresses are still in the process of altering the environmental system, and what is the forecast of a new stable equilibrium? Are the changes accelerating? Is there a danger of stressing the system as a whole to the point of collapse?

The most direct human contact with the environment is mediated by the air, for a massive amount of this substance is continuously brought into intimate contact with internal metabolism through the lungs. Natural air contains only oxygen, nitrogen, water vapor, carbon dioxide, rare gases, some volatile biological products, and occasional dust. But the air that most of us breathe, especially in the cities, now contains as well: increasing amounts of oxides of nitrogen and sulfur, various kinds of dust and soot, particles of rubber and asbestos, carbon monoxide, and a wide array of poorly identified organic compounds.

Ten years ago automotive smog was a problem found almost entirely in Los Angeles, and sulfur dioxide hazards were apparent only in isolated industrial regions such as Donora, Pennsylvania. Now, New York City experiences acute episodes involving both automotive smog and sulfur dioxide. I know from personal observations that the incidence and extent of smog pollution in St. Louis has increased sharply in the last 20 years. Denver, once famed for its clear mountain air, is now subject to smog. Clearly this stress on the environment is worsening.

And while the general level of air pollution is rising there is reason to believe that the incidence of disease associated with it will rise more rapidly than the pollutant concentrations themselves. Consider, for example, the problem of lung cancer arising from chemicals such as benzopyrene which are found in the polluted city air. Air-borne organic carcinogens such as benzopyrene are capable of inducing lung cancer because of their influence on cells that line the air passages of the lungs. Laboratory studies show that the degree of the carcinogenic hazard rises with the concentration of carcinogen to which the cells are exposed and with the duration of contact between the carcinogen and the susceptible cells. There are protective mechanisms in the lung that tend to limit exposure to materials drawn in from the air, and any additional air pollutant that inhibits these mechanisms will influence the effect of a given concentration of the air-borne carcinogen. For example, sulfur dioxide tends to paralyze the ciliated cells of the lung air passages and thereby cut down the self-protective cleansing process in the lung. For this reason sulfur dioxide will extend the time of contact between a carcinogen such as benzopyrene and the lung. In this situation the risk of carcinogenesis must be measured by the *product:* benzopyrene concentration multiplied by sulfur dioxide concentration. If the concentrations of both pollutants double, we must expect that the risk of carcinogenesis may rise by as much as a factor of four.

Unfortunately, we do not yet have sufficient public health data to generalize about the quantitative relations between the level of air pollution and the medical effects associated with it. However, in the relatively sparse data available there is already some evidence that the health effects associated with pollution may be rising faster than the over-all level of pollution itself. Thus, although the concentration of organic air pollutants (a class that includes carcinogens such as benzopyrene) increases more or less proportionally with city size, the incidence of cancer in cities of different sizes seems to rise with city size not linearly but exponentially. Obviously there are other factors involved in this problem, but the present information should certainly warn us that the health effects from air pollution may worsen faster than the pollution level itself—a result expected from the multiplicative effects of air pollutants.

The dependence of human society on large supplies of fresh water is deep and pervasive. In addition to its direct biological necessity to man, water is essential in vast amounts for almost every industrial process. In natural lakes and rivers, animal organic wastes are degraded by the action of bacteria of decay which convert them into inorganic substances: carbon dioxide, nitrates, and phosphates. In turn these substances nourish plants, which provide food for the animals. In sunlight, plants also add to the oxygen content of the water and so support animals and the bacteria of decay. All this makes up a tightly woven cycle of mutually dependent events, which in nature maintains the clarity and purity of the water and sustains its population of animals, plants, and micro-organisms.

We use this natural self-purifying system to control urban wastes. Sewage treatment plants add considerable amounts of organic substances to the lakes and rivers that receive their outflow, although the increment is reduced by the treatment. If all goes well the biological cycle assimilates the added organic materials, and, maintaining its balance, keeps the water pure. But such a complex cyclical system, with its important feedback loops, cannot indefinitely remain balanced in the face of a steadily increasing organic load. Sufficiently stressed it becomes vulnerable at certain critical points. For example, the bacteria that act on organic wastes must have oxygen, which is consumed as the waste is destroyed. If the waste load becomes too high, the oxygen content of the water falls to zero, the bacteria die, the biological cycle breaks down, the purification process collapses, and the water becomes foul.

The water pollution problem has become urgent chiefly because we are allowing the organic content of surface waters to approach the breaking point. The first large-scale warning is the death of Lake Erie, where, as a result of the rapid accumulation of wastes, most of the central portion of the lake has gone to zero oxygen. The lake's life-cycle has been forced out of balance and what was, for tens of thousands of years, a beautifully clear and productive inland sea in a decade has become a rank, muddy sink.

Even universal use of present waste disposal technology will not get us out of trouble, for the treatment systems themselves elevate the nitrate and phosphate content of the receiving waters. These substances are always present in natural waters — but in amounts far less than those generated by the huge waste load imposed on them by man. And at such abnormally high levels, nitrate and phosphate become a new hazard to the biological balance. These concentrated nutrients may induce a huge growth of algae — an algae "bloom." Such an enormously dense population tends to die off with equal suddenness, again overloading the water with organic debris, and disrupting the natural cycle. And nitrate, if sufficiently concentrated, may be toxic to man. About 8-9 parts per million of nitrate in an infant's drinking water may interfere with hemoglobin function; in a number of areas of the United States, water supplies have reached nitrate levels of 3 parts per million. In some places, physicians have been forced to replace tap water in infant diets.

In 1900 the total amount of nitrogen discharged to U.S. streams by municipal sewage was about 200 million pounds per year. Rising since then at an accelerating rate, the amount reached 1200 million pounds per year in 1963 and is expected to reach about 2000 million pounds per year by 2000. From 1900 to 1940 phosphate discharged into U.S. streams by municipal sewage rose from about 10 million pounds (as phosphorus) per year to about 30 million pounds per year. But, thereafter, the rate of increase accelerated so rapidly that in 1963 the annual phosphorus burden was 250 million pounds and is expected to double again by 2000. The total oxygen demand on surface waters for degradation of organic materials in municipal sewage more than doubled between 1900 and 1960. The increase has been held in check by the production of new sewage treatment plants, but these plants do not, of course, reduce the burden of inorganic residues, such as nitrate, imposed on surface water.

Clearly our aqueous environment is being subjected to an accelerating stress, which will become so severe in the next few decades as to threaten to collapse the self-purifying biological system on which we rely for usable water.

Finally we can look at the status of the nation's soil. The soil is, of course, the basis for the initial production of nearly all of our food resources, and many industrial raw materials as well. The soil is a vastly complex ecosystem, its fundamental capabilities for supporting plant life being the resultant of an intricate balance among a wide variety of micro-organisms, animals, and plants, acting on a long-established physical substrate.

The complicated biology of the soil ties the fate of the city and industrial plant to the farm. Crop plants convert nitrates and other plant nutrients to protein. In nature, let us say a plant growing in a wood or meadow, nitrate reaches the soil chiefly as the product of bacterial decay of organic wastes — manure and the bodies of animals and plants. The natural concentration of nitrate in the soil water is very low and the roots need to work to pull it into the plant. For this work the plant must expend energy which is released by biological oxidation processes in the roots.

These processes require oxygen, which can reach the roots only if the soil is sufficiently porous. Soil porosity is governed by its physical structure; in particular a high level of organic nitrogen, in the form of humus, is required to maintain a porous soil structure. Thus, soil porosity, therefore its oxygen content, and hence the efficiency of nutrient absorption, is closely related to the organic nitrogen content of the soil.

When the United States was settled, the soil system was in this natural condition; the soil cycle was in balance maintaining its nitrogen reserve in the stable organic form. Only small amounts of inorganic salts drained off into the rivers, which remained clear and unburdened with pollutants. As the continent was settled, the natural soil system was taken over for agricultural purposes. Plants were grown on the soil in amounts much greater than they would sustain in nature. The organic store of nutrients was gradually depleted and crop yields declined year by year. With virgin lands always available, farmers moved westward, repeating the process of skimming from the soil the most available nutrient and leaving it when its productivity fell below a certain point, which made westward migration more attractive. This process, of course, came to an end about 1900 and from then on as crop production became intensified to meet the demands of a growing population, more and more of the original store of organic nutrients was withdrawn from the soil in the form of crops. In the Midwest the organic content of soil has declined about 50 per cent in the last 100 years. As a result, the productivity of the soil has declined.

For a time nutrients were returned to the soil by use of animal manures and imported fertilizers, especially guano. With the growth of the chemical industry it became possible to produce much cheaper inorganic nutrients as fertilizer. The heavy use of inorganic fertilizer began especially in the cotton and tobacco land of the South. Here, because of high climatic temperatures which stimulate the breakdown of the organic stores of the soil, the soil was particularly impoverished and spectacular gains in yields could be obtained from inorganic fertilizers. In the 1940s there began a striking increase all over the nation in the use of inorganic fertilizers. The use of inorganic nitrogen fertilizer has increased about sevenfold in the last 25 years.

The result has been a massive stress of the soil ecosystem by the addition to it of huge and increasing quantities of nitrogen, phosphorus, potassium, and other plant nutrients. During heavy rains there is a natural tendency for the added inorganic fertilizers to wash out of the soil into rivers, especially in the case of nitrates. The available data show that under most field conditions an appreciable part of the added nitrogen fertilizer fails to enter the crop and instead leaves the soil in one of two forms. Part of this lost nitrogen, probably of the order of from 10 to 25 per cent of the total fertilizer placed on the soil, drains out of the soil into rivers and lakes, the amount varying greatly with local soil conditions. Another part of the added nitrogen (perhaps 5 to 10 per cent) leaves the soil because the excess nitrate and low soil oxygen content tend to stimulate bacterial formation of volatile forms of nitrogen (nitrogen oxides and ammonia). This volatilized nitrogen is caught up in rain and is washed down again to the ground, and eventually into rivers and lakes where it adds to the inorganic nitrogen already present. Investigators have been continually surprised of late to find large amounts of nitrogen in rainfall. For example, studies in Wisconsin show that rainfall now often contains as much as one part per million of nitrogen. In contrast earlier studies showed nitrogen content of rain to be of the order of .2 of one part per million.

The seriousness of the agricultural contribution to water pollution is evident from the following data: In 1964 municipal sewage in the United States contributed a total of about 1200 million pounds of nitrogen to surface waters, ultimately in the form of nitrate. In that same year agriculture added about 8000 million pounds of nitrogen to the soil in the form of inorganic fertilizers. If only 15 per cent of this fertilizer leached out of the soil into surface waters—a percentage often observed in field experiments—the amount of nitrogen imposed on surface waters would be equivalent to the amount originating in municipal sewage. And, it should be added, there is no sign that the increasing use of inorganic fertilizer will slacken in the next decade.

Thus, universal use of secondary treatment methods for urban sewage, and corresponding control of industrial organic wastes, will nevertheless burden surface waters with large amounts of the inorganic residues of treatment, especially nitrate. At the same time, nitrate leaching from fertilized farmland will probably double this burden, leading to massive overgrowths of algae which, on their death, cause a new cycle of organic pollution. By means of advanced treatment methods, it would be possible to remove inorganic nutrients from the effluent of municipal and industrial waste systems, but a corresponding control of nutrients from farmland runoff would require treatment of the total mass of surface water—a forbidding task. We might undertake a huge program of controlling sewage and industrial waste only to find that rivers and lakes were dying from overfeeding by farmland fertilizer runoff.

In large part, agricultural production has increased in the United States in order to sustain the increasing population in this country and elsewhere and also to support a rising U.S. per capita consumption. In order to accomplish this increased food production we have massively stressed the nitrogen cycle in the soil by the introduction of inorganic fertilizer and this process, in turn, may stress to the breaking point the self-purifying aqueous systems upon which we depend for our urban waste disposal. This process may well turn out to be the most immediate mechanism whereby increasing population exerts a negative feedback on the quality of the environmental system sustaining it.

We have only begun to perceive the vast economic, social, and political conflicts that are being generated by the crisis in the environment. The nation is already in the throes of a tangled struggle with the problem of urban air pollution. This involves pervasive issues in transportation, power production, and basic urban design, which add enormously to the complex situation in the ecosystem itself. If coal-burning power plants contaminate the air with sulfur dioxide, shall we replace them with apparently "clean" nuclear reactors—and run the risks of radioactive contamination from waste-handling and the small but catastrophic risks of an accident in a highly populated area? If, in order to cure the smog problem we need to replace gasoline-burning vehicles with electric ones, how can the power industry and the petroleum industry accommodate this massive change?

Subtle, but vital, interactions operate in this area. For example, the New York City power industry is preparing to build a proposed water-storage generating plant on the Hudson River at Storm King Mountain in order to use excess nighttime generating capacity to store energy for daytime use. But if New York's vehicles are to be driven by electric motors, their batteries will need to be charged at night, and this will surely wipe out the nighttime excess in generating capacity that is the basis for the Storm King proposal.

Similar conflicts surround most of our environmental problems, but the ones that we have yet to confront will be vastly more serious. The economic and political impact of farm productivity on the nation is, of course, massive and pervasive. The present financial status of American agriculture is heavily based on the massive use of inorganic fertilizer. Since 1950 the cost to the American farmer of the land, machinery, and labor that he uses has increased about 80, 40, and 60 per cent respectively. In contrast, the cost of fertilizer has *dropped* about 20 per cent. The values of land, machinery, and labor inputs into farming have all declined in that period; in contrast, the input value of fertilizer has increased more than 80 per cent. Clearly any effort to limit the use of inorganic fertilizer on U.S. farms—and I can foresee no other way of ensuring the integrity of our waste disposal systems—will set off a series of explosive economic and political problems.

The crisis in the environment reveals a potentially fatal flaw in the social use of modern science and technology. We have developed an enormous competence to intervene in the natural world: We can release fearful nuclear explosions, spray insecticides over the countryside, and produce millions of automobiles. But at the same time we are unable to predict the full biological consequences of nuclear war or to avoid risks to our livelihood and health from the side effects of the insecticides or from the smog that our autos produce. In the eager search for the benefits of modern science and technology we have blundered into the accompanying hazards before we were aware of them.

In 1956 the government thought there was no harm associated with nuclear tests; but we now know from the thyroid nodules in Utah children that this was a tragic mistake. We exploded the bombs *before* we had the scientific knowledge to understand the biological and medical consequence.

We produced power plants and automobiles which envelop our cities in smog—before we understood its harmful effects on health. We learned how to synthesize and use new insecticides—before we learned that they also kill birds and might be harmful to people. We produced detergents and put billions of pounds on the market—before we realized that they would make water supplies foam and should be taken off the market. We are ready to conduct a nuclear war—even though we do not know whether the effect of the vast catastrophe on life, on soil, and the weather will destroy our civilization.

Despite their complicated scientific background, the issues generated by environmental pollution do not lie in the domain of science. No scientific evaluation can determine how to share the inevitable costs of controlling water pollution among cities, industries, and farms. Scientific method cannot determine whether it is better to suffer the hazards of smog, or to undertake the huge economic cost of reorganizing urban transportation. No scientific principle can tell us how to make the choice between the prosperity of the farm and the welfare of the city. These are social and political issues and can only be resolved by social and political processes.

What can be done? Sometimes it is suggested that since scientists and engineers have made the bombs, insecticides, and autos, they ought to be responsible for deciding how to deal with the resultant hazards. But this would deprive everyone else of the right of conscience and the political rights of citizenship. This approach would also force us to rely on the moral and political wisdom of scientists and engineers, and there is no evidence that I know of that suggests they are better endowed in this respect than other people.

There is an alternative, which is feasible though difficult. I believe that citizens can continue to rely on their own collective judgment about the issues of environmental conservation—if they take steps to inform themselves. The nuclear test-ban treaty is a good example of how this can be done. It seems clear that one of the important reasons this treaty was approved by a vote of the Senate is that the Senators were informed by their constituents of their opposition to the radioactive poisoning of our foods by fallout. Where did the letter writers get the necessary facts? Largely from public education by many scientists who believe that these issues ought to be decided by public judgment.

Out of an original concern with fallout and nuclear war we have developed a new "information movement" among academic scientists, designed to educate the public about the scientific and technological facts relevant to the major issues of the day. This is the alliance between the scientist and the citizen, which Margaret Mead has called "a new social invention." On this alliance depends the hope that the morality of man can, at last, turn the enormous new power that science has given us from the path of catastrophe toward the goal which is common both to science and humanity—the welfare of man.

Conservation Law

LUTHER J. CARTER*

Few terms have greater currency in the United States today than "environmental quality," a cliché that is constantly on the lips of politicians and luncheon speakers. Yet few knowledgeable people believe that, despite successes scored in skirmishes here and there, the battle for environmental quality really is being won. There is growing evidence that pollution problems, noise, urban sprawl, and other environmental ills are generally becoming worse and that an effective overall strategy for

*Reprinted with permission from *Science*, Vol. 166 (December 19, 1969), pp. 1487-1491 and Vol. 166 (December 26, 1969), pp. 1601-1606. Copyright 1969 by the American Association for the Advancement of Science. Edited and abridged.

coping with these problems is yet to be found. It seems likely, however, that if a workable strategy is found, it will include, among other things, the rapid and imaginative development of what is coming to be called environmental or conservation law.

Environmental problems usually represent conflicts between competing uses of natural resources — for example, a virgin forest may be preserved as wilderness or reduced to pulpwood, and a city park may be kept for recreation or given over as right-of-way for a freeway. It is natural, therefore, that lawyers, who are supposed to have some expertise at resolving conflicts, should be called upon to help resolve problems concerned with the environment. Numerous legal actions over environmental issues are now pending before various courts and administrative agencies around the country.

These include, for instance, suits and petitions to outlaw use of DDT (which no doubt influenced the Nixon Administration's recent decision to institute a partial ban on this pesticide in the United States); to prevent completion of a Corps of Engineers cross-Florida barge canal project that is flooding much of the Oklawaha River basin and causing what some scientists say are disastrous ecological changes; to keep the U.S. Forest Service from allowing Walt Disney Productions to build a commercial resort at Mineral King in the Sierra Nevada; and to bring anti-trust charges against major automobile manufacturers for an alleged conspiracy not to compete in the development of exhaust-control devices (damage suits are being brought by the State of New York, two Chicago aldermen, and Los Angeles County). Scientists and other academicians figure importantly in many pending actions, in part because they are strongly represented in the membership of groups such as the Sierra Club which are bringing suits, and in part because they often testify as expert witnesses.

Lawyers and law school professors are becoming aware of conservation law as a potentially important field. This year the American Trial Lawyers Association has established an environmental law committee, which is arranging a series of seminars and is planning to establish an environmental law reporting service. Significantly, the American Bar Association, a generally conservative organization which tends to resist new trends until they are certified as thoroughly respectable, also is setting up a committee on environmental quality....

Furthermore, law schools, under growing pressure from students to make their programs more responsive to the public interest, have been adding courses on environmental law as well as courses on such topics as consumer and poverty law. And some long established courses on natural resources law are being reoriented to reflect concerns broader than those of the exploitative industries which law schools and many of their law graduates have always served. Some prestigious law firms, such as the Washington firm of Arnold & Porter, which once had their pick of the ablest law graduates, are now finding that to attract such graduates it is helpful to offer opportunities for *pro bono publico* (public service) work in environmental law and other fields....

For 2 years now the Environmental Defense Fund (EDF), a Long Island-based group organized in late 1967, has been asserting in anti-DDT cases and other actions that people have a constitutional right to a clean environment. For example,

EDF makes such a claim in the federal suit that it filed last year in Montana to force the Hoerner Waldorf Paper Company to provide an adequate air pollution control process at its Missoula pulp mill. Victor J. Yannacone, Jr., an EDF attorney, speaks of the Missoula suit as the "perfect air-pollution test case." The Hoerner Waldorf mill, he says, is responsible for heavy emissions of active sulfur compounds that are polluting the regional air shed. (The company recently announced plans to try out some new pollution-control equipment.) Such pollution, Yannacone argues, represents a "nonnegotiable hazard" from which citizens should be able to obtain relief under the Constitution's Ninth Amendment, which states that the enumeration of certain rights elsewhere in the Constitution does not deny other rights (such as the right, says Yannacone, to breathe clean air) retained by the people. The Missoula case has not yet been set for trial, and, if and when it is tried, the outcome may turn on legal arguments that are more conventional than Yannacone's Ninth Amendment argument.

Many lawyers doubt that the courts are ready to accept that argument. Most judges are extremely wary about venturing beyond precedent and known law and about deciding questions, such as the general public's interest in clean air (as opposed to a mill's interest in cheaply disposing of its wastes), normally left for legislative determination.

Yet E. F. Roberts, professor of law at Cornell, said at the September conference on environmental law that the Ninth Amendment allows enough "growth" in the interpretation of the Constitution to extend constitutional protection to the environment. The Ninth Amendment, he noted, was cited by the Supreme Court a few years ago in invalidating a Connecticut law against dissemination of birth-control information. This statute was declared an unconstitutional infringement on personal privacy, even though a right of privacy is not explicitly mentioned in the Constitution.

Enunciation of a right to environmental protection, Roberts said, would "require every agency of government, whether a local zoning board or a federal home mortgage lending agency, to review their plans to make certain that their activities did not actually exacerbate deterioration of the environment." Obviously, however, recognition of a right to environmental protection would have to be reconciled with such necessities as carrying on industrial and commercial activities, providing systems of mass transport, and building homes for an expanding population.

The "trust doctrine" also was discussed at the September conservation law conference. This ancient doctrine holds that all land was once held in trust for the people by the sovereign—or government—and that the government cannot divest itself entirely of responsibility for the uses to which land is put, even though most of it long since has passed into private hands. The government must, according to the trust doctrine, see that no land, public or private, is abused or otherwise used in ways contrary to the public interest. The trust doctrine, though recognized by the courts in certain cases involving submerged lands and publicly owned lands, has not been applied to lands generally.

Joseph Sax, a University of Michigan law professor and specialist in the field of conservation law, views the trust doctrine as a particularly useful and flexible legal concept. A court's finding that a particular proposal or action violates this doctrine, he says, would rarely result in the invalidation of a legislative act. Massachusetts courts, in a series of public trust cases decided in recent years, have set aside administrative decisions in controversial land-use cases when the legislative authority on which those decisions were supposedly based was not clearly spelled out.

In one such case, for example, the state highway department was not allowed to use a public marshland for right-of-way, even though state law seemed to permit such action. The court said that, if it were the legislature's intent to allow such a diversion of parkland to highway use, it should say so explicitly. Sax believes that rulings of this kind have a desirable "squeezing" effect on a legislature, forcing it to face up to the implications of vaguely stated policies which it writes into law.

Sax is the author of a bill now pending in the Michigan legislature which would give Michigan conservationists a potent new weapon. Under this measure, any citizen could bring suit against any person or agency to safeguard the natural resources of the state and to protect the "public trust."

If courts should ever apply the trust doctrine or the Ninth Amendment argument in a wide variety of environmental cases, this would force the executive and legislative branches to move at a faster pace in setting and enforcing standards for environmental protection. Although the environmental problem and the racial problem are not closely parallel, it may be instructive to recall that the Supreme Court's 1954 ruling against racial segregation in public schools triggered the release of dynamic social and political forces that produced the major civil rights legislation of the 1960's.

If courts leap too far ahead of public opinion, they do so at their peril, for, being empowered of neither the "sword nor the purse," they depend on the executive and legislative branches — and ultimately on the electorate — to see that their edicts are obeyed. But today courts are probably behind public opinion with respect to questions of environmental protection. During the 19th century and the early 20th century the courts became, in a real sense, the instruments of laissez-faire economics. In one classic case, decided by a Tennessee court in 1904, two copper smelting companies were allowed to continue their practice of reducing copper ore by cooking it over open-air wood fires, a process that produced billowing clouds of sulfur dioxide smoke which made a wasteland of the surrounding valley.

Farmers who had complained were told by the court that they were not entitled to injunctive relief because "the law must make the best arrangement it can between the contending parties, with a view to preserving to each one the largest measure of liberty possible under the circumstances." Roberts, the Cornell law professor, observes that "'liberty' here meant that the companies were free to create a wasteland if they paid for it [some damages were awarded], whereas the farmers were free to take jobs with the industry and continue to reside in a valley totally polluted with chemicals."

Judicial attitudes have of course been evolving and, in a variety of matters involving the public interest and the social welfare, the private entrepreneur no longer enjoys the freedom of action he once did. Nevertheless, in environmental cases some courts still have not progressed far beyond the kind of balancing of interests that characterized the ruling in the Tennessee case just cited. For example, as Roberts has noted, a New York court recently allowed a new cement plant, which had been erected in an Albany neighborhood, to continue polluting the air with cement dust, provided it gave money damages to residents of the area.

With concern about the environment now widespread, it seems likely that the public and most elected officials would support strong court action to curb pollution and other forms of environmental degradation. The "new conservation," calling for the rational use of the environment in the interest of a high quality of life, is as much concerned with the urban environment as it is with wilderness and other natural areas. The conservation movement no longer can be regarded as a "special interest" of concern chiefly to sportsmen, wilderness "preservationists," and the like. On the contrary, conservation has a fast broadening constituency.

Problems such as noise and air pollution bear especially heavily on low-income people who cannot escape from industrial districts and who cannot afford air-conditioned homes or weekends at Aspen or Sea Island. These people, and in many cases their labor unions, are becoming increasingly concerned about environmental issues. Political careers are being built on the environmental protection issue. For example, Representative Bob Eckhardt (D-Texas), before his election to Congress in 1966, had made a record in the state legislature as a crusader on that issue. Many of Eckhardt's constituents are workers who suffer daily the odors and eye-smarting fumes that are emanating from plants along the Houston ship canal.

There is even a strong possibility that the conservation and civil rights movements may form an alliance. Controversies growing out of urban freeway projects, for example, already are bringing together black people threatened with displacement and others who are concerned about worsening air pollution, traffic congestion, and other problems. A leader of the National Association for the Advancement of Colored People in Texas recently joined with several Texas conservation groups, such as the local chapters of the Sierra Club and the National Audubon Society, in a suit to block construction of a golf course in Meridian State Park. The complaint alleges in part that the project would impose a kind of "de facto segregation"—by taking a public park area open to all races and income groups and replacing it with a golf course open only to those with money enough to pay green fees and buy golfing paraphernalia.

Further evidence of the growing interest in environmental protection can be seen in the recent adoption by New York voters of a "conservation bill of rights" as an amendment to the state constitution. If it is true, as Oliver Wendell Holmes once said, that judges must respond to the "felt necessities of the times," it would seem that the time has come when the courts will begin to play an important role in helping to resolve the environmental crisis.

If the genius of a well functioning democratic system is to have reasonable compromises emerge from the clash of countervailing forces, one can say that the forces working for environmental quality have been undermanned and outgunned. At the moment, however, anti-pollution and other conservation issues have taken hold politically, and prospects for achieving gains for conservation have seldom been better. Conservationists are seeking to commit to the battle all the branches of government, the legislative, the executive, and—the judicial.

In view of the size and complexity of the environmental crisis, the best hope for coping with it surely lies in action by the legislative and executive branches. Citizens' suits and court rulings alone can never do more than a patchy, limited job of environmental protection. But environmental lawsuits, such as those which will be described here, are likely to play a significant role, especially by making the process of decision-making followed by government administrative and regulatory agencies more responsive to environmental concerns.

For instance, a suit now pending before a U.S. district court in Colorado is being closely watched by conservationists. If it succeeds, the U.S. Forest Service and other federal agencies will know that, in making plans to dispose of resources under their control, they had better be prepared, through careful assessments of the alternative uses for those resources, to justify their decisions publicly—and perhaps in court. The Colorado case boils down to a charge by the Sierra Club, the Colorado Open Space Coordinating Council, and other parties that the Forest Service has, in deciding on a sale of old-growth timber near the Gore Range-Eagle Nest Primitive Area, neglected its statutory obligations by not properly assessing the wilderness and recreation values affected....

Conservationists are beginning to make effective use of the courts, although the usable precedents are still relatively few.

One such precedent may have been set last July when a federal appeals court, responding to the eleventh-hour petition of some Colorado scientists, prevented the destruction of the 34-million-year-old Florissant Fossil Beds by land developers. The court enjoined the development activity long enough for Congress to complete action on legislation establishing a fossil beds national monument. Estella B. Leopold, a paleobotanist at the University of Colorado (and daughter of the late Aldo Leopold, a noted conservationist), had testified that "the Florissant Fossil Beds are to geology, paleontology, and evolution what the Rosetta Stone was to Egyptology and what the Dead Sea Scrolls are to Christianity."

Citizens have often been denied "standing" to bring suit to block government actions or to have a nuisance abated unless they personally faced or were suffering loss or injury, to a degree not shared by the public generally. However, two Wisconsin conservation groups, with the help of the Environmental Defense Fund, the Long Island-based legal action group . . . were able to petition—in an exhaustive state administrative hearing—for a ban on the use of DDT. And although the Wisconsin statute (enacted in 1943) allowing such proceedings is unusual, citizens in many states may now go to court and challenge government policies and activities which they deem to be harmful to the environment.

In a paper presented in September at the Conservation Foundation's conference on environmental law, Louis L. Jaffe, a Harvard law professor, said that 29 states allow any citizen to file suit to contest official conduct which is alleged to be illegal and that, in at least 27 states, any taxpayer has this privilege. "I would conclude that the constitutional obstacles to [such citizens'] suits . . . are becoming less and less significant," Jaffe added.

Scenic Hudson is a case, which, although the dispute that gave rise to it is still unresolved, has established two important precedents—federal regulatory bodies have been told to give greater weight to esthetic values and to allow conservation organizations to intervene in cases that raise environmental issues. In 1965, the U.S. Second Circuit Court of Appeals set aside an order of the Federal Power Commission (FPC) granting the Consolidated Edison Company a license to build a pumped-storage hydro-power facility at Storm King Mountain on the Hudson River. The court directed the commission to reopen the matter and to consider the preservation of natural beauty as well as such factors as the economics of power generation. The decision was appealed, but the Supreme Court declined to review the ruling.

In later FPC proceedings, the Scenic Hudson Preservation Conference, the Sierra Club, and other conservation organizations sought to show that Storm King Mountain is not merely pretty but uniquely beautiful. Specialists in cartography, landscape architecture, and art history were called to testify. They pointed out, for example, that although a number of rivers cut through the Appalachian Mountains, only the Hudson cuts through at sea level and achieves the effect of a fjord. Thus, these experts argued, even though the appreciation of natural beauty is subjective, certain objective esthetic standards can be applied. An FPC hearing examiner has since recommended that the Storm King project be approved, and the Commission may yet grant the license. But the precedents established in *Scenic Hudson* already have proved useful to conservationists in other suits.

For example, the Sierra Club, citing *Scenic Hudson* and certain other precedents, gained standing to bring suit against federal agencies to block construction of an expressway along the Hudson River, a segment of which was to be built on filled land in the river itself. The Sierra Club's attorneys dredged up an old statute pertaining to navigable waters which says that no dike or causeway may be built in the river without the consent of Congress. A U.S. district judge, ruling that this statute applies, has decided the case in the Sierra Club's favor. The defendants have appealed.

In another suit, the Sierra Club is trying to keep the U.S. Forest Service from allowing Walt Disney Productions, Inc., to build a ski resort in Mineral King Valley in the Sierra Nevada. As in the expressway case, the club's attorneys have searched the statutes and come up with provisions which they contend make the proposed development illegal. They also say that public hearings are required by law and have not been held. A federal district court has temporarily enjoined the carrying out of plans for the resort, but the case has not yet been decided.

As in the question of whether a party has standing to sue, burden-of-proof rules can be critical to the outcome of a court case. And, in the past, the burden of proof generally has fallen on the conservationists bringing the suit. However, a 1966 ruling of the New Jersey Supreme Court is viewed by some legal scholars as a sign that judicial attitudes on this point are changing. Texas East Transmission Company was condemning a right-of-way for a gas pipeline across a wooded tract owned by Wildlife Preserves, Inc., a private nonprofit organization, which insisted that the project would be less damaging ecologically if the pipeline were routed across a marsh.

The court held that, since Wildlife Preserves, Inc., was devoting its land to conservation objectives often pursued by government itself, it should not be required to carry as heavy a burden of proof as the ordinary property owner who protests that the condemnation of a particular piece of land is arbitrary. It said, in effect, that if Wildlife Preserves, Inc., made out a *prima facie* case, the burden of proof would shift to the company. The case ultimately was decided in the pipeline company's favor, but not until the trial judge was satisfied that the upland route for the pipeline was as acceptable ecologically as the marshland route and that special protective measures would be taken.

Environmental lawsuits are often supported on a shoestring by the fund-raising efforts of local conservation groups, whereas the defendants are generally well financed industries or government agencies. The struggle is not so unequal as it might seem, however, for the conservationists frequently can call as expert witnesses environmental scientists who are leading men in their fields. These scientists usually receive no more for their services than expense money and the satisfaction of striking a blow in a holy war....

Clearly, if conservationists should find the courts increasingly willing to help protect the environment, a heavy debt will be owed ecologists and other environmental scientists. In fact, the conservation movement probably would be doomed to deepening frustration and failure if it were not taking on a scientific rationale. In a crowded world, with increasing competition for resources, the most persuasive appeals for conservation are likely to be those supported by hard evidence of impending environmental upsets, large or small....

Ecology is not yet a mature science, and ecologists sometimes cannot predict with certainty the consequences of human intervention in an ecosystem. However, as the predictive capabilities of ecology are improved, this rapidly developing glamour science will become increasingly important to the resolution of environmental issues, in the courtroom as well as elsewhere.

David Gates, director of the Missouri Botanical Garden and leader of a new discipline dubbed "biophysical ecology" (wherein the relationship between an organism and its environment is analyzed as a function of energy, gas, and nutrient exchange), believes that eventually predictive models will be developed that will allow scientists to forecast the effect on the environment of various kinds of human activities, such as the clearing of forests from wide areas and the polluting of the atmosphere.

Of course, a court confronted with a lawsuit involving highly complicated environmental questions may doubt its competence to handle the matter. But courts can and sometimes do appoint technically trained special masters to hear cases believed to be beyond the ken of trial judges. The Wisconsin DDT hearings, a quasi-judicial proceeding, were conducted by an experienced examiner who had some background in chemistry and biology; no one doubted his grasp of the scientific issues raised.

Yet it is not uncommon for an ordinary trial judge to sort out and decide the issues successfully in an environmental law case. The judge in the New Jersey wildlife preserves case has confessed that, early in the proceedings, he went to the dictionary to look up "ecology," a word at that time unfamiliar to him. But, according to Joseph Sax of the University of Michigan Law School, who has made a study of the

New Jersey case, the judge did a masterful job and rendered an opinion with which it is difficult to quarrel.

As Sax points out, there was never a question of the judge's substituting his judgment for that of the pipeline engineers on any matter in which these engineers were the acknowledged experts. Rather, his task was to hear the environmental experts who testified—some representing the plaintiffs and others representing the defendants—and to decide whether, from the standpoint of protecting the wildlife preserve from needless damage, the utility's administrators and engineers had planned wisely. Neither judges nor the administrators who run utilities and public works agencies are experts on environmental issues. But judges, who ordinarily are not ax grinders, should be better than the administrators at listening impartially to those who are experts on these issues.

As the cases discussed here suggest, conservationists look to the courts for help in making industry, public utilities, and administrative and regulatory agencies give substantial weight to natural values and environmental protection. Such considerations often have been treated as matters of secondary concern by industry and by these agencies, as well as by the stockholders, special "clientele," and political interests which influence their policies. Sax points out the irony of the situation: "To make the democratic system respond properly to the environmental crisis, conservationists are going to the judiciary, the least democratic branch of government."

The Economics of Pollution

EDWIN L. DALE, JR.*

Now that environment has become a national concern, it might be well to clean up some of the economic rubbish associated with the subject. There are, alas, a few "iron laws" that cannot be escaped in the effort to reduce the pollution of our air and water, in disposing of solid waste and the like. The laws do not necessarily prevent a clean environment, but there is no hope of obtaining one unless they are understood.

We have all become vaguely aware that there will be a cost—perhaps higher monthly electric bills, perhaps higher taxes, perhaps a few cents or a few dollars more on anything made from steel—if there is a successful and massive effort to have a better environment. But that is only a beginning. There are other problems....

The Law of Economic Growth

Whether we like it or not, and assuming no unusual increase in mass murders or

* From *The New York Times Magazine* (April 19, 1970), pp. 27–29+. © 1970 by The New York Times Company. Reprinted by permission. Edited and abridged.

epidemics, the American labor force for the next 20 years is already born and intends to work. It is hard for any of us—myself included—to imagine a deliberate policy to keep a large portion of it unemployed. But that simple fact has enormous consequences.

For more than a century, the average output of each worker for each hour worked has risen between 2 and 3 per cent a year, thanks mainly to new machines, but also to better managerial methods and a more skilled labor force. This increase in what is called *productivity* is by far the most important cause of our gradually rising standard of living—which, pollution aside, nearly all of us have wanted. In simplest terms, each worker can be paid more because he produces more and he consumes more because he earns more. Inflation only increases the numbers and does not change the facts. Machines increase the productivity of an auto worker more than a barber, but both rightly share, through the general rise in real income, in the expansion of productivity in the economy as a whole.

It is difficult to conceive of our society or any other wanting to halt the rise in productivity, or efficiency, which has made real incomes higher for all of us. But even if "we" wanted to, in our kind of society and economy "we" couldn't. The profit motive will almost always propel individual, daily decisions in the direction of higher productivity. A business will always buy a new machine if it will cut costs and increase efficiency—and thank goodness! That is what has made our standard of living—and we do enjoy it—rise.

It is not a matter of enjoying it, however. By any fair test, we are not really affluent; half of our households earn less than $8,500 a year. Apart from redistributing income, which has very real limits, the only way the society can continue to improve the well-being of those who are not affluent—really the majority—is through a continued increase in productivity. Anyone who wants us to go back to the ax, the wooden plow, the horse carriage and the water wheel is not only living a wholly impossible dream, he is asking for a return to a society in which nearly everybody was poor. We are not talking here about philosophical ideas of happiness, but of what people have proved they want in the way of material things. This society is not about to give up productivity growth. But every increase in productivity adds to output.

·   ·   ·

What does output mean?
It means electric power produced—and smoke produced.
It means cans and bottles produced.
It means steel produced—and, unless something is done about it, water and air polluted.
It means paper produced—with the same result as for steel.
And so on and on.

·   ·   ·

The law of economic growth says, then, that we already know that the national output in 1980 will be, and almost must be, some 50 per cent higher than it is now.

President Nixon has said so publicly, and he is right. That is the result of an annual rate of real growth of about 4 per cent, compounded. It is terrifying. If an economy of $900-billion in 1969 produces the pollution and clutter we are all familiar with, what will an economy half again as large produce?

Is there no escape from this law? The answer, essentially, is no. But there is one possible way to mitigate the awesome results. We might reduce the labor input (but, we hope, not the productivity input), without creating mass unemployment.

Each working person has a workday, workweek, workyear and worklife. Any one of them could be reduced by law or otherwise. We could reduce the legal workweek from the present 40 hours. We could add more holidays or lengthen vacations to reduce the workyear. We are already shortening the worklife, without planning it that way: increased participation in higher education has meant later entry into the labor force for many, and retirement plans, including Social Security, have brought about earlier retirement than in the past for others.

If, by chance or by law, the annual man-hours of employment are reduced in the years ahead, our output will grow a little less rapidly. This is the only way to cut our economic growth, short of deliberate unemployment or deliberate inefficiency.

There is a cost. It is most easily seen in a union-bargained settlement providing for longer vacations without any cut in annual wages, or a legal reduction in the workweek from 40 to 35 hours, with compulsory overtime payments after that. In each case, more workers must be hired to produce the same output, and if the employer—because of market demand—goes on producing at the same level, wage costs for each unit of output are higher than they otherwise would have been. Prices will therefore be higher. This is widely recognized. Maybe we would be willing to pay them.

But we cannot guarantee less output. Only if employers produce less—because of the extra cost—would that happen. And in that larger sense, the cost of a reduction of our annual labor input is simply less production per capita because the labor force is idle more of the time.

But less production was the objective of the exercise—the antipollution exercise. If we start with the proposition that the growth of production is the underlying cause of pollution, which has merit as a starting point, the only way we can get less growth in production, if we want it, is to have more of our labor force idle more of the time. In that case, we will have more leisure without mass unemployment, as we usually think of the term. Our national output, and our standard of living, will rise less rapidly.

That last idea we may learn to take, if we can cope with the leisure. But under any foreseeable circumstances, our output will still go on rising. With the most optimistic assumptions about a gradual reduction of the workday, workweek, workyear and worklife, we shall undoubtedly have a much higher output in 1980 than we have in 1970. To a man concerned about the environment, it might seem a blessing if our economic growth in the next 10 years could be 2 per cent a year instead of 4 per cent; he cannot hope for zero growth.

The law of economic growth, then, tells us a simple truth: "we" cannot choose to reduce production simply because we have found it to be the cause of a fouled environment. And if we want to reduce the rate of growth of production, the place to look is in our man-hours of work.

The Law of Compound Interest

It is a fair question to ask: Why weren't we bothered about pollution 12 or 15 years ago? In October, 1957, to pick a date, the Soviet Union sent the first earth satellite into orbit. The American economy had just begun a recession that was to send unemployment to 7 per cent of the labor force. The late George Magoffin Humphrey, who had just resigned as Secretary of the Treasury, was warning of what he saw as vast Government spending, at that time $77-billion, and saying it would bring "a depression that would curl your hair." There were plenty of things to think about.

But nobody was worried about pollution. Conservation groups were properly bothered about parts of the wilderness (the Hell's Canyon Dam in Idaho, for example), but that was an entirely different thing. That was an issue of esthetics, not health. Nobody seemed to mention air pollution or waste that might overwhelm the space in which to put it. In a peculiarly sad irony, the late Adlai E. Stevenson had fought and lost an election against Dwight D. Eisenhower in 1956 partially on a "pollution" issue—radiation in the atmosphere from the explosion of atomic weapons.

The question, to repeat: Why didn't we worry about pollution then? The answer is that, relatively speaking, there *was* no pollution. Yes, there were electric power plants then, too. Yes, there were paper mills polluting streams. Yes, there were tin cans and paper and bottles. Some snowflakes, though we didn't know it, were already a bit black, and Pittsburgh got national attention because it tried to do some cleaning up.

But here we come to the law of compound interest. In 1957—*only 13 years ago*—our gross national product was $453-billion. In 1969, in constant dollars, it was $728-billion. That is an increase of nearly $300-billion in tin cans, electric power, automobiles, paper, chemicals and all the rest. It is an increase of 60 per cent.

So what? That was not the result of an unnaturally rapid growth rate, though a bit more rapid than in some periods of our past. The *so what* is this: in the preceding 13 years the growth had been *only $100-billion*. We were the same nation, with the same energy, in those preceding 13 years. We invested and we had a rise both in productivity and in our labor force. But in the first 13 years of this example our output rose $100-billion, and in the second 13 it rose $300-billion.

In the next 13 it will rise more than $500-billion.

That is the law of compound interest. These are not numbers; they are tin cans and smoke and auto exhaust. There is no visible escape from it. Applying the same percentage growth to a larger base every year, we have reached the point where our growth in one year is half the total output of Canada, fully adjusting for inflation. Another dizzying and rather horrifying way of putting it is that the real output of goods and services in the United States has grown as much since 1950 as it grew in the entire period from the landing of the Pilgrims in 1620 up to 1950. . . .

The Law of the Mix Between Public and Private Spending

Robert S. McNamara, the eternally energetic and constructive former Secretary of Defense and now president of the World Bank, gave a speech in February about the plight of the poor countries. In the speech he understandably criticized the

United States for reducing its foreign aid effort. But in supporting his point he adopted, almost inadvertently, a piece of partly fallacious conventional wisdom:

"Which is ultimately more in the nation's interest: to funnel national resources into an endlessly spiraling consumer economy—in effect, a pursuit of consumer gadgetry with all its senseless by-products of waste and pollution—or to dedicate a more reasonable share of those same resources to improving the fundamental quality of life both at home and abroad?"

Fair enough. It means tax increases, of course, though Mr. McNamara did not say so. That is what the "mix" between public and private spending is all about. But for our purposes the point is different. Let us look more closely at the phrase: ". . . a pursuit of consumer gadgetry with all its senseless by-products of waste and pollution. . . ."

As it stands, it is true. Private consumption does create side effects like waste and pollution. But now, assume a Brave New World in which we are all happy to pay higher taxes and reduce our private consumption so that the Government may have more money with which to solve our problems—ranging from poor education to poverty, from crime to inadequate health services. We shall not examine here the issue of whether more Government money solves problems. It is obviously more effective in some areas than in others. But anyway, in our assumption, we are all willing to give the Government more money to solve problems, including pollution.

Now let us see what happens.

☐ The Government spends the money to reduce pollution. Sewage plants are built. They need steel. They need electric power. They need paperwork. They need workers. The workers get paid, and they consume.

☐ The Government spends the money on education. New schools are built, which need steel, lumber and electric power. Teachers are hired. They get paid, and they consume. They throw away tin cans.

☐ The Government spends the money on a better welfare system that treats all poor people alike, whether they work or not. Incomes among the poor rise by some amount between $4-billion and $20-billion, and these people consume. Electric power production rises and appliance and steel production rises, and so on and on.

The point is obvious by now. A shifting in our national income or production between "public goods" and "private goods" hardly changes the environment problem at all because it does not reduce total spending, or output, in the economy. . . .

Conclusion

Three nice, depressing laws. They give us a starting point for any rational discussion of the environment problem. Our output is going to go on growing and growing under any conceivable set of choices we make.

But the starting point does not mean despair. It simply means that trying to solve the problem by reducing output, or the growth of output, is waste of time and energy. It won't and can't work.

How is the problem solved then? The purpose here is not, and has not been, to solve any problems. It has been to try to head off useless solutions. But a few things can be said:

There is, first, technology itself. The very energy and inventiveness that gave us this rising output—and got us to the moon—can do things about pollution. A fascinating case is the sulphur dioxide put into the air by coal-burning electric power plants. A very strong argument can be made that under any foreseeable circumstances we will have to burn more and more coal to produce the needed growth of electric power. And the ground does not yield much low-sulphur coal. Thus, somebody is going to have to have the incentive to develop a way to get the sulphur out before it leaves the smokestack; and if this costs the utilities money, the regulatory commissions are going to have to allow that cost to be passed along in electric bills.

Next, there is the related idea—being increasingly explored by economists, regulators and some legislators—of making antipollution part of the price-profit-incentive system. In simplest terms, this would involve charging a fee for every unit of pollutant discharged, with meters used to determine the amount. There would be an economic incentive to stop or reduce pollution, possibly backed up with the threat to close down the plant if the meter readings go above a specified level. The company—say a paper company—would be faced with both a carrot and a stick.

There is also the simple use of the police power, as with poisonous drugs or, lately, D.D.T. It is the "thou shalt not" power: automobiles can emit no more than such-and-such an amount of this or that chemical through the exhaust pipe. Once again, if the engineers cannot find a way out, the car simply cannot legally be sold. There will be, and should be, all sorts of debate "at the margin"—whether the higher cost of the different or improved engine is worth the extra reduction of pollution. The argument exists now over D.D.T.; there are clearly costs, as well as benefits, in stopping its use. But the "thou shalt not" power exists.

Finally, there are many possibilities for using a part of our public spending for environmental purposes. Sewage plants are the obvious case. President Nixon has proposed a big expansion of the current level of spending for these plants, though not as much as many interested in clean water—including Senator Edmund Muskie —would like to see.

In this case, and only in this case, a greater effort at curing pollution must be at the expense of some other Government program unless we pay higher taxes. It is proper to point out here the subtle dimensions of the issue. There are all sorts of possible gimmicks, like tax rebates for antipollution devices for industry and federally guaranteed state and local bonds. One way or another, spending more for pollution abatement will mean spending that much less for something else, and the something else could mean housing or medical services. Every local sewage plant bond sold means that much less investment money available for mortgages, for example.

A final reflection is perhaps in order, though it is almost banal. Our rising G.N.P. gives us the "resources" to do the antipollution job. These resources include rising Government receipts. Our technology, which has given us the rising G.N.P., might find the way out of one pollution problem after another—and they are all different.

But, in the end, we cannot be sure that the job will be done. Growth of total output per capita will continue. The long-term relief is perfectly obvious: *fewer "capita."* That sort of "solution" might help, in our country, by about 1990. If we survive until then, the law of compound interest will be much less horrifying if the population is 220 million instead of 250 million.

Authority and Responsibility for Environmental Administration

LYNTON K. CALDWELL*

Laws and institutions must go hand in hand with the progress of the human mind. As that becomes more developed, more enlightened, as new discoveries are made, new truths disclosed, the manners and opinions change with the change of circumstances, institutions must advance also, and keep pace with the times.

Thomas Jefferson to Samuel Kercheval
July 12, 1816

Jefferson's didactic assertion is obviously and unfortunately untrue. Laws and institutions do not necessarily go hand in hand with the progress of the human mind —or at least with the minds of those who influence the character of social arrangements at any given time. The lag of laws and institutions behind the changing state of society has become a sociological commonplace. Since Jefferson's day, an accelerated rate of change in laws and institutions has, nevertheless, fallen farther and farther behind the rate of social and technological innovation. One major consequence of this widening gap has been the declining ability of society to cope with its environmental problems. A secondary consequence has been the growing environmental and ecological crisis of our time. But a dual crisis of attitudinal and institutional inadequacy must be surmounted if the crisis of the environment is to be overcome. It is in this context that the organization of authority and responsibility for the administration of man-environment relationships becomes a matter of major social importance. If one cares about the future of man, the impact of human society upon the environment has now become too great safely to allow man's future circumstances to be determined by random and inadvertent consequences of obsolete, ineffectual, or socially dysfunctional mechanisms for social control.

Defining the Organizational Problem

Except in the most abstract terms, one cannot embrace all human society in

*Reprinted with permission from the author and the editors of *The Annals of The American Academy of Political and Social Science* (May 1970), pp. 107-115.

generalizations concerning management of the physical environment. And considering the diversity of human values, attitudes, and institutions, to extrapolate the conditions and behaviors of any single society to human society generally is not feasible. Nevertheless, there are aspects of man-environment relationships that are substantially the same for all mankind. One can examine the influence or response of the human animal with respect to these relationships, making allowance for differences of culture. The number of these universal man-environment relationships is tentative and uncertain. Some relate to man's dependence upon the environment for life support; others relate to the impact of man upon his environment and upon its life-support capabilities. The social problem of man-environment relationships arises as a consequence of the frequently destructive character of this impact. Illustrative of these destructive consequences are the eutrophication of lakes and rivers, the exhaustion of soil fertility, the extermination of wildlife, and the degradation of the landscape. It is possible to take the environmental experience of a particular society or nation as a case in point and to draw from it certain generalizations regarding man's ability to manage his environment. These generalizations may have an heuristic value even though they may not be validly applied without qualification to the total range of human relationships within the physical world. The method employed in this article is to use the problems of the United States in establishing an environment policy to formulate and illustrate a number of projections and conjectures regarding the ability of modern man to bring his environmental relationships under rational and self-renewing control.

There are several abstract or generalized criteria that may be used to describe how societies organize to govern the relationships of their members to their environment. Public safety and welfare would be logical criteria for evaluating man-environment relationships, and such criteria are often, but not always, employed among relatively primitive or simple societies. In large, complex, and cosmopolitan societies, such as those of the United States, social convention, reinforced by law and institutions, supports a variety of arrangements that, with hard-to-explain frequency, sacrifice the safety and welfare of society, as a whole, to the immediate and often short-term interests of relatively few individuals. This paradoxical circumstance in a nation governed of, by, and for the people is most readily, but not fully, accounted for by a persistent carry-over of pioneer and frontier attitudes and values into a space-ship society. Traditional criteria for environmental policy in the United States today are largely inappropriate to the circumstances of the times. To understand why they have become inappropriate, it is necessary to examine the substance of the attitudes and assumptions under which environmental policies are made and administered and to see how their application affects the quality of life.

Contrary to widely held opinion, the least significant factors in public decisions on environmental issues are the technical-functional aspects. Technology has not "run rampant" in America, but technology has been distorted, misused, and suppressed for reasons politely described as "economic" or "political." It helps to preserve the American obsession with service-club congeniality to impute abstract causes to social developments that disturb or offend. Such abstract expressions as "development," "private property," "price of progress," "technological inevitability," "national defense," "jobs," or "taxes" are invoked to explain away environment-impairing action without justifying what is actually happening through recourse to actual facts, reasons, and alternatives. The vocabularies of all modern societies are as full of thought-stopping clichés as the life of primitive man was filled with uncomprehended taboos. The mental processes of many "practical" people have been so firmly programmed in response to these mind-stoppers that their interjection into debate on environmental policy is often sufficient totally to block further rational consideration of the issues.

Decisions regarding the environment and all other public issues are influenced positively by the dominant and activist elements in society and negatively by the relative inertia of the uninterested mass. But it is easier to ascertain whose *purposes* are being served than whose *interests* are being served. History is filled with examples of dominant groups who injured themselves in pursuit of purposes that not only were not in their best interest, but contributed directly to their downfall; and because politically dominant groups are able to make *their* purposes *public* purposes, we find governments in the United States and elsewhere in vigorous pursuit of policies that could be said to be in the public interest only by legal definition. Therefore, when one considers the organization of government for the administration of environmental policy, one cannot begin to think realistically about the problem until the policy itself is *defined* and its implications are understood.

There is no universally "best" way to organize public authority and responsibility for environmental administration. In the absence of a defined (but not necessarily publicly stated) policy, there is no way to evaluate any administrative structure or function, even by means of the sterile criteria of economy and efficiency. The present structure of the government of the United States has been widely indicted for its inadequacy in providing a coherent and ecologically sound administration for natural resources and the environment. The indictment is valid but, until now, it has been politically irrelevant. It is valid *if* an ecologically sound environmental policy is what the critic believes to be the desirable norm. It is invalid if projected against the objectives of the *ad hoc* architects of the historical political structure. Ecological considerations are *not* what the National Reclamation Association, the Rivers and Harbors Congress, the National Forest Products Association, the American Farm Bureau, and the many other specialized resource-user groups and organized clients of the federal natural resource agencies have had in mind. The present structure suits many client groups admirably—it serves their immediate and specific purposes. Whether it also serves the national interest depends upon a broader range of considerations.

But there is more to the problem of organizing public authority and responsibility than the perceived, and perhaps mistaken, self-interest of groups and individuals. As we have already noted, people frequently do not act in their actual self-interest. They are often locked into behavior patterns, assumptions, and responses that cannot possibly serve them well. Confusion of form and substance has caused large numbers of otherwise intelligent Americans to support and defend anachronistic forms of law and government in the mistaken belief that they are upholding traditional principles. They are, in fact, acting in contradiction to the highly rational assumptions of the eighteenth-century founders of independent government in North

America. Nothing could be more contrary to the spirit of Jeffersonian political philosophy than the stubbornness with which many Americans resist the reformation and revitalization of local government. The mummification of the Egyptian dead has proved a boon to archaeologists and historians. The American mummification of townships, counties, and almost innumerable inefficient units of local and state government is less rational and less meritorious. There is need for a latter-day political prophet who will free Americans from their superstitious reverence for forms of government that are functionally "dead," in a utilitarian sense, even though still manipulated by men who are tenacious in their pursuit of personal ambitions and ego gratifications.

To deal effectively with America's environmental problems it will be necessary first to modify prevailing conventional assumptions regarding the nature of social responsibility, the scope of public and administrative authority, and the level of professional and institutional competence required for the discharge of public functions. Popular acceptance of responsible public control in preference to non-responsible private control will have to increase markedly before stable, high-quality environments become more than rare accidents or exceptions throughout the United States. But along with these needs, and concomitant with them, there must also emerge a coherent and persuasive doctrine to legitimize and reinforce an ecological approach to man-environment relationships *if* environmental quality is to become a social objective.

Dynamics of Attitudinal Change

Because prevailing attitudes toward authority and responsibility for environmental administration are not conducive to its effective implementation, changes in these attitudes must precede or accompany significant changes in environmental policy. Social or attitudinal change is difficult to describe or analyze because of its complex and dynamic character. Social changes do not occur as monistic transitions, uniform throughout society and over extended periods of time. Characteristically, any major social change is the result of multiple interacting changes. Among the frequently identified components of major social change are those classified as physical, perceptual, conceptual, behavioral, and institutional. Interaction among these aspects of social change is now reshaping public attitudes toward environmental policy in the following manner.

Few nations, if any, have experienced the necessity for a more radical revision of social attitudes toward the environment than that which now confronts the United States. The pioneer experience, the frontier tradition, individualism, the illusion of endless natural wealth, and a strongly materialistic view of values have cumulated in a social attitude that has long inhibited public efforts to protect or manage the national environment. The "coonskin cap" tradition still exerts a powerful, if in-articulated, bias against public authority and responsibility for the quality of the environment. Included in this tradition are the following widely held beliefs: (1) speculation in land values is a legitimate way to "windfall" wealth, (2) government must help enterprise, but not attempt to control it, (3) growth (especially economic growth) is an absolute good, (4) people have a right to do as they please with their property, and (5) government by judges is preferable to government by administrators.

These attitudes are not universal in American society. Their practical realization has been abridged by contrary doctrines of policy and law. Nevertheless, they are still widely influential, and in some places dominant, especially at local levels of government. Verifiable evidence concerning their prevalence, and the degrees and direction of attitudinal change, are needed. The evidence at hand, most of it indirect and circumstantial, suggests that these traditional views are being displaced by a new set of public attitudes, but at what rate and in what political or social context, it is difficult to say. The persistence of older attitudes will obstruct any serious effort to bring America's worsening environmental trends under ecologically oriented control. Yet, it is probably true (although no proof is presently available) that few Americans realize that protection or improvement of the environment requires or implies the radical alteration of these attitudes or beliefs.

The direction of attitudinal change implied by a national environmental-quality effort would bring public opinion to the following novel state of affairs. *First,* unearned or speculative profits in the sale of land or any other natural resource would be viewed as illegitimate and would be prohibited by law or expropriated by taxation. *Second,* government subsidy to "private" enterprise would invest it with a public character, subjecting it to an appropriate degree of public control. *Third,* uncritical pursuit of indiscriminate growth would be replaced by a preference for dynamic stability, selective growth in some areas, and reduction of economic activity in others. *Fourth,* the concept of usufruct would replace ownership as a realistic and socially acceptable relationship between man and property. *Five,* litigation would increasingly give way to administrative adjudication in the enforcement of law and the settlement of disputes over environmental and natural-resources questions.

"Whate'er Is Best Administer'd"

If Americans in politically significant numbers have begun to depart from traditional biases that inhibit environmental policy, it is clear that they have not arrived at the set of attitudes just described. How, then, can public authority and responsibility be organized to formulate and implement policies that large numbers of people do not understand well enough to know what must be done to make them effective? How high a price are Americans prepared to pay for environmental quality? For many of them, perhaps for most, the monetary price is the least costly; the psychological cost of abandoning illusions may be the most difficult price to pay. To give up the golden dream of something-for-nothing in land speculation, and to concede that the government that helps to enrich may also have a voice in what happens in the process, are examples of the concessions that may be very hard for most Americans to make. Even though the vast majority of them have no possibility of realizing any material benefit whatever from certain of their traditional attitudes, and, in fact, are disadvantaged by them, it will be difficult to pry them loose from time-honored prejudices.

If this interpretation of the unsettled state of public opinion is correct, several implications follow for the organization of environmental administration. The *first* of these is that Alexander Pope's phrase has no meaning until the goals and necessities of administrative policy can be specified. "Whate'er is best administer'd" can only be "best" when the policy to be administered is known; otherwise there is no test of the quality or effectiveness of administration. If the objective of administration is to impede the functioning of government, as it once was in the Vichy government of France, then the most inefficient administration may be the best. If the structure of authority and responsibility is designed primarily to serve the interests of groups seeking private benefits through public-resource development or exploitation, as it has often been in the United States, then the diffused and fractionated organization of public environmental policy is unobjectionable and even advantageous.

If "Whate'er is best administer'd" is paraphrased to read "What *can* be best administered," a *second* implication appears. If the state of public opinion in a democratic society is unsettled or in flux, administrative policy cannot safely be dogmatic or inflexible. When people appear to be seeking remedies for their dissatisfactions that (although they do not understand it) imply new interpretations of law and policy, then leadership in attitudinal change becomes a task of politics and a responsibility of public administration. Assumption of this task is necessary because only insofar as a politically significant degree of popular consensus or consent can be developed will it be possible also to develop an effective public policy and administration.

By the end of 1969 there had developed in the United States a "critical mass" of public opinion sufficient to prompt the adoption of a national statement of policy for the environment in the form of statute law. The National Environmental Policy Act (Public Law 91-190) signed by the President on January 1, 1970 declared a national policy for the environment, provided general criteria and procedures to guide the actions of the federal government in relation to the environment, and established a three-member Council on Environmental Quality in the Executive Office of the President. By Executive Order 11514 on March 5, 1970, "Protection and Enforcement of Environmental Quality," President Nixon defined the jurisdiction of the Council in broad terms. And so the United States entered the decade of the nineteen-seventies with an explicit national policy for the environment and with one new piece of policy-guiding machinery to make the declared policy a policy in fact. The visible upsurge of public concern over environmental quality issues during the latter half of 1969 brought about enactment of the National Environmental Policy Act with no extended debate or opposition that might have been expected to accompany the legislative course of so fundamental and novel a measure. The political forum for environmental policy-making has been moved to a significant, but as yet indeterminate, extent from the legislative to the executive branch of government. Nevertheless, additional legislation will be required to overcome some of the constitutional constraints of the American federal system. For example, the proposed National Land Use Policy Amendment to the Water Resources Planning Act (S.3354) introduced into the Ninety-First Congress, Second Session (January 29, 1970) by Senator Henry M. Jackson declares a nation-wide policy for land use and provides a framework for the development of interstate, state, and local land use policy. As governmental action moves from formulation of principles to practical application the nature and extent of public receptivity to environmental administration will become clearer. There are substantial interests and sectors in the American economy that have heretofore shown little concern for the growth of the environmental-quality movement or for the enactment of what they perceive as generalizing and theoretical laws. But when the practical consequences of the new environmental policies are brought to bear upon their ambitions, bank accounts, or business activities, a political response may be expected.

The *third* implication that follows from the preceding discussion of attitudinal change is that the American people are concerned not only with *what* government does but also with *how* public power is organized and exercised. Americans have not, however, troubled themselves greatly about the constitutional structure of authority since the ratification of the Constitution in 1789. Thoroughgoing environmental administration might reactivate this concern—which, of course, has never been wholly absent from political discussion and debate. Several constitutional questions are near to being concomitants of a national policy for the environment that is based on ecological assumptions. Among them, the relationships between federal, state, local, interstate, regional, and international responsibilities with relation to environmental policy will inevitably require attention. The planetary unity of the biosphere and the apparent inability of any nation unilaterally to control or protect the open seas, outer space, or the world wide movements of the weather, among other global phenomena, suggests the early emergence of one or more international environmental control agencies, probably under the authority of the United Nations. And if environmental problems are perceived and defined in terms of such nonpolitical and often unstable ecological boundaries as air-sheds, watersheds, ecosystems, migratory organisms, or flow phenomena, questions of relationships among political jurisdictions within many countries compound the broader problem of international relationships.

Another area of constitutional uncertainty arises, or should arise, concerning the responsibilities, authorities, and tasks appropriate to the federal government of the United States. The present *ad hoc* structure of federal jurisdiction gives no apparent clue to what are or should be the responsibilities and the functions of the federal government. This remark implies no lofty disparagement of political convenience as a criterion for the allocation of administrative functions. But the logic of political convenience, useful on some occasions, provides no guidance for the organization of authority and responsibility where the effective control of man-environment relationships is the goal. In the long run, a more solid basis than an ephemeral *ad hoc* convenience will be necessary if the environmental problems of contemporary society are to be attacked with determination and some promise of success. As of early 1970, the President's Advisory Council on Executive Reorganization was endeavoring to establish rational principles for limited reorganization of the executive branch. How its recommendations would affect the implementation of environmental policy was not evident at the time that this [article] went to press.

Prospects and Conjectures

Collective self-control is perhaps the most difficult task that any society can attempt. Whether human society in the United States or elsewhere can cope with an environmental crisis of its own making has yet to be demonstrated. There are obvious limitations to human capabilities in this respect. Among them are the limits of rationality, foresight, technical knowledge, altruism, and ability to co-operate and co-ordinate (psychologically as well as through institutions). It would appear especially difficult for a democratic society to discipline itself. The challenge of science and advanced technology to social responsibility has no true historical precedent. New forms of public decision-making, and redefinitions of authority, responsibility, and democracy may become necessary concomitants to effective public control of the uses of science and technology, and especially to the management of the environment.

No modern society appears to be coping adequately with its environmental problems. Laws and institutions for the administration of environmental policy will everywhere require substantial change before significant improvement can occur. Meanwhile, where and how does the process of reform begin?

Effective reform must begin in more than one place. A mutually reinforcing relationship among major social institutions is needed. Schools, laws, and the administrative agencies of government are especially critical, but certain sectors of the professions and the business community must also be brought into a concerted effort toward environmental protection and improvement. Active support for a public policy on behalf of environmental quality is needed from the communities of scientists, engineers, and lawyers. Efforts toward professional reorientation have been started among each of these groups, but continuing and increased effort is needed. An environmental-quality sector of the business community is emerging, over and beyond the older fields of architecture, landscaping, and environmental planning. Industrial corporations for pollution control, waste management, ecological research, and community development can and should be brought into a supporting relationship to environmental-quality programs. The restructuring of government for environmental administration is an important element in this process of social reinforcement. How rapidly this development can occur is conjectural, but the most productive strategy would be for the proponents of environmental quality to use whatever avenues toward national policy commitment become available. This has been the approach taken by the sponsors of the environmental quality legislation enacted to date.

The novelty, complexity, variety, and interlocking character of environmental-policy issues indicate an extended period of trial, error, and reexamination before the laws and institutions of the United States and of modern nations generally can be adapted to accommodate the necessities of the over-stressed ecosystems of Spaceship Earth. The effects of present efforts in environmental education and of the massive outpouring of literature on environmental quality should be considered in conjecturing the rapidity and extent of public action on environmental policy in the future. Ecological disasters, such as the Santa Barbara oil spill, have moved public opinion in the past and will probably continue to do so in the future. It is difficult to predict how long the present high level of public concern over the quality of the environment will be sustained. But there are no indications that the environmental and ecological problems of our times will cease to annoy, arouse, and alarm people in large numbers. The causal factors underlying the environmental-quality movement are not going to disappear. They will in all probability intensify.

Must society adopt an ecologically sound approach to its environmental relationships in order to survive? Will modern, and especially democratic, societies pay the cost of such a policy in order to obtain the presumed benefits or to avoid the penalties for ecological folly? The answer to the first query is more easily obtained than is that to the second. In a finite world, the only escape from the penalties of ecological error would appear to be technological evasion. There are "optimists" in contemporary society who are confident that many ecological costs can be counterbalanced by technologically induced benefits. How far this philosophy of trade-offs and substitutes can safely be carried is conjectural. And even more uncertain are which criteria can be relied upon to enable society to determine wisely when to substitute artifice for nature.

In summation, the restructuring of authority and responsibility for the management of man's environmental relationships is not a suitable topic for confident or simplistic assertion. The relevant factors are complex, and many are obscure. Yet, certain probabilities are evident—as, for example, that delay in developing a more ecologically valid approach to environmental relationships is already damaging human welfare, and may threaten human survival. Modern society needs a coherent politico-ethical ideology to make the meaning of an ecologically based environmental policy clear and believable to an, at present, only partially comprehending public. Such an activating belief-system is the operational answer to the conservational or environmental ethic which has long been the objective of environmental reformers. Such an ethic is needed to legitimize the new tasks of authority and responsibility that an ecological environmental administration would require.

The Iron Law of Environmental Disorder

JOHN A. STRAAYER

ROY L. MEEK*

There has been increasing recognition of the interrelatedness of public services and public programs in America, and of the urgent need to study and plan the environment within a systems context.[1] For example, links have been uncovered between transit systems and air pollution, between the availability of consumer credit

* An earlier draft of this paper appeared in *Intergovernmental Relations in Water Resource Planning,* Proceedings of Army Engineer Conference, Colorado State University, Department of Political Science Policy Science Papers, No. 1 (1970), pp. 247–256.

[1] For just a few of the numerous examples of literature which uses or advocates the systems perspective, see Stewart Marquis, "Economic Systems, Societies and Cities," *American Behavioral Scientist,* Vol. XI (July–August, 1968), pp. 11–16; Henry Fagin, "Planning for Future

and suburban land use, and between public attitudes and the support for funding public problem-solving efforts.

Numerous attempts have been made and are now underway to improve the environment by thinking and acting from a systems perspective. Much research today is either interdisciplinary or multidisciplinary; and at the urging of federal agencies, metropolitan councils of governments have been formed and the U.S. Army Corps of Engineers is attempting to engage in comprehensive river basin planning.[2]

Our thesis is that while research and planning within a comprehensive and systems framework is long overdue and vitally needed, there are limits to what both can accomplish—there are limits to what we can reasonably expect from systematic planning for development and environmental quality. The argument which follows is that much of our planning must remain short-run, localized, and largely uncoordinated; that it cannot be truly comprehensive; and that we can do no more than continue to chip away at the edges of the more serious problems. Social scientists and planners should admit this.

Four interacting factors underlie this theory. They are: (1) the existence of multiple decision-centers in the American political system; (2) the nature of contemporary environmental problems; (3) the nature of decision-making in situations where demands outstrip resources; and (4) an ideology which supports local and decentralized decision-making prerogatives. This law of collective decision-making is similar to Roberto Michels' "Iron Law of Oligarchy" in that, like Michels' law, the underlying factors are not likely to undergo any sudden, radical change.

Multiple Decision-Centers

One of the most obvious and salient characteristics of American government is the degree to which decision-making authority is dispersed. Combining the federal, state, and local levels we have approximately 100,000 units of government. Employment of the principles of separation of powers and bicameralism within many of these units fragments decision-making authority still further.[3] Many of these governmental units feature numerous boards, commissions, departments, agencies, divisions, and offices. None of the decision-centers or decision-makers within them is fully autonomous. Decision-making prerogatives are restricted by such factors as the availability of resources; formal constitutional, statutory, and administrative rules; political relationships with other public and private decision-centers; and, of course, both public opinion and the value systems of the decision-makers. Nevertheless, each decision-center and decision-maker does possess some degree of autonomy. Further, the decisions produced by each have both internal and external

Urban Growth," *Law and Contemporary Problems,* Vol. 30 (Winter, 1965), pp. 9–25; Lynton K. Caldwell, "Environment: A New Focus for Public Policy," *Public Administration Review,* Vol. 23 (September, 1963), pp. 132–139; John Friedmann, "A Conceptual Model for the Analysis of Planning Behavior," *Administrative Science Quarterly,* Vol. 12, No. 2 (September, 1967), pp. 225–252; and Arthur Maass, Maynard Hufschmidt, and others, *Design of Water Resource Systems* (Cambridge: Harvard University Press, 1962).

[2] The term "comprehensive planning" is not used here in any technical sense.

[3] See U.S. Bureau of Census, *Census of Governments,* 1967.

consequences and so, as in the economic market system, decisions made in each decision-center affect not only that center itself, but also the external environment, i.e., externalities.[4] The collective result is that no decision-makers and no decision-centers are capable of exercising *full* control over their environment. Whereas they can and do have some impact on the environment, the external effects of decisions made elsewhere affect them and the environment itself. To some degree, in a systems sense, everyone is affected by everyone else, while at the same time nobody fully controls the environment.

Environmental Problems

The fact that America is beset by numerous environmental problems is obvious to even the most casual observer. Included among them are problems of water pollution, water supply, mass transit, urban housing, education, civil disorder, and unemployment. These problems tend to center in, but are not exclusive to, the urban areas. They are extremely complex and expensive to deal with. Most demand treatment and analysis in a systems context. Many are the result of technological advances and public policy. Problems of water pollution, mass transit, black ghettos, and unskilled and unemployed workers can be traced in whole or in part to the process of industrialization in general, and to such items as the automobile in particular. In addition, the development of suburbia, the exodus from core cities, and the pressing of minorities into ghettos, along with certain other problems already mentioned, can be shown to be related to public development of road and expressway systems, to governmental generation of consumer credit, to government insured home loans, and, of course, to industrial and technological factors.

Further, many of these problems tend to be comprehensive, mainly in two important respects. First, they are products of not one but a combination of factors. These factors themselves result from a multiplicity of decisions. They result, in short, from a process of "market place" decision-making. And second, these problems affect large and irregularly shaped geographic areas, thus having implications for numerous decision-making centers.

Decision-Making and Scarce Resources

The goals and constraints involved in decision-making vary widely, of course, from one decision-center to another, from problem to problem, and from decision to decision. But to state that the circumstances surrounding decisions are unique is not to say that decision-making cannot be treated abstractly, or that decisions themselves represent phenomena that are inappropriate for comparison and immune from scientific analysis. Most decisions concerning collective public action are similar to other decisions along a number of dimensions.

---

[4] Just as the market mechanism in economics does not necessarily produce a state of affairs which anyone likes, neither is a desired state of affairs the necessary product of thousands of individual and semi-individual decisions. On this subject, see James N. Buchanan and Gordon Tullock, *The Calculus of Consent* (Ann Arbor: University of Michigan Press, 1962), p. 332.

First, each decision-making situation contains a multiplicity of values, any one of which decision-makers would maximize. These values are generally related to each other hierarchically, some being more important than others. These values derive from demands from a multiplicity of problems and publics, as well as from the decision-makers' own personal value systems. Thus each decision-center is subject to numerous and varied demands to commit organizational resources to a variety of needs or problems. The nature and strength of the demands help to determine the decision context and influence decision-making behavior. In addition, the values, perceptions, and psychic needs of each decision-maker and his organization will influence the decision. In every decision situation, therefore, decision-makers are subject to a host of cross-pressures.

Second, both the demands upon an organization and the problems its decision-makers face will vary greatly. Some demands and problems will relate to the short run while others will have implications for the longer run. Some will relate to localized values while others will bear on comprehensive matters. For example, a school board decision to anticipate future suburban development and build a junior high school in a cornfield may prove very rational relative to a goal of saving money and holding back an increase in the property tax. But to build in a cornfield may mean foregoing improvement of older buildings—a decision which may decrease the attractiveness of older sections of town to families with children, and thus hasten the decay of the core city. Therefore, in a comprehensive sense, to build in a cornfield is irrational, whereas in a localized sense it is highly rational. Most decisions involve similar dilemmas; what is rational in the short run may not be so in the long run, and what is rational from a local perspective may, in a comprehensive sense, be highly irrational.

Third, since demands outstrip organizational resources, some discrimination is required in every decision situation. Some demands will be met while others will not. Some problems will be dealt with and some ignored. Some programs will be created, funded, and operated and others will not. Thus, given a hierarchy of values, efforts will be made to realize some values but not others.

There is a dominant and understandable tendency for decision-makers to seek to maximize short-run, local goals rather than long-run comprehensive ones. Responding to their most immediate and proximate stimuli, they behave so as to achieve and retain job security, status, and advancement, and to keep themselves and their organization out of political, economic, or other sorts of trouble. Small group pressures and upward mobility usually demand loyalty and promotion of the organization and its goals. All of this means that there is seldom any payoff for deciding in favor of, and committing resources to, such long-run and comprehensive goals as joining in a group effort to rid an entire metropolitan area of air and water pollution. Everyone would benefit, of course, from the abatement of air and water pollution. But decision-making in the context of scarce resources usually precludes this, since it is cheaper in the short run—and even profitable—to pollute the air and water.

Finally, certain characteristics of large organizations preclude direction by the central organization and act instead to increase subsystem decision-making autonomy. As organizations increase in size, resources, and specialization, it becomes harder to control them. As the range and complexity of organizational activities increase, communications systems become more intricate and confused, executive spans of control increase, and bureaus, offices, and individuals rapidly develop increased decision-making autonomy. Central planning and clear, purposeful organizational action thus become more and more difficult to maintain.[5] A multiplicity of decision-centers, then, in the form of either independent governmental units or subsystems within large organizations, exercise a degree of legal or *de facto* autonomy in pursuing goals which may or may not relate to comprehensive environmental planning.

American Ideology

A long and deeply rooted American tradition of support for local decision-making, for political and administrative decentralization, and for the utilization of check and balance schemes promotes our present system of atomized decision-making. And it will probably continue to do so in the foreseeable future. As a number of political socialization studies so firmly document, behavior is based largely upon belief systems and directed by them;[6] and American support for states' rights, suburban autonomy, and the mythical right of local self-rule appears to preclude any substantial reduction in our vast array of decision centers (as has been demonstrated by the dismal success of metropolitan governmental consolidation efforts). The effectiveness of reorganization is doubtful anyway: a consolidation of autonomous decision-centers would simply result in a reduced number of larger organizations, which are themselves characterized by semi-autonomous subsystems.[7]

Some Conclusions

What this probably means is that as long as the four factors discussed at the outset exist, decisions which preclude comprehensive environmental planning will continue to be made. This conclusion comes about as follows: (1) where demands outstrip resources, some values will be maximized, while others will not; (2) some demands and values will deal with long-run, comprehensive matters, while others will relate to short-run, local matters; (3) decision-makers will most often respond to their most immediate and proximate stimuli, thus frequently failing to allocate

---

[5] Anthony Downs argues that as organizations increase in size and functional specialization, there develops a parallel increase in the decision-making autonomy of the various subsystems of which it is composed. See Downs' *Inside Bureaucracy* (Boston: Little, Brown, 1967), p. 143. This phenomenon is also treated in the writings of Herbert Simon, Victor Thompson, Robert Presthus, and others.

[6] On the impact of belief systems upon behavior, see Robert Lane, *Political Ideology* (Glencoe: The Free Press, 1962); David Easton and Robert D. Hess, "The Child's Political World," *Midwest Journal of Political Science,* Vol. 6 (August, 1962), pp. 229–246; Herbert McClosky, "Consensus and Ideology in American Politics," *The American Political Science Review,* Vol. 58 (June, 1964), pp. 361–379.

[7] See Anthony Downs, *op. cit.*

resources to long-run, comprehensive matters and problems; (4) decisions have both internal and external consequences; and (5) American ideology and political reality ensure the continuance of this type of decision-making and environmental noncontrol. The comprehensive nature of problems, scarcity of resources, multiplicity of decision-centers, and short-run nature of decisions are sure to persist.

The import of these realities is that conditions which no one chooses, and which no one may want, arise and endure. A host of decisions, each made individually and rationally, given the immediate decision-making context, result in universally abhorrent environmental conditions. They create an environment selected and controlled by no one.[8]

One could cite countless examples of this phenomenon, but let us note just two. No one acts purposefully to pollute the air. The auto industry manufactures internal combustion automobiles in order to make a profit. Cities, counties, states, and federal agencies build weblike metropolitan expressway systems in order to move more and more automobiles at what they hope to be an ever faster rate. Individual auto owners drive their machines on expressways to get to work, to the ball park, and to the shopping center. But the collective result of all these decisions is pollution—which nobody wants.

Consider secondly the increasingly serious, world-wide population problem. No one is in favor of overpopulation, crowded conditions, starvation, and human misery. In fact, everyone is against all of these. But most decisions regarding the size of the world's population are made individually. Millions of parents and parents-to-be make billions of decisions which individually hardly affect population growth, but which collectively bear heavily on the size of the world's population—and create a set of conditions nobody wants.

What we are saying, of course, is that society has no agency that can couple existing and newly developing knowledge with advance planning so as to minimize the unintended and unwanted consequences of purposeful behavior. This is obviously not due to a lack of knowledge about our environment; air, water, transit, and other types of technology are highly developed. Rather, the reason is simply that there exists no agency capable of identifying a universally desired state of affairs. In other words, we have not yet developed the institutional capacity to give meaning to the term "environmental quality." Of course, countless numbers of individuals and groups have defined environmental quality for themselves, and whereas the American democratic ideology legitimizes these efforts, it does not permit one segment of the population to impose its image of "the good" upon the rest of us.

Where does this leave our technological-urban-mass democracy? Some have argued that we may be able to preserve a good share of our ideological baggage, but we may have to rethink its basis and alter the institutions designed to implement it. That is, we may be able to preserve popular sovereignty, political equality, and majority rule, but unless we want to choke to death, starve to death, or be killed in an auto or plane crash, we may have to retool the institutions through which we

[8] This point resembles certain socialistic criticism of the capitalist market mechanism in the realm of economics. It is argued that no one controls the market and thus the economy is free to move in a direction acceptable to no one.

seek to maximize these values. Federalism, separation of powers, bicameralism, and the proliferation of local governments may simply require modification — and so may our permissive non-reaction toward interagency wrangling. As things now stand, such modification is not feasible, politically. As John Gaus has suggested, it may take a crisis of large proportions to open the door to a massive and fundamental redirection in public policy, or to reshape our decision-making apparatus.

Measured against a utopian preference for some sort of total solution to clearly defined problems, the picture we have been painting is rather pessimistic. But from another perspective it is not, for consider what the prerequisites would be for total solutions. There would have to be a hierarchical rank order of values, a parallel authoritative and fairly detailed specification of the desired state of affairs, and the making operational of a complete set of programs to achieve these ends. One of two sets of conditions would, in turn, be prerequisite. Either there would have to be almost total community consensus on both ends and means; or someone or some group would have to impose its values on everyone else. The first, we submit, would be an unbearable bore; and the entire history of tyranny discredits the second. Thus, in short, there may be something to say for incremental and oftimes muddled planning; after all, it does suggest a society with a rather exciting variety of value systems and considerable freedom to pursue them. Both the new left and the old right are probably quite capable of comprehensive planning on almost any scale. The iron law of environmental chaos may be preferable.

The Future of the Environmental Struggle

DANIEL M. OGDEN, JR.

Environmental policy issues raise some of the most profound and basic questions facing mankind. In their broadest context they pose the fundamental questions of how many people the earth can support, of what quality of life man can hope to sustain, and of which philosophy man will use to guide his attitudes and actions toward his fellow men and the world about him.

In the years ahead, environmental issues will transcend in significance even the great perennial human problems of famine, pestilence, natural disasters, and war. Scientific agriculture has demonstrated that famine is conquerable. Modern medicine can erase pestilence. Modern conservation practices have controlled fire and floods. And the atom bomb may have rendered world war obsolete as a method of settling human disputes, even if mankind has not yet devised a viable worldwide alternative method for managing his affairs.

Man's headlong despoilation of the environment, however, now threatens his very existence. Man himself has become his own greatest problem.

At base, man's philosophical and religious concepts, his social patterns, his economic system, and his political processes will determine whether he can survive. The technology of survival largely exists or can be devised. The crucial question is whether man has the wisdom and the will to act effectively, in time.

Some alarmists are saying man will survive but 30 more years. Some polluters are claiming that man is not even close to tolerance levels and that nature has been a much greater polluter than man could ever be. The truth, of course, lies at neither extreme. Man can survive; the question is at what level of life and with what level of freedom and personal fulfillment. On the other hand, mankind dares not be lulled by the soothing phrases of the polluters. Deterioration of the quality of the environment is rapid and serious. Man is the principal cause of the deterioration and he need not be.

Three basic types of action must shape the course of environmental policy for the future: (1) the generation and dissemination of knowledge about the environment and its problems; (2) the taking of vigorous political action to protect environmental quality; and (3) a fundamental re-thinking of the philosophical concepts by which man justifies his actions about the environment.

Knowledge. Man's first task must be to learn about the environment, about himself in relation to the environment, and how to bring human society to act effectively to maintain quality of life. While detailed knowledge about the environment itself is, and probably must remain, the possession of a relatively few specialists, most of mankind may be able to comprehend some basic principles.

First, the general public should comprehend the balance of nature—the interdependence of animals and plants upon each other in the oxygen and carbon dioxide cycles and the dependence of animals upon plants and each other for food. The science of ecology, appropriately taught and popularized, should enable most human beings to grasp the fundamentals of life and to develop a reverence for it and its beauty.

Second, the public needs constant reminders of the well-established principles of conservation of natural resources which are needed to sustain human standards of living. The public should be led to appreciate its dependence upon scientific agriculture and range management for food and fibre; upon multiple-use forest management for wood products; upon prudent withdrawal of non-renewable resources to provide minerals, gas, and oil; upon sound multiple-purpose management of water resources to support domestic use, industry, agriculture, navigation, power, recreation, and animal life; upon power from water, fuel, and atomic energy to meet a myriad of human needs; and especially upon the preservation of natural areas, of wilderness, of open space, and of streams, estuaries, and seashores to permit human recreation and sustain the balance of nature.

Third, human abuses of nature merit special public attention. Water pollution in all its forms—from domestic sewage, industrial wastes, and silt to high water temperature—must be understood, along with known or potential remedies. Air pollution, its sources, its consequences, the means for control, and the standards of enforcement which will be necessary, all warrant public understanding. Fire control—long popularized by Smokey the Bear—must remain a continuing effort. The biocides—the pesticides, the herbicides, the fungacides, and their relatives— useful though they are to man, must be recognized as potential threats to the balance of nature. Their use and abuse should be widely understood for they are now readily available. Strip mining, in hilly terrain, especially merits public attention, for its principal justification is its apparent economy — an economy achieved by passing the bulk of the real cost on to society. Despoiled land, rendered unproductive for many generations by the giant gouging machines, cries out for a vasly different approach to mineral recovery by mankind. Similarly, solid waste disposal has become a major problem and a major abuse. Ocean dumping has already disturbed the fine balance of the sea. Collection, crushing, and burial of refuse on the earth's surface offer partial solutions to some of these problems.

Fourth, the public needs greater comprehension of the rudimentary elements of good urban design. All too often the public puts up with cities which are mercilessly depressing and inefficient. Antidotes must be developed — through appreciation of elementary esthetic quality in design, color, form and line; of the physical dispersal of residences, commercial enterprises, and industry; of the fundamentals of a mass transportation system; of the role of utilities for service and waste disposal; of the significance of cultural support from schools, churches, museums, libraries, parks, and auditoriums; and of the control of nuisances such as litter, noise, signs, and neighborhood degeneration.

Fifth, and most important of all, every living soul should comprehend and accept in his daily life, as fully as possible, the absolute necessity for population control. The runaway population growth which now besets mankind is the primary cause of many human problems today and will compound most of them tomorrow. At the present rate the world population will double in the next 39 years. Mankind may have to ration reproduction if life itself is to retain meaning and quality.

Limits, therefore, are essential: limits on population, pollution, growth and size, luxury, and profits.

If man is to establish and live within limits, he also must know and understand himself. In this regard, basic scientific knowledge is far more primitive, and the conclusions are far less exact, than in the physical and biological sciences. Even in the United States, the world's most research-oriented nation, relatively little public effort has been directed into the social sciences. America possesses perhaps more systematic knowledge about its economic system than about any other phase of human behavior. Its people badly need to increase their understanding of their social systems, and of how to use their democratic decision-making systems to achieve desired ends. Widespread mistrust of the political system, a mistrust bred of ignorance and misunderstanding, handicaps the American people in their efforts to shape public affairs.

To achieve this first task of learning about the environment, men, and effective political action, the systematic spread of knowledge and understanding is essential. The initial step, as in any learning process, is to arouse attention. For much of this century, conservationists have attempted to arouse public concern for the environment. In recent years such noted figures as Rachel Carson (*Silent Spring*), Stewart L. Udall (*The Quiet Crisis* and *1976: Agenda for Tomorrow*), and Ian McHarg (with films and lectures) have battled to focus public attention on environmental problems. Mrs. Lyndon B. Johnson, during her tenure as first lady, initiated a White House Conference on Natural Beauty and greatly stimulated public concern for environmental quality. Many groups like the League of Women Voters have drawn attention to these issues. In the future follow-up efforts should keep attention at a sufficient level to involve large numbers of people in environmental problems.

A second step involves the dissemination of basic knowledge. Environmental patterns should become a basic part like mathematics and English, of both elementary and secondary school curriculums. Universities should train specialists in environmental studies just as they now train social scientists and physical education instructors. Adult education, aimed at providing essential knowledge, should be widely offered as part of continuing education and cooperative extension work. Service clubs should make environmental education part of their indoctrination.

The generation of a propensity to act must be the third step. Public attention, and even public knowledge, will achieve little unless the educational process inculcates the widespread belief that action must follow. Instruction in politics can engender confidence in the efficacy of political action and of using democratic political processes to accomplish action in an orderly manner. A significant ingredient in man's struggle to survive, then, must be vast improvement in popular understanding of the use of the political process. Old-fashioned civics never did, and will not now do the job. The dynamics of politics as the way a free people shape public policy must become a part of the everyday public knowledge.

Politics. Man's second major step must be vigorous political action to protect environmental quality. Politics is the critical ingredient in environmental policy decisions. Good engineering plans and good economic analysis can determine *whether a development is possible.* Politics decides *whether it will be done.*

Environmental politics tends to be pressure politics, not partisan party politics. Both major American political parties are arenas of compromise — organizations of citizens primarily united by the desire to gain office. People of many different but broadly compatible views join the political party of their choice seeking particular policy achievements from government. By offering to support at least a reasonable part of the goals of others in his party, each member can in turn win support for some of his goals. Thus American parties are organized to win elections. Policy is a product of compromise among the active participants in the party at any election, not the application of the party's philosophy to the problems of the day.

American political parties are therefore primarily useful to determine *who* will hold public office, rather than *what* the public office holders will *do* once in office. Moreover, in their competition for power, both political parties are certain to favor quality environment, to oppose pollution, to support conservation, and to admit the need to control population. But they are unlikely to present a meaningful choice to the American voter on these issues.

Pressure groups, then, become essential to the shaping of public issues, in the presentation of alternative courses of action, in the mustering of public support for a policy position, and in spurring all branches of government to act in all aspects of environmental quality.

Pressure group activity seems certain to arise from at least three quarters. Many existing groups, organized for other purposes, will find environmental problems increasingly important to their members. Possessing organization, staff, funds, and political skill, they will be able to swing their resources into the fray—rapidly, and with effect. However, because their membership has joined for non-environmental reasons, many groups such as organized labor, chambers of commerce, churches, and farm organizations may experience internal dissension if they stress environmental issues at the expense of traditional goals.

Thus many people will turn to such existing goal groups as the Sierra Club, the Wilderness Society, and the National Parks Association which have environmental quality as their central purpose, and which have demonstrated their effectiveness in the political struggle. Successful goal groups of this type gain added strength by setting new, closely related goals by which they can attract new members.

In addition, new goal groups, some destined for great power, are certain to enter the political arena. Existing groups in the environmental field tend to line up along traditional natural resource conservation lines. With new issues arising from abuses of nature and from the population explosion, many people are sure to find that new goal groups, dedicated to the control of population, the eradication of air and water pollution, the control of biocides, or the ending of strip mining, will better serve their ends. The establishment of such new groups may draw members from many lines of endeavor who find that the organizations which they traditionally support are incapable of acting firmly and effectively to fight the environmental evils.

Some new groups will start with spontaneous local citizen committees for "clean water" or "clean air," and will then federate into effective national organizations capable of fighting for appropriations and against major industrial polluters. Others will begin as national organizations and will stimulate action wherever possible. But however they originate, such organizations seem destined to flourish in the 1970s. To both the new and the existing groups will fall the task of reducing abuses of nature, of controlling population, of teaching people the basic facts of life, and of instructing in methods of using the democratic system to protect humanity. Like the old Anti-Saloon League, the clean air and water leagues and the zero-population growth league may well become the great crusaders of the 1970s to which many successful political leaders will hitch their careers. The new groups will bring forth heroes, and castigate villains. The political struggle for the environment is certain to be dramatic, colorful, and exciting—as well as deadly serious.

Pressure and counter pressure, however, will require skillful resolution of conflicts if society is to take effective political action. Power holders in both the legislative and executive branches will have to exercise great skill in the delicate art of the possible. Working across party lines to find broad areas of agreement upon which sound legislation and effective administration can rest, they will have to make hard choices between competing groups and among conflicting ideas. Dedicated and skillful political leadership, then, is the essential ingredient to translate the knowledge and the group efforts into working change.

Pressure for a quality environment also will inevitably compete with other demands for legislative action and especially for public funds. Defense, space, atomic energy, urban problems, race relations, education, and many other pressing problems have equally powerful lobbies and well-established administrative units to present their cases. The environmental crisis demands a reordering of public priorities for money and attention—which in turn means that some programs which now enjoy high priority must be greatly curtailed or even laid aside. Because urban problems, race relations, and education are related to environmental issues, their priorities are not likely to come under attack. The targets in priority changes, consequently, are sure to be defense—which now consumes far more national wealth than at any previous time in history; space exploration, which increasingly seems to be an indulgence of human curiosity; and atomic energy, which after 30 years of astronomical investment has yielded but meager improvement to the lot of mankind. Yet these three programs consume enormous amounts of hardware and have spawned elaborate scientific research efforts by industry and the universities. These "kept" industries provide a self-serving lobby of formidable magnitude to perpetuate existing priorities regardless of their utility to society. Resolution of the inevitable conflict over priorities to insure adequate funding for environmental goals will require a high order of patience, leadership, and statesmanship from elected and appointed public officers.

Political action will have to move on several fronts simultaneously. Population control will not be achieved simply by ending all state prohibition on abortion and making contraceptive devices readily available. A maximum of two children per family must either become the effective moral standard for the entire society or government will have to license reproduction, just as it licenses marriage, driving, and certain other human activities.

To control pollution and other environmental abuse, society will be forced to outlaw pollution and other environmental abuses, and relentlessly punish violators. Costs will increase and profits will decline for enterprises which now pass wastes onto the public via the air, water, or land. Polluters are sure to fight pollution control laws and resist effective enforcement. The drafting of legislation, the establishment of enforcement agencies, the appointment of fearless public servants, the promulgating of rules, the provision of ample operating funds, the enforcement of law, and the supplying of continuous public support will therefore require massive public dedication, effort, and follow-through.

To reconstruct our cities and make them livable and governable may require a radical change in our concept of urban organization. For example, political scientists, economists, and sociologists might profitably be asked to determine the optimum size for cities—large enough to be economically viable, but small enough to permit widespread participation in political affairs and the imposition of effective, continuous, normal social controls over the entire range of interpersonal behavior. If such optimum urban areas can be defined, people should set about to create such cities along with transit links that permit society to retain its effectiveness of production, marketing, and communication while at the same time restoring lost human values to urban life.

While the established conservation goals will require continuous effort and support they should not create extended controversy. Strengthened laws, better organization, and adequate funding should enable the existing structure to conserve the major national resources along traditional lines.

Philosophy. In some ways the environmental crisis is philosophical, not political. Unless man can re-think the intellectual basis for his moral systems, and replace ancient misconceptions with supportable normative conclusions about the real world and his place in it, he may prove incapable of achieving the knowledge, the patterns of life, or the political action essential for survival. If he fails to engage in some basic re-thinking, the alarmists may well prove to be correct; and the end is likely to be both slow and painful, rather than swift and merciful. But if he can re-think some basic values, man may enter a prolonged era of peace, accomplishment, and individual fulfillment — beyond present imagination.

In the future, as in the past, man will have to re-evaluate the premises and re-examine the conclusions which underlie and shape the present ethical system. First, for two thousand years man believed that the earth was the center of the universe. He now knows instead that he inhabits a relatively small planet which revolves around a relatively unimportant star on the edge of a relatively small galaxy. There may be many thousands of such islands in the universe on which life may exist, or could exist. Yet this is the only such place he knows of and it may well be the only place he can reach. The islands may be so separated in space and in time as to render movement from one to the other impossible. Man may well have to get along with the earth he now has.

Second, man long has believed that the earth was created at a single point in time. He now knows that both the inanimate and the living world is ever changing. It is evolving and will continue to evolve both in terms of physical structure and life. Mountains will come and go; ice caps will melt and seas rise; glaciers will advance and recede; new forms of life will arise and old forms disappear. Man alone, of all the complex living creatures, seems capable of adapting to a changing environment. He should, therefore, possess the capacity for indefinite survival on this planet. But he is also able to change the course of evolution, for better or for worse, by accident or design. Man must, therefore, accept change as reality and plan for change so as to protect and preserve life on earth.

Third, while men have been told that they have dominion over all other things — they now know that man is a part of nature, a part of the oxygen-carbon dioxide cycle, a part of the food chain. Man cannot view himself as having dominion over all things, nor as free to do what he will with all living creatures. Like all living things, he is bound by nature's laws. He must learn them, and how to abide by them.

Fourth, man is capable of defining and achieving both good and evil. He is not utterly corrupt and capable of good only if he accepts supernatural intervention in his affairs. Nor will his innate goodness prevail if he destroys his evil institutions. Man shapes his own destiny. He can make the world a good place for himself and all living things, or he can turn it into a Hell. He can determine what is good by free democratic procedures so that all men may share in the determination of goals and the standards of conduct necessary to achieve them. He can plan and organize and implement to achieve what he deems good and wise.

Fifth, many men long believed that their fate was pre-ordained. Man now knows enough about himself to know that much of his fate is what he makes it. He has the skills and the know-how to set goals, to plan the fullfillment of goals, and to achieve them. If he needs more knowledge or techniques, he also has the skills and know-how to develop them.

Thus the moral philosophy for a quality environment must be a philosophy based upon realism about the physical world and realism about human society. It can neither predict inevitable success nor foretell inevitable doom. It must provide for mankind the moral underpinnings which will enable him to be free and to determine his destiny within the finite limits of the planet earth, and the natural laws which regulate it.

Bibliography

General

Books:

Boulding, Kenneth E. *Environmental Quality in a Growing Economy*. Baltimore: Johns Hopkins Press, 1966.
Ciriacy-Wantrup, S. V. and Parsons, J. J. (eds.). *Natural Resources: Quality and Quantity*. Berkeley: University of California Press, 1966.
Commoner, Barry. *Science and Survival*. New York: Viking, 1968.
Cooley, Richard A. and Wandesforde-Smith, Geoffrey (eds.). *Congress and the Environment*. Seattle: University of Washington Press, 1970.
Douglas, William O. *Wilderness Bill of Rights*. Boston: Little, Brown, 1965.
Dubos, René. *Reason Awake: Science for Man*. New York: Columbia University Press, 1970.
Ewald, William R., Jr. (ed.). *Environment and Change: The Next Fifty Years*. Bloomington: Indiana University Press, 1968.
Goldman, Marshall (ed.). *Controlling Pollution: The Economics of a Cleaner America*. Englewood Cliffs, N.J.: Prentice-Hall, 1967.
Helfrich, Harold W. *The Environmental Crisis: Man's Struggle to Live with Himself*. New Haven: Yale University Press, 1970.
Herfindahl, Orris C. and Kneese, Allen V. *Quality of the Environment*. Baltimore: Johns Hopkins Press, 1965.
Odum, Eugene. *Ecology*. New York: Holt, Rinehart and Winston, 1963.
Stewart, George R. *Not So Rich As You Think*. Boston: Houghton Mifflin, 1968.
Udall, Stewart L. *Agenda for Tomorrow*. New York: Harcourt, Brace & World, 1968.

Articles:

Ayres, Robert U. and Kneese, Allen V. "Production, Consumption, and Externalities." *American Economic Review* (June 1969), 282-97.
Caldwell, Lynton K. "Environment: A New Focus for Public Policy." *Public Administration Review* (September 1963), 132-39.
—————————. "A Symposium: Environmental Policy: New Directions in Federal Action." *Public Administration Review* (July/August 1968), 301-47.
Cousins, N. (ed.). "Cleaning Humanities' Nest Symposium." *Saturday Review* (March 7, 1970), 47-54.
Kartman, Leo. "Human Ecology and Public Health." *American Journal of Public Health* (May 1967), 737-50.
Kennan, George F. "To Prevent a World Wasteland." *Foreign Affairs* (April 1970), 401-13.
Krutilla, J. V. "Some Environmental Effects of Economic Development." *Daedalus* (Fall 1967), 1058-70.
McNaughton, S. J. and Wolf, L. L. "Dominance and the Niche in Ecological Systems." *Science* (January 9, 1970), 131-39.
Michael, Donald N. "On Coping with Complexity: Planning and Politics." *Daedalus* (Fall 1968), 1179-93.
Nelson, Gaylord A. "Our Polluted Planet." *Progressive* (November 1969), 13-17.

Nixon, M. and Muskie, E. S. "Environment: A National Mission for the Seventies." *Fortune* (February 1970), 98+.

Wollman, N. "New Economics of Resources." *Daedalus* (Fall 1967), 1099-114.

Woodwell, G. M. "Science and the Gross National Pollution." *Ramparts* (May 1970), 51-4.

Population

Books:

Ehrlich, Paul R. *The Population Bomb.* New York: Ballantine Books, 1969.

Ehrlich, Paul R. and Ehrlich, Anne H. *Population, Resources, Environment: Issues in Human Ecology.* San Francisco: W. H. Freeman, 1970.

Hardin, Garrett (ed.). *Population, Evolution, and Birth Control.* San Francisco: W. H. Freeman, 1969.

Hauser, Philip M. *The Population Dilemma.* Englewood Cliffs, N.J.: Prentice-Hall, 1963.

Paddock, William and Paddock, Paul. *Famine — 1975.* Boston: Little, Brown, 1967.

Articles:

Cain, Stanley A. "Man and His Environment." *Population Bulletin* (November 1966), 96-103.

Ehrlich, Paul R. "Population, Food and Environment: Is the Battle Lost?" *Texas Quarterly* (Summer 1968), 43-54.

McNaughton, S. J. "Rising Population: Its Effect On Environment." *The Conservationist* (June/ July 1970), pp. 14-16.

Sternglass, E.; Friedlander, M. W.; and Klarmann, J. "How Many Children?" *Environment* (December 1969), 2-13.

Sulloway, Alvan W. "The Legal and Political Aspects of Population Control in the United States." *Law and Contemporary Problems,* 25 (1960), 593-99.

Sundquist, James L. "Where Shall They Live?" *The Public Interest* (Winter 1970), 88-100.

Taeuber, Irene B. "Demographic Transitions and Population Problems in the United States." *The Annals of the American Academy of Political and Social Science* (January 1967), 131-40.

Urban Environment

Books:

Battan, Louis J. *The Unclean Sky.* New York: Doubleday (Anchor), 1966.

Carr, Donald E. *The Breath of Life.* New York: W. W. Norton, 1965.

Dales, J. H. *Pollution, Property and Prices.* Toronto: University of Toronto Press, 1968.

Havighurst, Clark C. (ed.). *Air Pollution Control.* New York: Oceana, 1969.

Jacobs, Jane. *The Death and Life of Great American Cities.* New York: Random House, 1961.

Mayer, Albert. *The Urgent Future: People, Housing, City, Region.* New York: McGraw-Hill, 1967.

Mumford, Lewis. *The Urban Prospect.* New York: Harcourt, Brace & World, 1969.

Articles:

Antrop, D. F. "Environmental Noise Pollution: A New Threat to Sanity." *Bulletin of Atomic Scientists* (May 1969), 11-16.

Ayres, Robert U. "Air Pollution in Cities." *Natural Resources Journal* (January 1969), 1-22.

Cassell, Eric J. "The Health Effects of Air Pollution and Their Implications for Control." *Law and Contemporary Problems* (Spring 1968), 197-217.

Crocker, Thomas D. "Some Economics of Air Pollution Control." *Natural Resources Journal* (April 1968) 236-258.

Demaree, A. T. "Cars and Cities on a Collision Course." *Fortune* (February 1970), 124-8+.

Fagin, Henry. "Planning for Future Urban Growth." *Law and Contemporary Problems* (Winter 1965), 9-25.

Gans, H. J. "Doing Something About the Slums." *Commonwealth* (March 18, 1966), 688-93.

Graham, F. "Ear Pollution!" *Audubon* (May 1969), 34-9.

Kennedy, Robert F. "Air Pollution and the Death of Our Cities." *Social Action* (May 1968), 38-46.

Kryter, D. K. "Psychological Reactions to Aircraft Noise." *Science* (March 18, 1966), 1346-55.

Smith, Bruce L. R. "The Politics of Air Pollution in New York City." *Interplay* (March 1970), 4-7.

Spengler, Joseph J. "Megalopolis: Resource Conserver or Resource Waster?" *Natural Resources Journal* (July 1967), 376-95.

Teller, A. "Air-Pollution Abatement: Economic Rationality and Reality." *Daedalus* (Fall 1967), 1082-98.

Land

Books:

Carson, Rachel. *Silent Spring.* Boston: Houghton Mifflin, 1962.

Graham, Frank, Jr. *Since Silent Spring.* Boston: Houghton Mifflin, 1970.

Headley, J. C. and Lewis, J. N. *The Pesticide Problem.* Baltimore: Johns Hopkins Press, 1967.

Novick, Sheldon. *The Careless Atom.* Boston: Houghton Mifflin, 1968.

Rudd, Robert L. *Pesticides and the Living Landscape.* Madison: University of Wisconsin Press, 1964.

Van Dersal, William R. *The Land Renewed.* New York: Henry Z. Walck, 1968.

Whyte, William H. *The Last Landscape.* Garden City, N.Y.: Doubleday, 1968.

Articles:

"Agricultural Pesticides: The Need for Improved Control Legislation." *Minnesota Law Review* (June 1968), 1242-60.

Brooks, David B. "Strip Mining, Reclamation, and the Public Interest." *American Forests* (March 1966), 18-19.

Butler, George J. "Pesticides: Potions of Death." *Progressive* (March 1969), 28-31.

Commoner, Barry. "Myth of Omnipotence, Hidden Costs of Nuclear Power." *Environment* (March 1969), 8-13+.

Green, M. D. "Politics of Pesticides." *Nation* (November 24, 1969), 569-71.

Harmer, R. "Poisons, Profits and Politics." *Nation* (August 25, 1969), 134-37.

Novick, Sheldon. "New Pollution Problem: Mercury Contamination of Food, Air and Water." *Environment* (May 1969), 2-9.

Ridgeway, J. "Para-Real Estate: The Handing Out of Resources." *Ramparts* (May 1970), 28-33.

Soth, Lauren. "The Counterrevolution in Chemical Farming." *Interplay* (February 1970), 18-20.

Van Den Bosch, R. "Pesticides: Prescribing for the Ecosystem." *Environment* (April 1970), 20-5.

Weisberg, B. "Raping Alaska: Ecology of Oil." *Ramparts* (January 1970), 25-33.

Water

Books:

Carr, Donald E. *Death of the Sweet Waters.* New York: W. W. Norton, 1966.

Graham, Frank, Jr. *Disaster by Default: Politics and Water Pollution.* Philadelphia: Lippincott, 1966.

Kneese, Allen V. and Bower, Blair T. *Managing Water Quality.* Baltimore: Johns Hopkins Press, 1968.

Marx, Wesley. *The Frail Ocean.* New York: Doubleday (Anchor), 1967.

White, Gilbert (ed.). *Water, Health and Society.* Bloomington: Indiana University Press, 1969.

Wright, Jim. *The Coming Water Famine.* New York: Coward-McCann, 1966.

Articles:

Bryan, Edward H. "Water Supply and Pollution Control Aspects of Urbanization." *Law and Contemporary Problems* (Winter 1965), 176-92.

Carter, L. J. "Thermal Pollution: A Threat to Cayuga's Waters?" *Science* (February 7, 1969), 517-18.

Commoner, Barry. "Lake Erie, Aging or Ill?" *Scientist and Citizen* (December 1968), 254-63.

Douglas, William O. "An Inquest on Our Lakes and Rivers." *Playboy* (June 1968), 96-8+.

Freeman, A. M. III and Ross, L. "Cleaning Up Foul Waters: Proposals for Pollution Base and Regional Treatment Authorities." *New Republic* (June 20, 1970), 13-16.

Gotaas, H. B. "Outwitting the Patient Assassin: The Human Use of Lake Pollution." *Bulletin for Atomic Scientists* (May 1969), 8-10.

Lieber, Harvey. "Water Pollution." *Current History* (July 1970), 23-30+.

Muskie, E. S. "Fresh Water: A Diminishing Supply." *Current History* (June 1970), 329+.

Powers, C. F. and Robertson, A. "Aging Great Lakes." *Scientific American* (November 1966), 94-100+.

Warne, William E. "The Water Crisis is Present." *Natural Resources Journal* (January 1969), 53-62.

Wenk, E., Jr. "Federal Policy Planning for the Marine Environment." *Public Administration Review* (July 1968), 312-20.

List of Contributors

R. Stephen Berry is Professor of Chemistry, University of Chicago.

Clifford R. Bragdon is associated with the U.S. Army Environmental Hygiene Agency, Edgewood Arsenal, Maryland.

Gene Bylinsky is an Associate Editor of *Fortune* magazine.

Lynton K. Caldwell is Professor of Political Science, Indiana University.

Luther J. Carter is a member of the staff of *Science* magazine.

Barry Commoner is Chairman of the Department of Botany and Director of the Center for the Biology of Natural Systems, Washington University, St. Louis.

Edwin L. Dale, Jr., is a member of the Washington bureau of the *New York Times,* specializing in economic news.

Judith Blake Davis is Professor and Chairman of the Department of Demography, University of California at Berkeley.

Marjory Stoneman Douglas has taken an active part in the fight to save the Everglades.

Frank E. Egler is a vegetation scientist with Ecosystem Research Station, Aton Forest, Norfolk, Connecticut.

Paul Ehrlich is Professor of Biology, Stanford University.

Robert S. Gilmour is Assistant Professor of Public Law and Government, Columbia University.

Robert R. Grinstead is a senior chemist at the Western Division Research Center of the Dow Chemical Company, Walnut Creek, California.

Ralph Z. Hallow is an editorial writer for the Pittsburgh *Post-Gazette.*

Arnold Hano is a freelance writer who lives in Southern California.

Harvey Lieber is Assistant Professor and academic director of the Washington Semester Program, School of Government and Public Administration, The American University.

Stewart Marquis is Associate Professor of Regional Planning, School of Natural Resources, University of Michigan.

Roy L. Meek is Associate Professor of Political Science, Colorado State University.

Harvey Molotch is Assistant Professor of Sociology, University of California at Santa Barbara.

Daniel M. Ogden, Jr., is Dean of the College of Humanities and Social Science and Professor of Political Science, Colorado State University.

Claire and W. M. S. Russell are British social biologists.

Robert Rienow is Professor of Political Science, State University of New York at Albany; co-author of *Moment in the Sun,* and creator of *Man Against His Environment,* a TV series.

Peter Schrag is an editor-at-large for *Saturday Review* magazine.

John A. Straayer is Assistant Professor of Political Science, Colorado State University.

Harvey Wheeler is a Senior Fellow, Center for the Study of Democratic Institutions.

Aaron Wildavsky is Professor of Political Science, University of California at Berkeley.

D. Wolfers is associated with the Population Bureau, London, England.

ABCDEFGHIJ— SM —7654210